# PROFESSIONAL F# 2.0

**FOREWORD** . . . . . . . . . . . . . . . . . . . . . . . . . . . . . . . . . . . . . . . . . . . . . . . . . . . . . . . . . . . . . . . . . . . . . . . . . . xxi

**INTRODUCTION** . . . . . . . . . . . . . . . . . . . . . . . . . . . . . . . . . . . . . . . . . . . . . . . . . . . . . . . . . . . . . . . . . xxiii

▶ **PART 0       BEGINNINGS**

**CHAPTER 1**     Primer . . . . . . . . . . . . . . . . . . . . . . . . . . . . . . . . . . . . . . . . . . . . . . . . . . . . . . . . . . 3

▶ **PART I       BASICS**

**CHAPTER 2**     Lexical Structure . . . . . . . . . . . . . . . . . . . . . . . . . . . . . . . . . . . . . . . . . . . . . .31

**CHAPTER 3**     Primitive Types . . . . . . . . . . . . . . . . . . . . . . . . . . . . . . . . . . . . . . . . . . . . . . 37

**CHAPTER 4**     Control Flow . . . . . . . . . . . . . . . . . . . . . . . . . . . . . . . . . . . . . . . . . . . . . . . . 47

**CHAPTER 5**     Composite Types . . . . . . . . . . . . . . . . . . . . . . . . . . . . . . . . . . . . . . . . . . . . 55

**CHAPTER 6**     Pattern Matching . . . . . . . . . . . . . . . . . . . . . . . . . . . . . . . . . . . . . . . . . . . 85

▶ **PART II       OBJECTS**

**CHAPTER 7**     Complex Composite Types . . . . . . . . . . . . . . . . . . . . . . . . . . . . . . . . . . . 105

**CHAPTER 8**     Classes . . . . . . . . . . . . . . . . . . . . . . . . . . . . . . . . . . . . . . . . . . . . . . . . . . . . 125

**CHAPTER 9**     Inheritance . . . . . . . . . . . . . . . . . . . . . . . . . . . . . . . . . . . . . . . . . . . . . . . .161

**CHAPTER 10**    Generics . . . . . . . . . . . . . . . . . . . . . . . . . . . . . . . . . . . . . . . . . . . . . . . . . . . 183

**CHAPTER 11**    Packaging . . . . . . . . . . . . . . . . . . . . . . . . . . . . . . . . . . . . . . . . . . . . . . . . . .191

**CHAPTER 12**    Custom Attributes . . . . . . . . . . . . . . . . . . . . . . . . . . . . . . . . . . . . . . . . . . 197

▶ **PART III       FUNCTIONAL PROGRAMMING**

**CHAPTER 13**    Functions . . . . . . . . . . . . . . . . . . . . . . . . . . . . . . . . . . . . . . . . . . . . . . . . .209

**CHAPTER 14**    Immutable Data . . . . . . . . . . . . . . . . . . . . . . . . . . . . . . . . . . . . . . . . . . .225

**CHAPTER 15**    Data Types . . . . . . . . . . . . . . . . . . . . . . . . . . . . . . . . . . . . . . . . . . . . . . . . 247

**CHAPTER 16**    List Processing . . . . . . . . . . . . . . . . . . . . . . . . . . . . . . . . . . . . . . . . . . . . 257

**CHAPTER 17**    Pipelining and Composition . . . . . . . . . . . . . . . . . . . . . . . . . . . . . . . . . .269

*Continues*

▶ **PART IV   APPLICATIONS**

**CHAPTER 18**   C# . . . . . . . . . . . . . . . . . . . . . . . . . . . . . . . . . . . . . . . . . . . . .283

**CHAPTER 19**   Databases . . . . . . . . . . . . . . . . . . . . . . . . . . . . . . . . . . . . . 297

**CHAPTER 20**   XML. . . . . . . . . . . . . . . . . . . . . . . . . . . . . . . . . . . . . . . . . . . . . .317

**CHAPTER 21**   ASP.NET MVC. . . . . . . . . . . . . . . . . . . . . . . . . . . . . . . . . . . 341

**CHAPTER 22**   Silverlight. . . . . . . . . . . . . . . . . . . . . . . . . . . . . . . . . . . . . . . . 357

**CHAPTER 23**   Services . . . . . . . . . . . . . . . . . . . . . . . . . . . . . . . . . . . . . . . . . 377

**INDEX**. . . . . . . . . . . . . . . . . . . . . . . . . . . . . . . . . . . . . . . . . . . . . . . . . . . . . . . .391

PROFESSIONAL

# F# 2.0

Ted Neward
Aaron C. Erickson
Talbott Crowell
Richard Minerich

Wiley Publishing, Inc.

## Professional F# 2.0

Published by
Wiley Publishing, Inc.
10475 Crosspoint Boulevard
Indianapolis, IN 46256
www.wiley.com

Published simultaneously in Canada

ISBN: 978-0-470-52801-3

ISBN: 978-1-118-00713-6 (ebk)

ISBN: 978-1-118-00827-0 (ebk)

ISBN: 978-1-118-00828-7 (ebk)

Manufactured in the United States of America

10 9 8 7 6 5 4 3 2 1

For general information on our other products and services please contact our Customer Care Department within the United States at (877) 762-2974, outside the United States at (317) 572-3993 or fax (317) 572-4002.

Wiley also publishes its books in a variety of electronic formats. Some content that appears in print may not be available in electronic books.

Library of Congress Control Number: 2010932419

*To Charlotte: thank you.*

—TED NEWARD

*For my grandmother who gave me confidence to write,
and for my kids for giving me a reason to.*

—AARON C. ERICKSON

*This book is dedicated to my family.*

—TALBOTT CROWELL

*To Lou Franco, beyond being a mentor and friend,
you showed me that what I once thought hard was in
fact easy.*

—RICHARD MINERICH

# CREDITS

**ACQUISITIONS EDITOR**
Paul Reese

**DEVELOPMENT EDITOR**
Kelly Talbot

**TECHNICAL EDITORS**
Jason Mauer
Matthew Podwysocki
Al Scherer
David Morton

**PRODUCTION EDITOR**
Rebecca Anderson

**COPY EDITOR**
San Dee Phillips

**EDITORIAL DIRECTOR**
Robyn B. Siesky

**EDITORIAL MANAGER**
Mary Beth Wakefield

**PRODUCTION MANAGER**
Tim Tate

**VICE PRESIDENT AND EXECUTIVE GROUP PUBLISHER**
Richard Swadley

**VICE PRESIDENT AND EXECUTIVE PUBLISHER**
Barry Pruett

**ASSOCIATE PUBLISHER**
Jim Minatel

**PROJECT COORDINATOR, COVER**
Lynsey Stanford

**PROOFREADER**
Sheilah Ledwidge,
Word One New York

**INDEXER**
Johnna VanHoose Dinse

**COVER DESIGNER**
Michael E. Trent

**COVER PHOTO**
© hfng/istockphoto.com

# ABOUT THE AUTHORS

**TED NEWARD** is the Principal with Neward & Associates, a consulting firm that works with clients of all sizes, from Fortune 500s to small startups. He is fascinated with programming languages, virtual machines, and enterprise-class systems, spends a lot of his time in the Java and .NET ecosystems, and has recently begun to explore the world of mobile devices and games. He resides with his wife, two sons, and eight laptops in the Pacific Northwest.

**AARON C. ERICKSON** is a Principal Consultant with ThoughtWorks. His life's work is helping organizations better leverage technology by contributing to solutions that have substantial positive economic impact for his clients. He is an enthusiast of agile techniques for delivery of software, and he has a special interest in helping companies understand how to leverage functional programming techniques to perform meaningful business analytics, particularly using natural language processing and Monte Carlo simulation.

**TALBOTT CROWELL** is a Solution Architect and founder of ThirdM responsible for designing and building enterprise applications with a focus on Microsoft technologies including SharePoint, BizTalk Server, and the .NET framework. His company delivers solutions and services to large and small companies, including Fortune 500s. ThirdM also assists companies with the development process by using a blend of Agile and traditional methodologies, Team Foundation Server and Visual Studio Team System, Scrum, Test Driven Development (TDD), performance testing, and other proven tools and practices. Involved in the developer community, Talbott co-founded the F# User Group, http://fsug.org, and serves as a lead for other community events and groups such as SharePoint Saturday Boston and the Boston Area SharePoint User Group. You can follow him on twitter, @talbott, or http://twitter.com/talbott.

**RICHARD MINERICH** began to notice a problem in the software industry only a few years after graduating from UMass Amherst. He saw a deep divide between the remarkable advancements being made in computer science and the aged tools still in use by software engineers and domain experts. Through writing, speaking, and consulting, Richard hopes to bring these advances to a broader audience, to facilitate the creation of intelligent software, and to bring disruptive change to stagnant industries. Richard is currently a Microsoft MVP for the F# programming language and is one of three leaders of the New England F# User Group.

# ACKNOWLEDGMENTS

**FIRST AND FOREMOST**, I would like to thank Aaron, Rick, and Talbott for swooping in at the last second, carving off chunks of the vastly-overwhelming "TODO" list remaining to me, and knocking them off with nary a complaint or challenge. You guys have been a delight to work with. A tip of the hat must also go to Don Syme, Luke Hoban, Chris Smith, and the others on the F# team, who patiently answered stupid question after stupid question. Thanks must also go out to the various attendees who've listened to me prattle on about F#, both those who knew more about the subject than I, as well as those who knew less — all of you have been extremely helpful in honing the delivery of the answer to the question, "What is F#, why do I care, and how do I use it?" Matt Podwysocki in particular gets a hearty kudo for helping me understand some of the thornier functional concepts, and Kevin Hazzard gets one just for being himself.

Lastly, no book gets written without a support structure, and in this case, that structure consists principally of my wife, Charlotte, who patiently endured night after night of "I promise I'll be home by midnight" and wound up waiting for me 'til 3 or 4 AM, just to hear how my day (er... night) went. Hon, you deserved much better than me, but I'll never tell, on the off chance that you haven't figured it out yet.

—TED NEWARD

**I WOULD LIKE TO** thank, my wife, my kids, and my professional colleagues for their support through this process. Of course, a hearty thanks goes to the folks at Wrox who have been very patient along the way, especially during those times where billable consulting time conflicted with book writing time. Of course, without all the great people in the F# community, this book would not have happened. Particular thanks goes to Alex Pedenko, who helped me vet the Relational Record Mapper concept, nicely extending the work I started in the data chapter.

—AARON C. ERICKSON

**I WOULD LIKE TO** thank my family, especially my wife Pradeepa and two sons, Tristan and William, for their support and patience while I worked on this book. I would also like to thank my parents and siblings who have also been major supporting factors in my life. I would like to extend my gratitude toward my co-authors, Ted Neward, Aaron Erickson, and Rick Minerich for their dedication to getting this book published, Michael de la Maza for spearheading the F# User Group, Don Syme and Microsoft Research for their brilliant work creating F#, plus Luke Hoban and the Microsoft product team for bringing F# into Visual Studio as part of the product.

—Talbott Crowell

**NO AMOUNT OF THANKS** to my co-authors would be enough. Ted, for bringing vision and leadership to this project. Aaron, for his frequent advice on dealing with the many small dramas of the authoring and consulting world. Talbott, for recommending me for this project and for being my New England F# brother-in-arms. I'd also like to thank Michael de la Maza who came up with the idea to start a New England F# User Group, everyone at Atalasoft for supporting me in this and my parents for cheering me up when the pressures seemed worst. Finally, I'd like to thank the F# community; each of you proves the superiority of statically-typed functional programming on a daily basis.

—Richard Minerich

# CONTENTS

*FOREWORD*                                                    *xxi*

*INTRODUCTION*                                                *xxiii*

## PART 0: BEGINNINGS

### CHAPTER 1: PRIMER                                          3

Setup                                                         5
It's that Time of Year Again...                               7
Strategy                                                      10
The Delegate Strategy                                         12
Lambda Calculus (Briefly)                                     17
Type Inference                                                22
Immutability                                                  26
Expressions, not Statements                                   27
Summary                                                       28

## PART I: BASICS

### CHAPTER 2: LEXICAL STRUCTURE                               31

Comments                                                      31
Identifiers                                                   32
Preprocessor Directives                                       33
Significant Whitespace                                        34
Summary                                                       35

### CHAPTER 3: PRIMITIVE TYPES                                 37

Boolean                                                       37
Numeric Types                                                 38
Bitwise Operations                                            40
Floating-Point Types                                          40
Arithmetic Conversions                                        41
String and Character Types                                    42
Unit                                                          43
Units of Measure Types                                        43

Literal Values     44
Summary     45

**CHAPTER 4: CONTROL FLOW**     47

Basic Decisions: if     47
Looping: while/do     49
Looping: for     50
Exceptions     50
    try...with     51
    try...finally     52
    Raising and Throwing Exceptions     52
    Defining New Exception Types     53
Summary     53

**CHAPTER 5: COMPOSITE TYPES**     55

Option Types     55
    Option Functions     57
Tuples     58
Arrays     60
    Array Construction     60
    Array Access     62
    Array Functions     62
Lists     65
    List Construction     66
    List Access     68
    List Methods     70
Using Lists and Arrays     72
Sequences     74
Maps     79
    Map Construction     79
    Map Access     80
    Map Functions     81
Sets     82
Summary     83

**CHAPTER 6: PATTERN MATCHING**     85

Basics     85
Pattern Types     88
    Constant Patterns     88
    Variable-Binding ("Named") Patterns     89

AND, OR Patterns 90
Literal Patterns 90
Tuple Patterns 91
as Patterns 92
List Patterns 92
Array Patterns 93
Discriminated Union Patterns 93
Record Patterns 93
**Pattern Guards** **94**
**Active Patterns** **95**
Single Case 96
Partial Case 97
Multi-Case 99
**Summary** **102**

**PART II: OBJECTS**

**CHAPTER 7: COMPLEX COMPOSITE TYPES** **105**

**Type Abbreviations** **105**
**Enum Types** **106**
**Discriminated Union Types** **109**
**Structs** **114**
Value Type Implicit Members 117
Structs and Pattern-Matching 118
**Record Types** **119**
Record Type Implicit Members 123
**Summary** **123**

**CHAPTER 8: CLASSES** **125**

**Basics** **125**
Fields 126
Constructors 127
Creating 131
**Members** **132**
Properties 132
Methods 140
**Static Members** **146**
Operator Overloading 147
**Delegates and Events** **149**
Subscribing 150
Delegates 150

DelegateEvents                                      152
Beyond DelegateEvents: Events                       154
**Access Modifiers**                                **155**
**Type Extensions**                                 **157**
**Summary**                                         **159**

**CHAPTER 9: INHERITANCE**                          **161**

**Basics**                                          **161**
Fields and Constructors                             163
**Overriding**                                      **166**
Abstract Members                                    168
Default                                             169
**Casting**                                         **171**
Upcasting                                           172
Downcasting                                         172
Flexible Types                                      173
Boxing and Unboxing                                 174
**Interfaces**                                      **177**
Implementation                                      177
Definition                                          180
**Object Expressions**                              **181**
**Summary**                                         **181**

**CHAPTER 10: GENERICS**                            **183**

**Basics**                                          **183**
Type Parameters                                     185
**Type Constraints**                                **186**
Type Constraint                                     187
Equality Constraint                                 187
Comparison Constraint                               188
Null Constraint                                     188
Constructor Constraint                              188
Value Type and Reference Type Constraints           188
Other Constraints                                   189
**Statically Resolved Type Parameters**             **189**
Explicit Member Constraint                          189
**Summary**                                         **190**

**CHAPTER 11: PACKAGING**                           **191**

**Namespaces**                                      **191**
Referencing a Namespace                             191

Defining a Namespace 192
**Modules** **193**
Referencing a Module 193
Defining a Module 193
**Summary** **195**

**CHAPTER 12: CUSTOM ATTRIBUTES** **197**

**Using Custom Attributes** **197**
EntryPoint 198
Obsolete 199
Conditional 200
ParamArray 200
Struct, Class, AbstractClass, Interface, Literal, and Measure 201
Assembly Attributes 201
DefaultMember 202
Serializable, NonSerialized 202
AutoOpen 202
Other Attributes 202
**Creation and Consumption** **203**
Creation 203
Consumption 205
**Summary** **206**

**PART III: FUNCTIONAL PROGRAMMING**

**CHAPTER 13: FUNCTIONS** **209**

**Traditional Function Calls** **209**
**Mathematical Functions** **210**
**Coming from C#** **211**
**Function Arguments and Return Values** **211**
Automatic Generalization and Restriction 211
The inline Keyword 212
Type Annotations 213
Generics and Type Constraints 214
Statically Resolved Type Parameters 215
**Partial Application** **215**
Currying 216
Restrictions on Functions and Methods 217
**Functions as First Class** **218**
Recursive Functions 218
Higher Order Functions 219
Storing Functions 221

Creating Functions at Runtime 221

**Summary** 223

## CHAPTER 14: IMMUTABLE DATA 225

**The Problem with State** 225

**State Safety** 226

Programwide State Safety 226

Local Data State Safety 229

**Data Mutation** 232

Avoiding Mutation 233

Bubble and Assign 235

Reference Cells 236

Passing by Reference 238

Message Passing 238

**Performance Considerations** 239

Lists 239

Arrays 242

Sequences 242

Tuples 243

Records 243

structs 243

**Summary** 245

## CHAPTER 15: DATA TYPES 247

**Ambiguously Typed Data** 247

**Failing Fast** 248

**Specificity** 248

Option as an Example 249

Encapsulating State in Types 249

Avoiding Exceptions 251

Data and State Flow 252

Recursively Defined Data Types 253

**Summary** 255

## CHAPTER 16: LIST PROCESSING 257

**Collection Abstractions** 257

**Module Functions** 258

**Collection Subsets** 258

filter 259

partition 259

**Element Transformations**     **260**
map     260
choose     262
collect     262
**Accumulators**     **263**
reduce     264
fold     265
scan     266
**Summary**     **267**

**CHAPTER 17: PIPELINING AND COMPOSITION**     **269**

**Basic Composition and Pipelining**     **269**
Pipelining     270
Composition     272
**Applying Pipelining and Composition**     **275**
From Loops to Pipelining     276
From Pipelining to Composition     277
Advanced Composition     278
**Summary**     **280**

**PART IV: APPLICATIONS**

**CHAPTER 18: C#**     **283**

**Overview**     **283**
**Calling C# Libraries from F#**     **284**
Simple Method Calling Scenarios     284
C# Object Construction     285
F#, C#, and null     286
F# and C# Methods that Expect Delegates     287
F# and C# Events     288
F# to C# Summary     289
**Calling F# Libraries from C#**     **289**
Basics of Calling F#     290
F# Tuples in C# Programs     290
Dealing with F# Records from C#     291
Passing Functions to F# Functions     292
Dealing with F# Discriminated Unions from C#     292
Working with F# Option Types from C#     293
**Rules of Thumb for Writing F# APIs**     **294**
**Summary**     **295**

**CHAPTER 19: DATABASES** — **297**

Overview — 297
Retrieving Data Using ADO.NET — 298
  Creating a Database Connection — 298
  Reading Data — 299
  Filtering Data — 300
  Insert, Update, and Delete — 301
F# and Object Relational Mapping — 302
Introducing F# Active Record (FAR) — 303
  Reading Data — 303
  Querying Data — 304
  Adding Data — 304
  Updating Data — 305
  Deleting Data — 305
  What Isn't Supported — 306
  Coming Soon — 306
How FAR Works — 306
  Dependencies — 306
  Utility Routines — 307
  Table Creation — 308
  Query Processing — 309
  Implementation of Other FOR Operations — 314
Summary — 315

**CHAPTER 20: XML** — **317**

Overview — 317
F# and LINQ-to-XML — 318
  Reading — 318
  Querying — 320
  Processing — 322
  Writing — 325
  Writing XML to Memory or Other Stream-Based Resources — 325
F# and XML DOM — 325
  Reading — 326
  Querying — 327
  Processing — 328
  Writing — 329
F#, XML, and Active Patterns — 329
  Multi-case Active Patterns — 330

Partial-Case Active Patterns | 336
**Summary** | **339**

**CHAPTER 21: ASP.NET MVC** | **341**

**Overview** | **341**
**FORECAST'R — The World's Simplest Weather Forecast Site** | **342**
Modeling the Domain | 343
Creating a Repository | 344
Creating the Controller | 349
Creating Some View Helpers | 351
Creating the View | 352
**Summary** | **355**

**CHAPTER 22: SILVERLIGHT** | **357**

**Overview** | **357**
Software Runtime and Developer Requirements | 359
**Visual Studio Project Templates** | **360**
The Silverlight Application | 361
The F# Silverlight Library | 363
**The Silverlight Toolkit** | **365**
Line Charts and Area Charts | 365
Designer Tools | 366
**Data Binding** | **368**
Design Time Data Binding | 368
Programmatic Data Binding | 371
**Calculating Moving Average** | **372**
**Putting It All Together** | **373**
**Summary** | **376**

**CHAPTER 23: SERVICES** | **377**

**Overview** | **377**
**An F#-Based Weather Service** | **378**
The Service Contract | 378
**Leveraging the Domain Model** | **380**
**Writing the Service Controller** | **381**
Rendering Weather | 381
Helping the Service Controller | 381
Service Controller Implementation | 382

Service Implementation 383
Implementing the Service Host 383
**Consuming Services** **385**
Generating a Service Stub 385
Writing the Service Consumer 388
**Summary** **390**

*INDEX* *391*

# FOREWORD

There's Left, Right, and there's Center. There's peanut butter, chocolate, and then there's peanut butter cups. C#, Visual Basic...and now there's F#. There have always been effectively only two choices for programmers that target .NET, and for many that's been no choice at all. Take a look at F#. It's a functional language, to be clear, but it's also object-oriented and a bridge between two worlds. It's all the goodness of a peanut butter cup, and more.

To many, F# feels new and dramatic. Its values are rooted not just in some of the first programming languages, but the lambda calculus itself. F# may feel new to you and me, but it's based on 80 years of deep mathematical proof and respected thought.

When the get-er-done programmer hears names like Scheme, OCaml, Haskell, Erlang, and F#, these languages conjure up visions of crazy-eyed computer scientists and bearded hermits. You can't expect to really sell software written in these languages any more than John Grisham can sell a legal mystery written in Latin, right? That's madness.

Actually not. F# needs to be a new tool in your toolbox. Imagine not thinking about variables changing their value. Imagine no global state and no side effects. Imagine not worrying about deadlocks and race conditions because you aren't using any locks. Consider not just testing your application but proving that it works and being able to count on it.

F# reminds us that writing stateful code in a procedural language for a machine that has 12 cores is, well, freaking hard to get right. F# reminds the .NET programmer that there is life beyond the simply procedural. F# gives you this, and the familiarity of the .NET runtime and Base Class Library that you already know how to use. You can write F# not just with .NET on Windows, but also on Xbox 360, Silverlight, and Mono on Linux.

There's another way of thinking out there and it's functional. Study this book's take on F#. It's clear, code-focused, realistic, and pragmatic. This is a real language that you can solve real problems with. I hope you enjoy reading this book as much as I did.

—Scott Hanselman
*Principal Program Manager Lead*
—*Server and Tools Online - Microsoft*

# INTRODUCTION

This is a book on the F# programming language.

On the surface of things, that is a nonsensical and/or intuitively obvious statement, given the title of this book. However, despite the apparent redundancy in saying it aloud, the sentence above elegantly describes what this book is about: We are not attempting to teach developers how to accomplish tasks from other languages in this one, nor are we attempting to evangelize the language or its feature set or its use "over" other languages. We assume that you are reading this book because you have an interest in learning the F# language: its syntax, its semantics, its pros and cons, and its use in concert with other parts of the .NET ecosystem.

## WHO THIS BOOK IS FOR

In order to keep to the core focus of the book, we assume that you, the reader, are a journeyman .NET developer, familiar with at least one of the programming languages in the .NET ecosystem: C# or Visual Basic will be the most common language of choice for those in the .NET community — but if you've learned C++/CLI or even one of the lesser-known .NET languages (IronPython or IronRuby, perhaps, or even one of the dozens or so of "alternative" languages for the CLR), you'll still be able to follow along without too much difficulty.

In particular, we assume that you're already comfortable with concepts like assemblies, managed code, and executing on top of a virtual machine, so none of that ".NET 101" topical material appears here, as it would be redundant to what you've already read in a beginning or intermediate C# or Visual Basic book. You've probably used Reflection at some point in your career, and/or XML, WinForms, Windows Presentation Foundation (or its web-based successor, Silverlight), Windows Communication Foundation, with maybe a little database access thrown in for good measure.

In short, we assume that you've been developing in the .NET environment for the past couple of years. If that's not you, you may want to start with one of the introductory .NET titles, such as *Beginning C# 3.0* or *Beginning Visual Basic 2010*. For that reason, there are no "hand-holding" steps found in a variety of other books when it comes to creating Visual Studio Solution files or creating new Projects; not only would those steps be useless to the journeyman .NET developer (not to mention somewhat insulting), but they are also useless to the F# developer who wants to use MonoDevelop and the Mono implementation of the Common Language Runtime for writing and executing F# code. Considering that F# has held full compatibility with Mono as a goal since its inception, ignoring that crowd felt rude.

If you are of the handful of functional programmers who've been working in Haskell, Ocaml, ML, or some Lisp-based derivative, you're probably not going to like this book. We spend no time discussing monads, monoids, or catamorphisms here, nor do we consider that a missing part of the book that "we just didn't have time to cover;" the book you want will be written entirely differently than this one, in a different style than this one, and probably by entirely different authors.

This book assumes you are comfortable with object-orientation and want to start down the path of learning not only how to program with functional concepts, but that you want to work with both functions and objects, in some kind of pleasant harmony, on top of the CLR.

If you're still not sure if you're the right reader for this book, take this little test: read Chapter 1, Primer, and see if that makes sense to you. If it seems way too simple, you're probably more functionally-minded than we assumed the average reader to be; you'll find the book useful as a reference, perhaps, or as a skimmable guide to the syntax, but you won't find mind-popping concepts in here. If it seems way too difficult, then don't despair — that chapter is intended as a microcosm of where we want you to end up.

If that chapter seems "just right," though, head on over to the register.

## WHAT THIS BOOK COVERS

This book takes a four-part approach to the F# language (officially, the F# 2.0 version of the language): basics, objects, functions, and "integration" (meaning how F# interacts with various .NET technologies like Silverlight or relational databases). We go over the 90% of the F# programming language that we think you're going to need.

Note that we're not a complete reference on the language. We ignore the 10% of the language specification that we think most .NET developers will never run into, on the grounds that if you do run into one of those edge-case constructs, you'll have enough familiarity with the F# syntax to figure it out, or you'll look it up in the F# 2.0 Language Reference (or ask somebody in forums or on a mailing list) for the exact details. (Our guess is that it'll be at least a year or so as a practicing F# developer before you run into one of those constructs.)

## HOW THIS BOOK IS STRUCTURED

The book is arranged in, we think, the order a practicing .NET (which means, "object-trained") developer will find most useful.

Part 0 is the Primer, a gentle up-sloping introduction to the concepts that the F# language incorporates as first-class citizens as well as a hint of some of the ways in which functional programming can be useful within the .NET environment.

Part I covers Basics. Here, you'll find definitions of the primitive types, flow control, syntax rules, and other such things that have to be defined before anything else can be discussed.

Part II covers Objects. F# permits the creation of new classes, interfaces and other object-oriented types, as well as the traditional set of object-oriented features such as implementation inheritance, and they're all covered here. In keeping with the tone of the book, we don't spend a lot of time teaching you what "IS-A" means; as a practicing .NET developer, you already know that. So this chapter focuses primarily on the syntax, and how F# "does objects" both similarly to, and differently from, its sibling languages C# and Visual Basic.

Part III takes on an entirely different tone, that of Functions, and will be the new material and concepts for most readers. Instead of using Visual Studio, you use the REPL (Read-Evaluate-Print-Loop) for writing snippets of code and seeing them execute immediately. Instead of building up objects, you create functions. And so on. Readers could stop after the end of Part II and have F# as "a better C#," but doing so would be missing out on some of the very things that make F# vastly more interesting than C#.

Part IV, then, shows how to use F# with a variety of different technologies (XML, Silverlight, services, and so on), and tries to show one way — not *the* way — to use F# beyond straight console-mode applications. As tempting as it might be to jump straight here and cut-and-paste the code into your own applications, resist the urge until you've read through the first three parts. It's vastly more satisfying to be able to predict what the code will look like as you read along, than to just see the code execute and have no real idea why.

## WHAT YOU NEED TO USE THIS BOOK

We assume that you have Visual Studio 2010 installed on your system. As of this writing, unfortunately, no "Visual 2010 F# Express" edition download exists from Microsoft, so you'll need to have Visual Studio 2010 Professional installed, with (obviously) the Visual F# feature set installed with it.

If you have a Visual Studio 2008 installation, you can still play in the F# playground, but it's a bit harder: You must find and download the Visual F# install bits for Visual Studio 2008 (it's a Visual Studio package), and install them. Technically, this is the "F# 2.0 for Windows + Visual Studio 2008 (April 2010 release)" version.

If you don't have any version of Visual Studio and are unwilling to acquire one, another option is available to you: a self-constructed version of "Visual F# Express." By installing the Visual Studio 2008 Shell and the aforementioned "F# 2.0 for Windows..." bits, you will have a version of Visual Studio 2008 that contains only the F# language compiler and nothing else — no ASP.NET, no Silverlight, nothing. (As of this writing, the F# team was exploring whether the Visual Studio 2010 Shell would work as a host for the F# 2.0 bits, and while it's likely that such a combination will work, none of the authors here can verify that for a fact.)

If you are looking to use F# on Mono, then you want to download the "F# 2.0 for Mono/Mac/Linux (compiler binaries)" and install according to the instructions there.

As of this writing, the "F# Downloads" page on Microsoft Research (research.microsoft.com) has links to all of the different flavors discussed here.

Our assumption is that the vast majority of our readership will be using Visual Studio 2010 or Visual Studio 2008, so if you're one of the readers outside of that population set, we apologize ahead of time for whatever conflicts you will find with command-prompt output, screen shots, or references to IDE instructions.

## CONVENTIONS

To help you get the most from the text and keep track of what's happening, we've used a number of conventions throughout the book.

> *Boxes with a warning icon like this one hold important, not-to-be-forgotten information that is directly relevant to the surrounding text.*

> *The pencil icon indicates notes, tips, hints, tricks, or asides to the current discussion.*

As for styles in the text:

➤ We show keyboard strokes like this: Ctrl+A.

➤ We show file names, URLs, and code within the text like so: `persistence.properties`.

➤ We present code like this:

```
We use a monofont type for code examples.
```

## SOURCE CODE

As you work through the examples in this book, you may choose either to type in all the code manually, or to use the source code files that accompany the book. All the source code used in this book is available for download at `www.wrox.com`. When at the site, simply locate the book's title (use the Search box or one of the title lists) and click the Download Code link on the book's detail page to obtain all the source code for the book. Code that is included on the website is highlighted by the following icon:

**Available for download on Wrox.com**

Listings include the filename in the title. If it is just a code snippet, you'll find the filename in a code note such as this:

*Code snippet filename*

 *Because many books have similar titles, you may find it easiest to search by ISBN; this book's ISBN is 978-0-470-52801-3.*

Once you download the code, just decompress it with your favorite compression tool. Alternately, you can go to the main Wrox code download page at www.wrox.com/dynamic/books/download .aspx to see the code available for this book and all other Wrox books.

## ERRATA

We make every effort to ensure that there are no errors in the text or in the code. However, no one is perfect, and mistakes do occur. If you find an error in one of our books, like a spelling mistake or faulty piece of code, we would be very grateful for your feedback. By sending in errata, you may save another reader hours of frustration, and at the same time, you will be helping us provide even higher quality information.

To find the errata page for this book, go to www.wrox.com and locate the title using the Search box or one of the title lists. Then, on the book details page, click the Book Errata link. On this page, you can view all errata that has been submitted for this book and posted by Wrox editors. A complete book list, including links to each book's errata, is also available at www.wrox.com/misc-pages/ booklist.shtml.

If you don't spot "your" error on the Book Errata page, go to www.wrox.com/contact/techsupport .shtml and complete the form there to send us the error you have found. We'll check the information and, if appropriate, post a message to the book's errata page and fix the problem in subsequent editions of the book.

## P2P.WROX.COM

For author and peer discussion, join the P2P forums at p2p.wrox.com. The forums are a Web-based system for you to post messages relating to Wrox books and related technologies and interact with other readers and technology users. The forums offer a subscription feature to e-mail you topics of interest of your choosing when new posts are made to the forums. Wrox authors, editors, other industry experts, and your fellow readers are present on these forums.

At p2p.wrox.com, you will find a number of different forums that will help you, not only as you read this book, but also as you develop your own applications. To join the forums, just follow these steps:

1. Go to p2p.wrox.com and click the Register link.

2. Read the terms of use and click Agree.

3. Complete the required information to join, as well as any optional information you wish to provide, and click Submit.

4. You will receive an e-mail with information describing how to verify your account and complete the joining process.

 *You can read messages in the forums without joining P2P, but in order to post your own messages, you must join.*

Once you join, you can post new messages and respond to messages other users post. You can read messages at any time on the Web. If you would like to have new messages from a particular forum e-mailed to you, click the Subscribe to this Forum icon by the forum name in the forum listing.

For more information about how to use the Wrox P2P, be sure to read the P2P FAQs for answers to questions about how the forum software works, as well as many common questions specific to P2P and Wrox books. To read the FAQs, click the FAQ link on any P2P page.

# PART 0
# Beginnings

▶ **CHAPTER 1:** Primer

# 1

# Primer

**WHAT'S IN THIS CHAPTER?**

➤ Understanding strategies

➤ Reviewing Lambda calculus

➤ Infering types

➤ Understanding mutability

➤ Creating your own bindings

Object-oriented programming has been with us for close to two decades, if not longer; its expressions of those concepts via the languages C# and Visual Basic, and the platform on which they run, the CLR, have been more recent, only since 2002. The community and eco-system around the object-oriented paradigm is vast, and the various traps and pitfalls around an object-oriented way of thinking has seen copious discussion and experience, and where disagreements occur, reasoned and heated debate. From its inception more than 40 years ago, through its exploration in languages invented yesterday, an object-oriented approach to languages has received the benefit of the attention of some of the smartest language and tool designers in the industry, and a highly permutational approach to ancillary features around the language, such as garbage collection, strong-versus-weak typing, compilation-versus-inter-pretation, and various hybrids thereof, full-fidelity metadata, parameterized types, and more; no stone, it seems, remains unturned.

One of the principal goals of an object-oriented language is the establishment of user-defined types (UDTs) that not only serve to capture the abstractions around the users' domain, but also the capability to reuse those types in a variety of different scenarios within the same domain without modification. Sometimes this domain is a business-flavored one — at the start of the 21$^{st}$ century these kinds of types were called *business objects* and later *domain types*. Sometimes the domain is an infrastructural one, such as presentation or communication, and these types are frequently collected together in a large bundle known as a *framework* or *class library*. And despite the relatively slow start that C++ class libraries saw during C++'s heyday, the combination of fast, cheap network access and volunteers willing to share their efforts has led to a proliferation of these infrastructural bundles that dwarfs anything the industry has seen before.

Unfortunately, despite the huge success of C++, Java, and .NET, the original premise of the object-oriented, that developers could take objects "off the shelf" and reuse them without modification, has yet to occur for anything but the infrastructural domain. Even in that domain, debate and duplication rages over subtle points of design that can only be changed by changing the underlying source code making up those infrastructural types.

More important, as the 20th century came to a close and the 21st loomed on the horizon, developers began to find "edges," limitations to the object-oriented paradigm that saw no easy answer. These edges pushed the object-oriented community to amend its approach slightly, placing those objects into *containers* and relying on the container to provide a set of services that could not easily be captured by object-oriented methodology. These *component containers*, exemplified by the Enterprise Java Beans standard (and its later lighter-weight successor, Spring) and COM+/EnterpriseServices found some traction but were never wholly adored by the developers who used them.

In time, those containers were amended to take a more coarse-grained approach, seeking a certain degree of simplification to enable for a more interoperable capacity, and these new domain bundles received a new name: *services*. Although Service-Oriented Architecture (SOA) sounded an entirely new style of programming, developers seeking to take their traditional object-oriented concepts into the service-oriented realm found themselves struggling with even the simplest of designs.

Despite the guidance of well-honed discussions around object-oriented design (called *design patterns* at first, then later just *patterns*), the more developers sought to model their software after the reality of the businesses around them, the more they struggled to achieve the reusability promised them. Coupled with this came the disquieting realization that object languages had not only failed to produce that set of "Tinkertoys" that developers or users could just reuse off the shelf, but also that some domains defied some of the modeling characteristics of object languages entirely — some domains were just complicated and awkward to model in objects.

Then, subtly, a new problem emerged: the underlying hardware ceased its steady march of improved performance and instead began to respond to the beat of a different drum, that of *multicore*. Suddenly, where programmers used to face problems in a single- or slightly-multi-threaded environment, now the hardware demanded that additional performance would come only from greater and greater parallelization of code. Where the object-oriented developers of the 20th century could assume that only a single logical thread of execution would operate against their objects, the developers of the 21st century has to assume that many logical threads of execution will all be hammering on their objects simultaneously. The implication, that developers must now consider all possible interactions of multiple threads on every operation available on the types they define, continues to hang like a proverbial Sword of Damocles over the heads of object-oriented programmers even as the first decade of the new century came to a close.

This chapter attempts to demonstrate some of the technical challenges C# and Visual Basic developers (and, to a logical extent, their cousins and predecessors in Java and C++) have faced when using the object-oriented paradigm exclusively. In the beginning, challenges will be addressed with programming techniques available to the developer using off-the-shelf tools and technology, but as the problems surmount, so will the desire to change those tools into something more, something that demonstrates the need for a new approach to programming beyond the traditional object-oriented one, and a new language to explore and expose those concepts more succinctly and directly.

## SETUP

Imagine a system, a simple one (to start) for tracking students and instructors and the classes they teach. In keeping with traditional object-oriented thought, several domain types are defined, here in C# 2.0, though the actual language — C#, Visual Basic, C++/CLI (any .NET language would work) — in which they are defined makes little difference:

```csharp
class Person
{
    private string m_first;
    private string m_last;
    private int m_age;

    public Person(string fn, string ln, int a)
    {
        FirstName = fn;
        LastName = ln;
        Age = a;
    }
    public string FirstName
    {
        get { return m_first; }
        set { m_first = value; }
    }
    public string LastName
    {
        get { return m_last; }
        set { m_last = value; }
    }
    public int Age
    {
        get { return m_age; }
        set { m_age = value; }
    }
}

class Student : Person
{
    private string m_major;

    public Student(string fn, string ln, int a, string maj)
        : base(fn, ln, a)
    {
        Major = maj;
    }
    public string Major
```

```
    {
        get { return m_major; }
        set { m_major = value; }
    }
}

class Instructor : Person
{
    private string m_dept;

    public Instructor(string fn, string ln, int a, string dept)
        : base(fn, ln, a)
    {
        Department = dept;
    }
    public string Department
    {
        get { return m_dept; }
        set { m_dept = value; }
    }
}

class Class
{
    private string m_name;
    private List<Student> m_students = new List<Student>();
    private Instructor m_instructor;

    public Class(string n)
    {
        Name = n;
    }
    public string Name
    {
        get { return m_name; }
        set { m_name = value; }
    }
    public Instructor Instructor
    {
        get { return m_instructor; }
        set { m_instructor = value; }
    }
    public List<Student> Students
    {
        get { return m_students; }
    }
}
```

As with most systems of its type, the system begins simply: there are two kinds of "Person"s in the system, Students and Instructors, and Classes are taught to Students by Instructors. So, building up from basic parts, lists of Instructors and Students might look like this:

```
class Program
{
    static List<Student> Students = new List<Student>();
    static List<Instructor> Instructors = new List<Instructor>();
```

```
static Program()
{
    Instructors.Add(new Instructor("Al", "Scherer", 38,
                    "Computer Science"));
    Instructors.Add(new Instructor("Albert", "Einstein", 50,
                    "Physics"));
    Instructors.Add(new Instructor("Sigmund", "Freud", 50,
                    "Psychology"));
    Instructors.Add(new Instructor("Aaron", "Erickson", 35,
                    "Underwater Basketweaving"));

    Students.Add(new Student("Matthew", "Neward", 10,
                "Grade school"));
    Students.Add(new Student("Michael", "Neward", 16,
                "Video game design"));
    Students.Add(new Student("Charlotte", "Neward", 38,
                "Psychology"));
    Students.Add(new Student("Ted", "Neward", 39,
                "Computer Science"));
}
}
```

Obviously, in a real-world program, these lists of objects will be stored in some form of long-term storage, such as a relational database, but this suffices for now.

## IT'S THAT TIME OF YEAR AGAIN...

At the beginning of the school year, new classes are created and entered into the system — again, this is modeled in the example as a simple list:

```
List<Class> classesFor2010 = new List<Class>();
classesFor2010.Add(new Class("Scala for .NET Developers"));
classesFor2010.Add(new Class("F# for .NET Developers"));
classesFor2010.Add(new Class(
                    "How to play pranks on teachers"));
classesFor2010.Add(new Class(
                    "Baskets of the Lower Amazon"));
classesFor2010.Add(new Class("Child Psych"));
classesFor2010.Add(new Class("Geek Psych"));
```

And when the classes have been set up (Instructors will be assigned later, after the Instructors have determined who is lowest on the totem pole and has to actually teach this year), the students need to log in to the system and register for classes:

```
Console.Write("Please enter your first name:");
string first = Console.ReadLine();
Console.Write("\nPlease enter your last name:");
string last = Console.ReadLine();
```

After the student has entered this information, the two strings must somehow be reconciled into a Student object, a process that usually involves searching the list:

```
foreach (Student s in Students)
{
```

```
            if (s.FirstName == first && s.LastName == last)
            {
                // ... Do something
            }
        }
```

This feels sloppy somehow — after some deeper thought, several things emerge as "wrong."

First, an obvious bottleneck emerges if this list becomes large; for a school of a half-dozen Instructors and a few dozen Students, this simple one-at-a-time comparison works well enough, but if the system grows to incorporate campuses all across the world and millions of Students, this is going to break down quickly.

Second, when it comes time to select an Instructor for a class, similar kinds of search needs to happen, and simply repeating the foreach loops over and over again is a violation of the DRY (Don't Repeat Yourself) principle — there's no reusability. This problem will only magnify itself if the searches are somehow optimized, because the optimizations will need to happen for each search.

*It may seem tempting to brush these concerns off as irrelevant, because if the data is stored in a relational database, the performance and scalability concerns become issues of SQL and database tuning. Stay with the point for now, and trust in that this is merely the tip of the iceberg.*

The obvious object-oriented solution to the problem, then, is to create custom data structures for storing the Students and Instructors:

```
class InstructorDatabase
{
    private List<Instructor> data = new List<Instructor>();
    public InstructorDatabase() { }

    public void Add(Instructor i) { data.Add(i); }
    public Instructor Find(string first, string last)
    {
        foreach (Instructor i in data)
        {
            if (i.FirstName == first && i.LastName == last)
                return i;
        }
        return null;
    }
}

class StudentDatabase
{
    private List<Student> data = new List<Student>();
    public StudentDatabase() { }

    public void Add(Student i) { data.Add(i); }
```

```
public Student Find(string first, string last)
{
    foreach (Student i in data)
    {
        if (i.FirstName == first && i.LastName == last)
            return i;
    }
    return null;
}
}
```

At first glance, this seems like a good idea, but a longer look reveals that these two classes differ in exactly one thing — the kind of data they "wrap." In the first case, it's a list of Instructors, and in the second, a list of Students.

The sharp C# 2.0 programmer immediately shouts out, "Generics!" and after enduring the quizzical looks of the people sharing the room, looks to create a single type out of them, like this:

```
class Database<T>
{
    private List<T> data = new List<T>();
    public Database() { }

    public void Add(T i) { data.Add(i); }
    public T Find(string first, string last)
    {
        foreach (T i in data)
        {
            if (i.FirstName == first && i.LastName == last)
                return i;
        }
        return null;
    }
}
```

but unfortunately, the C# compiler will balk at the code in Find(), because the generic type T can't promise to have properties by the name of FirstName and LastName. This can be solved by adding a type constraint in the generic declaration to ensure that the type passed in to the Database is always something that inherits from Person, and thus has the FirstName and LastName properties, like this:

```
class Database<T> where T: Person
{
    private List<T> data = new List<T>();
    public Database() { }

    public void Add(T i) { data.Add(i); }
    public T Find(string first, string last)
    {
        foreach (T i in data)
        {
            if (i.FirstName == first && i.LastName == last)
                return i;
        }
```

```
            return null;
        }
    }
```

which works, for now. Unfortunately, although this solves the immediate problem, what happens when the `Database` needs to search for a `Student` by major, or an `Instructor` by field? Because those are properties not specified on the `Person` type, once again the `Database` class will fail.

What's actually needed here is the ability to search via some completely arbitrary criteria, specified at the time the search is to happen — if this search were being done in SQL, the programmer could pass in a `WHERE` clause, a search predicate, by which the database could evaluate all the potential matches and return only those that met the criteria.

This sounds like a pretty good idea and one to which object-orientation has an answer: the Strategy pattern.

## STRATEGY

In design patterns parlance, a Strategy is a setup where an object that implements an algorithm can be passed in for execution without the client knowing the actual details of the algorithm. More important, an appropriate Strategy can be selected at runtime, rather than being decided (some might say hard-coded) at compile-time. This is almost spot-on to what's needed here, except in this case the "algorithm" being varied is the criteria by which each potential match is evaluated.

In the classic Strategy implementation, an interface defines the parameters and result type to the algorithm:

```
interface ISearchCriteria<T>
{
    bool Match(T candidate);
}
```

This, then, enables the `Database` to be written to be entirely ignorant of the criteria by which to search:

```
class Database<T> where T : class
{
    private List<T> data = new List<T>();

    public T Find(ISearchCriteria<T> algorithm)
    {
        foreach (T i in data)
        {
            if (algorithm.Match(i))
                return i;
        }
        return null;
    }
}
```

The type constraint is still necessary, because the Database needs to return "null" in the event that the search fails. But now at least the Database is once again generic. Unfortunately, using it leaves something to be desired:

```csharp
class Program
{
    static Database<Student> Students = new Database<Student>();
    static Database<Instructor> Instructors =
        new Database<Instructor>();

    class SearchStudentsByName : ISearchCriteria<Student>
    {
        private string first;
        private string last;
        public SearchStudentsByName(string f, string l)
        {
            first = f;
            last = l;
        }
        public bool Match(Student candidate)
        {
            return candidate.FirstName == first &&
                candidate.LastName == last;
        }
    }

    static void Main(string[] args)
    {
        // ...
        Student s = null;
        while (s == null)
        {
            Console.Write("Please enter your first name:");
            string first = Console.ReadLine();
            Console.Write("\nPlease enter your last name:");
            string last = Console.ReadLine();
            s = Students.Find(
                new SearchStudentsByName(first, last));
            if (s == null)
                Console.WriteLine("Sorry! Couldn't find you");
        }
        // Do something with s
```

Yikes. The code definitely got a little bit easier to use at the point of doing the search, but now a new class has to be written every time a different kind of search needs to happen, and that class will have to be accessible every place a search could be written.

Fortunately, the savvy C# 2.0 developer knows about delegates and their extremely powerful cousins, anonymous methods. (Equally as fortunate, the savvy C# 2.0 developer knows not to shout things out in a room full of people while reading a book.)

# THE DELEGATE STRATEGY

The whole interface-based Strategy approach can be eliminated in favor of a well-defined delegate type and an instance of an anonymous method:

```
delegate bool SearchProc<T>(T candidate);
class Database<T> where T : class
{
    private List<T> data = new List<T>();
    public Database() { }

    public void Add(T i) { data.Add(i); }
    public T Find(SearchProc<T> algorithm)
    {
        foreach (T i in data)
        {
            if (algorithm(i))
                return i;
        }
        return null;
    }
}
```

The real savings comes at the point where the student login code does the lookup; because the search now takes a delegate instance, the criteria by which the Student is looked up can be as rich or as simple as the case demands:

```
Student s = null;
while (s == null)
{
    Console.Write("Please enter your first name:");
    string first = Console.ReadLine();
    Console.Write("\nPlease enter your last name:");
    string last = Console.ReadLine();
    s = Students.Find(delegate (Student c) {
                         return
                             c.FirstName == first &&
                             c.LastName == last
                      });
    if (s == null)
        Console.WriteLine("Sorry! Couldn't find you");
}
// Do something with s
```

Now, all kinds of performance optimization can be done in the Database<T> class, because the client code remains ignorant of *how* the search is done. Instead, it simply specifies *what* to match (or if you will, how the *match* is done, instead of how the *search* is done).

However, the Database isn't done yet: if the Database is later going to find all Instructors that teach a particular subject, it needs the capability to return more than one object if the criteria is matched:

```
class Database<T> where T : class
{
```

```
    private List<T> data = new List<T>();

    // ...

    public T[] FindAll(SearchProc<T> algorithm)
    {
        List<T> results = new List<T>();
        foreach (T i in data)
        {
            if (algorithm(i))
                results.Add(i);
        }
        return results.ToArray();
    }
}
```

C# 2.0 saw much of this coming and predefined those delegate types already as part of the FCL: the Predicate<T> and Func<T> delegate types, the first used to yield a bool result (like the SearchProc previously defined) and the other used to simply "act" upon the value passed in (such as printing it to the console or something similar). In the spirit of "Code not written or removed means code not written with bugs, or maintained so that bugs are introduced later," this means that the code can be refactored to remove the redundant delegate type declaration and use those already defined:

```
class Database<T> where T : class
{
    private List<T> data = new List<T>();
    public Database() { }

    public void Add(T i) { data.Add(i); }
    public T Find(Predicate<T> algorithm)
    {
        foreach (T it in data)
            if (algorithm(it))
                return it;
        return null;
    }
    public T[] FindAll(Predicate<T> algorithm)
    {
        List<T> results = new List<T>();
        foreach (T it in data)
            if (algorithm(it))
                results.Add(it);
        return results.ToArray();
    }
}
```

Other kinds of operations on the Database not yet implemented (but should be) quickly come to mind, such as taking some kind of action on each of those returned objects. To be precise, three kinds of operations should be supported on Database<T>: Filter, Map, and Reduce:

```
delegate U Accumulator<T, U>(T src, U rslt);
class Database<T> where T : class
{
    private List<T> data = new List<T>();
```

```
    public Database() { }

    public void Add(T i) { data.Add(i); }

    public IEnumerable<T> Filter(Predicate<T> pred)
    {
        List<T> results = new List<T>();
        foreach (T it in data)
            if (pred(it))
                results.Add(it);
        return results;
    }
    public IEnumerable<U> Map<U>(Func<T, U> transform)
    {
        List<U> results = new List<U>();
        foreach (T it in data)
            results.Add(transform(it));
        return results;
    }
    public U Reduce<U>(U startValue, Accumulator<T, U> accum)
    {
        U result = startValue;
        foreach (T it in data)
            result = accum(it, result);
        return result;
    }

    public T Find(Predicate<T> algorithm)
    {
        return Filter(algorithm).GetEnumerator().Current;
    }
    public T[] FindAll(Predicate<T> algorithm)
    {
        return new List<T>(Filter(algorithm)).ToArray();
    }
}
```

When those three operations are in place, any other operation can be defined in terms of those three through various combinations of them.

By defining their parameters in terms of IEnumerable<T>, instead of as a raw array as the earlier definitions did, any sort of IEnumerable<T> could be used, including lists, arrays, or even the anonymous iterator defined using the C# 2.0 yield return statement:

```
    public IEnumerable<T> Filter2(Predicate<T> pred)
    {
        foreach (T it in data)
            if (pred(it))
                yield return it;
    }
    public IEnumerable<U> Map2<U>(Func<T, U> transform)
```

```
    {
        foreach (T it in data)
            yield return (transform(it));
    }
```

In terms of their purpose, `Filter` is the easiest to grasp — it applies the `Predicate` to each element in the `Database` and includes that element if the `Predicate` returns true.

`Map` is less obvious — it applies a `Func` (an operation) to each element in the `Database`, transforming it into something else, usually (though not always) of a different type. If, for example, the system needs to extract a list of all the `Students`' ages, `Map` can transform the `Student` into an age:

```
foreach (int a in
    Students.Map(delegate(Student it)
    { return it.Age; }))
{
    Console.WriteLine(a);
}
```

The last, `Reduce`, is the most complicated, largely because it is the most fundamental — both `Map` and `Filter` could be rewritten to use `Reduce`. `Reduce` takes the collection, a delegate that knows how to extract a single bit of information from the element and perform some operation on it to yield a rolling result and hand that back. The easiest thing to do with `Reduce` is obtain a count of all the elements in the collection, by incrementing that accumulator value each time:

```
int count =
    Students.Reduce(0, delegate(Student st, int acc)
                    {
                        return acc++;
                    });
```

Or if for some reason the total of all the `Students`' ages added together were important, `Reduce` can produce it by adding the age to the accumulator each time through:

```
int sumAges =
    Students.Reduce(0, delegate(Student st, int acc)
                    {
                        return st.Age + acc;
                    });
```

In truth, this is useless information — what would be much more interesting is the average of all the `Students`' ages, but this is a bit trickier to do with Reduce — because the average is defined as the total divided by the number of elements in the collection, Reduce has to be used twice:

```
float averageAge =
    (Students.Reduce(0, delegate(Student st, float acc)
                    {
                        return st.Age + acc;
                    }))
    /
    (Students.Reduce(0, delegate(Student st, float acc)
```

```
                    {
                        return acc + 1;
                    }));
```

But even more intriguingly, a collection of Students can be "reduced" to an XML representation by applying the same approach and transforming a Student into a string representation:

```
string studentXML =
    (Students.Reduce("<students>",
                        delegate(Student st, string acc)
                        {
                            return acc +
                                "<student>" +
                                st.FirstName +
                                "</student>";
                        })) + "</students>";
```

If some of this sounds familiar, it is because much of this was later expanded to be a major part of the C# 3.0 release. LINQ, Language-Integrated Query, centers on these same core principles. Using C# 3.0's capability to define new methods from "outside" a class (extension methods), C# 3.0 defined a series of these methods directly on the collection classes found in the .NET Framework Class Library, thus making the Database type even simpler:

```
class Database<T> where T : class
{
    private List<T> data = new List<T>();
    public Database() { }

    public void Add(T i) { data.Add(i); }
    public T Find(Predicate<T> algorithm)
    {
        return data.Find(algorithm);
    }
    public T[] FindAll(Predicate<T> algorithm)
    {
        return data.FindAll(algorithm).ToArray();
    }
}
```

And, of course, if the List<T> holding the Student objects is available for public consumption, perhaps via a property named AsQueryable, as is the convention in LINQ, the Students' ages can be counted, summed, and averaged using a LINQ expression:

```
count =
    Students.AsQuerayable.Aggregate(0, (acc, st) => ++acc);
sumAges =
    Students.AsQuerayable.Aggregate(0,
        (acc, st) => st.Age + acc);
averageAge =
    Students.AsQuerayable.Aggregate(0.0F,
        (acc, st) => ++acc)
    /
    Students.AsQuerayable.Aggregate(0.0F,
        (acc, st) => st.Age + acc);
```

As can be surmised from the preceding code, the LINQ `Aggregate` extension method is the moral equivalent of the `Reduce` written earlier. And as was demonstrated, this means LINQ can be used to "reduce" a collection of Students into an XML representation.

C# 3.0 also offered a slightly more terse way of specifying those delegates to be passed in to the `Database`, something called a *lambda expression*:

```
Student s = null;
while (s == null)
{
    Console.Write("Please enter your first name:");
    string first = Console.ReadLine();
    Console.Write("\nPlease enter your last name:");
    string last = Console.ReadLine();
    s = Students.Find(c => c.FirstName == first &&
                           c.LastName == last );
    if (s == null)
        Console.WriteLine("Sorry! Couldn't find you");
}
// Do something with s
```

The etymology of this name stems quite deeply in computer science history, to a mathematician named Loronzo Church, who discovered a subtle yet very powerful idea: if mathematical functions are thought of as things that can be passed around like parameters (just as delegates can), then all mathematical operations can be reduced to functions taking functions as parameters. And this body of work came to be known as the *lambda calculus*, after the Greek symbol that served as the placeholder symbol for the function name.

## LAMBDA CALCULUS (BRIEFLY)

Without getting too deeply into the academic details, Church observed that if the actual function could be passed around, then various operations that normally seem distinct and individual could be collapsed together into a single *higher-order* function.

Consider the following two basic math operations and their C# equivalents:

```
static int Add(int x, int y) { return x + y;  }
static int Mult(int x, int y) { return x * y; }
static void MathExamples()
{
    int x = 2;
    int y = 3;
    int added = x + y;
    int multed = x * y;
    int addedagain = Add(x, y);
    int multedagain = Mult(x, y);
}
```

What Church realized is that if the actual operation — adding, multiplying, whatever — is abstracted away as a parameter, then both of these operations can be described using a single function:

```
delegate int BinaryOp(int lhs, int rhs);
static int Operate(int l, int r, BinaryOp op)
```

```
    {
        return op(l, r);
    }
    static void MathExamples()
    {
        int x = 2;
        int y = 3;
        // using explicit anonymous methods
        int added = Operate(x, y,
                            delegate(int l, int r){ return l+r; });
        int multd = Operate(x, y,
                            delegate(int l, int r){ return l*r; });
        // using lambda expressions
        int addedagain = Operate(x, y, (l, r) => l + r);
        int multdagain = Operate(x, y, (l, r) => l * r );
    }
```

When used this way, it doesn't make a lot of sense, because it would seem obvious to just write x + y, but now that the operation is abstracted away from the actual point of performing the operation, any kind of operation can be passed in.

This has some interesting implications. Consider, for example, an all-too-common business rule: Classes are associated with a given field of study (which must now appear on the Class object as another property, Field), because only certain kinds of Students can take certain kinds of Classes — for example, a Student studying Computer Science can take Computer Science classes, as can Students studying video game design, but Computer Science students are forbidden from taking anything that won't help them learn computer science better, such as Underwater Basketweaving classes. Meanwhile, Video game design is a pretty open-ended major and accepts just about anything except Fashion Design classes, whereas Physics majors will need to know some Physics and Computer Science but nothing else, and so on. (Like so many of its kind, this business rule made all kinds of sense back when it was first created, and nobody still with the company remembers why it was created in the first place, so don't question it now.) When a Student signs up for a Class, this business rule needs to be enforced, but where?

This kind of validation has historically plagued the object-oriented designer; effective enforcement of the rule requires knowledge coming from two different places, the Student and the Class. As such, it seems to defy logical placement: If the validation routine lives on the Student, the Student class then has to have awareness of every kind of Class in the system, a clear violation of separation of concerns, and vice versa if the validation routine lives on the Class.

If the validation is abstracted away, however, now the validation can occur without having to know the actual details yet:

```
delegate bool MajorApproval(Class cl);
class Student : Person
{
    // ...
    private MajorApproval m_majorApproval;

    // ...

    public MajorApproval CanTake
    {
```

```
            get { return m_majorApproval; }
        }
    }

    class Class
    {
        // ...

        public bool Assign(Student s)
        {
            if (s.CanTake(this))
            {
                Students.Add(s);
                return true;
            }
            return false;
        }
    }
```

Now, the validation code can be kept in a third place, thus localizing it to neither the Student nor the Class, but someplace accessible to either, such as a ProgramSignup collection someplace that the Student constructor can access (or the Class.Assign method could consult directly, depending on the developer's sense of aesthetics):

```
ProgramValidation["ComputerScience"] =
    c => c.Field == "Computer Science";
ProgramValidation["Physics"] =
    c => c.Field == "Computer Science" ||
        c.Field == "Physics";
ProgramValidation["Psychology"] =
    c => c.Field == "Psychology" ||
        c.Field == "Grade school";
ProgramValidation["Grade school"] =
    c => false;
ProgramValidation["Video game design"] =
    c => c.Field != "Underwater Basketweaving";
```

It should be noted that yes, something similar to this could be modeled in a traditional object-oriented way, usually by modeling the rules as function objects (like the Strategy approach earlier), also sometimes referred to as *functors*, and has been around for quite a while; C and C++ used pointers-to-functions to do things like this for decades.

The lambda calculus also permits more than just "lifting" the operation out and capturing it, though. As originally expressed, the lambda calculus also states that if a function can accept a function as a parameter, then all functions are essentially functions of one parameter, even though they may appear otherwise.

For example, returning to the basic mathematic operation of addition, the basic C# method of earlier:

```
static int Add(int x, int y) { return x+y; }
static void MoreMathExamples()
{
    int result = Add(2, 3);
}
```

In the lambda calculus, this operation can be thought of as asking a function to take an `int` and another function, where that second function takes an `int` and returns an `int` back. So, in C# 2.0, converting this to look like what the lambda calculus implies, starting with the `Add` method converted to a delegate operation:

```
private delegate int Operation(int l, int r);
static void MoreMathExamples()
{
    int result = Add(2, 3);

    Operation add = delegate(int l, int r) { return l + r; };
    int result2 = add(2, 3);
}
```

then means the delegate can be broken up into two different delegates — the first handing back a delegate that in turn knows how to do the actual operation:

```
delegate InnerOp DelegateOp(int r);
delegate int InnerOp(int l);
static void MoreMathExamples()
{
    int result = Add(2, 3);

    Operation add1 = delegate(int l, int r) { return l + r; };
    int result2 = add1(2, 3);

    DelegateOp add2 = delegate(int l)
                          {
                              return delegate(int r)
                                  {
                                      return l + r;
                                  };
                          };
    int result3 = add2(2)(3);
}
```

This process is known as *currying*, named after Haskell Curry, another mathematician who was famous (among mathematicians, at least). Because this sequence of steps should be applicable for more than just integers, a quick application of generics makes it available for any type:

```
Func<int,Func<int, int>> add4 =
    delegate(int l)
        {
            return delegate(int r)
                {
                    return l + r;
                };
        };
    int result4 = add4(2)(3);
```

Then, on top of all this, the whole process can be further genericized by creating a standard-purpose method for doing it:

```
delegate U Op<T1, T2, U>(T1 arg1, T2 arg2);
delegate U Op<T1, U>(T1 arg1);
```

```
    static Op<T1, Op<T2, U>> Curry<T1, T2, U>(Op<T1, T2, U> fn)
    {
        return delegate(T1 arg1)
                    {
                        return delegate(T2 arg2)
                                    {
                                        return fn(arg1, arg2);
                                    };
                    };
    }
    static void MoreMathExamples()
    {
        int result = Add(2, 3);

        Operation add2 = delegate(int l, int r) { return l + r; };
        int result2 = add2(2, 3);

        DelegateOp add3 = delegate(int l)
                            {
                                return delegate(int r)
                                        {
                                            return l + r;
                                        };
                            };
        int result3 = add3(2)(3);

        Func<int,Func<int, int>> add4 =
            delegate(int l)
                {
                    return delegate(int r)
                            {
                                return l + r;
                            };
                };
        int result4 = add4(2)(3);

        Op<int, int, int> add5 =
            delegate(int l, int r) { return l+r; };
        int result5 = add5(2, 3);
        Op<int, Op<int, int>> curriedAdd = Curry(add5);
        int result6 = curriedAdd(2)(3);
    }
```

It's horribly obtuse, and no sane C# developer would write add this way...unless they wanted to build up chains of functions calling functions in a highly generic way:

```
        Op<int, int> increment = curriedAdd(1);
        int result7 = increment(increment(increment(2)));
```

Although it seems awkward to think about at first, composing functions in this way means a new level of reusability has opened up, that of taking operations (methods) and breaking them into smaller pieces that can be put back together in new and interesting ways.

The most obvious use of this is to "pipeline" functions together in various ways, permitting reuse of behavior at a level previously unheard of in the object-oriented space. Functionality can now be written in small chunks, even as small as simple operations and then composed together, such as what might be needed for input validation code for a web application. However, making this work in a syntax that doesn't drive the average C# developer insane (if it hasn't already) is difficult, which leads to the next question — what if we could somehow make the syntax cleaner and easier to read and understand?

## TYPE INFERENCE

One thing is apparent from all this, particularly the definition of the `Curry` method: This is heavily genericized code, and it's not easy to read. It's a long way from `List<T>`! Fortunately, C# 3.0 introduced anonymous local variables, effectively informing the compiler that it is now responsible for determining the type of the declared local variable:

```
var add9 = Curry(add5);
int result9 = add9(2)(3);
```

Here, the compiler uses the context surrounding the variable declaration to figure out, at compile-time, precisely what the type of the local variable should be. In other words, despite the vague-sounding `var` syntax, this is still a full statically-typed variable declaration — it's just that the programmer didn't have to make the declaration explicit because the compiler could figure it out instead.

Theoretically, this means now that the compiler can remove responsibility for the "physical details" about the code from the programmers' shoulders:

```
var x = 2;
var y = 3;
var add10 = add9(x)(y);
```

Are x and y local variables, or are they property declarations? If these were members of a class, would they be fields or properties or even methods? Is add10 a method or delegate? More important, does the programmer even care? (In all but a few scenarios, probably not.)

Ideally, this is something that could be layered throughout the language — such that fields, properties, method parameters, and more, and could all be inferred based on context and usage, such as:

```
// This is not legal C# 3.0
class Person
{
    public Person(var firstName, var lastName, var age)
    {
        FirstName = firstName;
        LastName = lastName;
        Age = age;
    }
    public string FirstName { get; set; }
    public string LastName { get; set; }
    public int Age { get; set; }
    public string FullName {
      get { return FirstName + " " + LastName; }
    }
}
```

C# 3.0 provides some of this, via the automatic property declaration — it assumes the task of creating a field and the get/set logic to return and assign to that field, respectively, but unfortunately, C# 3.0 will choke on the var declaration as a method parameter or as a field. And 3.0 allows only inference for local variable declarations — any attempt to use these things as fields in an object will require the explicit declaration and, potentially, all the disconcerting angle brackets.

Additionally, looking at the previous example, some of C#'s syntactic legacy begins to look awkward — specifically, the use of the var as a type prefix is somewhat redundant if the compiler is going to infer the type directly, so why continue to use it?

```
// This is not legal C# 3.0
class Person
{
    public Person(firstName, lastName, age)
    {
        FirstName = firstName;
        LastName = lastName;
        Age = age;
    }
    public FirstName { get; set; }
    public LastName { get; set; }
    public Age { get; set; }
    public FullName {
      get { return FirstName + " " + LastName; }
    }
}
```

Despite the compiler's best efforts, though, it may be necessary to provide the type as a way of avoiding ambiguity, such as when the compiler cannot infer the type or finds any number of potential inferences. FirstName and LastName can be assumed to be strings, since the FullName property adds them together against a constant string, something (presumably) only strings can do. Age, however, is an ambiguity: It could be just about any object type in the system, because it is never used in a context that enables the compiler to infer its numerical status. As a result, the compiler needs a small bit of help to get everything right.

If the type declaration prefix syntax has been thrown away, though, then something else will have to take its place, such as an optional type declaration suffix syntax:

```
// This is not legal C# 3.0
class Person
{
    public Person(firstName, lastName, age : int)
    {
        FirstName = firstName;
        LastName = lastName;
        Age = age;
    }
    public FirstName { get; set; }
    public LastName { get; set; }
    public Age { get; set; }
    public FullName {
      get { return FirstName + " " + LastName; }
    }
}
```

Of course, types need not be the only thing inferred by the compiler; because `public` is the most common access modifier for methods, constructors and properties, and `private` is most common for fields, let those be the inferred default:

```
// This is not legal C# 3.0
class Person
{
    Person(firstName, lastName, age : int)
    {
        FirstName = firstName;
        LastName = lastName;
        Age = age;
    }
    FirstName { get; set; }
    LastName { get; set; }
    Age { get; set; }
    FullName {
      get { return FirstName + " " + LastName; }
    }
}
```

While syntax is under the microscope, the constructor syntax is a bit strange — why is repeating the type's name necessary? And because most types have a principal constructor to which all other constructors defer, if it even has multiple constructors at all, that constructor should have a more prominent place in the type's declaration:

```
// This is not legal C# 3.0
class Person(firstName, lastName, age : int)
{
    FirstName { get; set; }
    LastName { get; set; }
    Age { get; set; }
    FullName {
      get { return FirstName + " " + LastName; }
    }
}
```

Problem is, the constructor body is now missing, and the assignment of the constructor parameters to the respective properties is lost, unless somehow the body of the class can serve as the body of the constructor, and the property declaration can know how to "line up" against those parameters:

```
// This is not legal C# 3.0
class Person(firstName, lastName, age : int)
{
    FirstName { get { firstName } set; }
    LastName { get { lastName } set; }
    Age { get { age } set; }
    FullName {
      get { return FirstName + " " + LastName; }
    }
}
```

Unfortunately, the syntax is getting tricky to parse, particularly if the constructor body is now implicitly "inside" the class. It's going to have difficulty knowing what denotes a member of the class and what denotes a local variable inside the constructor body. Even if the compiler could, the programmer may not, so an explicit declaration of what is a member and what isn't would be helpful:

```
// This is not legal C# 3.0
class Person(firstName, lastName, age : int)
{
    member FirstName { get { firstName } set; }
    member LastName { get { lastName } set; }
    member Age { get { age } set; }
    member FullName {
      get { return FirstName + " " + LastName; }
    }
}
```

If the compiler's going to infer properties, let it infer the default property implementation, a get/set pair against a field backdrop, and assign its first value:

```
// This is not legal C# 3.0
class Person(firstName, lastName, age : int)
{
    member FirstName = firstName;
    member LastName = lastName;
    member Age = age;
    member FullName = FirstName + " " + LastName;
}
```

Methods, of course, would have similar inferential treatment:

```
// This is not legal C# 3.0
class Person(firstName, lastName, age : int)
{
    member FirstName = firstName;
    member LastName = lastName;
    member Age = age;
    member FullName = FirstName + " " + LastName;
    override ToString() {
        return String.Format("{0} {1} {2}",
            FirstName, LastName, Age);
    };
}
```

Language-wide type inference is turning out to be quite the beneficial thing to have. Fortunately, the compiler is still fully aware of the types of each of these constructs, so static type safety remains viable. But if this compiler is going to continue to take burdens off the programmer's shoulders, then some kind of facility to address the burdens of concurrent-safe programming is necessary.

On top of all this, the language can start to make the explicit "generic" declarations of the earlier C# operations less necessary, because now the compiler will have the ability to infer the actual types of the parameters, and with it, the ability to infer them as generic type parameters:

```
var swap = delegate (l, r) {
    var temp = r; r = l; l = temp;
};
```

Here, the compiler can infer that l and r are of the same type, but that actual type is entirely irrelevant, because any type (class or struct, user-defined or BCL) can satisfy the inferred type parameters for l and r.

This would make much of the earlier code around currying so much, much easier to write and understand.

## IMMUTABILITY

As an old joke goes, a man walks into a doctor's office and says, "Doctor, it hurts every time I do this" and jabs his thumb into his eye. The doctor, without missing a beat, says "Well, don't do that, and you'll be fine." Concurrency experts have long had a similar joke: If it hurts to write the locking code around every time the program changes state, then don't change state and you'll be fine. After all, if the variable never changes its state, then no update operation is possible and thus no locking code around those updates are necessary.

Although the proponents of fully-immutable variable state (also known as the "pure functional language") continue to wage loud and copious arguments against those who favor the merits of partially mutable variable state (the "impure language"), too many systems and libraries in the .NET ecosystem rely on the capability to change variable state in a running program to abandon the idea of mutable state entirely. That said, many objects in a .NET program remain immutable when initialized, and many other types could do so with little concern or change to their use:

```
Person talbott = new Person("Talbott", "Crowell", 29);
Person olderTalbott = new Person(talbott.FirstName,
    talbott.LastName, talbott.Age + 1);
```

Enforcing this, however, requires the developer writing the class type to ensure there's no way to modify the contents of those instances. This means that fields must be marked as read-only and properties with just a "get" handler.

If, however, the presumption is that most objects will remain unchanged when created, then rather than assuming the objects should be mutable by default, the language can make the opposite assumption and require the use of a keyword to indicate mutability.

Thanks to the power of inference, the programmer no longer has to stress over the low-level physical details of how the code projects itself onto the underlying CLR. Plus, perhaps surprisingly, none of the earlier syntax needs to change — the compiler simply chooses to generate the code differently, to be immutable by default instead of mutable.

Of course, now that the situation has reversed itself, if the programmer does want the ability to modify the internals of an object, the programmer must explicitly mark the parts of the class that need to be mutable:

```
// This is not legal C# 3.0
class Person(firstName, lastName, age : int)
{
    member FirstName = firstName;
    member LastName = lastName;
    mutable member Age = age;
    member FullName = FirstName + " " + LastName;
    override ToString() {
        return String.Format("{0} {1} {2}",
            FirstName, LastName, Age);
    };
}
```

This will not be enough to make the world safe for multiple threads of execution, but it will reduce the amount of thinking required to write thread-safe code.

## EXPRESSIONS, NOT STATEMENTS

While the language syntax and semantics are up for discussion, an inconsistency within the traditional imperative language presents itself for possible correction: Certain constructs within the imperative language are expressions, yielding a result value, while other constructs are statements, yielding no value whatsoever. And in some languages, particularly those descending from the C++ wing of the language family tree, the ultimate inconsistency presents itself: Two different language constructs that do almost the same thing, except that one is a statement and the other an expression:

```
var anotherResult = false;
  if (x == 2)
      anotherResult = true;
  else
      anotherResult = false;
var yetAnotherResult = (x == 2) ? true : false;
```

The inconsistency is maddening. Particularly when it could be applied to a variety of other constructs — why doesn't switch/case have a similar kind of expression construct?

```
var thirdResult =
    switch (x)
    {
        case 0: "empty"; break;
        case 1: "one"; break;
        case 2: "two"; break;
        default: "many"; break;
    };
```

If every (or most every) language construct is an expression, it means the language takes a more input-yields-output style to it, which reinforces the general nature of testable programs, rather than just as a series of statements.

## SUMMARY

This chapter began with a litany of the flaws of the object-oriented mindset and detailed what a new language might look like — one in which functions and methods were given first-class citizen status, the compiler could infer static type information from more of the language constructs, variable and field immutability serves as the default, and expressions formed the core of the language instead of imperative statements.

In short, we have just authored a language strikingly similar to the F# programming language. The remainder of this book details that language.

# PART I
# Basics

▶ **CHAPTER 2:** Lexical Structure

▶ **CHAPTER 3:** Primitive Types

▶ **CHAPTER 4:** Control Flow

▶ **CHAPTER 5:** Composite Types

▶ **CHAPTER 6:** Pattern Matching

# 2

# Lexical Structure

**WHAT'S IN THIS CHAPTER?**

➤   Understanding basic syntax

➤   Defining values and identifiers

In any language, some basic lexical ideas have to be laid down before programmers can begin to understand the concepts behind the language — questions such as "What makes a comment?" or "What is allowed in identifier names?," although intrinsically boring in many ways, have to be defined before any further progress into the language's structure and form.

F#'s lexical structure derives strongly from its immediate ancestor, OCaml, which is itself a derivative of the pure functional language ML. This means that for the most part, although F# strives to be .NET-friendly in terms of its syntax, the C# and Visual Basic developer can find a number of new and interesting syntactic ideas, some of which will be surprising. Fortunately, most of those will be pleasant surprises because much of the syntax is less restrictive than the other .NET languages offered from Microsoft.

## COMMENTS

The easiest place to begin with any language is a simple definition of what makes a comment (meaning, syntax that the compiler will ignore during processing). F# supports three different styles of comments:

➤   Multi-line comments using the (* and *) delimiters, such as:

```
(* This is
a multi-line
comment *)
```

Note that multi-line comments nest, meaning that the multi-line comment will only be terminated when the number of end-comment pairs match the number of begin-comment pairs preceding it.

➤ Single-line comments using the `//` delimiter, which signals a comment until the next end-of-line, such as

```
// This is a single-line comment
```

➤ Documentation comments using the `///` delimiter, which signals a special form of comment (similar to the C# comment of the same form) that can be used to extract documentation for the element that follows.

Of the three, the multi-line comment form isn't seen much in general F# usage, and for the most part is present solely to support F# cross-compiling OCaml code.

The documentation comment supports much, if not all, of the same kinds of XML documentation "hints" that the C# documentation syntax supports, such as:

```
/// <summary>This is a cool function</summary>
/// <remarks>Use it wisely</remarks>
```

Note that if developers stick primarily to the single-line and documentation comment forms for regular use, swatches of code can be temporarily removed from use via the multi-line comment form, which can be particularly useful given the nesting nature of multi-line comments.

## IDENTIFIERS

Identifiers in F# generally follow the same rules as C# or C++, in that any combination of Unicode characters defined as letters (uppercase or lowercase), digits, and the underscore are allowed, provided that the first character is a letter. For the C# developer, this is identical to how C# operates.

Like most languages, F# reserves certain character combinations for its own use, typically as keywords in the language. F# defines the following as unacceptable identifiers, either because they are keywords, or because the F# team wants to reserve them for future use (meaning they might become keywords in a future release of the F# language):

```
abstract and as asr assert atomic base begin break checked class component
const constraint constructor continue default delegate do done downcast
downto eager elif else end event exception extern external false finally
fixed for fun function functor global if in include inherit inline
interface internal land lazy let lor lsl lsr lxor match member method mixin
mod module mutable namespace new null object of open or override parallel
private process protected public pure rec return sealed sig static struct
tailcall then to trait true try type upcast use val virtual void volatile
when while with yield
```

Not all these identifiers are currently used, and some may end up never being used, depending on future directions the language takes. Even should the language later permit using them, none of the preceding words should ever be used as an identifier, for developer sanity if nothing else.

In addition, F# reserves a special syntax when an identifier ends in ?, !, or # for its own use. The most obvious example of this is the `let!` syntax used for asynchronous workflows. Again, even should the language permit their use in later versions of the language, avoid using them.

Some sample identifiers, and illegal identifiers, appear here:

```
let y = 1
let aReallyLongIdentifierName = 2
let _underscores_are_OK_too = 3
let soAreNumbers123AfterALetter = 4
```

Note that, as with all Microsoft Visual Studio-integrated languages, the IDE flags illegal identifiers with the ubiquitous "red-squiggly."

> *Like most languages, F# has its share of surprise moments, in which something that works generates unexpected results. One interesting edge case emerges within the language; if an identifier containing the & symbol is used, it appears to work. For example, consider* `let abc&foo = 5`. *However, what's happening here is* not *the creation of a single identifier, but two identifiers (one on each side of the &), each with the same value.*

For those situations in which F# has to consume an identifier (a class, method, field, property, or some other element) from an assembly that happens to have the same syntax as a reserved word, F# enables for a double-backtick syntax that permits the "escaping" of the identifier: Simply wrap the otherwise prohibited term in double-backtick characters (as in ``assert``), and the F# parser will obligingly accept it. As a general rule, however, F# developers should avoid using this syntax for the purpose of overloading existing F# keywords or reserved words, and should take care to avoid creating identifiers that will conflict with other languages' reserved words that are likely to consume F# assemblies (such as C# and Visual Basic), assuming it can be helped at all. This syntax is mostly intended for making it easier to consume assemblies written in non-F# languages, where other programmers accidentally created identifiers that conflict with F# reserved words.

## PREPROCESSOR DIRECTIVES

F#, like C#, uses "hash tags" to indicate preprocessor directives, directions to the parser on how to consider the act of parsing. F# employs a small number of preprocessor directives, all of which use the traditional C-style hash syntax, such as #line or #light. These are processed by the compiler before considering any other aspect of the language, and aside from whatever effect they have during compilation, provide no runtime overhead or impact. The full list of preprocessor directives recognized by the F# compiler is given here:

➤ #line: Sets the line number for the source file immediately following this line. By default, the first line in an F# file is 1.

➤ #if #else #endif: As the names imply, these directives evaluate whether an identifier has been defined (typically using the –define flag given to the compiler) at compile-time, and take either the code between the `#if` and `#else`, or between the `#else` and `#endif`, for processing. Note that this means that any syntactic or semantic errors in the block of code not taken are never checked by the compiler.

Other preprocessor directives may be added to the language later, depending on future directions.

## SIGNIFICANT WHITESPACE

Languages frequently need to find some way to "set off" a block of code from the code around it — the "true" branch of a decision statement or the body of a function or method, for example — and where some languages choose to use some kind of syntactic "pairing," such as C#'s "{"/"}" characters or Visual Basics "Begin"/"End" tokens, F# chooses instead to use *significant whitespace*, using block indentation as the means by which blocks of code are set off from surrounding context.

Additionally, F# also requires no explicit end-of-line terminator,* which means overall that the language has far fewer syntactic "marker"s in the code, relying instead on the implicit structure of the indentation to indicate the structure of the code. Note that this means that developers must be careful to line up indentation levels consistently across the body of the program, because F# uses the indentation level of the "previous" lines to know precisely when a block has ended. For example, in the following:

```
let outer =
    let x = 1
    if x = 1 then
        System.Console.WriteLine("Hello, F#")
    else
        System.Console.WriteLine("Uh... how did this happen?")
```

the outer declaration creates one scope block, and inside of that, a new value, x, is declared, and an if/then/else statement (discussed in more detail in Chapter 4) whose true and false branches each form a new block.

If, for some reason, the else block is off by one or more whitespace characters — either indented too far or too little — the language may not know which `if` block this `else` is paired up against, and will flag the entire construct as an error (actually, for this precise example, the compiler will be able to adjust... but the programmer may not be so lucky, and other, less-trivial, examples will flag an error):

```
let outer =
    let x = 2
    if x = 1 then
        System.Console.WriteLine("Hello, F#")
        if x = 1 then
            System.Console.WriteLine("Again!")
      else
        System.Console.WriteLine("Uh... how did this happen?")
```

---

* Except when writing statements in the interactive F# window inside Visual Studio or the fsi.exe F# interpreter window, when ";;" is used to indicate that the user is not continuing input onto a new line.

Note that F# can be made back into a whitespace-insignificant language by turning off `#light` mode, but this then forces the use of `begin`, `end`, `in` and `;` tokens to denote blocks, according to the syntax of the OCaml language (to which F# originally intended to be syntax-equivalent, back when it was "just" a research language). Most F# developers agree that `#light` mode is the superior mode to use, and it will be the assumed mode for the code samples for the rest of this book.

## SUMMARY

F# uses a number of lexical constructs similar to existing .NET languages, but also several lexical conventions that are brand-new to the platform. For the most part, experienced .NET developers can adjust to F#'s quirks without much work, but a few "gotchas" compared to C#/Visual Basic do exist. Fortunately these disappear quickly as the new F# developer gains experience with the language.

# 3

# Primitive Types

**WHAT'S IN THIS CHAPTER?**

➤ Understanding primitive types

➤ Declaring primitive type instances

➤ Applying operators

Like all languages that run on top of the CLR, the F# language provides a core set of primitive types that offer basic integer and floating-point arithmetic capabilities, character string support, Boolean types, and so on. In general, these map to the corresponding CLS types (`System.Int16`, `System.Int32`, and so on), as described next, but a few types are new to F# and come from the F# libraries. These types are fully accessible to other languages, such as C# and Visual Basic but obviously have no native language support there and need to be used as any other .NET type is (that is, via fully qualified type names).

## BOOLEAN

Probably the simplest primitive type in F# is the `bool` type, which corresponds to the CLR's underlying `System.Boolean` type, and has two possible values, `true` and `false`.

Booleans support the usual range of logical operations, including `&&` (logical AND) and `||` (logical OR), and otherwise behave just as Boolean values do in any other .NET language.

## NUMERIC TYPES

F# supports a wide range of numeric types, 8 bits in size to 64, in both signed and unsigned versions, as shown here:

| TYPE | DESCRIPTION | .NET NAME | LITERALS |
|------|-------------|-----------|----------|
| Byte | 8-bit unsigned integer | System.Byte | 3uy, 0xFuy |
| Sbyte | 8-bit signed integer | System.SByte | 3y, 0xFy |
| int16 | 16-bit signed integer | System.Int16 | 3s, 0xFs |
| uint16 | 16-bi unsigned integer | System.UInt16 | 3us, 0xFus |
| int, int32 | 32-bit signed integer | System.Int32 | 3, 0xF |
| uint32 | 32-bit unsigned integer | System.UInt32 | 3u, 0xFu |
| int64 | 64-bit signed integer | System.Int64 | 3L, 0xFL |
| uint64 | 64-bit unsigned integer | System.UInt64 | 3UL, 0xFUL |
| nativeint | Machine-sized integer | System.IntPtr | 3n, 0xB8000n |
| unativeint | Machine-sized unsigned integer | System.UIntPtr | 3un, 0xB8000un |
| bigint | Arbitrarily large integer | System.Numerics. BigInteger | 3I |

Each of these types can be initialized to decimal, hexadecimal, octal, or binary constants. Decimal constants are represented simply with the numeric value itself, whereas the other three must be prefixed with a flag indicating whether it should be hexadecimal (0x or 0X), octal (0o or 0O), or binary (0b or 0B). This means that the following literals, 0xF, 0o20, 15 and 0b1111, are all the same value (15).

For each of these types, with the exception of the bigint type, the traditional algebraic operators are supported, providing unchecked (that is, wraparound in the event the value exceeds the available representation size) operations for addition, subtraction, multiplication, division, and modulo. Operations that should throw an exception if they overflow (of type System.OverflowException) are defined in the Microsoft.FSharp.Core.Operators module; opening modules and using operations defined therein is discussed in more detail in Chapter 11. Any sort of integer division by zero raises a standard System.DivideByZeroException.

Because of the dangers of overflow, even with the largest-precision types, the bigint type is the preferred type for handling exceedingly large values, such as the total size of the U.S. budget or the royalty checks for programming language book authors. (Technically, the bigint type isn't a primitive type, according to the language specification, but given its syntax and role, it's helpful to think of it as such for all practical purposes.)

The `nativeint` and `unativeint` types are typically used only for interoperability with native code that receives and produces machine word-sized values, that is, pointers. They are rarely, if ever, used for arithmetic purposes.

The `Microsoft.FSharp.Core.Operators` module also defines a number of mathematical operations, listed here, which behave as their names imply. (These operators are also defined for the floating-point types, described later.)

➤ abs

➤ cos

➤ sin

➤ tan

➤ cosh

➤ sinh

➤ tanh

➤ acos

➤ asin

➤ atan

➤ ceil

➤ floor

➤ truncate

➤ exp

➤ log

➤ log10

➤ **

This is not an exhaustive list, but a representative sample of the operators found in that namespace. Each of these behaves as its name implies; `ceil` returns the ceiling (rounded up), `floor` returns the floor (rounded down), and `truncate` returns the rounded (traditional closest-to-zero semantics) integer value for floating-point values. Exponentiation (power) is done using the `**` operator.

Opening a module (needed in order to use these operators) is discussed in Chapter 11.

In addition, the following comparison operations are all defined:

➤ <

➤ <=

➤ >

➤ >=

➤ =

➤ <>

➤ min

➤ max

And again, each behaves as its name implies. (C# and C++ developers, take special note that equality uses one =, not two, and that not-equals uses <> instead of the C-family !=. Assignment is done differently in F#, as discussed in Chapter 13.)

## BITWISE OPERATIONS

All the previous integer types support bitwise operations — operations that take into account the underlying bitwise representation — such as AND, OR, eXclusive OR, and so on. The operators to carry out these operations are definitely nontraditional, compared to the C family of languages, but aren't difficult to understand or follow. Consider the following:

| OPERATOR | DESCRIPTION | EXAMPLE (WITH RESULTS) |
|---|---|---|
| &&& | bitwise AND | 0b1111 &&& 0b1100 -> 0b1100 |
| \|\|\| | bitwise OR | 0b1111 \|\|\| 0b1100 -> 0b1111 |
| ^^^ | bitwise exclusive OR | 0b1111 ^^^ 0b1100 -> 0b0011 |
| ~~~ | bitwise NOT | ~~~ 0b11110000uy = 0b00001111uy |
| <<< | bitwise shift left | 0b0110 <<< 1 -> 0b1100 |
| >>> | bitwise shift right | 0b0110 >>> 1 -> 0b0011 |

Generally, bitwise operations are not necessary in F# because their principal use in traditional C/C++ code was to carry a variety of "flag"-style information or concise values packed into a single variable to save space; "flags" are typically better represented in other ways in F# (see Chapter 5 for details), and the CLR will do its own packaging of values to save space, so such measures are often counterproductive.

## FLOATING-POINT TYPES

Floating-point types in the F# language hold values that should not or cannot be rounded up to whole numbers.

| TYPE | DESCRIPTION | .NET NAME | LITERALS |
|---|---|---|---|
| single, float32 | 32-bit IEEE floating-point | System.Single | 3.2f, 1.3e4f |
| double, float | 64-bit IEEE floating-point | System.Double | 3.2, 1.3e4 |

| TYPE | DESCRIPTION | .NET NAME | LITERALS |
| --- | --- | --- | --- |
| decimal | High-precision decimal | System.Decimal | 19M, 3.2M |
| bignum | Arbitrary-precision rationals | Microsoft.<br>FSharp.Math.<br>bignum | 19N, 3.2N |

Like all CLR-based languages that use the System.Single and System.Double IEEE-based types, floating-point arithmetic is inherently inaccurate — adding the values 1.0 and 1.0 does not necessarily produce 2.0, but could produce 1.9999999. For this reason, any operations that require high accuracy should use the decimal or bignum types instead of single/float32 or double/float.

The bignum type, unlike decimal or single or double, does not store its representation in a decimal format, instead preferring to store it as an actual fraction, tracking both numerator and denominator. This guarantees the highest degree of precision, but at the cost of having to do the fractional mathematics directly when looking to convert it to a floating-point representation. Fortunately, F# supports all the major mathematical operations on bignum types, performing the appropriate fractional math.

 *With the release of Visual Studio 2010, Microsoft moved the* bignum *definition to the F# PowerPack, which is a useful and near-mandatory set of supplemental material available for free download at* http://fsharppowerpack.codeplex.com.

Note also that F# understands two special floating-point constants, (positive) Infinity and (negative) -Infinity, which will be the result of any floating-point division by zero.

## ARITHMETIC CONVERSIONS

Unlike the C-family of languages, F# will not do implicit type conversion among numeric types, instead requiring manual conversion. This is different from C# or C++, where conversion from integer to floating-point values is commonly expected; this means that the following C# code:

```
int x = 12;
float y = 2.0;
var result = x / y; // returns 6.0
```

when translated to F#, has to be explicitly converted, like this:

```
let i = 4   // int constant
let f = 4.0 // float32 constant
// let result = i * f will fail; i and f not the same type
let result = (float32 i) / f
```

The conversion is done by explicitly naming the type to convert to, in much the same way that a downcast is written in C#, without the parentheses. Note, however, that the parentheses around the conversion are necessary — without them, the compiler sees the multiplication first, and tries to multiply i and f and then take the result and convert it to a float32, which will fail to compile, because again now i and f are not the same type.

## STRING AND CHARACTER TYPES

F#, like all CLR-based languages, has an intrinsic notion of a string type, a sequence of characters manipulated as a single entity. The string type is a synonym for the System.String type from the Base Class Library and supports all the methods defined there; therefore, to obtain the length of a string, simply use the Length property, just as C# or Visual Basic would do.

| TYPE | DESCRIPTION | LITERALS | .NET NAME |
|------|-------------|----------|-----------|
| string | String | "Katie" | System.String |
| byte[] | Literal byte array | "ABCD"B | System.Byte[] |
| char | Character | 'c' | System.Char |

Note that strings can be either "escaped," meaning that strings normally recognize the backslash character (\) as an "escape" to allow for nonprintable character sequences (such as the linefeed or newline characters) in strings, or "verbatim," meaning that the string contents are never escaped. Verbatim strings must be prefixed with the @ character (just as in C#), as in:

```
// This is an escaped string--double backslashes are
// necessary to represent a single backslash character
"C:\\Prg\\FSharp\\Examples" // escaped string;

// Verbatim string--no escaping takes place
@"C:\Prg\FSharp\Examples"
```

Note that in F#, strings can also span lines without having to close off the string, re-open a new string on the next line, and concatenate the two (as is necessary in C#). This is known as a *multi-line string literal*.

The literal byte array type is useful when working with binary protocols and file formats, particularly for magic numbers and begin/end sequences that appear in the content stream.

Strings can also be concatenated using the + operator or the .NET Framework Class Library class System.Text.StringBuilder, just as other CLR languages can.

Because the F# string is a System.String at the CLR level,* all the members of the System.String class are also accessible to F# code, so the usual litany of operations familiar to C# and Visual Basic programmers, such as the Length property to return the length of the string, are all accessible. More on F# compatibility and interoperability with other CLR languages is given in Chapter 18.

---

*Actually, this isn't quite 100% true — an F# string is an instance of F#'s own string type, but all the System.String members are available on an F# string, so practically the statement holds true.

# UNIT

The Unit type in F# is a special type, one that has no direct equivalent in traditional object-oriented or imperative programming languages. In practice, to the C# and Visual Basic developer, Unit is a combination of both `null` and `System.Void`. In essence, `unit` is the type that represents no type (similar to `System.Void`) and has one value only (given by the literal `()`, similar to `null`). It is used in those situations in which the value returned from an expression needs to represent the case where there is no value to be returned.*

Developers familiar with C# and Visual Basic may find the general disdain for null and void to be confusing at first; null, in particular, is a staple resource for those languages to indicate a lack of response in a return value. F# provides alternative ways to represent the lack of a response — the option type — and is described in more detail in Chapter 5.

 *Note that F# does support the keywords `null` and `void`, and they are used as one might expect — the first as a value and the second as a type, but the principal use for these two centers around the area of .NET interoperability. More on `null` and `void` can be found on Chapter 18.*

# UNITS OF MEASURE TYPES

In addition to the primitive types provided here, F# provides a feature, colloquially known as units-of-measure, that allows an F# programmer to annotate an instance of a primitive type with some additional information intended to describe the "units" for this value. This is intended to better support the real-world, in which calculations frequently are done with a unit system either explicitly or implicitly applied to the calculation.

For example, consider a function in a physics simulation program that needs to calculate the trajectory of an artillery shell fired from a gun.** The shell will have an initial velocity, but this velocity will decrease over time, based on its angle and the pull of gravity.

Without getting into the mathematics too deeply, several different "units" are being expressed here, and if the programmer is not careful, mistakes in the code can appear if the right values are not converted to the appropriate "units" type during the calculations. This is less trivial than it might seem at first — both space programs (NASA and the European Space Agency, to name a few) and financial institutions have suffered losses measured in millions of $US because of flawed unit-based calculations.

---

*Obviously, this is a confusing statement and isn't necessary for the practicing programmer to spend a lot of time worrying about — simply know that when void or null might have applied in C#, or Nothing in VB, use unit and () instead.

**The full source for this program is found on Chris Smith's blog, under the name "Burning Land."

Defining a new unit of measure requires a simple declaration of what name the unit-of-measure will use, annotated by the Measure attribute recognized by the compiler. (Attributes are described in more detail in Chapter 12.) When declared, this unit-of-measure can be used to "annotate" a primitive type value or variable (typically of `float`, `float32`, or `decimal` type, though signed integer types are also acceptable) and provide the additional type checking to ensure that units-of-measure are not combined in illegal ways. So, given the following declaration:

```
[<Measure>] type usd
[<Measure>] type euro
```

the compiler recognizes two new unit-of-measure types to be defined, one representing (presumably) U.S. dollars, the other, European euro.

Thus, the following function defines a usd-to-euro conversion, and the compiler understands the unit-of-measure conversions as part of the function's signature:

```
let usdRoyaltyCheck = 1500000.00<usd>
let usdToEuro (dollars : float<usd>) =
    dollars * 1.5<euro/usd>
```

When described in the compiler's Intellisense window, it clearly indicates that the `usdToEuro` function takes a single parameter of type `float<usd>` as input and returns a value of type `float<euro>` as the result from the function. It knows this by virtue of the conversion constant being defined as a unit-of-measure that, as all conversion constants do, is expressed as a ratio of <euro> to <usd>, in this case, 1.5 <euro> to the <usd>.

Note that this doesn't mean that the F# compiler has built-in knowledge of physics or accounting or mathematics or any other domain — the units are simply parsed and compared as-is, leaving F# developers free to create their own units and unit systems as necessary or desirable. The units can be called by any legitimate identifier, and no particular relationship is assumed by their names, so that <m> and <km> aren't intrinsically understood — the programmer seeking to convert <m> to <km> must write that function explicitly.

## LITERAL VALUES

It's important to note that the F# compiler takes great pains to hide some of the physical characteristics of the mappings to the underlying CLR from the developer.

For example, consider the following F# code:

```
let s = "Hello world!"
```

Contrary to what the C# or Visual Basic developer assumes, this does not create a constant value, but a property whose contents are pre-initialized to the value previously defined.

Normally, this is not a problem; this is arguably a good thing — C# and Visual Basic developers spend far too much time thinking about the physical layout characteristics of their code, explicitly declaring fields and properties as separate entities, when 95% of the time the two will map in a one-to-one manner. Even given the presence of automatically generated properties in C# 3.0, the developer must still think explicitly about physical layout — for example, should a name intended to yield a constant value be a property, a field, or a method? Should it yield a singleton object via a static method? And so on. By removing some of these "low-level" issues from the language syntax, F# manages to avoid much of the unnecessary debate around those decisions.

There are a few cases, most notably in C#/F# interop (see Chapter 18) and pattern matching (see Chapter 6) where ensuring that a name/value binding is defined as a constant field value is necessary; to do this, annotate the name with the Literal attribute:

```
[<Literal>]
let S2 = "Hello world again!"
```

This now forces the F# compiler to compile s2 as a constant static field in the class created for the F# file.

## SUMMARY

F# has a similar set of basic types to that of other CLR-based languages, with some slight differences in syntax and semantics, and some extended types that the traditional CLR languages (C#, Visual Basic) don't have directly. Many of these additional types were originally created to support F#'s original research role as a "math/science" language but turn out to be useful in the general programming space as well; for example, `bigint` will be useful in accounting applications, and both `decimal` and `bignum` will have particular application for monetary calculations and high-precision mathematics.

F# developers can also find the units-of-measure capabilities within the language to be helpful anywhere real-world calculations are done — obviously mathematical calculations, such as those routinely done in physics (either simulators or guidance-control software) can find units-of-measure useful but so will accounting programs, particularly those that deal with a known set of currencies or calculations dealing with time.

# Control Flow

**WHAT'S IN THIS CHAPTER?**

➤  Branching with if/else

➤  Looping with while/do

➤  Looping with for

➤  Handling exceptions

Much, if not all, of the power of a programming language derives from its capability to branch based according to particular criteria and values in various ways, also known as *control flow* expressions. Like its sister languages on the .NET platform, F# has a wide range of powerful control flow constructs, including one whose power is such that it merits its own chapter, *pattern-matching*, discussed in Chapter 6.

## BASIC DECISIONS: IF

The simplest control flow construct to understand and come to know, of course, is the simple branching construct based on a single Boolean decision criteria: the `if` construct:

```
let x = 12
if x = 12 then
    System.Console.WriteLine("Yes, x is 12")
```

The `then` keyword is mandatory, indicating the end of the criteria test and the start of the body of the code to execute in the case when the test passes true. For this reason, parentheses are unnecessary around the criteria test.

Also, similar to how C# refuses to allow anything other than a Boolean expression to be used in the comparison clause of its `if` statement, F# refuses to automatically convert non-`bool` values into `bool` values, so the following refuses to compile:

```
let x = 12
if x then
    System.Console.WriteLine("Yep, x")
```

The issue here isn't one of trying to prevent programmers from accidentally performing an assignment (as was the case in C/C++ years ago), but that the F# language refuses to perform implicit primitive type conversions. The solution, therefore, is to always make sure the test criterion is a Boolean one, by adding a <> null or <> 0 as the case requires.

Also, F# uses the mathematical = (single-equals) operator to do relativity/equality comparisons, and <> to do inequality comparisons, as opposed to the C-family traditional == and !=. This is common practice in functional languages, largely because functional languages (including F#) don't use = for assignment.

For those cases where either/or kinds of decision making needs to be done, if/then also supports an else clause, like this:

```
let x = 12
if x = 12 then
    System.Console.WriteLine("Yes, x is 12")
else
    System.Console.WriteLine("Nope, it's not 12")
```

Again, as discussed in Chapter 2, the code blocks corresponding to the if/then and else clauses are defined by their indentation from the previous lines, regardless of the actual number of spaces from the left margin. As a result, else must always appear on a separate line from the end of the if/then code block in front of it. But, this also means that there is no dangling else problem as seen in other languages — the else block is associated with the if/then block that starts at the same level of indentation.

In some scenarios, a particular decision may not be binary in nature, but trinary or quadrinary, testing multiple conditions before ultimately yielding a final value; in F#, these can be made all part of one if/then construct by using the elif keyword to perform another conditional test and (possible) block of code to execute:

```
let x = 12
if x = 12 then
    System.Console.WriteLine("Yes, x is 12")
elif x = 24 then
    System.Console.WriteLine("Well, now x is 24")
else
    System.Console.WriteLine("I have no clue what x is")
```

Any number of elif clauses can be defined, and the else clause is not required, regardless of however many elif clauses there might be.

As discussed in Chapter 1, as with most functional languages, in F# most language constructs are not statements but expressions, which yield values, and this is true of the if/then as well. This means that the preceding could be rewritten to the arguably more readable form:

```
let x = 12
let msg = if x = 12 then "Yes, x is 12" else "Nope, not 12"
System.Console.WriteLine(msg)
```

In this respect, C# developers will recognize that if/then/else is actually more like the ternary operator from C# (the so-called ?: operator) than the traditional if/else from that language. In the preceding example, the expression result from the then clause is used as the value for the entire if/then/else expression if x is 12; and if not, then the expression result from the else clause is used. (This also holds true for the `if/then/elif/else` construct, regardless of the number of elif clauses used.)

This has a deeper ramification that might throw C# developers off at first. Because the entire `if/then/else` yields a value, it means that both sides (or in the case of `if/then/elif/else`, all sides) of the expression must yield the same *kind* of value, meaning that the following will not compile:

```
let x = 12
let msg = if x = 12 then "Yes" else false
System.Console.WriteLine(msg)
```

This fails to compile, pointing at the false portion of the expression and saying, "This expression has type bool but is here used with type string." This is potentially confusing at first; the F# compiler is stating that the expression `false` has type `bool` (which is obvious), which is clearly at odds with the expected return type of `string`, as established by the `if/then` clause in front of it.

It may seem odd, at first, to consider that if/then returns a value, particularly given the preceding examples, in which no obvious value is returned. It may help to realize that an F# `if/then` always returns a value, even if that value is the functional value `()`, also known as `unit`. Executing the previous examples in F# Interactive can help drive this point home:

```
C:\Projects\Publications\Books\ProF#> fsi.exe

Microsoft F# Interactive, (c) Microsoft Corporation, All Rights Reserved
F# Version 1.9.6.2, compiling for .NET Framework Version v2.0.50727

Please send bug reports to fsbugs@microsoft.com
For help type #help;;

> let x = 12;;

val x : int

> if x = 12 then System.Console.WriteLine("Yep, 12")
- else System.Console.WriteLine("Nope, something else");;
Yep, 12
val it : unit = ()
>
```

The F# Interactive console, after executing the `if/then/else` expression, prints the result of that expression, which is `()`, of type `unit`. (Remember, from Chapter 3, that `unit` and `()` are roughly equivalent to C#'s null-and-void or Visual Basic's Nothing-and-Nil.)

## LOOPING: WHILE/DO

Branching decisions provide one form of flow control, and an obvious extension to that is the branching-to-a-previous-execution-point style of control flow, also known as looping. F# supports a number of different looping constructs, the simplest of which is the `while` construct, which executes a block of code so long as a Boolean condition remains true:

```
while (System.DateTime.Now.Minute <> 0) do
    System.Console.WriteLine("Not yet the top of the hour...")
```

In this particular case, so long as the current time remains any number of minutes past 0, the Boolean condition remains true, and the body of the loop will execute. Again, as with the preceding if construct, the block of code defining the body of the while loop is set off by some number of spaces from the left margin. And, again, as with if/then conditions, the condition against which the while tests must be explicitly a Boolean expression.

Unlike the if/then/else construct, while is a statement and thus yields no value. For this reason (among others), while is less preferred in functional-leaning code, replaced instead by recursion over functions, as discussed in Chapter 13.

## LOOPING: FOR

Similarly, just as while/do can execute blocks of code over and over again depending on the value of a Boolean condition each time before executing the code block, the for construct can be used to execute a block of code based on a variable that increments somehow each time through the loop, and tested against a Boolean criterion each time the block of code is entered:

```
for i = 1 to System.DateTime.Now.Hour do
    System.Console.Write("Cuckoo! ")
```

Note that for expressions become significantly more powerful (and for that reason, will be revisited again) in Chapter 16, when the sequence type is discussed. The for expressions of the preceding form are known as *simple for expressions* in the F# Language Definition and can only be used with integer bindings (such as i in the preceding example); any attempt to use any other kind of primitive type or nonprimitive type in a simple for expression will result in an error.

In addition, simple for expressions have one additional form, performing decrement operations instead of increment:

```
for i = 10 downto 1 do
    System.Console.WriteLine("i = {0}", i)
```

Officially, the downto syntax is supported solely for OCaml backward compatibility but shows no signs of being removed from the language any time soon.

Simple for expressions are statements, not expressions, and as such yield no resulting values. (However, the more generic and powerful for constructs over sequences discussed in Chapter 16 can yield values, using a slightly different syntax.) Again, as with while, in more functional-leaning code, simple for expressions are replaced with a more functional style, also discussed in Chapter 14.

## EXCEPTIONS

On the .NET platform, exceptions represent a universal way of signaling and handling failure, and the F# language is (if you'll pardon the pun) no exception to this rule. F# can throw exceptions, catch thrown exceptions, and define new kinds of exception types.

Handling exceptions in F# works in much the same fashion as it does across the rest of the .NET ecosystem. A *guarded block* is defined and is so named because it will be guarded by either a set of exception-catching clauses (given by the with keyword) or a general clause (given by the finally keyword) that will be executed regardless of how the guarded block is exited, whether by exceptional or regular means. Note that in what will come as a surprise to C# developers, F# does not support *both* — there is no try...with...finally construct in the F# language.

## try...with

In both the try...with and try...finally forms, the try keyword begins the (indented) guarded block, and the with keyword sets off the various clauses against which the exception instance, if an exception is thrown, is compared against to determine which clause should be executed as the exception-handling mechanism:

```
let results =
    try
        let req = System.Net.WebRequest.Create(
                        "Not a legitimate URL")
        let resp = req.GetResponse()
        let stream = resp.GetResponseStream()
        let reader = new System.IO.StreamReader(stream)
        let html = reader.ReadToEnd()
        html
    with
        | :? System.UriFormatException ->
            "You gave a bad URL"
        | :? System.Net.WebException as webEx ->
            "Some other exception: " + webEx.Message
        | ex -> "We got an exception: " + ex.Message
    results
```

*Code snippet FlowControl.fs*

This particular example attempts to download and return the results of an HTTP request to a URL, but because the URL given is not a legitimate URL, the System.Net.WebRequest class will throw an exception. The exception instance thrown is compared against the three clauses in the with section, and the first match (in top-down order) executes the body of the clause, which is on the right side of the -> syntax.

The different possibilities of the with section are separated by a vertical pipe (|) character, in a manner deliberately reminiscent of pattern-matching (described in Chapter 6). This is a limited form of pattern-matching, and the patterns used here will be consistent in both parts of the language.

The first two clauses in the with section (also known as the "rules" clause) are *type patterns*, essentially testing the exception against the type given to the right of the :? token, in much the same way that C# or Visual Basic do. If the exception is of that given type (or a derived type), then a match has fired and the right side of the -> is executed. Notice that in the first form, the exception instance itself is not needed or available; to make the instance available for use (so as to obtain information from inside the exception instance, for example, such as its Message property), it must be named in an as clause.

The third clause matches any exception and binds the exception instance into the name given (in this case, ex) for use in the right side of the -> body. The named value will be of System.Exception type, so all its members will be available for use.

Additionally, a fourth type of clause, the *wildcard pattern*, serves the case where the exception instance isn't needed and the F# programmer desires a "catch-all" case. The wildcard pattern is given by the _ character.

Notice that, as shown in the preceding example, the try...with construct is an expression, and as such yields a value. This means that, like the if construct described earlier, the various "branches" of the try...with must all yield a value that is type-compatible; in the preceding case, both the body of the try block and each of the with clauses return a string (which is then returned as the result of the whole expression).

## try...finally

The try...finally form of the exception-handling behavior is similar to try...with, with the difference that the finally clause has no exception instance specified, because it will be executed regardless of how the guarded block is exited. Note that, like its sister language C#, the finally clause does not handle the exception if one is thrown from within the guarded block, but simply executes and then proceeds to allow the exception to circulate further back up the call stack.

```
let results =
    try
        (12 / 0)
    finally
        System.Console.WriteLine("In finally block")
```

Again, like the try...with form, the try...finally form is an expression, meaning it yields a return value; however, because the finally clause itself isn't an actual result but merely a way in which to provide cleanup, "returning" a value out of the finally clause will have no effect on the code. In other words, this version of the previous example

```
let results =
    try
        (12 / 0)
    finally
        System.Console.WriteLine("In finally block")
        5
```

will *not* yield the value 5 but will still circulate the exception to higher stack frames because the exception has not yet been caught.

It is also possible to rethrow an exception that has been thrown and caught in a catch block, using rethrow:.

As with all .NET languages, rethrowing an exception causes the runtime to immediately begin looking for catch handlers above the current stack frame — there is no difference between a thrown exception and a rethrown exception.

## Raising and Throwing Exceptions

Raising an exception in F# is accomplished via raise, as demonstrated here:

```
try
    raise (new System.Exception("I don't wanna!"))
finally
    System.Console.WriteLine("In finally block")
```

Raising an exception in F# is effectively the same behavior as using `throw` in C# or `Throw` in Visual Basic, constructing an `exception` instance (capturing a snapshot of the thread stack at the time) and immediately beginning the stack-frame-exiting to find an appropriate exception handler.

## Defining New Exception Types

Although the entire range of .NET exception types are available to the F# programmer for raising, in general it is considered bad form to throw an exception type that isn't particular to that library; in other words, when designing a new component, F# programmers should take care to define exception types that are specific to that component, so that programmers catching exceptions can discriminate exceptions thrown by different components and handle each accordingly.

F# provides two mechanisms by which new exception types can be defined: One that provides maximum compatibility with the rest of the .NET ecosystem, and one that requires a near-trivial amount of work. The first, which is to define a new class type, in a manner reminiscent of C# or Visual Basic, is discussed in more detail in Chapter 8: simply create a new class that derives (either directly or indirectly) from `System.Exception`.

The second involves the F# `exception` keyword, and at its simplest, defines an exception type that inherits from the F# base exception class `exn`:

```
exception MyException
```

The `MyException` type, defined like this, defines a new .NET class type that looks like the following, if it were to be written in C#:

```
public class MyExceptionException : Exception
{
    public MyExceptionException() { ... }
    public int CompareTo(Exception ex) { ... }
    public int CompareTo(object o) { ... }
    public bool Equals(Exception ex) { ... }
    public bool Equals(object o) { ... }
    public int GetHashCode() { ... }
    public int GetStructuralHashCode() { ... }
}
```

Note the name of the class — the F# compiler has silently appended the suffix `Exception` to the name of the exception type defined in F#, because it is a .NET convention that all exception type names be so named. Inside of F#, this will have no effect, but when calling F# code from other languages, it will need to be taken into account.

## SUMMARY

The control handling primitives of F# are, for the most part, identical to control primitives of other languages, with the difference that functions (described in Chapter 13) will often step in to take over some of the flow-control behaviors C# and Visual Basic programmers are used to using other language constructs to handle. For example, much of the imperative looping (`while`/`do` and the simple `for` expression) will be instead written to use recursion and pattern-matching. Much of the flow-control constructs in F# can be rewritten entirely using pattern-matching constructs, as discussed in more detail in Chapter 6.

# 5

# Composite Types

**WHAT'S IN THIS CHAPTER?**

➤ Understanding option types

➤ Working with tuples

➤ Using arrays, lists and sequences

➤ Creating and using maps and sets

Like many other .NET languages, F# provides not only a set of primitive types for describing the basic atoms of data (strings, integers, and so on), but also a set of types for gathering those atoms into larger structures. These *composite types* are also built into the language, and in some cases directly mirror capabilities found within the .NET Base Class Library or the CLR.

In many cases, F# developers will find that these composite types can serve where normally developers in other languages would have to create a complete class type. For example, as with many functional languages, F# developers can find that a collection of functions plus a tuple type instance or list instance can be sufficient to model the problem domain, without having to create a standalone class to represent the data. Much of the F# library is built in precisely this manner, wrapped into a module (see Chapter 11 for lexical scoping).

## OPTION TYPES

The simplest composite type to understand is the *option type*, which is effectively an either/ or type similar in some ways to the Boolean data type, but with an entirely different purpose and use.

Options are similar to Booleans in that there are only two acceptable values for a given option, None, indicating an absence of value, and Some, which indicates a value. As can be easily inferred from the description here, options are used as a replacement for the null-checking that object-oriented languages traditionally use to determine the difference between "nothing" and "something":

```
let nothing : string option = None
let something : string option = Some("Ted Neward")
System.Console.WriteLine("nothing = {0}", nothing)
System.Console.WriteLine("something = {0}", something.Value)
```

As is demonstrated here, options are tied to another type, the actual type "carried" as part of the Some value, which in this case, is a string. (The Option type is a generic type, which should be familiar to .NET developers; generics in F# are discussed in Chapter 10). F# allows us two different ways to specify an option type, one using the T option syntax (as shown here), or to use a more .NET/BCL-like syntax, which may seem more comfortable to the C# crowd:

```
let nothing : Option<string> = None
let something : Option<string> = Some("Ted Neward")
System.Console.WriteLine("nothing = {0}", nothing)
System.Console.WriteLine("something = {0}", something.Value)
```

It's important to note that the two syntaxes are entirely equivalent and produce exactly the same IL; the former is preferred among functional-language programmers, but the latter may be more comfortable for object-oriented developers until the functional style becomes more intuitive. (We'll see similar kinds of syntax when looking at list declarations later in this chapter.)

The option type serves as a simple type designed to differentiate between (as its name implies) "some" data and "no" data. Pragmatically, Option acts as a measure to avoid developers having to worry about null-object values and the inevitable NullReferenceException that gets thrown when forgetting to test for null before dereferencing the possibly-null value. Because None is an object instance just as any other object is,* None is perfectly acceptable as a target for comparisons and method calls:

```
let possibleValue =
    if (System.DateTime.Now.Millisecond % 2) = 0 then
        None
    else
        Some("Have a happy day!")
if possibleValue.IsSome then
    System.Console.WriteLine("Ah, we got a good value. Good!")
    System.Console.WriteLine(possibleValue.Value)
```

This makes the use of Option vastly superior to the use of null and goes a long way toward removing a significant source of exceptions thrown at runtime. (Consider this a prescriptive piece of advice: Prefer Option to null as a return type indicating a lack of data or response.)

As is shown in the preceding code, testing an option value for Some-ness can be done several different ways. The Option type has several properties defined on it directly, such as the IsSome property already shown, which returns true if the underlying Option is a Some of some value, just as IsNone returns true if the underlying Option instance is set to None. Accessing the value of a Some is done through the Value property, but it is important to note that for None, Value will return null, so only access it when IsSome is true.

---

* Technically, this isn't true — the None value is, in truth, null under the covers (for optimization reasons), but many of the F# APIs are written specifically to handle the null-ness silently. This lends the idea that None is a "real" object value.

Any of the following code, when invoked, will throw an exception, so careless use of None can still create NullReferenceExceptions:

```
let nothing : string option = None
if nothing.Equals(None) then
    System.Console.WriteLine("None.Equals(None)")
System.Console.WriteLine(nothing.GetHashCode())
System.Console.WriteLine(nothing.ToString())
```

F# does this for efficiency and performance reasons, so although the compiler does attempt to make None appear as if it is a legitimate value, be careful when trying to peek too far under the hood. More often than not, using IsSome (or relying on the functions described below) is the preferred approach to test for Some-ness or None-ness.

## Option Functions

F# provides a suite of functions in the Option module that also provide access to the members of the Option type, and some enhanced capabilities over using the properties directly. For example, Option.iter is a method that executes a passed-in function against an Option instance, but only if that Option instance is a Some rather than a None (in which case it does nothing):

```
let possibleValue =
    if (System.DateTime.Now.Millisecond % 2) = 0 then
        None
    else
        Some("Have a happy day!")
Option.iter (fun o -> System.Console.WriteLine(o.ToString()))
        possibleValue
```

Following are some of the Option module methods:

| NAME | EFFECT |
| --- | --- |
| bind fn o | Executes the function fn against the Option instance o, returning a value, but only if o is a Some |
| count o | Returns 0 if o is None, 1 if o is Some |
| exists fn o | Executes the function fn against the Option instance o, returning true or false, but only if o is a Some |
| forall fn o | Executes the function fn against the Option instance o, passing o.Value into fn, expecting a true or false value back, but only if o is a Some |
| get o | Returns the value in the option (if o is a Some), or else throws an exception (if o is a None) |
| iter fn o | Executes the function fn against the Option instance o, passing o.Value into fn, but only if o is a Some |
| isNone o | Returns true if o is None, false if o is Some |

*continues*

*(continued)*

| NAME | EFFECT |
|---|---|
| isSome o | Returns false if *o* is None, true if *o* is Some |
| toArray o | Converts the Option instance o into an array of size 0 or 1, depending on whether o is Some or None |
| toList o | Converts the Option instance o into a list of length 0 or 1, depending on whether o is Some or None |

Observant readers will notice that many of these methods make more sense on collection classes, and much of the Option API is designed around the concept that an Option is a single-slot collection. This also creates a consistent API when working with other composite types (such as Lists or Arrays).

## TUPLES

Tuples group two or more unnamed values into an ordered collection of values described as a single value:

```
let myName = ("Ted", "Neward")
let myDescription = ("Ted", "Neward", 38, 98053)
```

Tuples are described by comma-separated values in between parentheses, so in the preceding snippet, the two tuples listed are of string and string type, and of string and string and int and int or more accurately, (string * string) and (string * string * int * int) in the F# syntax. These are two separate and unique types, even if they have no formal name assigned to them so that any attempt to use a (string * string) where a (string * string * int * int) is expected will fail.

Any tuple whose list of types — in both number and order — is equivalent to another is thus considered to be of the same type. Thus, in the following:

```
let myName = ("Ted", "Neward")
let herName = ("Sarah", "Michelle", "Gellar")
```

the two values, myName and herName, are of entirely separate types and therefore incompatible, whereas in:

```
let myName = ("Ted", "Neward")
let cityState = ("Phoenix", "AZ")
```

the values myName and cityState, despite representing obviously different intended values, are both (string * string), and therefore are type-equivalent. Formally, this kind of equivalence is known as *structural equivalence*, meaning that the two values are equal in terms of their contents, even if they may or may not be of the same type.* Thus, when the following is run:

---

* In truth, this isn't a precise definition of the term, but it suffices for the discussion here.

```
System.Console.WriteLine("myName = herName? {0}",
    myName.GetType().Equals(herName.GetType()))
System.Console.WriteLine("myName = cityState? {0}",
    myName.GetType().Equals(cityState.GetType()))
```

the resulting printed values will be False and True.

Accessing the individual values inside the tuple is typically done through one of three methods. First, the F# library provides functions (fst and snd) that return individual elements from inside the tuple. Second, pattern-matching can be used to extract elements from within the tuple (and is described in Chapter 6), or third, a new set of individual values can be bound based on values from inside the tuple.

The first approach uses F# library functions fst and snd ("first" and "second") to extract either the first or second element from inside the tuple value:

```
let me = ("Ted", "Neward")
let firstName = fst me
let lastName = snd me
System.Console.WriteLine("Hello, {0} {1}", firstName, lastName)
```

Each returns only that particular element, and restrictions on the fst and snd functions require that the tuple be a pair (2-element tuple). For this reason, any triple (3-element tuple) or tuple with elements beyond that will not be accessible via this approach.

The third approach uses new values to pull elements out of the tuple, as in the following:

```
let me = ("Ted", "Neward", 38, "Redmond", "WA")
let (firstName, lastName, age, city, state) = me
System.Console.WriteLine("Hello, {0} {1}", firstName, lastName)
```

This is actually a short form of pattern-matching (discussed in Chapter 6) so the use of the wildcard (_) to ignore certain elements of the tuple also works:

```
let me = ("Ted", "Neward", 38, "Redmond", "WA")
let (firstName, _, _, city, _) = me
System.Console.WriteLine("Hello, {0}, how's {1}",
    firstName, city)
```

Note that any sort of name-binding can be used, so if we have an array (see the next section for more on arrays) of tuples that we need to extract values from individually, we can do so using for again:

```
let people = [|
    ("Ted", "Neward", 38, "Redmond", "WA")
    ("Katie", "Ellison", 30, "Seattle", "WA")
    ("Mark", "Richards", 45, "Boston", "MA")
    ("Rachel", "Reese", 27, "Phoenix", "AZ")
    ("Ken", "Sipe", 43, "St Louis", "MO")
    ("Naomi", "Wilson", 35, "Seattle", "WA")
|]
for (firstName, lastName, _, _, _) in people do
    System.Console.WriteLine("{0} {1}", firstName, lastName)
```

Where other .NET languages tend to use custom value types (those types that inherit from System .ValueType, also known as structs in C# or as Structures in Visual Basic), F# encourages the use of tuples instead. Note that it is still possible to create value types in F# (see Chapter 7 for details), but that should be reserved for the specific case where a new kind of "primitive type" needs to be created, rather than simply creating a "bundle of values," which is the province of the tuple type.

## ARRAYS

Arrays, as most .NET developers know, are homogenous collections that are laid out sequentially in memory, providing fast random-access capabilities. Because arrays of objects are just arrays of mutable references to objects, however, arrays are discouraged as constructs for use in functional programming. As a fully vested member of the CLR platform, the F# language provides a complete set of functionality to arrays that is similar to that for lists and other collection types, but aside from interoperability with the underlying CLR platform and assemblies written in other languages, F# code "in the wild" rarely uses it. For new F# programmers, the general recommendation is to reach for a list (seen next) rather than an array.

### Array Construction

The simplest array to understand is the empty array, denoted by an empty pair of array brackets:

```
let emptyArray = [| |]
```

Arrays can also be initialized with contents by semicolon-separating the values, as in:

```
let arrayOfIntegers = [| 1; 2; 3; 4; |]
```

or by separating the contents onto their own line:

```
let arrayOfStrings = [|
    "Fred"
    "Wilma"
    "Barney"
    "Betty"
|]
```

Either style works equally well, leaving the choice to be based primarily on which one reads more clearly to the developers involved.

If the array is to contain all the same value, the `create` function from the `Array` module can be used to construct an array:

```
let arrayOfZeroes = Array.create 10 0
let arrayOfTeds = Array.create 10 "Ted"
```

The `Array.create` function takes an initial size and an initial value as parameters and constructs the array accordingly.

Arrays can also be initialized by *range expressions*, in which a starting and ending value are provided to the language, and it infers the rest, initializing the list with starting and ending values and the contents in between:

```
let arrayOfIntegers = [| 1 .. 10 |]   // [ 1; 2; 3; ... 10; ]
```

The range expression can also have a "step" to it, an increment value that will be added to the starting value repeatedly so long as the value produced is smaller or equal to the ending value:

```
let arrayOfEvenIntegers = [| 0 .. 2 .. 10 |]
    // [ 0; 2; 4; ... 10; ]
```

The step can be any numeric step, and the range expression can also support floating-point values:

```
let arrayOfFloatsToTen = [ 0.0 .. 0.5 .. 10.0 ]
```

 *Note that as of this release, F# will continue to support floating-point range expressions, but a warning will be generated because the language designers reserve the right to remove that functionality in a later release.*

For those cases where the "step" form of a range expression isn't quite powerful enough to create the array desired, such as creating an array of the squares of 1 through 10 (1, 4, 9, 16, and so on), you could construct an array using the `Array.create` function and then fill the values with the desired squares using a looping construct:

```
let mutableArray = Array.create 10 0
for i = 0 to 9 do
    mutableArray.[i] <- i*i
```

Note that in F#, array indexing begins at 0, as God intended.

Although this is a "traditional" way to accomplish this, F# provides a better way, by using the looping construct directly inside of the array initializer:

```
let arrayBuiltList = [ for i in 1 .. 10 -> i * i ]
```

In this particular case, we use a second form of the "for" construct, a *sequence expression*, described later in this chapter in the section on sequences. The net result is that the loop is effectively expanded "inside" the initializer, each result creating a new value initialized into the array. In this case, the result is an array of int, 10 cells in size, containing 1, 4, 9, 16, and so on.

The F# syntax for describing the type of the array is, as with Option, to append "array" to the end of the type descriptor so that an array of integers in F# is described as int array. This can be important in certain scenarios, where the array type must be explicitly described, such as when constructing an array of objects:

```
let (arrayOfObjects : obj array) = [|
    (1 :> obj)
    ("two" :> obj)
    (3.0 :> obj)
|]
```

In this case, not only does the array itself need to be explicitly described as an obj array (where obj is the synonym for System.Object in F#), but the individual elements must also be explicitly upcast as obj types.

## Array Access

Accessing the members of the array, as shown earlier in the discussion of looping through the list to initialize its members, is done through the [] method on the array:

```
let people = [|
    ("Ted", "Neward", 38, "Redmond", "WA")
    ("Mark", "Richards", 45, "Boston", "MA")
    ("Rachel", "Appel", 27, "Pittsburgh", "PA")
    ("Neal", "Ford", 43, "Atlanta", "GA")
    ("Naomi", "Wilson", 35, "Seattle", "WA")
|]
let thirdPerson = people.[2]
```

Note that the "dot" in the usage here is required — the F# language wants to be consistent, and so treats the [] as a method invocation, to keep it in line with the other methods, such as those inherited from System.Array, that are accessible. (Fortunately, the F# compiler will "do the right thing" with this expression, turning it into a single-opcode expression when emitting the bytecode, so no performance is lost by doing so.)

Modifying the contents of the array is as easy as putting the access expression on the left side of the assignment operator:

```
// Happy Birthday, Mark!
people.[2] <- ("Mark", "Richards", 46, "Boston", "MA")
```

As with any use of arrays on the .NET platform, this modifies the array by storing a new reference to an object and has no effect on the object originally referenced.

## Array Functions

The Array module provides a large number of methods that can operate on arrays and provides a much richer set of functionality for arrays than that provided by the BCL. Using them typically requires nothing more than to provide the array instance on which to operate and any parameters needed by the operation (such as the function to apply to each of the array elements). For example, to iterate over an array and display its contents, the C# or Visual Basic programmer may be tempted to write the iteration loop manually:

```
let array = Array.create 10 0
for i = 0 to array.Length - 1 do
    System.Console.WriteLine(array.[i])
```

Doing this requires the developer to extract the element out of the array using the integer index and can be awkward in certain situations. Like C# and Visual Basic, F# permits a form of for to handle the details of iteration internally and simply provide the element to the body of the loop for processing:

```
for p in array do
    System.Console.WriteLine(p)
```

However, functional programmers find this more easily done by passing a (typically anonymous) function containing the "operation" code (the body of the loop, in this case) directly to the

`Array.iter` function, which iterates over the array, extracts the current element, and passes it in to the "operation" function for processing:

```
Array.iter (fun it -> System.Console.WriteLine(it.ToString()))
           array
```

It may seem odd to the traditional O-O developer to do this at first, but doing so actually creates more opportunities for reusability and easier extension. To understand why, imagine that the array is a large one, consisting of thousands of elements. To iterate over each in a serial fashion is a huge performance hit, particularly when each element is being processed independently and therefore could be processed on its own thread (and depending on the underlying hardware, CPU core). But to write the code that spins up threads (or borrows them from the system thread pool) can be awkward to write and hard to debug, and certainly won't be something we want to write twice.

Fortunately, if the parallel-iteration code is written once and placed into a function inside a module (calling it `ParallelArray`, perhaps), we can modify the previous example to take advantage of it, yielding a (fictitious) example of:

```
ParallelArray.iter
    (fun it -> System.Console.WriteLine(it.ToString()))
    array
```

This is a powerful form of reusability and is supported in .NET 4 using `Array.Parallel`.

Some of the functions offered by the Array module are given next, grouped loosely by category.

## Array Meta Functions

These functions (in a general sort of way) operate on the array itself, rather than individual elements within the array, to do things such as create a new array, concatenate two arrays together, and so on. These are documented in the F# documentation, so look there for more details.

| | |
|---|---|
| `append ar1 ar2` | Creates a new array containing the elements of `ar1` and `ar2` (in that order) |
| `average ar` | Assuming the array type supports three members (+, `DivideByInt` and `get_Zero`), calculates the average of the elements in `ar` |
| `averageBy fn ar` | Assuming the array type supports three members (+, `DivideByInt` and `get_Zero`), calculates the average of the elements by calling `fn` on each element of `ar` |
| `blit ar1 st1 ar2 st2 len` | Reads `len` elements from `ar1` starting at `i` and copies them to `ar2` starting at `st2` |
| `concat seq` | Creates an array consisting of all the elements of the given sequence of arrays `seq` |
| `copy src` | Creates a copy of the array `src` |
| `create sz init` | Creates a new array of size *sz* with an initial value (and type) of `init` |
| `empty<'t>` | Returns an empty array of the given type `t` |

*continues*

*(continued)*

| | |
|---|---|
| `fill ar st len val` | Fills the array ar with `len` number of `val` values, starting from `st` |
| `get ar i` | Returns the i'th element from the array ar; synonymous with ar.[i] |
| `init sz gen` | Creates an array of size `sz` and uses the `gen` function to compute the initial contents |
| `isEmpty ar` | Returns true if the array ar is empty |
| `length ar` | Returns the length of ar; synonymous with ar.Length |
| `ofList lst` | Converts the list `lst` to an array |
| `ofSeq seq` | Converts the sequence `seq` to an array |
| `partition predFn ar` | Splits *ar* into two arrays (returned as a tuple), containing the elements for which `predFn` returns true and false, respectively |
| `rev ar` | Returns a new array containing the contents of ar in reversed order |
| `set ar i val` | Sets the i'th element in ar to `val`; synonymous with ar.[i] <- val |
| `sub ar st len` | Creates a new array containing the subrange from ar starting at `st` for `len` elements |
| `toList ar` | Converts the array ar to a list |
| `toSeq ar` | Converts the array ar to a sequence |
| `unzip ap` `unzip3 ap` | Converts the array of pairs ap into two (or three) separate arrays, returned as a tuple |
| `zip ar1 ar2` `zip3 ar1 ar2 ar3` | Combines the elements of ar1 and ar2 (and ar3) into an array of pairs (or triplets), where the 0'th elements of ar1 and ar2 will be paired up, and so on |

## Array Application Operations

These functions operate on the contents of the array, typically by taking a function as a parameter and using it against each of the elements in the array to produce a result, either a single value or another array.

| | |
|---|---|
| `choose fn ar` | Applies fn to each element in ar, and if fn returns `Some(x)` for that element, includes it in the returned array |
| `exists fn ar` | Returns true if any of the elements in ar, when passed to fn, return true |
| `filter fn ar` | Returns an array consisting of the elements in ar that, when passed in to fn, causes it to return true |
| `find fn ar` | Returns the first element in ar that returns true when passed to fn; if no such element exists in ar, throws an exception |

| | |
|---|---|
| `findIndex fn ar` | Returns the index of the first element in `ar` that returns true when passed to `fn`; if no such element exists, throws an exception |
| `fold fn s ar` | Applies `fn` to each element in `ar`, passing `s` in with the element, allowing `s` to act as an accumulator across all the calls; starts with the 0'th element in `ar` |
| `foldBack fn s ar` | Applies `fn` to each element in `ar`, passing `s` in with the element, allowing `s` to act as an accumulator across all the calls; starts with the last (n'th) element in `ar` |
| `forall fn ar` | Returns true if all of the elements in `ar`, when passed to `fn`, returns true |
| `iter fn ar` | Applies `fn` to each element in `ar`; `fn` is expected to return unit |
| `iteri fn ar` | Applies `fn` to each element in `ar`; `fn` receives both the element and its index and is expected to return unit |
| `map fn ar` | Applies `fn` to each element in `ar`; `fn` is expected to yield a value, which is put into an array and returned |
| `mapi fn ar` | Applies `fn` to each element in `ar`; `fn` receives both the element and its index and is expected to yield a value, which is put into an array and returned |
| `reduce fn ar` | Applies `fn` to each element in `ar`; `fn` receives both the element and its next element, starting from the 0'th element |
| `reduceBack fn ar` | Applies `fn` to each element in `ar`; `fn` receives both the element and its previous element, starting from the last (n'th) element |
| `try_find fn ar` | Returns the first element in `ar` for which `fn` returns true, or `None` if no such element exists |
| `try_findindex fn ar` | Returns the index of the first element in `ar` for which `fn` returns true, or `None` if no such element exists |
| `try_findindexi fn ar` | Returns the index of the first element in `ar` for which `fn` returns true, or `None` if no such element exists; `fn` receives both the element and its index as parameters |

There are some additional functions in the `Array` module, but many of these are just additionally varied versions of the these functions (`iter2`, for example, is just a form of `iter` that can operate on two arrays simultaneously), or "bake in" the function to apply to each of the elements (such as the max and min functions, which do as their names imply).

# LISTS

Lists are an ordered collection of a single type and, like tuples, form a major backbone of functional programming. Internally, lists are singly linked lists, meaning that list construction and extraction is extremely fast and space-efficient. However, random access to elements in the list will be far slower than arrays; fortunately, most functional programming prefers recursion over iteration, and recursion works well to extract elements one at a time out of the list for processing.

# List Construction

The simplest list to understand is the empty list, denoted by an empty pair of brackets:

```
let emptyList = []
```

Lists that have something inside of them are vastly more interesting, however, and can be initialized by including values (again, all of the same type) in between the brackets, separated either by semi-colons or carriage-returns:

```
let listOfIntegers = [ 1; 2; 3; 4; ]
let listOfStrings = [
    "Fred"
    "Wilma"
    "Barney"
    "Betty"
    ]
```

As with arrays, either style works equally well — although the former is preferred for short or easily initialized lists, the latter is useful when each element in the list takes up more space, either because it needs to be accompanied by a comment describing its contents, or for scenarios where each element's initialization takes up more than a few characters:

```
let listOfStrings = [
    "Fred"      // Flintstone
    "Wilma"     // Flintstone
    "Barney"    // Rubble
    "Betty"     // Rubble
    ]
let listOfPeopleTuples = [
    ("Ted", "Neward", 38, "Redmond", "WA")
    ("Katie", "Ellison", 30, "Seattle", "WA")
    ("Mark", "Richards", 45, "Boston", "MA")
    ("Rachel", "Reese", 27, "Phoenix", "AZ")
    ("Ken", "Sipe", 43, "St Louis", "MO")
    ("Naomi", "Wilson", 35, "Seattle", "WA")
    ]
```

Like arrays, lists can also be initialized by *range expressions*:

```
let listOfIntegersToTen = [ 1 .. 10 ]  // [ 1; 2; 3; ... 10; ]
let listOfEvenIntsToTen = [ 0 .. 2 .. 10 ]
    // [ 0; 2; 4; ... 10; ]
let listOfFloatsToTen = [ 0.0 .. 0.5 .. 10.0 ]
```

It is also possible to take an existing list and prepend new elements to it using the :: (pronounced "cons") operator, which takes an element on the left side and a list on the right side and produces a new list out of the results:

```
let consedList = 1 :: 2 :: 3 :: 4 :: []
```

Two things are important to note about consedList: First, notice that the right-most element is the empty list. This is because the cons operator must have a list as its right-most argument, or the operation will fail. This also leads to the second point, which is that the cons operator is *right-associative*, meaning that the preceding code, written in a more explicit (and tedious) form, looks like

```
let consedList = 1 :: (2 :: (3 :: (4 :: [])))
```

which illustrates that in each case, the right item to the operator will be a list. Note that this also implies that for each operation, a new list object will be created and handed back, until the final list object created will be bound to `consedList`. In this respect, lists behave similar to how .NET `System.String` objects behave, for many of the same reasons.

Developers with an eye on performance-sensitive code may find that last paragraph disconcerting. The implication that each `cons` operation requires the contents of the list to be copied over into a new list, only to in turn be copied again into the new list after that, and so on, smacks of a horrible waste of effort.

Fear not. Two things make this situation more palatable. First, the list is a singly linked list, meaning that each value is stored in its own node. Second, because lists are immutable, they can share nodes across lists, thus reducing the total cost of "copying" the list. (It's worth noting that this "sharing" of nodes could never be possible in a mutable list, reinforcing the intrinsic usefulness of immutable data structures, making this use of immutable lists often much faster than working with mutable lists.)

For those cases where the "step" form of a range expression isn't quite powerful enough to create the list desired, such as creating a list of the squares of 1 through 10 (1, 4, 9, 16, and so on), you could use a looping construct (from Chapter 4) to build up a list, something along the lines of the following:

```
let mutable forBuiltList = []
for i = 1 to 10 do
    forBuiltList <- (i * i) :: forBuiltList
```

but this feels horribly awkward, for a variety of reasons. First, because lists are immutable, concatenating against `forBuiltList` will produce only a new list, not modify the original, and thus needs to be captured into a mutable local variable (using the mutable keyword, described in Chapter 8) across each step in the loop. Second, because `forBuiltList is` now a mutable reference, any developer can come along and modify the contents after its initial construction, creating a potential logic hole.

Fortunately, as with arrays, the F# language permits the use of a sequence expression inside of the list initializer:

```
let forBuiltList = [ for i in 1 .. 10 -> i * i ]
```

As with the array case, the result is a list of int containing the squares of the values 1 through 10.

*If you are diligently typing in the examples in as you read this book, you might notice that the two lists aren't exactly the same. Although they're both lists of int containing the squares of 1 through 10, the first list is a list of squares counting down from 10, and the second is a list counting up from 1. This is because in the second case the elements are automatically appended to the list, whereas in the first case they're manually prepended. This just reinforces the idea that the second syntax is the preferential one to use, since it will more likely be what the developer really intended.*

For those situations where a developer wants to smash two lists together, F# provides the @ (concatenation) operator, which takes two lists and produces a new list out of the combined contents:

```
let concattedList = listOfIntegers @ consedList
    // [ 1; 2; 3; 4; 1; 2; 3; 4; ]
```

In each of these cases, the resulting list is a list of a single type, whether int, string or the tuple type (string * string * int * string * string).

Because lists are so common in F# code, the language provides a particular type syntax for describing lists, that of appending the list element type with the suffix "list." Thus, the respective types of the lists viewed so far would be described by F# as:

```
listOfIntegers : int list
listOfStrings : string list
listOfPeopleTuples : (string*string*int*string*string) list
listOfFloatsToTen : float list
consedList : int list
forBuiltList : int list
concattedList : int list
```

In certain scenarios, it will be helpful (or necessary) to create a list that contains more than one type, but trying the naïve approach fails miserably:

```
let notWorkingList = [ 1; "2"; 3.0; ]
```

This is because the compiler looks at the first element of the list, an int, and assumes that the rest of the list should also be int values, which the successive two values clearly are not.

For those situations demanding a "list of everything," the F# language allows for an "object list," though the syntax will often require a type descriptor to force the compiler to see it as such:

```
let (objectList : obj list) = [
    (1 :> obj)
    ("2" :> obj)
    (3.0 :> obj)
]
```

The "upcast" operators are required here for the F# compiler to see them in their obj form (instead of assuming them, as it would naturally, to be literals of their declared type — int, string, and float, respectively), and the parentheses around the upcast is necessary to see it all as one expression. (The awkwardness here is arguably a deliberate decision, because F# would much rather programmers figure out more strongly typed ways of interacting with lists.)

## List Access

When initialized, elements of a list can be accessed using a variety of approaches.

The first approach is to use the Head and Tail properties on the list instance itself, which returns the first object in the list and the remainder of the list (as a list), respectively:

```
let people = [
    ("Ted", "Neward", 38)
    ("Mark", "Richards", 45)
```

```
        ("Naomi", "Wilson", 38)
        ("Ken", "Sipe", 43)
    ]
    let peopleHead = people.Head
    System.Console.WriteLine(peopleHead)
```

In the case of a single-element list, Head will return that element, and Tail will return an empty list. Unlike the array, however, the list provides no efficient random-access operation — lists can only be accessed as head and tail elements. However, should the .NET developer desire access to the *n*th item of a list, it can be obtained via the "Item" indexer property defined on the List<> class. However, doing so has two drawbacks. One, because the list is a singly linked list, accessing elements further from the head of the list will be increasingly slower. Two, doing so will potentially create confusion in those who read the code, because functional languages have not traditionally had arbitrary access to elements of the list. As a result, it's best to consider this method and its performance implications carefully before using.

The Head and Tail properties provide effectively the same result as the List module methods* head and tail, respectively:

```
    let people = [
        ("Ted", "Neward", 38)
        ("Mark", "Richards", 45)
        ("Naomi", "Wilson", 38)
        ("Ken", "Sipe", 43)
    ]
    let firstPerson = List.head people
    System.Console.WriteLine(firstPerson)
```

Which of these two styles F# programmers should use depends somewhat on programmer aesthetics and comfort. Having said that, however, the programmer seeking to understand and master functional style will prefer the use of the List methods because those can be partially applied; see Chapter 13 for more details.

Like arrays, lists can also be extracted through the use of variable bindings, but this is less common and potentially dangerous; for example, the following code will compile and run, but generates a warning that not all possible matches are accounted for. (This is discussed further in Chapter 6.)

```
    let people = [
        ("Ted", "Neward", 38)
        ("Mark", "Richards", 45)
        ("Naomi", "Wilson", 38)
        ("Ken", "Sipe", 43)
    ]
    let (personOne :: rest) = people
    System.Console.WriteLine(personOne)
```

As a result, this form is less used, in favor of recursively using Head/List.head and Tail/List.tail instead.

Lists can also provide access to the *n*-th item in the list using the .[] method (the Item property at the IL level) or the List.nth function, but this is rarely done in F# code, because each such access

---

* Note that in previous releases of F#, these were known as hd and tl, and lots of F# code and samples still use them as such.

will require traversing the linked list from the beginning until the *n*-th item is found (O(*n*) performance). Given how trivially easy it is to convert between arrays and lists, using the `toArray` or `toList` functions found on each, in general it will be preferable to convert the list to an array to do random access.

# List Methods

The `List` module (see Chapter 11 for details on modules and namespaces) provides a large number of `functions` for use with lists, even more than those provided for `Array`. As with the `Array` module functions, the `List` module functions frequently take a function as a parameter to apply to the various elements within the `List`, and many of the same functions appear in both modules under the same names and declarations so as to maintain consistency.

Some of the `List` functions appear next, loosely grouped by category.

## List Meta Functions

These functions, like those listed for the `Array` module, manipulate lists rather than the contents within them. In general, these functions create or copy lists, or do something to the list as a whole, in much the same way that the functions described in the `Array` section do. There is a great deal of duplication here, so that the F# programmer familiar with how an operation works on an array already knows how an operation will work on a list, and vice versa.

| | |
|---|---|
| `append lst1 lst2` | Creates a new list containing the elements of `lst1` and `lst2` (in that order) |
| `concat seq` | Creates a list consisting of all the elements of the given sequence of lists `seq` |
| `empty<'t>` | Returns an empty list of the given type `t` |
| `head lst` | Returns the head (first element) of `lst`; synonymous with `lst.Head`; unlike `tl`, `hd` always returns a single object, not a list |
| `init sz gen` | Creates a list of size `sz`,using the `gen` function *sz* times to compute the initial contents |
| `isEmpty lst` | Returns true if the list `lst` is empty |
| `length lst` | Returns the length of `lst`; synonymous with `lst.Length` |
| `nth lst i` | Returns the i'th element from the list `lst`; synonymous with `lst.[`*i*`]` |
| `ofArray ar` | Converts the array `ar` into a list |
| `ofSeq seq` | Converts the sequence *seq* to a list |
| `partition predFn lst` | Splits *lst* into two lists (returned as a tuple), containing the elements for which `predFn` returns true and false, respectively |
| `rev lst` | Returns a new list containing the contents of `lst` in reversed order |
| `tail lst` | Returns the tail (remainder) of `lst`; synonymous with `lst.Tail`; unlike hd, `tl` always returns a list, even if it is of zero or one elements in length |

| | |
|---|---|
| `toArray lst` | Converts the list `lst` to an array |
| `toSeq lst` | Converts the list `lst` to a sequence |
| `unzip lp`<br>`unzip3 lp` | Converts the list of pairs (or triplets) `lp` into two (or three) separate lists, returned as a tuple |
| `zip lst1 lst2`<br>`zip3 lst1 lst2 lst3` | Combines the elements of `lst1` and `lst2` (and `lst3`) into a list of pairs (or triplets), where the 0'th elements of `lst1` and `lst2` (and `lst3`) will be paired up (or tripled up), and so on |

## List Application Operations

These functions operate on the contents of the list, typically by taking a function as a parameter and invoking it once for each of the elements, passing that element in as a parameter (also known as "applying" the function to each of the elements), to produce a result, either a single value or with all the results grouped into another list.

| | |
|---|---|
| `choose fn lst` | Applies `fn` to each element in `lst`, and if `fn` returns `Some(x)` for that element, includes it in the returned list |
| `exists fn lst` | Returns true if any of the elements in `lst`, when passed to `fn`, returns true |
| `filter fn lst` | Returns a list consisting of the elements in `lst` that, when passed in to `fn`, causes it to return true |
| `find fn lst` | Returns the first element in `lst` that returns true when passed to `fn`; if no such element exists in `lst`, throws an exception |
| `findIndex fn lst` | Returns the index of the first element in `lst` that returns true when passed to `fn`; if no such element exists, throws an exception |
| `first fn lst` | Applies `fn` to each of the elements in `lst`, returning as soon as `fn` finds `Some(x)` for an element; if none are found, it returns `None` |
| `fold fn s lst` | Applies `fn` to each element in `lst`, passing `s` in with the element, allowing `s` to act as an accumulator across all of the calls; starts with the 0'th element in `lst` |
| `foldBack fn s lst` | Applies `fn` to each element in `lst`, passing `s` in with the element, allowing `s` to act as an accumulator across all of the calls; starts with the last (n'th) element in `lst` |
| `forall fn lst` | Returns true if all of the elements in `lst`, when passed to `fn`, returns true |
| `iter fn lst` | Applies `fn` to each element in `lst`; `fn` is expected to return unit |
| `iteri fn lst` | Applies `fn` to each element in `lst`; `fn` receives both the element and its index and is expected to return unit |

*continues*

*(continued)*

| | |
|---|---|
| `map fn lst` | Applies `fn` to each element in `lst`; `fn` is expected to yield a value, which is put into a list and returned |
| `mapi fn lst` | Applies `fn` to each element in `lst`; `fn` receives both the element and its index and is expected to yield a value, which is put into a list and returned |
| `map_concat fn lst` | Applies `fn` to each element in `lst`; `fn` receives both the element and its index and is expected to yield a value, which is put into a list and returned |
| `reduce fn lst` | Applies `fn` to each element in `lst`; `fn` receives both the element and its next element, starting from the 0'th element |
| `reduceBack fn lst` | Applies `fn` to each element in `lst`; *fn* receives both the element and its previous element, starting from the last (n'th) element |
| `tryFind fn lst` | Returns the first element in `lst` for which `fn` returns true, or `None` if no such element exists |
| `tryFindIndex fn lst` | Returns the index of the first element in `lst` for which `fn` returns true, or `None` if no such element exists |

There are some additional functions in the `List` module, but many of these are just additionally varied versions of these functions (iter2, for example, is just a form of `iter` that can operate on two lists simultaneously), or "bake in" the function to apply to each of the elements (such as the average function, which calculates the average of an array whose elements support addition and division operations).

## USING LISTS AND ARRAYS

Because using the functions described in the `List` and `Array` modules can be confusing at first to the traditional object-oriented programmer, a few examples may help clear up their use.

In C# and Visual Basic, when looking through an array (or list) of `Person` objects for a `Person` whose last name is "Neward", most programmers write a `for-each` loop, looking through at the `LastName` property of the `Person` object to see if it matches the criteria in question. To do this in F#, assuming the existence of a class type called `Person` was already defined, you would write instead:

```
let people = [|
    new Person("Ted", "Neward", 38)
    new Person("Mark", "Richards", 45)
    new Person("Ken", "Sipe", 43)
    new Person("Naomi", "Wilson", 38)
    new Person("Michael", "Neward", 16)
    new Person("Matthew", "Neward", 9)
|]
let newardsFound =
    Array.find (fun (it : Person) -> it.LastName = "Neward")
            people
System.Console.WriteLine(newardsFound)
```

If, instead, the goal was to know all the people who were of drinking age, however, the find operation would want all the `Persons` whose age was greater or equal than 21. Because this could be any number of `Persons`, and all of them need to be returned, this is better returned as another array:

```
let drinkers =
    Array.filter (fun (it : Person) -> it.Age > 21) people
```

Of course, everybody who's over 21 deserves a beer, and that's something that needs to be applied to each element in the array:

```
Array.iter (fun (it : Person) ->
    System.Console.WriteLine("Have a beer {0}!", it.FirstName))
    drinkers
```

The real power of this functional style becomes apparent when used with the pipeline operator (discussed in Chapter 13) to string each of these operations together:

```
people
    |> Array.filter (fun (it : Person) -> it.Age > 21)
    |> Array.iter (fun (it : Person) ->
        System.Console.WriteLine("Have a beer, {0}!",
            it.FirstName))
```

When the filtered and iterated functions are named, the code becomes almost a natural language:

```
people |> Array.filter isADrinker |> Array.iter haveABeer
```

Or the functions involved in the `filter` and `iter` operations can be named to make it look even more readable:

```
let isADrinker (ar : Person array) =
    Array.filter (fun (p : Person) -> p.Age > 21) ar
let haveABeer (ar : Person array) =
    Array.iter (fun (p : Person) ->
        System.Console.WriteLine("Have a beer, {0}!",
            p.FirstName) )
        ar
people |> isADrinker |> haveABeer
```

Of course, all these operations are equally applicable to either arrays or lists, simply by either converting the type descriptors to use `Person` list instead of `Person` array, or in some cases by omitting the type descriptor entirely and allowing F# to infer the types.

F#, like most functional languages, is without peer when working with collections this way. Most C# and VB developers, after having used LINQ for a while, discover that many of the exact same concepts built into LINQ are here in F# (and other functional languages). Even more deeply, if the budding F# programmer wants to spend a few mind-blowing moments, they should go back to their old SQL code, replace the columns with tuples and the tables with lists of tuples, and see how quickly list access and manipulation in F# using functions feels almost identical to the canonical SQL operations (SELECT, INSERT, UPDATE, DELETE).

More on using F# against a relational database is given in Chapter 19.

# SEQUENCES

A sequence, according to the formal definition of the F# language, is simply a synonym for the IEnumerable type defined in the .NET platform. As such, anytime an F# function produces an iterator across a collection, it is typically a sequence type. However, because functional languages have a rich history of using generators (functions that produce values, including functions that appear to be infinitely large or lazily computed) as the source of values to other functions, F# has a much wider suite of functions for sequence types (seq) than the .NET developer might expect.

By default, the sequence type is just a producer of values; in other words, when a sequence is obtained, the sequence itself has no sense of what values it holds and will hand back — instead, it has code internally that knows how to produce the next-expected value. For this reason, sequences are frequently thought of as *lazy*, meaning they do not initialize to contain all the values they will eventually produce.*

By far, the easiest way to obtain a sequence is to create one, using the seq keyword and a block of code that yields a result each time the sequence is asked to produce one, as in:

```
let x = seq { for i = 1 to 10 do yield i }
```

It's important to note that the sequence will not have yet produced any values — x is simply a generator of values, and each time it is asked to generate the value, it will execute the next branch of the for construct. This means that the loop inside of the sequence isn't really a loop at all, but a sequence of executable statements — contrary to what might seem obvious, there isn't a collection of 10 integers waiting to be handed back.

This becomes more obvious when we put some obvious side effect into the sequence loop, such as:

```
let y = seq { for i = 1 to 10 do
                System.Console.WriteLine("Generating {0}", i)
                yield i }
```

When run, no such "Generating" lines appear on the screen, because as of this point, the sequence has only been created, not asked to produce a value. The Console.WriteLine action won't take place until the sequence is asked to produce a value, such as when we convert the sequence into an IEnumerable and ask it for its current value:

```
let y = seq { for i = 1 to 10 do
                System.Console.WriteLine("Generating {0}", i)
                yield i }
let yEnum = y.GetEnumerator()
if yEnum.MoveNext() then
    System.Console.WriteLine(yEnum.Current)
```

This will produce "Generating 1" to the screen as soon as MoveNext() is called, because it is at that point that the sequence is asked to produce its first value. No other value is generated, because only that particular value is needed — any future values will be waiting to be generated on demand.

Note that sequences can be "reset" at any time by obtaining a new IEnumerator from the GetEnumerator() method on the sequence, or by simply using the sequence in a different Seq

---

* This is not quite what functional programmers think of when they use the term lazy, but it is a related concept and will feel pretty lazy to programmers not used to the functional lingo.

module call. It is important to realize, however, that it is the IEnumerator that holds the "current state" of the sequence and not the sequence itself.

This means that F# can permit what other languages would consider to be "impossible" sequences, such as a sequence that never terminates. Imagine for a moment that we have a program that needs to simulate rolling three six-sided dice several times.* This can be approximated by an infinite sequence generating random numbers between 3 and 18, inclusive. We can generalize the function that creates it to generate random numbers between any minimum and maximum values:

```
let randomNumberGenerator minVal maxVal =
    let randomer =
        new System.Random()
    seq {
        while (true) do
            yield (randomer.Next(maxVal - minVal) + minVal)
    }
let diceRolls = (randomNumberGenerator 3 18) |> Seq.take 6
Seq.iter
    (fun (roll : int) ->
        System.Console.WriteLine("You rolled a " +
            roll.ToString()))
    diceRolls
```

(See Chapter 13 for details on writing functions.) This code uses the Seq.take function to obtain the first six values from the sequence, which should range between the values 3 and 18 and then takes that resulting sequence of six "die rolls" and hands that into the Seq.iter function for printing each roll to the console.

In Chapter 4, we saw that for loops could be initialized with range expressions that made it fairly easy to iterate through a collection of numbers in a sequential stepped format. It turns out that the range expression is a kind of sequence expression so that the expression seq {0 .. 2}; produces a sequence consisting of the values 0, 1, and 2. However — the difference between this expression and the list or array examples we saw earlier is that, as discussed already, the sequence has not yet produced those values but will do so on demand.

> As a side note, this behavior of the range expression is actually open to any user-defined type, not just numeric values. Any type that defines member methods (..) and (.. ..), as discussed in the section on defining operator methods in Chapter 8, can be used in a range expression.

Combining sequences with a "for comprehension" is a trivial and natural thing to do, as in:

```
let squares = seq { for i in 0 .. 10 -> (i, i*i) }
```

This produces a sequence of int * int tuples consisting of the numbers 0 through 10 and their squares; but again, the lazy nature of the sequence means that the body of the for loop has not yet been fired but is waiting to be asked for the first value.

*Yes, I'm looking at all of you who used to (or still do) play *Dungeons & Dragons*.

Sequences have broad application beyond just the computation of numbers, particularly anywhere a stream of data instances from outside the program itself is the principal data item. For example, developers frequently iterate through a directory or series of directories looking for files of a particular type for processing. If we consider the file itself to be the data item in question, then the directory or set of directories becomes the scaffolding for the sequence:

```
let dir d =
    let di = new System.IO.DirectoryInfo(d)
    seq { for fi in di.GetFileSystemInfos() -> fi }
```

This makes it easy to get all the files in the root directory on the system:

```
let rootFiles = dir "C:\\"
```

Now, of course, given the sequence, it becomes trivial to walk through those files and display their names:

```
let printFileInfo (fi : System.IO.FileSystemInfo) =
    System.Console.WriteLine("{0}", fi.FullName)
for fi in rootFiles do printFileInfo fi
```

But the real power of the sequence again comes in its laziness; normally, trying to build a list of all the files on the system requires the program to do a harsh bit of I/O gathering up all the data required, but if a sequence is generated instead of an ordinary list, no disk I/O is performed until the developer starts to look through the sequence:

```
let rec recursiveDir d =
    let di = new System.IO.DirectoryInfo(d)
    seq {
        for f in di.GetFiles() do yield f
        for sd in di.GetDirectories() do
            yield! recursiveDir sd.FullName }
let allFiles = recursiveDir @"C:\"
for fi in allFiles do printFileInfo fi
```

A couple things are happening here simultaneously: One, the sequence is being built from two sources, rather than the single source expression that's been demonstrated so far, and two, rather than using the yield keyword to return a single instance back to the sequence, we use the yield! keyword to yield back a sequence into the sequence, essentially appending the results of that (recursively obtained) sequence to the one being generated. This second sequence, the one generating an additional sequence, must be the last expression in the sequence block. Any number of item-generating expressions can be used prior to that, however.

Like the array and list types, the sequence has a large number of functions defined in the Seq module and can be thought of in a few loosely grouped categories which are described next.

## Seq "Meta" Functions

These functions, like those listed for the Array module, manipulate lists rather than the contents within them. In general, these functions create or copy sequences, or do something to the sequence as a whole, in much the same way that the functions described in the Array section do. There is a great deal of duplication here so that the F# programmer familiar with how an operation works on an array already knows how an operation will work on a sequence, and vice versa.

| `append seq1 seq2` | Creates a new sequence containing the elements of `seq1` and `seq2` (in that order) |
| --- | --- |
| `cache seq` | Creates a cached sequence with the same values in `seq`, but only requiring calculation/computation once |
| `cache seq` | Creates a sequence out of another sequence of the same type |
| `concat sseq` | Creates a single sequence consisting of all the elements in the sequence of sequences `sseq` |
| `delay fn` | Returns a sequence that is built by `fn` (which is expected to take unit and return a sequence) every time an `IEnumerator` for the sequence is requested |
| `distinct seq` | Creates a sequence consisting of all the unique elements of the given sequence `seq` |
| `empty<'t>` | Returns an empty list of the given type `t` |
| `head seq` | Returns the head (first element) of `seq` |
| `initInfinite fn` | Creates a sequence that uses `fn` (which takes an int `i`) to generate the desired `i`'th element of the sequence |
| `isEmpty seq` | Returns true if `seq` is empty |
| `length seq` | Returns the length of `seq` |
| `nth seq i` | Returns the `i`'th element from the sequence `seq` |
| `ofArray ar` | Converts the array `ar` into a sequence |
| `ofList lst` | Converts the list `lst` to a sequence |
| `readonly seq` | Creates a new sequence that delegates to the passed sequence `seq`; this ensures that `seq` cannot be mutated or modified by a type cast |
| `singleton obj` | Creates a sequence consisting of the single object `obj` |
| `skip n seq` | Creates a sequence out of the items of sequence `seq`, skipping the first n items |
| `skipWhile fn seq` | Creates a sequence out of the items of sequence `seq`, skipping items if `fn` returns true for a given item |
| `take n seq` | Creates a sequence out of the first n items of the sequence `seq` |
| `takeWhile fn seq` | Creates a sequence out of the items of the sequence *seq* only if `fn` returns true for a given item |
| `toArray seq` | Creates an array from the sequence `seq` |
| `toList seq` | Creates a list from the sequence `seq` |
| `truncate n seq` | Returns a sequence consisting of no more than *n* items from the sequence *seq* |
| `windowed n seq` | Returns a sequence of "sliding windows" of the sequence `seq` as a sequence of arrays of n size |

## Seq "Application" Operations

These functions operate on the contents of the sequence, typically by taking a function as a parameter and invoking it once for each of the elements, passing that element in as a parameter (also known as "applying" the function to each of the elements), to produce a result, either a single value or with all the results grouped into another sequence.

| | |
|---|---|
| `choose fn seq` | Applies `fn` to each element in `seq`, and if `fn` returns `Some(x)` for that element, includes it in the returned sequence |
| `compareWith fn sq1 sq2` | Compares each element of `sq1` to `sq2` using the comparison function `f` (which is expected to take two parameters, one for each element, and return an `int`), returning an int |
| `exists fn seq` | Returns true if any of the elements in `seq`, when passed to `fn`, returns true |
| `filter fn seq` | Returns a sequence consisting of the elements in *seq* that, when passed in to `fn`, cause it to return true |
| `find fn seq` | Returns the first element in *seq* that returns true when passed to `fn`; if no such element exists in `seq`, throws an exception |
| `findIndex fn seq` | Returns the index of the first element in *seq* that returns true when passed to `fn`; if no such element exists, throws an exception |
| `fold fn s seq` | Applies `fn` to each element in `seq`, passing `s` in with the element, allowing `s` to act as an accumulator across all of the calls |
| `forall fn seq` | Returns true if all of the elements in `seq`, when passed to `fn`, return true |
| `iter fn seq` | Applies `fn` to each element in *seq*; `fn` is expected to return unit |
| `iteri fn seq` | Applies `fn` to each element in *seq*; `fn` receives both the element and its index, and is expected to return unit |
| `map fn seq` | Applies `fn` to each element in *seq*; `fn` is expected to yield a value, which is put into a sequence and returned |
| `mapi fn seq` | Applies `fn` to each element in *seq*; `fn` receives both the element and its index, and is expected to yield a value, which is put into a sequence and returned |
| `reduce fn seq` | Applies `fn` to each element in *seq*; `fn` receives both the element and its next element |
| `tryFind fn seq` | Returns the first element in `seq` for which `fn` returns true, or None if no such element exists |
| `tryFindIndex fn seq` | Returns the index of the first element in *seq* for which `fn` returns true, or None if no such element exists |

There are some additional functions in the `Seq` module, but many of these are just additionally varied versions of the preceding functions (`iter2`, for example, is just a form of `iter` that can operate on two sequences simultaneously), or "bake in" the function to apply to each of the elements (such as the average function, which calculates the average of a sequence whose elements support addition and division operations).

## MAPS

Maps, or dictionaries as the .NET FCL tends to call them, are collections of object-to-object pairings, most often used as name-value or key-value pairs, where the key is typically a string and the value is any particular type. Although not officially supported as an F# language construct, maps are commonly enough used that we can think of them as such, and have a number of interesting library supporting functions that make them almost trivial to use.

## Map Construction

Creating a new map is relatively easy. If we visualize a map as a list of pairs, then the Map.ofList function makes it easy to transform a list of two-element tuples into a Map:

```
let nicknames = Map.ofList [
                "Ted",new Person("Ted", "Neward", 38);
                "Katie",new Person("Katie", "Ellison", 30);
                "Mike",new Person("Michael", "Neward", 16)
            ]
```

Officially, the type returned by this function is a Map<string, string>, and the returned object is fully compatible with the rest of the .NET FCL — it implements the IDictionary<> interface and the ICollection<> interface yet is still "F#"-ish, in that this is also a sequence of System.Collections .Generic.KeyValuePair<string,string> items.

Maps can also be constructed from arrays (using Map.ofArray) or sequences (using Map.ofSeq); the syntax is almost identical to the preceding code, using sequence or array notation as appropriate.

Like arrays and lists, maps are type-safe, type-parameterized constructs that refuse to accept something (as either key or value) that is not type-compatible, so a Map<string, string> will not accept anything other than a string for the key or value. Also, like lists, when constructed, maps are immutable, so any "modification" operation (Add or Remove) on the map doesn't modify the contents of the map but returns a new map with the modification in it:

```
let moreNicknames =
    nicknames.Add("Mark", new Person("William","Richards",45))
```

An IDictionary<> instance can also be constructed explicitly from a sequence of two-element tuples using the dict function:

```
let numberMappings = dict [
                (1, "One"); (2, "Two"); (3, "Three")
            ]
```

However, despite the surface similarities, dict doesn't return an F# map, per se — the returned object doesn't quite implement all the same APIs as the returned object from Map.ofList, and as a result, the dict-returned object won't be acceptable as a parameter to the various Map functions (listed next). This also has other implications; for example, calling `Add()` on the `dict`-returned object modifies the internal collection rather than returning a new one.

For the most part, prefer to use the `Map` functions to create a map when writing F# code, and use `dict` to create .NET FCL-compatible `Dictionary<>` objects for easier interoperability with the rest of the .NET ecosystem. (See Chapter 18 for details on F#/.NET interoperability.)

## Map Access

Accessing the values in a map can be done in one of two ways, and just as with the list and array types, one of them is more .NET-like, and the other is more F#-like. Both rely conceptually on using the "key" of the pair to find the "value" of the pair.

Accessing values of the map in the .NET style involves using the built-in `Item` property in the traditional manner, as if the collection were an array taking the key type as a parameter:

```
let ted = nicknames.["Ted"]
System.Console.WriteLine(ted)
```

The other approach, preferred by functional programmers, involves the `find` function defined on the `Map` module:

```
let ted = Map.find "Ted" nicknames
System.Console.WriteLine(ted)
```

The reason for the two different approaches will become more clear in Part 3, "Functional Programming," when functions and function composition is introduced and explained; for now, just recognize that either style yields exactly the same result, the `Person` object whose value matches that of the string key passed in, or an exception if the key isn't found in the map:

```
try
    let noone = nicknames.["Katie"]
    System.Console.WriteLine(noone)
with
| ex -> System.Console.WriteLine("Katie not found")

try
    let noone = Map.find "Katie" nicknames
    System.Console.WriteLine(noone)
with
| ex -> System.Console.WriteLine("Katie not found")
```

Exception-handling is discussed in Chapter 4.

After having read the section on the `Option` type, it may seem that F# should support some kind of lookup operation that returns an `Option` instance, either `Some(value)` if found or `None` if the key isn't present, rather than throw an exception in the case of failure. Said readers would be correct; again, two different forms of lookup-without-exception are available, one a more FCL-ish style, the other a more F#-ish style:

```
let notfound = nicknames.TryFind("Katie")
System.Console.WriteLine(
    if notfound = None then "Not found"
    else notfound.Value.ToString()
```

```
        )
        let notfound = Map.tryFind "Katie" nicknames
        System.Console.WriteLine(
            if notfound = None then "Not found"
            else notfound.Value.ToString()
        )
```

 *The more idiomatic way to write this would be to use a pattern-match on the returned Option, as discussed in Chapter 6.*

Additionally, if you want to test to see if the key is in the map rather than return the value corresponding to the key, you can use either the `ContainsKey()` instance method or the `Map.tryFindKey` function.

## Map Functions

The `Map` module has a number of functions that can operate on maps, as shown here:

| | |
|---|---|
| `add k v map` | Adds the pair (k, v) to map and returns the new collection |
| `containsKey k map` | Returns true if map contains the key k |
| `exists fn map` | Returns true if there is at least one key/value pair in map that returns true when passed to fn |
| `filter fn map` | Returns a new map containing the bindings for which fn returns true |
| `find k map` | Finds the element k in the map, or else throws an exception if not present |
| `findKey fn map` | Finds the key for which fn returns true, or throws an exception if none of the keys match |
| `fold fn s map` | Executes fn over each of the key/value pairs in the map, passing an accumulated state s to each function and capturing the returned state (to be passed to the next pair) |
| `foldBack fn s map` | Similar to fold, but starts from the end of the map and works forward |
| `forall fn map` | Returns true if fn evaluates to true for all the pairs in the map |
| `isEmpty map` | Returns true if map is empty |
| `iter fn map` | Executes fn on each key/value pair in map |
| `map fn map` | Creates a new map by executing fn over each key/value pair in map |

*continues*

*(continued)*

| | |
|---|---|
| `ofArray ary` | Returns a new map made up of the elements in `ary` |
| `ofList lst` | Returns a new map made up of the elements in `lst` |
| `ofSeq seq` | Returns a new map made up of the elements in `seq` |
| `partition fn map` | Builds two maps (returned as a tuple), the first consisting of those key/value bindings which return true from `fn`, the second for the rest |
| `pick fn map` | Returns the first element in `map` for which `fn` returns `Some` |
| `remove k map` | Returns a map without the pair given by the key `k` |
| `toArray map` | Converts `map` into an array of (key, value) tuples |
| `toList map` | Converts `map` into a list of (key, value) tuples |
| `toSeq map` | Converts `map` into a sequence of (key, value) tuples |
| `tryFind` | Like find, but without the exception, returning an option (`Some` or `None`) instead |
| `tryFindKey` | Like `findKey`, but without the exception, returning an option (`Some` or `None`) instead |
| `tryPick` | Like pick, but without the exception, returning an option (`Some` or `None`) instead |

Most of these are self-explanatory, particularly when compared to the similarly named methods of `List` and `Array` and after higher-order functions are introduced in Part 3.

## SETS

Sets are another example of a type in F# that isn't implemented as a built-in type, yet has syntactic support enough to make it "feel" as it if were built-in, like maps. Fundamentally, a set is a strongly typed collection of objects that enforces a "no duplicates" principle:

```
let setOfPeople = Set.ofList [ new Person("Ted", "Neward", 38);
                               new Person("Ted", "Neward", 38);
                               new Person("Ted", "Neward", 38); ]
for p in setOfPeople do
    System.Console.WriteLine(p)
```

When run, only one object will display, the other two having been determined to be duplicates and therefore discarded.

The object that is returned is a `Set<>`, in this particular case, a `Set<Person>`, and like the preceding map, implements many of the .NET FCL types that .NET developers would expect for a collection type: `IComparable`, `ICollection`, and `IEnumerable` to be precise. (See Chapter 9 for details on interface inheritance in F#.) It also implements the interface corresponding to sequences, so any place a sequence is expected, a correspondingly strongly typed set can be passed in its place.

Like the map, sets can also be constructed using the set function that takes a list and converts it to a set:

```
let setOfNicknames = set [ "Ted"; "Theo"; "Tio";
                           "Ted"; "Ted"; "Teddy" ]
for p in setOfNicknames do
    System.Console.WriteLine(p)
```

In the case of set, however, the returned object is the exact same type as that returned from Set .ofList (or Set.ofArray or Set.ofSeq, used to construct sets from arrays or sequences, respectively), so there is no practical difference between the two.

One thing that differentiates sets from other collections is that types that are placed into a set must be comparable somehow so that the set can determine if the object instance is already present inside the set. In F#, this means the type in question must implement the IComparable interface (as described in Chapter 9), and as a result any type which doesn't support IComparable, such as the base type System.Object, won't go into a set; attempts to do so will generate an error, either at compile-time or at runtime.

Given that objects in a set are comparable, however, the set can provide some interesting additional functionality, such as finding the maximum and minimum value of all the items inside the set. These are available either as instance methods on the Set<> object, or as library methods from the Set module.

Again like its cousin the map, the set is an immutable collection, meaning that any attempt to modify the set will result in a new set being created and returned. More interestingly, however, beyond the simple add and remove from the set, the set also supports various "set theory" operations, such as intersection, union, difference, and testing for superset and subset comparison operations, all of which are possible because of the "comparison requirement" that sets impose on their contents.

In general, sets are good for domain objects, because domain objects frequently want or need to be unique within the domain, and the set operations can reduce the code developers need write.

## SUMMARY

F# provides a number of powerful composite types for the F# programmer, above and beyond those provided by the underlying .NET BCL. Lists are first-class citizens and the preferred way to collect a homogenous group of values together, but arrays are fully supported as well. Option types provide a safer means of dealing with the "no value" possibility, and tuple types provide a stronger method of working with a tightly grouped set of values without going to the trouble of creating a named, distinct type. Sequences are generic streams of objects and can either be a concrete finite set of data or lazily generated values produced on demand. Maps and sets are collection types that have some useful library support that allow them to look like language-supported built-in types and stand as an example of what additional functionality can be layered into F# without having to change the language itself, in addition to being useful entities in their own right.

# Pattern Matching

**WHAT'S IN THIS CHAPTER?**

➤  Understanding patterns and pattern-matching

➤  Using pattern matching types

➤  Applying pattern guards

➤  Using active patterns

More so than any other construct thus far explored, pattern matching is what distinguishes F# from the other languages in the .NET family. Pattern-matching is a hallmark of the functional language, and its power is something that is rapidly finding its way (in various guises) into other languages.

## BASICS

Fundamentally, pattern-matching looks, on the surface, like a variation on the switch/case construct from the C-family of languages: A value is tested, and depending on its contents, one of several different "branches" of code is evaluated:

```
let x = 12
match x with
| 12 -> System.Console.WriteLine("It's 12")
| _ -> System.Console.WriteLine("It's not 12")
```

The syntax is somewhat similar to the switch/case of C#; broken down, a pattern-match consists of the following:

➤  The match keyword, preceding the expression to be evaluated

➤  The with keyword, indicating the start of one or more various values to compare against

➤   The vertical pipe character (|) at the start of each match clause to evaluate against

➤   A match clause, which can take one of several different forms as described later in this chapter

➤   The arrow (->), separating the match clause from the expression to execute if the match clause succeeds

As is consistent with F#'s syntax, the underscore (_) character acts as a wildcard when used: anything that doesn't match against preceding clauses will match against this one.

Note that unlike the switch/case from imperative languages, the pattern-match is an expression, meaning that it, too, yields a value when evaluated:

```
let y = match x with
        | 12 -> 24
        | _ -> 36
```

This means that the various clauses in the pattern-match must all yield compatibly typed values, just as with the if/then construct (see Chapter 4 for details).

Leaving the discussion there, however, you miss out on all the other fun things that pattern-matching can do, such as value extraction into local variable bindings:

```
let people = [
    ("Ted", "Neward", 38)
    ("Mark", "Richards", 45)
    ("Naomi", "Wilson", 38)
    ("Ken", "Sipe", 43)
]
List.iter
    (fun (p) ->
        match p with
        | (fn, ln, a) ->
            System.Console.WriteLine("{0} {1}", fn, ln)
        | _ ->
            failwith "Unexpected value"
    )
    people
```

*Code snippet PatternMatching.fs*

In the preceding code, the List.iter function executes the anonymous function against each of the string/string/int tuples in the list. (For more on lists and tuples, see Chapter 5; for more on anonymous functions, see Chapter 13.) The important part of this example is the first match clause: If the value matched is a three-part tuple — which F# infers because the match clause uses a three-part tuple syntax ((fn, ln, a)) — then the individual elements of the tuple are each bound to the local variables fn, ln, and a, respectively. Because the previous example never actually uses the third part of the tuple, we can again leverage the wildcard pattern to indicate that it is irrelevant to the remainder of the expression:

```
let people = [
    ("Ted", "Neward", 38)
    ("Mark", "Richards", 45)
    ("Naomi", "Wilson", 38)
    ("Ken", "Sipe", 43)
```

```
    ]
    List.iter
        (fun (p) ->
            match p with
            | (fn, ln, _) ->
                System.Console.WriteLine("{0} {1}", fn, ln)
            | _ ->
                failwith "Unexpected value"
        )
        people
```

*Code snippet PatternMatching.fs*

The match expression itself doesn't just have to be a variable, and frequently serves as a way to make values easier to match inside of match clauses:

```
let p = new Person("Ken", "Sipe", 45)
let lastName = match (p.FirstName, p.LastName, p.Age) with
                | ("Ken", "Sipe", _) -> p.LastName
                | _ -> ""
```

> *Many of the examples in this chapter reference the* Person *class, which is defined in Chapter 8.*

In this case, the match expression is a three-part tuple, built from the three properties of the Person type (FirstName, LastName, and Age). Thus, only if p.FirstName matches against the constant value "Ken", p.LastName matches against "Sipe", and p.Age matches against any value (because of the use of the wildcard _ here) will the expression to the right side of the arrow be evaluated. If the match isn't made, the second match clause, the wildcard expression, will be matched, yielding an empty string.

Just because Person has three properties on it doesn't mean we have to use all those properties; because we don't care about the age of the Person p, the above expression could have been written more simply as:

```
let p = new Person("Ken", "Sipe", 45)
let lastName = match (p.FirstName, p.LastName) with
                | ("Ken", "Sipe") -> p.LastName
                | _ -> ""
```

Again, the match is defining a tuple out of p.FirstName and p.LastName and then matching it against possible expression types and values to find a block of code to execute.

This capability to match a variety of possible types and values and bind those values into local variables for later use makes pattern-matching a valuable construct for performing data-manipulation tasks against a collection, such as a list:

```
let persons = [
    new Person("Ted", "Neward", 38)
    new Person("Ken", "Sipe", 43)
    new Person("Michael", "Neward", 16)
    new Person("Matthew", "Neward", 9)
```

```
            new Person("Mark", "Richards", 45)
            new Person("Naomi", "Wilson", 38)
            new Person("Amanda", "Sipe", 18)
            ]
    List.iter
        (fun (p : Person) ->
            match (p.FirstName, p.LastName) with
            | (fn, "Sipe") ->
                System.Console.WriteLine("Hello, {0}!", fn)
            | (fn, "Neward") ->
                System.Console.WriteLine("Go away, {0}!", fn)
            | _ ->
                System.Console.WriteLine("Who the heck are you?")
        )
        persons
```

*Code snippet PatternMatching.fs*

Using pattern-matching to sift through a collection of data (such as the preceding Persons list) is a common idiom in F#, as is pattern-matching using the Option type to avoid null dereferences (and the subsequent exception) when searching through a collection of data. Of all the syntactic constructs in the F# language, pattern-matching is likely the most valuable — and thus the most important — to learn.

## PATTERN TYPES

A variety of different match constructs are available for use in the body of the match expression. Note that any of these can be combined with any other of the pattern types, allowing F# developers to "mix and match" as the mood suits them. This can sometimes create some surprising effects and can potentially lead to some surprising results — remember that matches are evaluated in a top-down fashion, and to help out, wherever possible the F# compiler will assist as best it can in finding matches that will never allow any further match to succeed, or when the pattern-match leaves some particular value or range of values out. The compiler isn't perfect, however, and when it detects an unmatched construct at runtime, a MatchFailure exception will be generated and thrown.

## Constant Patterns

As already demonstrated, a pattern-match can match against constant values in a manner entirely similar to that of the switch/case construct from any C-family language:

**Available for download on Wrox.com**

```
let x = (new System.Random()).Next(5)
let message = match x with
                | 0 -> "zero"
                | 1 -> "one"
                | 2 -> "two"
                | 3 -> "three"
                | 4 -> "four"
                | 5 -> "five"
                | _ -> "Unknown: " + x.ToString()
```

*Code snippet PatternMatching.fs*

As might well be expected, the match only works if the value stored in x is equal to the value in an individual match clause, such that if x holds the value 3, the corresponding result for message will be "three". Officially, this evaluation of equality is done using the F# method FSharp.Core .Operators.(=) (defining operator methods is described in more detail in Chapter 8).

Note that null is an acceptable constant value to match against, though F# code in general frowns on the use of null, preferring to use Option types (see Chapter 5) instead, using None to represent no value.

Unlike the switch/case, multiple constants can be matched, allowing easy construction of state machines or truth tables:

**Available for download on Wrox.com**

```
let x = (new System.Random()).Next(2)
let y = (new System.Random()).Next(2)
let quadrant = match x, y with
                | 0, 0 -> "(0,0)"
                | 0, 1 -> "(0,1)"
                | 0, 2 -> "(0,2)"
                | 1, 0 -> "(1,0)"
                | 1, 1 -> "(1,1)"
                | 1, 2 -> "(1,2)"
                | 2, 0 -> "(2,0)"
                | 2, 1 -> "(2,1)"
                | 2, 2 -> "(2,2)"
System.Console.WriteLine("We got {0}", quadrant)
```

*Code snippet PatternMatching.fs*

In the preceding code, the F# compiler will emit a warning about possible unmatched cases, because it cannot determine that the ranges of x and y are limited to 0 and 2. This is F# trying to help avoid a runtime exception, because it can't determine that the values of x and y will be limited to the range 0 to 2 (as defined by the Random.Next() method call).

## Variable-Binding ("Named") Patterns

If the match clause consists of a name beginning with a lowercase letter, then it is a variable-binding pattern, and it introduces a new local variable into which the value is bound for use in the expression to the right of the arrow:

```
let p = new Person("Rachel", "Reese", 25)
let message = match p.FirstName with
                | fn -> "Hello, " + fn
System.Console.WriteLine("We got {0}", message)
```

Admittedly, this particular example is a bit contrived, because we could just as easily have obtained said value by simply using the FirstName property on the Person object, but this will become much more useful when combined with some of the other patterns, such as tuple or list patterns. When combined with constant patterns, it allows for a useful "default" case:

```
let p = new Person("Rachel", "Appel", 25)
let message = match p.FirstName with
                | "Rachel" -> "It's one of the Rachii!!"
                | fn -> "Alas, you are not a Rachii, " + fn
System.Console.WriteLine("We got {0}", message)
```

Variables bound this way are scoped to the match construct itself.

## AND, OR Patterns

Patterns can combine using the Boolean operator "|" (for "or"), so that the right expression will be evaluated if either of the two clauses is a match:

```
let p = new Person("Rachel", "Reese", 25)
let message = match p.FirstName with
                | ("Rachel" | "Scott") ->
                    "Hello, " + p.FirstName
                | _ ->
                    "Who are you, again?"
System.Console.WriteLine("We got {0}", message)
```

Patterns can also use the & to connect two clauses that must both match for the right expression to fire, but for the most part, this will be limited to the use of active patterns discussed next.

## Literal Patterns

Given what's been said already about F#'s binding of values to names and the pattern-matching rules, it would seem reasonable to expect the following to work:

```
let rachel = "Rachel"
let p = new Person("Rachel", "Reese", 25)
let message = match p.FirstName with
                | rachel -> "Howdy, Rachel!"
System.Console.WriteLine("We got {0}", message)
```

And, it will — it will work too well as the compiler will tell us when we try to add any additional clauses to the pattern-match:

```
let Rachel = "Rachel"
let p = new Person("Rachel", "Reese", 25)
let message = match p.FirstName with
                | Rachel -> "Howdy, Rachel!"
                | _ -> "Howdy, whoever you are!"
System.Console.WriteLine("We got {0}", message)
```

The F# compiler will emit a warning that the wildcard clause will never be matched, which seems strange. However, a little bit further investigation reveals that despite the direct literal assignment, F# doesn't consider rachel to be a constant to compare against. Instead, it introduces a new binding; to be precise, F# binds the value of the match (p.FirstName) into a new name, rachel, for the duration of the pattern-match.

To tell F# that the binding "rachel" should be treated as a literal value in the pattern match, the .NET attribute "Literal" (introduced in Chapter 3) should be put on the let expression that introduces it:

```
[<Literal>]
let Rachel = "Rachel"
let p = new Person("Rachel", "Reese", 25)
```

```
let message = match p.FirstName with
                | Rachel -> "Howdy, Rachel!"
                | _ -> "Howdy, whoever you are!"
System.Console.WriteLine("We got {0}", message)
```

Now the warning goes away, and the pattern-match behaves as expected.

 *Notice that in order for the language to recognize the Literal as an actual literal, it must be uppercased; leaving the Literal identifier written as `"rachel"` will still fire the warning.*

## Tuple Patterns

Technically, we've already seen tuple matching; in the constant patterns section, we showed the following:

**Available for download on Wrox.com**

```
let x = (new System.Random()).Next(2)
let y = (new System.Random()).Next(2)
let quadrant = match x, y with
                | 0, 0 -> "(0,0)"
                | 0, 1 -> "(0,1)"
                | 0, 2 -> "(0,2)"
                | 1, 0 -> "(1,0)"
                | 1, 1 -> "(1,1)"
                | 1, 2 -> "(1,2)"
                | 2, 0 -> "(2,0)"
                | 2, 1 -> "(2,1)"
                | 2, 2 -> "(2,2)"
System.Console.WriteLine("We got {0}", message)
```

*Code snippet PatternMatching.fs*

What we didn't say at the time is that the F# language considers the x, y pair to be a tuple. F# allows tuples to be used both in the match value and the criteria, as the preceding code demonstrates. Tuple-based pattern-matching combined with named patterns is one of the most common ways to extract the values out of a tuple:

```
let t = ("Aaron", "Erickson", 35)
let message = match t with
                | (first, last, age) ->
                    "Howdy " + first + " " + last +
                    ", I'm glad to hear you're " +
                    age.ToString() + "!"
System.Console.WriteLine("We got {0}", message)
```

Tuples and pattern-matching go well together, so much so that it should be assumed that wherever tuples are used, pattern-matching will be used to extract and manipulate the data from inside the tuple.

## as Patterns

The as keyword allows us to do both extraction from a tuple and bind a new name to the original tuple at the same time:

```
let message = match t1 with
                | (x,y) as t2 ->
                    x.ToString() + " " +
                    y.ToString() + " " +
                    t2.ToString()
System.Console.WriteLine("We got {0}", message)
```

In this case, the original tuple value (t1) is not only extracted into the individual values x1 and y1, but also into the tuple value t2. This pattern-match type isn't common, at least not in this form; see the section "Beyond the Match" for details.

## List Patterns

Pattern-matching can also be used to match and extract values from lists, usually by extracting the head and the tail of the list into local values:

```
let numbers = [1; 2; 3; 4; 5]
let rec sumList ns = match ns with
                        | [] -> 0
                        | head :: tail -> head + sumList tail
let sum = sumList numbers
System.Console.WriteLine("Sum of numbers = {0}", sum)
```

Here the list is matched either against the empty list, or the head of the list is extracted into the local value "head" and the tail (which may be empty, if the incoming list is exactly one element long) is extracted into the local value "tail." This is an extremely common idiom in F#, particularly because of its thread-safe nature (because all state is held on the stack, rather than in a temporary variable; see Chapter 14 for more on F# and immutable state).

Note, however, that other forms of matching against the list are possible; for example the following is a more verbose way of extracting the first few values of a list:

```
let message = match numbers with
                | [] -> "List is empty!"
                | [one] ->
                    "List has one item: " + one.ToString()
                | [one; two] ->
                    "List has two items: " +
                    one.ToString() + " " + two.ToString()
                | _ -> "List has more than two items"
System.Console.WriteLine(message)
```

Again, because the pattern-match happens in a top-down fashion, the wildcard only matches if the list has three or more items in it. In general, however, because this style of list-matching has no convenient way to match against a list of arbitrary length, the preferred manner is to use the head :: tail pattern recursively.

## Array Patterns

Just as pattern-matching can match against lists, pattern-matching can also match against arrays:

```
let numbers = [|1; 2; 3; 4; 5|]
let message = match numbers with
                | [| |] -> "Array is empty!"
                | [| one |] ->
                    "Array has one item: " + one.ToString()
                | [| one; two |] ->
                    "Array has two items: " +
                    one.ToString() + " " + two.ToString()
                | _ -> "Array has more than two items"
System.Console.WriteLine(message)
```

However, because arrays lack an easy way to "tear off" a piece of the array and recursively process the remainder, as lists do, arrays are rarely used as a source or target of pattern-matching.

## Discriminated Union Patterns

Pattern-matching against discriminated unions (described in Chapter 7) is not much different than pattern-matching against other types, with the exception that the compiler sanity-checks to ensure that a match against a discriminated union value only has match clauses that could be remotely possible.

```
type Color =
    | Black
    | Blue
    | Cyan
    | Gray
    | Green
    | Magenta
    | DarkBlue
    | Red
    | White
    | Yellow

let color = Black
let message = match color with
                | Black -> "Black!"
                | Blue -> "Blue!"
                | _ -> "Something other than black or blue"
System.Console.WriteLine(message)
```

Discriminated unions are a powerful companion to pattern-matching, just as tuples are.

## Record Patterns

Record types, described more in Chapter 7, can also be pattern-matched (and values extracted) in much the same way that tuples are. In fact, since a record type is, in many ways, "just" a tuple, pattern matching with a record type is just an extension of doing it against a tuple type:

```
type Author =
    | Author of string * string * int

let ted = Author("Ted", "Neward", 38)
```

```
match ted with
    | Author(first, last, age) ->
        System.Console.WriteLine("Hello, {0}", first)
```

Record types are covered in more detail in Chapter 7, and more examples of pattern-matching with records are given there.

## PATTERN GUARDS

Despite all the power inherent in the various pattern types, F# developers will still periodically find situations where a pattern-match is clearly the best control construct to use, yet the match criteria just isn't quite a one-to-one match with one of the existing pattern types. For those situations, the F# language provides the capability to put a *when clause* on the pattern, effectively a Boolean check that must be passed for the clause to be fired:

```
let p = new Person("Rick", "Minerich", 35)
let message = match (p.FirstName) with
                | _ when p.Age > 30 ->
                    "Never found"
                | "Minerich" when p.FirstName <> "Rick" ->
                    "Also never found"
                | "Minerich" ->
                    "Hiya, Rick!"
                | _ ->
                    "Who are you?"
System.Console.WriteLine("We got {0}", message)
```

In essence, the when clause gives the F# developer the ability to attach any arbitrary criteria to the pattern-match, above and beyond those criteria defined by the various pattern-match rules already described. This capability can be badly abused, because any number of when clauses can be strung together using the Boolean operators, like so:

```
let p = new Person("Rick", "Minerich", 35)
let isOldFogey (person : Person) =
    match person with
    | _ when person.Age > 35 ||
        (person.FirstName = "Ted" &&
            person.LastName = "Neward") ||
        (person.FirstName = "Aaron" &&
            person.LastName = "Erickson") ->
        true
    | _ -> false
System.Console.WriteLine("{0} is an old fogey: {1}",
    p, isOldFogey p)
```

In these cases, it's often better to restructure the code to be more intentional about what the restrictions are, either by breaking the pattern-match into multiple matches, using active patterns, or out into separate functions entirely.

A first refactoring of the preceding code might produce:

```
let isOldFogey' (person : Person) =
    let isOld (p : Person) =
```

```
            p.Age > 35
      let isTed (p : Person) =
            p.FirstName = "Ted" && p.LastName = "Neward"
      let isAaron (p : Person) =
            p.FirstName = "Aaron" && p.LastName = "Erickson"
      match p with
          | _ when isOld p || isTed p || isAaron p ->
              true
          | _ ->
              false
System.Console.WriteLine("{0} is an old fogey: {1}",
      p, isOldFogey' p)
```

But it should be pointed out that it's possible to completely rewrite the match to take advantage of pattern-matching more effectively, and reduce the use of the when to its minimalist case:

```
      let isOldFogey'' (p : Person) =
          match p.Age, p.FirstName, p.LastName with
          | _, "Ted", "Neward" -> true
          | _, "Aaron", "Erickson" -> true
          | a, _, _ when a > 35 -> true
          | _ -> false
System.Console.WriteLine("{0} is an old fogey: {1}",
      p, isOldFogey'' p)
```

For the most part, when tempted to use a when clause, the neophyte F# developer should take an extra moment to see if another pattern-matching construct can achieve the same effect.

 *The use of the apostrophe and double apostrophe, deriving from the "prime" and "double-prime" in mathematics, in the two refactorings above may throw the hardened C# developer off (as it did one reviewer of the book). While legal, the use of the apostrophe may make it hard for F# neophytes to understand the syntax, and it will certainly make it hard for other .NET languages to consume a function or member using it in the name. As a result, F# developers should probably consider restricting its use to locally-scoped members (which won't be seen by external users of the code) and for temporary refactorings.*

## ACTIVE PATTERNS

If there is any criticism of pattern-matching, it is that the pattern-match is, at least so far, restricted to types understood by the F# compiler — meaning no complex composite types, like business object types, are eligible. This has historically meant that functional languages avoided "abstraction" in the traditional object-oriented sense, in favor of a "lightweight abstraction" by simply bundling data elements together and calling it a data type.

With F#, this limitation more or less goes away with the introduction of *active patterns*. In essence, active patterns are functions usable from within pattern-match rules, providing a degree of flexibility and extensibility beyond that of pattern-matching described thus far.

Active patterns can be thought of in three general forms: a single-case active pattern, which is used to convert data from one type to another for use in a pattern-match; a partial-case active pattern, which helps to match when data-conversion failures are possible or likely; and a multi-case active pattern, which can take the input data and break it into one of several different groupings.

## Single Case

The single-case active pattern is conceptually the easiest to understand: It allows the F# developer to specify a function that is called from inside the pattern-match — rather than before the match — so as to allow for processing or conversion of the data.

For example, when a developer starts to get used to using pattern-matching, it's fairly common to want to use it to handle all sorts of multi-case logic, such as situations where we want to determine if text matches a particular input pattern. It's not too difficult to imagine validation cases in a web application where a developer wants to determine if a text string contains "dangerous" input, such as embedded HTML tags of some form:

```
let inputData = "This is some <script>alert()</script> data"
let contains (inStr : string) =
    inStr.Contains "<script>"
System.Console.WriteLine("Does the text contain bad data? " +
    (contains inputData).ToString())
```

Obviously a real implementation would be screening for much more beyond <script> tags, so a refinement is necessary:

```
let inputData = "This is some <script>alert()</script> data"
let contains (srchStr : string) (inStr : string) =
    inStr.Contains srchStr
System.Console.WriteLine("Does the text contain bad data? " +
    (contains "<script>" inputData).ToString())
```

But using this requires us to list out all the possible "bad tags" that might appear in this user-input string, which can get tedious:

```
let inputData = "This is some <script>alert()</script> data"
let contains (srchStr : string) (inStr : string) =
    inStr.Contains srchStr
let goodInput inStr =
    contains "<script>" inStr ||
    contains "<object>" inStr ||
    contains "<embed>" inStr ||
    contains "<applet>" inStr
System.Console.WriteLine("Does the text contain bad data? " +
    (goodInput inputData).ToString())
```

Frankly, this is precisely the kind of thing that pattern-matching was originally intended to model, to avoid having to write this kind of code. Unfortunately, attempting to use contains() inside the pattern-match causes the pattern-match to match on the results of the contains() call, which isn't quite what's needed here, particularly because we need to call contains() over and over again (once for each potentially "bad" input).

Enter the single-case active pattern. By defining an active pattern — a function defined with "banana clips" around it — the function can be called as part of the pattern-match, as in:

```
let (|Contains|) srchStr (inStr : string) =
    inStr.Contains srchStr
let isSafeHtml inputData =
    match inputData with
    | Contains "<script>" true -> false
    | Contains "<object>" true -> false
    | Contains "<embed>" true -> false
    | Contains "<applet>" true -> false
    | _ -> true
```

Viewed this way, it may not seem like the active pattern is saving much time or space, but the logical equivalent, when written out, would be a series of nested "if" or pattern-match statements, testing each possibility one-by-one before finally resolving to some result.

The parameters to the Contains pattern function don't seem to match precisely against the use inside the pattern-match itself. This is because the first parameter (srchStr in the Contains() example) is coming from the match clause (<script>), and the second parameter (inStr) from the value being matched against (inputData). Regardless of the number of parameters to the active recognizer (the term the F# language uses for the Contains() function), the last parameter in the function definition is always the value being matched. The true at the end of the match clause is the actual test — if the Contains() call returns true, it matches against the value in the test (the literal "true"), and thus the match clause succeeds.

## Partial Case

The partial-case active pattern is, in many ways, a variant of the single-case active pattern, in that it allows for matches that may or may not always match successfully; in other words, it enables a "partitioning" of the input space into one or more possible variations. To understand what that means, let's return to the previous input-validation scenario. Much of the input validation itself would be made easier if we could incorporate a regular expression into the mix — in other words, if we could "partition out" the input into either something that matched a given regex or not. To do so, we can write a partial-case active pattern — again using the "banana clips" notation — to define it:

```
let inputData = "This is some <script>alert()</script> data"

let (|Contains|_|) pat inStr =
    let results =
        (System.Text.RegularExpressions.Regex.Matches(inStr, pat))
    if results.Count > 0
        then Some [ for m in results -> m.Value ]
        else None

let matchStuff inData =
    match inData with
    | Contains "http://S+" _ -> "Contains urls"
    | Contains "[^@]@[^.]+\.\W+" _ -> "Contains emails"
    | Contains "\<script\>" _ -> "Found <script>"
    | Contains "\<object\>" _ -> "Found <object>"
    | _ -> "Didn't find what we were looking for"

System.Console.WriteLine(matchStuff inputData)
```

The defining characteristic of a partial-case pattern match is twofold; first, the "wildcard" character defined as part of the function's name (such as (|Contains|_|) in the preceding code), intended to convey the idea that this is not always necessarily going to yield a successful result; and second, the return of the function being an Option type, with Some returning the results (which we ignore in our example), and None implying that the match didn't work.

Note that we can have numerous partial-case pattern matches; in fact, we can have as many as might be necessary to help complete the match. So, to use a different example (drawing from the Person class defined in Chapter 8), we can write several partial-case pattern match constructs to make it easier to use Reflection to find a particular part of a type:

```
let AllBindingFlags =
    BindingFlags.NonPublic ||| BindingFlags.Public |||
    BindingFlags.Instance ||| BindingFlags.Static
let (|Field|_|) name (t : System.Type) =
    let fi = t.GetField(name, AllBindingFlags)
    if fi <> null then Some(fi) else None
let (|Method|_|) name (t : System.Type) =
    let fi = t.GetMethod(name, AllBindingFlags)
    if fi <> null then Some(fi) else None
let (|Property|_|) name (t : System.Type) =
    let fi = t.GetProperty(name, AllBindingFlags)
    if fi <> null then Some(fi) else None
let pt = (new Person("", "", 0)).GetType()
let message =
    match pt with
    | Property "FirstName" pi ->
        "Found property " + pi.ToString()
    | Property "LastName" pi ->
        "Found property " + pi.ToString()
    | _ -> "There's other stuff, but who cares?"
System.Console.WriteLine(message)
```

 *Note that this example assumes that the* System.Reflection *namespace has been opened already, as described in Chapter 11.*

Contrary to what a Reflection-based example might imply, and what the preceding syntax seems to reinforce, this code won't find all the different properties, fields, and methods on the type passed in; instead, as is always the case with pattern-matching, it finds the first match that succeeds and returns that as the result of the pattern-match expression. This means that the partial-case pattern is good for finding a particular element (such as the FirstName property on any passed-in object) before extracting its value from that object:

```
let AllBindingFlags =
    BindingFlags.NonPublic ||| BindingFlags.Public |||
    BindingFlags.Instance ||| BindingFlags.Static
let (|Field|_|) name (inst : obj) =
    let fi = inst.GetType().GetField(name, AllBindingFlags)
    if fi <> null
```

```
            then Some(fi.GetValue(inst))
            else None
    let (|Method|_|) name (inst : obj) =
            let fi = inst.GetType().GetMethod(name, AllBindingFlags)
            if fi <> null
            then Some(fi)
            else None
    let (|Property|_|) name (inst : obj) =
            let fi = inst.GetType().GetProperty(name, AllBindingFlags)
            if fi <> null
            then Some(fi.GetValue(inst, null))
            else None

    let rm = new Person("Rick", "Minerich", 29)
    // Does it have a first name? Get the value if it does
    let message = match rm with
                    | Property "FirstName" value ->
                        "FirstName = " + value.ToString()
                    | _ -> "No FirstName to be found"
    System.Console.WriteLine(message)
```

This is sometimes known as duck typing ("If it walks like a duck and talks like a duck, treat it as a duck") in dynamic languages such as Python and Ruby.

This is also where AND patterns, briefly mentioned in the section "AND, OR Patterns" can be useful; if the object in question needs both a FirstName property and a LastName property before it can be considered a good object to work with, then the AND in the pattern-match will require both properties to be there before evaluating the action after the arrow:

```
    let rm = new Person("Rick", "Minerich", 29)
    // Does it have a first name AND a last name?
    let message = match rm with
                    | Property "FirstName" fnval &
                      Property "LastName" lnval ->
                        "Full name = " + fnval.ToString() +
                        " " + lnval.ToString()
                    | Property "FirstName" value ->
                        "Name = " + value.ToString()
                    | Property "LastName" value ->
                        "Name = " + value.ToString()
                    | _ ->
                        "No name to be found"
    System.Console.WriteLine(message)
```

Partial-case active patterns can obviously be used in a variety of other scenarios beyond Reflection; one such area is in processing XML documents, where judicious use of active patterns can act as a structured and type-safe form of XPath query. (More on using XML with F# can be found in Chapter 20.)

## Multi-Case

The previous Reflection-oriented example suffers from the fact that the match types a Type and uses that to try and find a match in top-down order, which succeeds the first time and then quits the rest of the match expression. This is fine if we want to test to see if a particular type supports a particular operation, but if the goal is to break down a given type into its constituent parts (such as what we see with tools such as ILDasm or Reflector), then the *multi-case* active pattern comes into play:

```
let (|Property|Method|Field|Constructor|) (mi : MemberInfo) =
    if (mi :? FieldInfo) then
        Field(mi.Name, (mi :?> FieldInfo).FieldType)
    elif (mi :? MethodInfo) then
        Method(mi.Name, (mi :?> MethodInfo).ReturnType)
    elif (mi :? PropertyInfo) then
        Property(mi.Name, (mi :?> PropertyInfo).PropertyType)
    elif (mi :? ConstructorInfo) then
        Constructor("", mi.DeclaringType)
    else
        failwith "Unrecognized Reflection type"
```

*Again, this example assumes that* System.Reflection *has been opened already in the code, as discussed in Chapter 11.*

In this case, we use dynamic type tests (see Chapter 9 for details on downcasting) to determine what subtype the MemberInfo instance is and extract values from that subtype for use.

Syntactically, notice that the multi-case active pattern includes all the possible result values within the banana clips, and the lack of the wildcard character implies that when this function is invoked, the results must, somehow, match into one of those values (Property, Method, Field, or Constructor in the previous example). The data that should be returned for use in the pattern-match is gathered into a tuple under the pattern-match name (Property, Method, and so on) and handed back.

When used, the multi-case active pattern (like all pattern-matching constructs) can bind values into a local value binding, which in this case, using the preceding definition, makes it relatively easy to extract the name and type of the reflective element in question:

```
for p in typeof<Person>.GetMembers(AllBindingFlags) do
    match p with
    | Property(nm, ty) ->
        System.Console.WriteLine(
            "Found prop {1} {0}", nm, ty)
    | Field(nm, ty) ->
        System.Console.WriteLine(
            "Found fld {1} {0}", nm, ty)
    | Method(nm, rt) ->
        System.Console.WriteLine(
            "Found mth {1} {0}(...)", nm, rt)
    | Constructor(_, _) ->
        System.Console.WriteLine("Found ctor")
```

Having done that, however, something jarring appears: Under the current definition of the multi-case pattern match, we lose the parameters from the method, and the constructor doesn't actually have a name or a return type, per se. This is because as written, the multi-case pattern match assumes that in each case, we want to return a string and a `System.Type` tuple.

Fortunately, the multi-case active pattern doesn't require that each possibility return the same type; it returns a `Choice<>` type, essentially creating a large tagged union type out of each of the potential types returned by the individual matches. So we can have the Constructor tuple return just the parameters to the constructor, and the `Method` tuple return the name, the return type, and the parameters to the method:

```
let (|Property|Method|Field|Constructor|) (mi : MemberInfo) =
    if (mi :? FieldInfo) then
        Field(mi.Name, (mi :?> FieldInfo).FieldType)
    elif (mi :? MethodInfo) then
        let mthi = (mi :?> MethodInfo)
        Method(mi.Name, mthi.ReturnType, mthi.GetParameters())
    elif (mi :? PropertyInfo) then
        let pi = (mi :?> PropertyInfo)
        Property(pi.Name, pi.PropertyType)
    elif (mi :? ConstructorInfo) then
        let ci = (mi :?> ConstructorInfo)
        Constructor(ci.GetParameters())
    else
        failwith "Unrecognized Reflection type"
```

This now gives us better data-extraction capabilities when displaying the individual parts of the type:

```
let pt = (new Person("", "", 0)).GetType()
let AllBindingFlags =
    BindingFlags.NonPublic ||| BindingFlags.Public |||
    BindingFlags.Instance ||| BindingFlags.Static
for p in pt.GetMembers(AllBindingFlags) do
    match p with
    | Property(nm, ty) ->
        System.Console.WriteLine(
            "Found prop {1} {0}", nm, ty)
    | Field(nm, ty) ->
        System.Console.WriteLine(
            "Found fld {1} {0}", nm, ty)
    | Method(nm, rt, parms) ->
        System.Console.WriteLine(
            "Found mth {1} {0}(...)", nm, rt)
    | Constructor(parms) ->
        System.Console.WriteLine("Found ctor")
```

The huge advantage to this approach, of course, is that as this code seeks to support additional Reflection types (events, delegates, generics, and so on), the active-pattern can simply be extended to add those additional types, and using them simply follows the traditional pattern-match style.

The multi-case active pattern is sometimes called data decomposition because it essentially allows an object (in this case, `System.Type` instance) to be broken down (decomposed) into its constituent parts and processed.

# SUMMARY

Pattern-matching is a fundamental part of the F# language, and of functional languages in general, that it should be considered to be absolutely critical to understanding any code written in F#. It provides well beyond the basic switch/case multi-if capabilities that C# or Visual Basic provide, to give developers the ability to do data decomposition and break complex data structures down into smaller parts for analysis and extraction.

# PART II
## Objects

▶ **CHAPTER 7:** Complex Composite Types

▶ **CHAPTER 8:** Classes

▶ **CHAPTER 9:** Inheritance

▶ **CHAPTER 10:** Generics

▶ **CHAPTER 11:** Packaging

▶ **CHAPTER 12:** Custom Attributes

# Complex Composite Types

**WHAT'S IN THIS CHAPTER?**

➤ Understanding type abbreviations

➤ Working with enums

➤ Creating discriminated unions

➤ Understanding structs

➤ Working with record types

Complex composite types serve as a bridge between the simple composite types explored in Chapter 5, such as tuples, options, and the collection types (list, array, sequence, set, and map), and the more traditional class types explored in Chapter 8. Unlike the simple composite type made up of multiple elements of a single type, the complex composite type is marked by the multiple parts that form the complex composite type, such as individual elements made up of other types.

## TYPE ABBREVIATIONS

One of the drawbacks to tuples is that the tuple, in its basic form, remains unnamed — lexically speaking, it's harder to talk about passing `string * string * int * float` types around than it is to talk about passing around instances of Employee.

Fortunately, F# alleviates this problem (for more than just tuples) by allowing for type abbreviations, which actually are nothing more than name declarations for existing type names:

```
type MenuItem =
    string * string * float

type RestaurantMenu =
    MenuItem list
```

In all other respects, the types behave as they've done normally:

```
let diner : RestaurantMenu = [
    ("Grand Slam", "Two eggs, two bacon, three hotcakes",2.99);
    ("Chicken strips", "Five strips and sauce", 3.99)
]
for (name, desc, price) in diner do
    System.Console.WriteLine("{0} costs {1}", name, price)
```

*Code snippet ComplexCompositeTypes.fs*

It's important to note that left to its own devices, the F# compiler will infer the `diner` instance to be a `string * string * float list` type, not a `RestaurantMenu` type, which is why the type annotation is necessary on the declaration in this sample.

It's also important to note that no new functionality has been introduced into the system, only a new name for types that were already present. The type is "erased" during compilation, so any attempt to find the type abbreviation name at runtime (via Reflection, for example) will fail. The type abbreviation simply adds a degree of readability to the source code.

Type abbreviations can also work on types other than tuples; if, for example, experience yields a better name for unsigned 32-bit integers, they can be named as such:

```
type ui32 = System.UInt32
```

However, blatantly renaming existing types should be done with care — mindlessly renaming types can render code less readable, rather than the opposite.

## ENUM TYPES

To create the C# or Visual Basic equivalent of the enumerated type, F# uses some slightly different syntax than what's been seen before; because this code introduces a new type into the program, the keyword `type` is used, and the various possibilities of the enumerated type are then listed in a form reminiscent of the pattern-match syntax (explored in Chapter 6):

```
type Soda =
    | Coke = 1
    | DietCoke = 2
    | SevenUp = 3
```

Unlike the C# or Visual Basic enumerated type, to create an enum, F# requires that each possible case be explicitly assigned a value — this is because in the CLR's view, an enumerated type is simply a placeholder over a more basic type, usually an unsigned int32. (F# has a better type, and nicer syntax, for its own notion of an enumerated type, called a discriminated union type, explored next.)

Each case in the enumerated type must be a constant value of one of the types permitted to underlie a .NET enumeration: sbyte, byte, int16, uint16, int32, uint32, int64 or uint64, or char. Any attempt to use a type outside that list will result in an error. More important, each of the cases in the enum must all be of the same type.

When used, the F# compiler insists on a syntax that's more or less commensurate with the syntax used for enum types in C# or Visual Basic, namely, that each use must be explicitly qualified with the type name when accessing one of its values:

```
let drink = Soda.DietCoke
```

Attempts to use just the value name, such as `DietCoke` directly, will fail. In particular, when used in a pattern-match construct, attempts to use the values directly will generate a warning, but more important, won't produce the results desired:

```
let drink = Soda.DietCoke
let message =
    match drink with
    | Coke -> "Ah, so refreshing!"
    | DietCoke -> "Just one calorie!"
    | _ -> "Bleah"
System.Console.WriteLine(message)
```

*Code snippet ComplexCompositeTypes.fs*

When this code is run, regardless of what the value in `drink` is, the first match always succeeds. Written properly, the pattern-match looks like

```
let drink = Soda.DietCoke
let message =
    match drink with
    | Soda.Coke -> "Ah, so sweet!"
    | Soda.DietCoke -> "Just one calorie!"
    | _ -> "Bleah"
System.Console.WriteLine(message)
```

> *For those who are curious, the reason the F# compiler knows to enforce this type-qualified access is because the F# compiler emits an attribute, the `RequiresQualifiedAccess` attribute, on the Soda type. This is an F#-specific attribute and is only recognized by the F# compiler; for more details on it, see Chapter 12.*

Because the underlying values beneath an enumerated type is another .NET atomic value, and because the other .NET languages permit it, F# allows for conversion from the enumerated type to its underlying value by prefixing the enumerated value instance with the primitive type:

```
let rawValue = int Soda.DietCoke
```

Converting it back again uses the `enum<>` syntax:

```
let rawInt = 2
let unknownDrink = enum<Soda>(rawInt)
let message =
    match unknownDrink with
```

```
    | Soda.Coke -> "Ah, so sweet!"
    | Soda.DietCoke -> "Just one calorie!"
    | _ -> "Bleah"
System.Console.WriteLine(message)
```

Doing this, however, is relatively dangerous, just as it is in C# or Visual Basic code, because the original value (`rawInt` in the preceding example) can be any acceptable 32-bit integer value, and the calculated enumerated type won't necessarily match up against the integer passed in. This makes the enumerated type "imperfect," in that it's possible for the enumerated type to hold a value outside the acceptable list of values for it:

```
let rawInt = 20
let unknownDrink = enum<Soda>(rawInt)
let message =
    match unknownDrink with
    | Soda.Coke -> "Ah, so sweet!"
    | Soda.DietCoke -> "Just one calorie!"
    | Soda.SevenUp -> "Clear soda!"
    | _ -> failwith "This should never happen!"
System.Console.WriteLine(message)
```

*Code snippet ComplexCompositeTypes.fs*

Unfortunately for the programmer who wrote this code, what should never happen, will.

For those cases where the values want to combine in a `flags`-style combination of values (such as summer camp, where campers routinely learn to mix sodas together in what was then called a "suicide soda"), F# permits the use of the CLR `System.Flags` attribute to the type declaration and hexadecimal values for the individual cases:

```
[<System.Flags>]
type SuicideSoda =
    | Coke = 0x0001
    | DietCoke = 0x0002
    | SevenUp = 0x0004
    | Grenadine = 0x0008
```

This allows the F# programmer the complete freedom to create their perfect drink:

```
let perfectDrink = SuicideSoda.Coke ||| SuicideSoda.Grenadine
```

The values that make up the perfect drink can then be extracted using typical bitmask coding:

```
System.Console.WriteLine("It contains Coke? {0}",
    (if perfectDrink &&& SuicideSoda.Coke = SuicideSoda.Coke
        then "true" else "false"))
System.Console.WriteLine("It contains DietCoke? {0}",
    (if perfectDrink &&& SuicideSoda.DietCoke =
        SuicideSoda.DietCoke then "true" else "false"))
```

Because the enumerated types created here are .NET-compatible enumerated types, all the methods defined by `System.Enum` are also accessible for them, which can sometimes simplify working with them:

```
let enumNames = System.Enum.GetNames(typeof<Soda>)
let enumValues = System.Enum.GetValues(typeof<Soda>)
```

Although certainly an acceptable style of programming, using enumerated types in F# pale in comparison to discriminated union types, and as a result, enumerated types are usually relegated to those situations where F# needs to interoperate against the remainder of the .NET framework.

In general, F# developers will not write many of these "old-school" enumerated types except for scenarios where the F# code needs to be easily accessible from other .NET languages; for most purposes, the discriminated union, described next, is vastly more powerful and flexible.

## DISCRIMINATED UNION TYPES

Discriminated unions are a particular kind of type whose possible values are limited to a bound set of possible values, similar to how an enumerated type works in C# or Visual Basic, but with some greatly enhanced functionality. Unlike an enumerated type in C# or Visual Basic, a discriminated union can define not only a bound set of values, but a set of types, as well, as acceptable values.

Consider, for example, the notion of "color." Color values can be seen in a variety of different formats: red/green/blue (RGB) triplet values, cyan/yellow/magenta/black (CMYK) quadruplet values, one of sixteen possible basic colors (red, blue, dark red, dark blue, and so on), and so on. Trying to capture all these different possibilities is difficult in C#, because each of the different kinds of representations must be modeled as a separate class, all inheriting from a base `Color` class whose only purpose is to act as a placeholder for the various derived types.

In F#, however, such a type naturally falls within the discriminated union's capabilities. To begin with, it's fairly easy to capture the idea of a `Color` being one of several predefined values:

```
type Color =
    | Black
    | Blue
    | Cyan
    | Gray
    | Green
    | Magenta
    | DarkBlue
    | Red
    | White
    | Yellow
```

And as might be expected, it's relatively easy to use, particularly because the F# type inferencer can be a bit more sure about how discriminated union values are used, compared to enumerated types:

```
let c = Black
System.Console.WriteLine(c)
```

Unfortunately, this produces rather disappointing output (`CompositeComplexTypes+Color`, assuming this code is compiled from "CompositeComplexTypes.fs" and not run from the interactive window or FSI.exe), so it's fortunate that the discriminated union works more nicely with pattern-matching than the enumerated type does:

```
let message =
    match c with
    | Black -> "Black"
    | _ -> "Not black"
System.Console.WriteLine(message)
```

However, as any interior design student will state, there are far more colors in the world than just these nine, and although it might be an interesting exercise to try and list them all in a single discriminated union case, a quick trip to the local art shop (or grocery store) to pick up a pack of 128-color crayon box will likely discourage that attempt fairly quickly. (Is Seashell really a color?) Fortunately, the discriminated union allows you to not only define discrete elements within it, such as previously shown, but also some "type cases" where data elements can be attached to it:

```
type Color =
    | Black
    | Blue
    | Cyan
    | Gray
    | Green
    | Magenta
    | DarkBlue
    | Red
    | White
    | Yellow
    | RGB of int * int * int
    | CMYK of int * int * int * int
```

Now, in addition to having the basic colors, the discriminated union permits users to describe colors in a variety of different color representation schemes:

```
let c = RGB(0,0,0)
```

And again, the discriminated union works exceedingly well in pattern-matching, making it relatively easy to produce nice strings regardless of whether the basic color name or its corresponding RGB or CMYK value were used:

**Available for download on Wrox.com**

```
match c with
    | Black | RGB(0,0,0) -> "Black"
    | White | RGB(255, 255, 255) -> "White"
    | Red | RGB(255, 0, 0) -> "Red"
    | Blue | RGB(0, 0, 255) -> "Blue"
    | Cyan | RGB(64, 128, 128) -> "Cyan"
    | Gray | RGB(192, 192, 192) -> "Gray"
    | Green | RGB(0, 255, 0) -> "Green"
    | Magenta -> "Magenta"
    | Yellow -> "Yellow"
    | RGB(r,g,b) ->
        System.String.Format("({0},{1},{2})",
            r, g, b)
    | CMYK(c,m,y,k) ->
        System.String.Format("[{0},{1},{2},{3}]",
            c,m,y,k)
```

*Code snippet ComplexCompositeTypes.fs*

Actually, this is probably code that should "stay with" the discriminated union type, as a way of producing the RGB triplet (as an `int * int * int` tuple) on demand; fortunately, the discriminated union, like the `struct`, can have custom methods defined on it, using the syntax described in Chapter 8:

```
type Color =
    | RGB of int * int * int
    | CMYK of int * int * int * int
    | Black
    | Blue
    | Green
    | Red
    | White
    | Cyan
    | Gray
    member this.RGBValue =
        match this with
        | RGB(r,g,b) -> (r, g, b)
        | Red -> (255, 0, 0)
        | Green -> (0, 255, 0)
        | Blue -> (0, 0, 255)
        | Black -> (0, 0, 0)
        | White -> (255, 255, 255)
        | Cyan -> (64, 128, 128)
        | Gray -> (192, 192, 192)
        | CMYK(c,m,y,k) ->
            failwith "I have no idea how to do that"
```

Similar methods to return the CMYK value of a given color can be imagined. (Returning the string representation, the job of the ToString() method, is deferred until overriding methods from base classes — in this case, System.Object — is covered in Chapter 9.)

It's important to note that the F# compiler can help with pattern-matching, evaluating to make sure that all possible matches are met in the match clauses, something that the compiler cannot do with enumerated types because of their "incompleteness" (meaning that an enumerated type can be spun out of thin air, because they are not much more than convenient names over constant numeric values).

Discriminated unions are also exceedingly common in defining tree-based structures, such as is commonly used in language design and parsing, or in any hierarchical structure.

```
type BinaryTree =
    | Node of BinaryTree * obj * BinaryTree
    | Empty
```

This is because, as demonstrated, the discriminated union allows for definitions of cases that include recursive definitions, such as the Node being a three-part tuple, the data element being stored and the left and right nodes that could be either an additional Node or Empty. Walking this tree becomes a fairly easy exercise, using either the member-method syntax described in Chapter 8 or the module-level function syntax described in Chapter 13:

```
type BinaryTree =
    | Node of obj * BinaryTree * BinaryTree
    | Empty
    member bt.Contents =
        match bt with
        | Empty -> ""
        | Node(data, left, right) ->
            "(" + left.Contents + ")" +
```

```
            ":" + data.ToString() + ":" +
            "(" + right.Contents + ")"
```

Using the tree can then be relatively easy:

```
let authorTree =
    Node("Ted",
        Node("Aaron",
            Empty,
            Empty),
        Node("Talbott",
            Node("Rick", Empty, Empty),
            Empty))
System.Console.WriteLine(authorTree.Contents)
```

When combined with higher-order functions (described in Chapter 13), it becomes positively trivial to operate on the elements in the tree:

```
type BinaryTree =
    | Node of obj * BinaryTree * BinaryTree
    | Empty
    member bt.Contents =
        match bt with
        | Empty -> ""
        | Node(data, left, right) ->
            "(" + left.Contents + ")" +
            ":" + data.ToString() + ":" +
            "(" + right.Contents + ")"
    member bt.iter (fn : (obj) -> unit ) =
        match bt with
        | Empty -> ()
        | Node(data, left, right) ->
            left.iter(fn)
            fn(data)
            right.iter(fn)
```

In essence, the `iter` method does a left-recursive-descent traversal of the tree:

```
authorTree.iter(System.Console.WriteLine)
```

which, given the previous `authorTree` example, would print `Aaron`, `Ted`, `Rick`, and `Talbott`. Right-recursive-descent or other paths through the tree could be added, if wanted.

Note that the F# compiler takes the preceding code and turns it into almost precisely the same construct that the object-oriented developer would ask for: The `BinaryTree` type becomes an abstract base class, with two subclasses defined, `Node` and `Empty`, so that either can be passed where a `BinaryTree` type is expected. Additionally, an `Is` property is inherited from the base class so that given any instance of `BinaryTree`, we can call `IsNode` or `IsEmpty` to determine if it is one of those two types. On top of that, because the `Empty` case holds no additional data, it can be represented via a singleton instance, and the F# compiler takes care of that by creating a single instance hiding behind a static property called, not surprisingly, `Empty`.

Remember that most of the time, the F# developer doesn't need to know all this detail about how the discriminated union matches up against the underlying CLR — in fact, we could argue that having all these details in mind distracts the F# developer. Mentioning this serves two purposes: One, because seeing how the language construct matches up against the CLR can sometimes offer insight into its use, and two, because it's an example of how the F# language wants to "hide" the physical details of how things compile from the developer to reduce the amount of complexity the developer must keep in mind.

In what will probably be viewed by some object-oriented purists as a heretical assertion, some of the simpler hierarchical structures traditionally represented in object-oriented languages using inheritance-based trees of classes can be more easily modeled using a discriminated union:

```
type Employee =
    | Grunt of string
    | Manager of string * Employee list
    member e.Name =
        match e with
        | Grunt(n) -> n
        | Manager(n, _) -> n
```

Because this is a discriminated union makes it trivial to determine how many employees a given Employee has working for them, with Grunts returning an empty list (because, after all, if one is a grunt, one has no direct reports):

```
type Employee =
    | Grunt of string
    | Manager of string * Employee list
    member e.Name =
        match e with
        | Grunt(n) -> n
        | Manager(n, _) -> n
    member e.Subordinates =
        match e with
        | Grunt(_) -> []
        | Manager(_, es) -> es
```

This can be even simpler using a judicious application of recursion, higher-order functions, and pattern-matching to make it absolutely trivial to calculate the size of a given Employee's empire:

```
type Employee =
    | Grunt of string
    | Manager of string * Employee list
    member e.Name =
        match e with
        | Grunt(n) -> n
        | Manager(n, _) -> n
    member e.Subordinates =
        match e with
        | Grunt(_) -> []
        | Manager(_, es) -> es
    member e.Empire =
        match e with
        | Grunt(_) -> []
        | Manager(_, es) ->
            List.collect
                (fun (e : Employee) -> e.Empire) es
```

To be straightforward about it, any case where a traditional object-oriented developer would consider using a Composite pattern (from *Design Patterns: Elements of Reusable Object-Oriented Software* by Erich Gamma, Richard, Helm, Ralph Johnson, and John Vlissides, also known as the Gang-of-Four book) can most likely be replaced by a discriminated union and result in a much smaller code base.

Discriminated unions also make the State pattern (again, from the Gang-of-Four book) trivial to code and implement:

```
type State =
    | New
    | Opened
    | Closed
    member s.Open() =
        match s with
        | New -> Opened
        | Opened ->
            failwith "Error to Open an Opened state"
        | Closed -> Opened
    member s.Close() =
        match s with
        | New ->
            failwith "Error to Close a New state"
        | Opened -> Closed
        | Closed -> Closed
```

And again, thanks to the compiler-checking the F# compiler can do in the pattern-matching constructs, if a new state is added to the discriminated union, any pattern-matching code that fails to incorporate that new state immediately triggers a compiler error.

## STRUCTS

Structs, also known within the .NET lexicon as "value types," are not objects in the traditional sense. Instead, value types are types that intend to be hosted inside other objects, or are simple enough that they represent a real, tangible value, à la numbers. All the .NET primitive types are value types — this was a deliberate design decision on the part of the .NET team, specifically so that the .NET environment can avoid the bifurcated type system that Java has, yet still avoid the overhead (such as garbage collection) that accompanies full objects.

*For more on .NET value types, see* http://msdn.microsoft.com/en-us/library/34yytbws(VS.71).aspx.

To create a value type in F#, the `type` keyword again comes into play, like so, for a value type that intends to represent a Cartesian point on a 2D graph:

```
[<Struct>]
type Point =
    member this.X = 0
    member this.Y = 0
```

A couple of things need to be highlighted here. First, the F# custom attribute Struct, applied to the type declaration, is what defines this is as a .NET value type — if it is left off, the type will be defined as a full-fledged class, implicitly inheriting from System.Object (as all good classes do), as opposed to being a value type and implicitly inheriting from System.ValueType and having the necessary CLR support to treat it as a value type (such as living on the stack when declared as a local variable in a method, and so on).

Second, this type has two available members, X and Y, which are, in this case, defined as returning the constant value 0. These will be compiled into read-only properties on the value type, without any further work required on the part of the F# developer — this is in support of F#'s desire to free the .NET developer from having to worry about low-level "physical" details such as fields-versus-properties where such details are irrelevant. Notice as well the this prefix to the two-member declarations — this self-identifier serves the same purpose as this in C# or Me in Visual Basic, except that F# allows the developer to choose what that prefix should look like. Thus, we can rewrite the previous code like so, if we think it makes the code more readable:

```
[<Struct>]
type Point =
    member pt.X = 0
    member p.Y = 0
```

The important thing to recognize is that the F# compiler "scopes" the self-identifier name to the member declaration itself, so if it makes sense to have different self-identifier names for different members, go for it. (You'll have a hard time convincing other F# developers that this is a good idea, mind you.) Developers coming from a C# background are advised to continue to use this as the common self-identifier prefix, and those coming from a Visual Basic background are advised to continue to use me. (Developers coming from a Perl background are probably beyond help.)

Using the Point value type is straightforward:

```
let origin = new Point()
System.Console.WriteLine("Point = {0},{1}", origin.X, origin.Y)
```

As it stands, however, the Point is not a useful value type, because it lacks any way to set the values of the X and Y coordinates of the graph when constructed. Normally, this is done via a constructor:

```
[<Struct>]
type Point(x : int, y : int) =
    member pt.X = x
    member pt.Y = y
```

Now things begin to really diverge from the other .NET languages; in this case, the "primary constructor" is declared inline alongside the type name itself, and it accepts two parameters, both of them 32-bit signed integer values. Notice that these parameters are then used in their respective property member; silently, the F# compiler has captured the parameters to the constructor and stored the values into field names of the same names (x and y, respectively) for use later in the type.

Using the Point type with its new constructor is simple:

```
let notOrigin = new Point(12, 12)
System.Console.WriteLine("Point = {0},{1}",
    notOrigin.X, notOrigin.Y)
```

Note that because this is a value type, and because the CLR requires it, a no-argument constructor is always defined for a value type:

```
let origin = new Point()
System.Console.WriteLine("Point = {0},{1}", origin.X, origin.Y)
```

This has two implications — it means that every value type created has a no-argument constructor, regardless of whether we defined one, and it means that we cannot define one of our own, even if we want to. (The CLR insists that the value type no-argument constructor does a zero-bit-pattern initialization on the entire contents of the value type. If we could define our own no-argument constructor, that constraint might be violated.)

Developers who experiment with the `Point` type as defined so far will notice that the `Point` type is a read-only value; attempts to change the value of `X` or `Y` will result in a compiler error. Normally, this is what's preferable for a value type, because not only does that help enforce a certain amount of thread-safety, but frankly, it just makes sense — we don't change the number 1 to hold a new value but instead manipulate it in some way and store that new value instead:

```
let newPoint = new Point((notOrigin.X - 6), (notOrigin.Y) - 6)
System.Console.WriteLine("Point = {0},{1}",
    newPoint.X, newPoint.Y)
```

However, sometimes the .NET developer insists that the value type must have mutable semantics, and F# supports this via the use of the `mutable` modifier:

```
[<Struct>]
type MutPoint =
    val mutable X : int
    val mutable Y : int
```

Doing so, however, means that the value type cannot have a custom constructor. F# also punishes the mutable-preferring developer by forcing them to use the `mutable` keyword when constructing the instance of the mutable `Point`, and by requiring a different syntax for doing destructive updates (what C# and Visual Basic developers call "assignments") to set the values of the `X` and `Y` members of the value type:

```
let mutable mutPt = new MutPoint()
mutPt.X <- 10
mutPt.Y <- 10
System.Console.WriteLine("Point = {0},{1}",
    mutPt.X, mutPt.Y)
```

Note that the F# compiler generates wildly different code when using this form — the `X` and `Y` members will now be generated as publicly accessible fields, rather than read/write properties. (Syntax for explicitly defining `X` and `Y` as read/write properties is given in Chapter 8.)

All this is designed to help the F# developer use immutable objects and types "by default," as described in more detail in Chapter 14, while still permitting access to the "old ways" of doing things in .NET. In general, the budding F# developer would be well-advised to adopt the immutable approach wherever possible, as soon as possible.

By the way, technically we lied to you earlier about the custom attribute `[<Struct>]` making this type declaration a value type; if you choose, you can use the alternative F# syntax:

```
type AnotherPoint(x : int, y: int) =
    struct
        member pt.X = x
        member pt.Y = y
    end
```

Some developers might consider this to be more readable than the attribute-annotated version, whereas some others prefer the earlier syntax. Use whichever aesthetically appeals; as of this writing, however, it seems that the attribute-based version is more widely accepted among F# developers.

Structs can have methods, properties, statics, and other member types defined on them, as described in Chapter 8, though generally value types should be relatively "lightweight" and support only those operations that make it easier to use the value type. In addition, although structs cannot inherit from other base classes (a restriction enforced by the underlying CLR), they can override methods defined in base classes; given that F# already does a good job for Equals() and GetHashCode(), the only member left to override would be ToString(), and the syntax for doing so is described in Chapter 9. As a preview, however, it appears here, along with the full definition of Point:

```
[<Struct>]
type Point(x : int, y : int) =
    member pt.X = x
    member pt.Y = y
    override pt.ToString() =
        System.String.Format("({0},{1})", x, y)
```

## Value Type Implicit Members

Experienced .NET developers can recall that a value type has several members it inherits from System.Object through System.ValueType; although we defer a full discussion of inheritance and overriding methods until Chapter 9, it is important to note that the value type created by F# obeys the general contract for value types and defines an Equals() method that automatically performs structural equality comparison:

```
let a = new Point(12, 12)
let b = new Point(12, 12)
System.Console.WriteLine("a = b? {0}",
    if (a = b) then "yes" else "no")
System.Console.WriteLine("a.Equals(b)? {0}",
    if (a.Equals(b)) then "yes" else "no")
```

From this, it makes sense that F# can also determine inequality just as easily as it can equality:

```
System.Console.WriteLine("a <> b? {0}",
    if (a <> b) then "yes" else "no")
```

However, F# can also do some inferred relativity comparisons, as well:

```
let c = new Point(6, 12)
let d = new Point(18, 12)
let e = new Point(12, 6)
let f = new Point(12, 18)
System.Console.WriteLine("a > c? {0}",
```

```
        if (a > c) then "yes" else "no") // yes
System.Console.WriteLine("a > d? {0}",
    if (a > d) then "yes" else "no") // no
System.Console.WriteLine("a > e? {0}",
    if (a > e) then "yes" else "no") // yes
System.Console.WriteLine("a > f? {0}",
    if (a > f) then "yes" else "no") // no
System.Console.WriteLine("a < c? {0}",
    if (a < c) then "yes" else "no") // no
System.Console.WriteLine("a < d? {0}",
    if (a < d) then "yes" else "no") // yes
System.Console.WriteLine("a < e? {0}",
    if (a < e) then "yes" else "no") // no
System.Console.WriteLine("a < f? {0}",
    if (a < f) then "yes" else "no") // yes
```

It can do this because the F# compiler defines the value type to implement the standard .NET interface `System.Collections.IComparer`, and uses a "generic comparer" defined in `Microsoft.FSharp.Core.LanguagePrimitives` to do the comparison against each of the fields in the value type one-by-one, returning "greater" or "lesser" as soon as it finds a discrepancy between the two value types being compared. For many types, such as our Point example, this will be sufficient. In general, though, relying on the built-in comparison logic is less desirable than defining explicitly the relationship between `Points`, so if this kind of relational comparison is desired, then those operators should be defined explicitly on the `Point`, as described in Chapter 9.

For the record, the generated value type also implements the standard .NET interface `System.Collections.IEqualityComparer` to make the F# value types "play nicely" when stored in .NET Collections.

Similarly, F# defines a `GetHashCode()` method that takes the internal bit-patterns of the value type into account when calculating the hashcode for the value type.

```
System.Console.WriteLine("a.GetHashCode() = {0}",
    a.GetHashCode())
System.Console.WriteLine("b.GetHashCode() = {0}",
    b.GetHashCode())
System.Console.WriteLine("a hash = b hash? {0}",
    a.GetHashCode() = b.GetHashCode()) // true
```

Note that this implies that if the internal contents of the value type change between calls to `GetHashCode()`, the returned hashcode could be different — yet another reason to prefer immutable value types.

## Structs and Pattern-Matching

In general, structs don't play well with pattern-matching; when attempting to use a `struct` in what would seem to be the most natural manner in a pattern-match, the compiler will complain:

```
let message =
    match a with
    | Point(0, 0) -> "You're at the origin!"
    | Point(12, 12) -> "You're at 12, 12!"
    | Point(_, _) -> "Who knows where you are?"
// "The pattern discriminator 'Point' is not defined"
```

In general, the easiest way to make `structs` work with pattern-matching is to break out the members of the value type into a tuple (or to a different primitive type, if the value type is easily convertible to an underlying primitive type, such as an int32) and match on that, like so:

```
let newPoint = new Point(0,0)
let message =
    match (newPoint.X, newPoint.Y) with
    | (0, 0) -> "You're at the origin!"
    | (12, 12) -> "You're at 12, 12!"
    | (_, _) -> "Who knows where you are?"
System.Console.WriteLine(message)
```

Alternatively, an active pattern rule can be defined describing how to convert to the value type during the pattern-match, as described in Chapter 6:

```
let (|Point|) (x : int, y : int) (inPt : Point) =
    inPt.X = x && inPt.Y = y
let message =
    match newPoint with
    | Point(0, 0) true -> "You're at the origin!"
    | Point(12, 12) true -> "You're at 12,12!"
    | _ -> "Who knows where you are?"
System.Console.WriteLine(message)
```

Different F# developers prefer one or the other, depending on the aesthetics of the situation.

## RECORD TYPES

The record type sits about halfway between a tuple and a classic "class" type, as defined in classical object-oriented languages. The tuple is a lightweight bundling of data, but the tuple suffers from the fact that the members of the tuple are unnamed, and the type as a whole is unnamed:

```
let ted = ("Ted", "Neward", 38)
let aaron = ("Aaron", "Erickson")
let rick = ("Rick", "Minerich", "I'd rather not say")
```

As described in Chapter 5, each of these is an instance of an entirely different type, because the contents of the tuple are different. We can fix this by creating a single-case discriminated union to give the tuple type a name, and making it easier to ensure that the various authors at least have the same basic structure:

```
type Author =
    | Author of string * string * int

let ted = Author("Ted", "Neward", 38)
let aaron = Author("Aaron", "Erickson", 35)
let rick = Author("Rick", "Minerich", 0)
```

But unfortunately, this doesn't do much to hide that the data is held in a tuple, and the lack of any sort of per-atom "name" to the constituent elements in the tuple mean that misunderstandings are still possible:

```
let talbott = Author("Crowell", "Talbott", 35)
```

Perhaps even more disturbingly, trying to extract one element out of the tuple can be painful, such as when we want to display the authors' first names:

```
let authors = [
    Author("Ted", "Neward", 38);
    Author("Aaron", "Erickson", 35);
    Author("Rick", "Minerich", 0);
    Author("Crowell", "Talbott", 35)
]
for a in authors do
    match a with
    | Author(first, last, age) ->
        System.Console.WriteLine("Hello, {0}", first)
```

As useful and powerful as pattern-matching is, we're not so enamored of it that we want to have to use it every time we want to extract a value out of the underlying tuple. Granted, we could define properties on the discriminated union to do this for each of the elements in the tuple, like this:

```
type Author =
    | Author of string * string * int
    member a.FirstName =
        match a with
        | Author(first, _, _) -> first
    member a.LastName =
        match a with
        | Author(_, last, _) -> last
    member a.Age =
        match a with
        | Author(_, _, age) -> age
```

but this is starting to look tedious and error-prone, and simply defining the `Author` as a value type starts to look a lot simpler by comparison.

What we'd actually like is a simple structure like the tuple but one we can put a name to and whose constituent elements we can also name:

```
type AuthorRecord =
    { FirstName : string
      LastName : string
      Age : int }
```

This is what F# calls a "record type," and in many respects, it looks like a standard .NET class. Despite that similarity, the record type has some advantages over a standard class, most notably in how it is used:

```
let ted = { FirstName = "Ted"; LastName = "Neward"; Age = 38 }
System.Console.WriteLine("Hello, {0}", ted.FirstName)
```

Unlike a traditional class, the record type is not identified as such simply because the programmer uses the type name in a "new" expression, but because the F# compiler looks at the individually named elements inside the bracketed expression and realizes that they line up one-for-one with the declared record type. This means that if the developer forgets to provide one of those named elements, it represents a compiler error:

```
let aaron = { FirstName = "Aaron"; LastName = "Erickson" }
```

The compiler will reject the preceding code with an error: No Assignment Given for Field 'Age' of Type 'ComplexCompositeTypes.AuthorRecord'. This gives us the type-safety that the tuple type leaves out, plus we get an added benefit:

```
let talbott = {
     LastName = "Crowell"; FirstName = "Talbott"; Age = 35 }
```

Because the fields are identified by name, they can be initialized in any order, so long as all the fields are eventually present in the construction.

There is a note of caution here, however: Because we're relying on the F# compiler's capability to infer the record type out of the fields being used, if there are two record types that have the same constituent fields, the compiler will have a hard time telling the two apart:

```
type ProgrammingLanguage =
     { Name : string
        YearsInUse : int }
type SpokenLanguage =
     { Name : string
        YearsInUse : int }
```

Unfortunately, the compiler won't always tell the developer when an ambiguity is present — it may simply pick the first (or the last) of the record types that match:

```
let english = { Name = "English"; YearsInUse = 1000 }
System.Console.WriteLine("english IS-A {0}",
     english.GetType()) // SpokenLanguage
let fsharp = { Name = "F#"; YearsInUse = 5 }
System.Console.WriteLine("fsharp IS-A {0}",
     fsharp.GetType()) // SpokenLanguage
```

In this case, the programmer must explicitly disambiguate by putting the type name in the fields when used:

```
let english = {
     SpokenLanguage.Name = "English"
     SpokenLanguage.YearsInUse = 1000 }
System.Console.WriteLine("english IS-A {0}",
     english.GetType()) // SpokenLanguage
let fsharp = {
     ProgrammingLanguage.Name = "F#"
     ProgrammingLanguage.YearsInUse = 5 }
System.Console.WriteLine("fsharp IS-A {0}",
     fsharp.GetType()) // ProgrammingLanguage
```

Record types also have an advantage when creating instances, in that the language permits "cloning" of records: A record type instance can be created using the values of another record type instance (of the same type, of course) as the default values:

```
type Person = {
     FirstName : string
     LastName : string
     FavoriteColor : string
}
let ted = {
```

```
        FirstName = "Ted";
        LastName = "Neward";
        FavoriteColor = "Black"
    }
let michael = { ted with FirstName = "Michael" }
let matthew = { ted with FirstName = "Matthew" }
```

This produces three `Person` instances, each with `LastName` set to `"Neward"` and `FavoriteColor` set to `"Black"`. Naturally, if later code comes along and sets one of these instance's `FavoriteColor` to `"Red"`, the other two are unaffected.

As with other F# types, the record type can also have members defined on it, such as:

```
type Person =
    { FirstName : string
      LastName : string
      FavoriteColor : string }
    member p.FullName =
        System.String.Format("{0} {1}",
            p.FirstName, p.LastName)
```

And the record type can be used as part of pattern-matching, such as:

```
let people = [
    ted; michael; matthew;
    { FirstName="Aaron"; LastName="Erickson";
        FavoriteColor="White" }
    { FirstName="Rick"; LastName="Minerich";
        FavoriteColor="Blue" }
    { FirstName="Talbott"; LastName="Crowell";
        FavoriteColor="Red" }
]

for n in people do
    match n with
    | { Person.LastName = "Neward" } ->
        System.Console.WriteLine("Hi, {0}!", n.FirstName)
    | _ ->
        System.Console.WriteLine("Who are you, {0}?",
            n.FullName)
```

This is an advantage over the traditional class, which would have to be either deconstructed into a primitive type or built up using an active pattern rule.

By default, the member fields of the record type are immutable; if a record type instance with mutable fields is wanted instead, again the `mutable` keyword must be applied:

```
type MutPerson =
    { mutable FirstName : string
      mutable LastName : string
      mutable Age : int }
```

Not all members of the record type need be mutable; pick and choose those members that need to be mutable, and leave the rest as immutable:

```
type MutPerson =
    { FirstName : string
```

```
          LastName : string
          mutable Age : int
          mutable Spouse : MutPerson }
```

But, as with other discussions around (im)mutability, the general preference is to prefer the immutable until the need for mutability has been proven.

## Record Type Implicit Members

Like the value type, F# provides some implementation of common members "for free." Specifically, like the value type, the F# compiler infers an implementation of `Equals()` and `GetHashCode()` based on structural equality — that is, if two record type instances are of the same record type and contain the same contents on a field-for-field basis, then they are considered equal and have the same hash code. In addition, as with the value type, a certain amount of relational comparison code can be inferred, making it possible for simple record types to be compared against one another:

```
          let a = { FirstName="Ted"; LastName="Neward"; Age=38 }
          let b = { FirstName="Ted"; LastName="Neward"; Age=38 }
          System.Console.WriteLine("a = b? {0}",
              if a = b then "yes" else "no")
          System.Console.WriteLine("a.Equals(b)? {0}",
              if a.Equals(b) then "yes" else "no")
          System.Console.WriteLine("a <> b? {0}",
              if a <> b then "yes" else "no")
```

As with the value type, the comparisons are done on a field-by-field basis; if more control over the various operations are needed, declare and implement those members on the record type directly.

## SUMMARY

F# defines a number of useful constructs that act as a kind of "run-up" to full-fledged class types, and these types are often very useful as supplements or replacements to a class hierarchy. Enumerated types are generally useful only in interop scenarios against other .NET languages, with the exception of those cases where `flags` and multiple-case values are needed. Discriminated unions are an exceptionally powerful way to represent a bound set of types and data values that define each of those bound set cases. Value types are useful to define new "primitive types" in the .NET environment. Record types provide a "classes light" ability that can be powerful as a "named tuple" type that also have some built-in behavior.

But when the .NET developer needs nothing less than a full-fledged class type, F# supports such definitions, as described in the next chapter.

# Classes

**WHAT'S IN THIS CHAPTER?**

➤ Defining classes

➤ Creating fields and constructors

➤ Declaring members

➤ Using access modifiers

➤ Using type extensions

For the experienced C# or Visual Basic developer, this chapter will likely be the least conceptually new material found thus far in the book — as the F# reference states clearly, object-oriented programming is the dominant paradigm of the .NET ecosystem, and classes form the core means by which .NET developers organize their code. As a result, classes and objects are (or at least, should be) familiar ground, and F# supports the full range of object-oriented facilities offered by other languages. Although the F# syntax frequently expresses the same concept in a more terse fashion, overall the developer experienced with objects in C# or Visual Basic will find classes in F# to be a comfortable transition.

A larger danger lurks — as a fusion of both objects and functions, F# offers more than "just" another syntax for building object-oriented applications. As the danger of C++ was in using it as "a better C" and not seeing its deeper capabilities, the danger to the budding F# developer is in using it as "a better C#" and not seeing beyond the object facilities, thus ignoring the potential power of the synthesis of object and function.

## BASICS

To create a new, empty, class, F# uses (again) the `type` keyword, and `class`/`end` markers to indicate the beginning and end of the class declaration:

```
type Example =
    class
    end
```

This introduces a new class into the assembly, although it doesn't do much. Because classes are generally of no use without either state or behavior (and, most often, both), it behooves us to first introduce some kind of state to be held inside of the class.

## Fields

The easiest way to introduce a field into a F# class is via the `val` keyword, which requires a type annotation to indicate the type the field should hold:

**Available for download on Wrox.com**

```
type Person =
    class
        val firstName : string
        val lastName : string
    end
```

*Code snippet Class.fs*

Contrary to what might seem obvious to the C# and Visual Basic developer, however, the `val` construct introduces more than just a field into the defined class. It will also introduce a read-only property of the same name, implicitly returning the value held in the field by that name.

It should be pointed out that the `class` and `end` markers, previously shown, are only necessary when the class has no members inside of it, which is an admittedly rare condition. When members are present, the markers can be left off completely:

```
type Person =
    val firstName : string
    val lastName : string
```

And the F# compiler is left to infer the actual type to compile (`class`, `interface`, or `struct`). Because inference can sometimes be wrong, however, F# provides a set of custom attributes to make explicit what the compiled form of this type should be, and so the most common declaration form of the preceding code will appear as:

```
[<Class>]
type Person =
    val firstName : string
    val lastName : string
```

By default, in keeping with the general style of the F# language, the fields described in this type are immutable and cannot change when initialized. To make them into mutable fields, F# requires the field declaration be decorated with the `mutable` keyword, and any modification to the field needs to be done with the "destructive update" operator (the left-arrow operator, written as `<-`):

```
[<Class>]
type Person =
    val firstName : string
    val mutable lastName : string
```

At this point, although the type has been defined, no method exists to allow for its creation. Unlike the C# or Visual Basic language, the F# compiler does not automatically create a constructor method. Thus, that exercise is left to us.

# Constructors

Recall from the object-oriented world that a constructor is a method invoked at the time that the object instance is being created, with the intent of initializing the object instance with the necessary data it requires to function properly. Being a good object-oriented citizen, F# naturally provides for the definition of constructors, using the new keyword and a parameter list of type-inferenced parameters:

```
[<Class>]
type Person =
    val firstName : string
    val mutable lastName : string
    new (fn, ln) = { firstName = fn; lastName = ln }
```

*Code snippet Class.fs*

Frequently, a class wants more than one constructor, and so long as the constructor method signatures are differentiated from one another either in number or type from one another, the class can have as many constructors as it wants:

```
[<Class>]
type Person =
    val firstName : string
    val mutable lastName : string
    new () = { firstName = ""; lastName = "" }
    new (fn, ln) = { firstName = fn; lastName = ln }
```

*Code snippet Class.fs*

As is often the case, one constructor will frequently want to "chain" into another one, reducing the potential for duplicated logic within constructors. In F#, this is done like this:

```
[<Class>]
type Person =
    val firstName : string
    val mutable lastName : string
    new () = Person("", "")
    new (fn, ln) = { firstName = fn; lastName = ln }
```

*Code snippet Class.fs*

If a chaining constructor (like the no-argument constructor previously defined) wants to do some additional logic after the chained-constructor call, this is done by appending the keyword then and defining a properly indented block of code:

```
[<Class>]
type Person =
    val firstName : string
    val mutable lastName : string
    new () = Person("", "") then
        System.Console.WriteLine("In Example ctor")
    new (fn, ln) = { firstName = fn; lastName = ln }
```

*Code snippet Class.fs*

Periodically, code written in a constructor wants to reference the object being instantiated. F# does not define a pre-existing "special name" identifying the object upon which methods, properties, or constructors are operating, like the `this` or `Me` references from C# or Visual Basic. Instead, F# uses a self-identifier declaration made explicitly on the constructor or member. In the case of a constructor, the self-identifier is done using an `as` clause after the constructor's declaration but before its body:

```
[<Class>]
type Person =
    val firstName : string
    val mutable lastName : string
    new () as this = Person("", "") then
        System.Console.WriteLine(this)
    new (fn, ln) = { firstName = fn; lastName = ln }
```

*Code snippet Class.fs*

The compiler will emit a warning if the `as` clause is present and the introduced name is never used (as is the case with the clause on the primary constructor in the preceding example). The names used are scoped to the constructor or class body, as appropriate, and need not be the same:

```
[<Class>]
type Person =
    val firstName : string
    val mutable lastName : string
    new () as this = Person("", "") then
        System.Console.WriteLine(this)
    new (fn) as p = Person(fn, "") then
        System.Console.WriteLine(p)
    new (fn, ln) = { firstName = fn; lastName = ln }
```

In general, most classes will be defined in terms of one principal constructor to which all others defer, such as the two-argument version in the preceding example. To reflect this, F# encourages the definition of a primary constructor, whose signature appears on the type-definition line, above all the other members in the class:

```
// NOTE: This will not compile as-is
[<Class>]
type Person(fn, ln) =
    val firstName : string
    val mutable lastName : string
    new () as this = Example("", "") then
        System.Console.WriteLine(this)
    new (fn, ln) = { firstName = fn; lastName = ln }
```

When we do this, however, a couple of things suddenly kick in.

First , the compiler complains about the definitions of two the `val`-declared fields — it will state that they need to be both made `mutable` and marked with the `DefaultValue` custom attribute, which we can easily do:

```
[<Class>]
type Person(fn, ln) =
```

```
[<DefaultValue>]
val mutable firstName : string
[<DefaultValue>]
val mutable lastName : string
new () as this = Person("", "") then
    System.Console.WriteLine(this)
```

However, the F# compiler has also done something interesting with the primary constructor — several "somethings." First, any parameters defined on the primary constructor are also implicitly declared as fields on the class. Thus, as previously written, the `Person` type now has four fields on it: `fn`, `ln`, `firstName` and `lastName`. Because the two `val`-declared fields were there essentially to hold two strings, it becomes unnecessary to declare those fields anymore, and we can strip the example down to:

```
[<Class>]
type Person(fn : string, ln : string) =
    new () as this = Person("", "") then
        System.Console.WriteLine(this)
```

Next, the primary constructor takes the typical constructor step of copying the data passed in over to the fields, saving the F# developer from having to make that explicit step. This is why the primary constructor, as written here, has no real "body" to it.

Despite this automatic behavior, the primary constructor may want to perform some additional logic, just as the other constructor does. This logic simply "appears" in the body of the class as `do`-prefixed expressions:

```
[<Class>]
type Person(fn : string, ln : string) =
    do System.Console.WriteLine("{0} {1}", fn, ln)
    new () as this = Person("", "") then
        System.Console.WriteLine(this)
```

The `do` is necessary because the language insists that any expression results (such as the "unit" result from calling the `Console.WriteLine` method) must be thrown away. Multiple statements can be chained under a single `do` expression:

```
[<Class>]
type Person(fn : string, ln : string) =
    do
        System.Console.WriteLine("{0}", fn)
        System.Console.WriteLine("{0}", ln)
    new () as this = Person("", "") then
        System.Console.WriteLine(this)
```

*The primary constructor now requires type annotations to its parameters because the compiler needs to know what the types of the two parameters are because* WriteLine *has so many possible overloads. This is a common situation in F#: The compiler can type-infer most situations but periodically gets confused and needs a bit of assistance in the nature of a type annotation or two.*

The do expression or block of code has one particular restriction on it, mostly that it must appear before any other member declarations or definitions (which we discuss later).

Frequently, however, the F# developer will want to define intermediate values that hold data calculated from the values passed in to the primary constructor; rather than having to define an explicit val-declared field and connect with a do expression (and requiring a self-identifier so that we can reference the field from inside the do expression):

```
[<Class>]
type Person(fn : string, ln : string) as this =
    [<DefaultValue>]
    val mutable fullName : string
    do
        this.fullName <- fn + " " + ln
    new () as this = Person("", "") then
        System.Console.WriteLine(this)
```

there is actually a shorter, easier, more F#-idiomatically correct way, via a let expression:

```
[<Class>]
type Person(fn : string, ln : string) =
    let fullName = fn + " " + ln
    new () as this = Person("", "") then
        System.Console.WriteLine(this)
```

Any binding introduced as a let binding in a class like this is a (by default) read-only private field within the class. They do not have to derive from constructor parameters, of course; any expression is acceptable here:

```
[<Class>]
type Person(fn : string, ln : string) =
    let fullName = fn + " " + ln
    let constructionDate = System.DateTime.Now
    let leapYearBaby =
        if constructionDate.Month = 2 &&
            constructionDate.Day = 29
        then true
        else false
    new () as this = Person("", "") then
        System.Console.WriteLine(this)
```

*Code snippet Class.fs*

As can be inferred from the preceding code, the compiler evaluates the body of the primary constructor in the order in which it appears in the declaration, making it perfectly legal to reference an earlier binding name in a later binding expression.

By default, when the compiler builds code referencing these fields (whether introduced by a let binding or in the primary constructor signature), the compiler assumes that these are immutable, read-only fields and disallows any attempt to modify them when initialized. This is a recurring theme throughout the F# language, and if the need for mutable elements is necessary, F# permits it via the `mutable` keyword modifier on the `let` binding declaration:

```
[<Class>]
type Person(fn : string, ln : string, a : int) =
    let mutable age = a
    let fullName = fn + " " + ln
    let constructionDate = System.DateTime.Now
    let leapYearBaby =
        if constructionDate.Month = 2 &&
            constructionDate.Day = 29
        then true
        else false
    do
        if constructionDate = System.DateTime.Now then age <- age+1
    new () as this = Person("", "",0) then
        System.Console.WriteLine(this)
    new (fn, ln) as this = Person(fn, ln,0) then
        System.Console.WriteLine(this)
```

*Code snippet Class.fs*

While the declared element is still internal to the class, it can now be modified, usually through a method call or property setter (described next).

Regarding the difference between using `let` versus `val` declarations, it is important to note that `val` always introduces a field, whereas a `let` binding can introduce either a method or a field, with the compiler determining which is more appropriate. For this reason, F# developers may find themselves occasionally reaching for `val` in those situations when they need to ensure a field is introduced, as opposed to a property or a method that returns a constant value.

## Creating

After the type is defined, creating an instance of the type is strikingly similar to the process in C# or Visual Basic: The `new` keyword, followed by the type name, followed by values intended for the constructor's parameter set, cause the CLR to create an instance of that type and invoke its constructor:

```
let p1 = new Person("Ted", "Neward", 38)
```

Any of the constructors defined on the type are available for use, and each returns a new object, as expected:

```
let p1 = new Person("Ted", "Neward", 38)
let p2 = new Person("Aaron", "Erickson")
let p3 = new Person()
```

In classic CLR tradition, each of these is a garbage-collected, reference-tracked object and will only be destroyed when the last reference to the object goes out of scope, which in this case will be when the method exits.

## MEMBERS

Much of the time, simply providing constructors to a type is not sufficient to make it useful — classes also generally want to have means by which to access the data passed in during construction (or derived from that data), and/or provide behavior that users of the class may want to use. For these situations, F# allows the provision of members to the class, typically using the member keyword, followed by a self-identifier prefix and then the name by which a member wants to be known; an example of such a member has already been demonstrated so far:

**Available for download on Wrox.com**

```
[<Class>]
type Person(fn : string, ln : string, a : int) =
    let fullName = fn + " " + ln
    let constructionDate = System.DateTime.Now
    let leapYearBaby =
        if constructionDate.Month = 2 &&
            constructionDate.Day = 29
        then true
        else false
    new () as p = Person("", "", 0) then
        System.Console.WriteLine(p)
    new (fn, ln) as this = Person(fn, ln, 0) then
        System.Console.WriteLine(this)
    member p.IsPerson = true
```

*Code snippet Class.fs*

In general, the F# compiler infers the type of the member — a method or property — based on the definition after the member name. In the preceding case, because the IsPerson member simply returns a constant value, F# infers the IsPerson member to be a read-only Boolean property.

## Properties

Defining additional properties on the type can often take the same form as the one previously demonstrated, often providing access to the data passed in during construction:

**Available for download on Wrox.com**

```
[<Class>]
type Person(fn : string, ln : string, a : int) =
    let fullName = fn + " " + ln
    let constructionDate = System.DateTime.Now
    let leapYearBaby =
        if constructionDate.Month = 2 &&
            constructionDate.Day = 29
        then true
        else false
    new () as p = Person("", "", 0) then
        System.Console.WriteLine(p)
    new (fn, ln) as this = Person(fn, ln, 0) then
        System.Console.WriteLine(this)
    member p.IsPerson = true
    member p.FirstName = fn
```

```
member p.LastName = ln
member p.Age = a
```

*Code snippet Class.fs*

In the continuing spirit of the type-inferencing nature of the F# language, the compiler infers that these three new properties are of type `string`, `string` and `int`, respectively. And, in the continuing spirit of the immutable-preference nature of the F# language, all three properties are assumed to be read-only.

Inference, however, can sometimes be wrong, and the F# language provides a syntax to make the member explicitly recognized as a property. Or in some scenarios, the property will require more code than simply returning a copy of a field value. In either case, the property need only specify a `with get()` clause, properly indented, and this will be the body of the getter method associated with the property name:

**Available for download on Wrox.com**

```
[<Class>]
type Person(fn : string, ln : string, a : int) =
    let fullName = fn + " " + ln
    let constructionDate = System.DateTime.Now
    let leapYearBaby =
        if constructionDate.Month = 2 &&
           constructionDate.Day = 29
        then true
        else false
    new () as p = Person("", "", 0) then
        System.Console.WriteLine(p)
    new (fn, ln) as this = Person(fn, ln, 0) then
        System.Console.WriteLine(this)
    member p.IsPerson = true
    member p.FirstName = fn
    member p.LastName = ln
    member p.Age = a
    member p.FullName with get() = fullName
    member p.NameAndAge
        with get() =
            System.String.Format("{0} ({1} years old)",
                p.FullName, p.Age)
```

*Code snippet Class.fs*

Note that in the preceding example, the `FullName` property uses the `let`-introduced `fullName` field, which is subtly different than if the `FullName` property did the concatenation; the `fullName` let-binding is evaluated once, during the object's construction, whereas if the property does the concatenation, it will be done on each and every property `get` reference. Given that these fields are all read-only (so far), such repeated concatenation would be a waste of CPU cycles.

In those situations where a read/write property is instead preferred, the member definition need only have a `with set` clause, specifying a single parameter to act as the implicitly passed-in value to the setter. As with most other cases in the F# language, this parameter type need not be specified explicitly if it can be inferred. Because most read/write properties want to act upon a backing field, the F# developer must explicitly define a mutable field that will be modified by the property, again typically with a `let` binding. And because most writable properties will also want to be readable, providing both a `get` and a `set` clause will require the first to be set off with the keyword `with` and the second with `and`; the common idiom looks like this:

```
[<Class>]
type Person(fn : string, ln : string, a : int) =
    let mutable age = a
    let fullName = fn + " " + ln
    let constructionDate = System.DateTime.Now
    let leapYearBaby =
        if constructionDate.Month = 2 &&
            constructionDate.Day = 29
        then true
        else false
    new () as p = Person("", "", 0) then
        System.Console.WriteLine(p)
    new (fn, ln) as this = Person(fn, ln, 0) then
        System.Console.WriteLine(this)
    member p.IsPerson = true
    member p.FirstName = fn
    member p.LastName = ln
    member p.Age
        with get() = age
        and set(newAge) = age <- newAge
    member p.FullName with get() = fullName
    member p.NameAndAge
        with get() =
            System.String.Format("{0} ({1} years old)",
                p.FullName, p.Age)
```

*Code snippet Class.fs*

Notice that the `set` clause again uses the destructive update operator (the left arrow operator, `<-`) to replace the value stored in the mutable field with whatever value is passed in.

Of course, normally some amount of validation will want to be done before blindly copying the new value over into the field, and as with almost all other .NET languages, F# allows for full method bodies in either the `get` or `set` clauses of the property member:

```
[<Class>]
type Person(fn : string, ln : string, a : int) =
    let mutable age = a
    let fullName = fn + " " + ln
    new () as p = Person("", "", 0) then
        System.Console.WriteLine(p)
    new (fn, ln) as this = Person(fn, ln, 0) then
        System.Console.WriteLine(this)
    member p.IsPerson = true
    member p.FirstName = fn
    member p.LastName = ln
    member p.Age
```

```
        with get() = age
        and set(newAge) =
            match newAge with
            | newAge when newAge > 0 ->
                age <- newAge
            | _ ->
                failwith "Age cannot be 0 or less"
    member p.FullName with get() = fullName
    member p.NameAndAge
        with get() =
            System.String.Format("{0} ({1} years old)",
                p.FullName, p.Age)
```

*Code snippet Class.fs*

Accessing properties is almost exactly identical to the form used in other .NET languages, through a dot-qualified use of the property name on an object reference:

```
let p1 = new Person("Ted", "Neward", 38)
let p2 = new Person("Aaron", "Erickson")
let p3 = new Person()
for p in [p1; p2; p3] do
    System.Console.WriteLine("{0} is {1} years old",
        p.FullName, p.Age)
```

If the property is writable, it is updated through (again) the use of the destructive update (left arrow) operator, like so:

```
p1.Age <- p1.Age+1
```

## Named Property Initialization

When constructing a new instance of an object, if the class has one or more properties defined on it, F# permits initialization of those properties in the constructor syntax:

```
let ted = new Person("Ted", "Neward", Age=38)
```

This permits a more expressive style of programming and cuts down on the number of assignment statements, effectively making the written code more functional in style, even if the class being instantiated is more of a traditional imperative type.

Using this style, a developer could allow for a highly flexible style of construction by providing a zero-argument constructor and a set of read/write properties:

```
[<Class>]
type FlexiPerson(fn, ln, a) =
    let mutable firstName = fn
    let mutable lastName = ln
    let mutable age = a
    new() = FlexiPerson("", "", 0)
    member fp.FirstName
```

```
        with get() = firstName and set(n) = firstName <- n
    member fp.LastName
        with get() = lastName and set(n) = lastName <- n
    member fp.Age
        with get() = age and set(n) = age <- n
```

This then allows the developer to select precisely which properties should be initialized during construction:

```
let p5 = new FlexiPerson()
let p6 = new FlexiPerson(FirstName="Ted")
let p7 = new FlexiPerson(LastName="Neward", Age=38)
```

However, doing this carries a few drawbacks, the first of which is that every property must be mutable and thus create potential thread-synchronization points, which can require additional coding and testing. The second drawback stems from the fact that the developer must make sure the object is viable for use regardless of which properties were or weren't set, which means considering the full permutation of all possible properties set during construction and testing each of those permutations.

Similar flexibility can be achieved using optional parameters, described later in this chapter (in the "Methods" section), in the constructor:

```
[<Class>]
type OptiPerson(?firstName, ?lastName, ?age) =
    member fp.FirstName
        with get() = firstName
    member fp.LastName
        with get() = lastName
    member fp.Age
        with get() = age
```

This permits similar flexibility in construction:

```
let op5 = new OptiPerson()
let op6 = new OptiPerson(firstName="Ted")
let op7 = new OptiPerson(firstName="Neward", age=38)
```

But the second drawback, that of making sure the class is still usable safely for all possible constructor permutations, remains.

In general, this property-based initialization syntax is used when constructing traditional imperative object-oriented types with large numbers of properties, such as the WinForms library.

## Indexer Properties

Within the CLR, it is common for a class to provide a kind of collection interface through a special kind of property called an indexer; in the C# language, this appears in the language using the square-bracket operators, whereas Visual Basic uses the round-bracket operators, both of which deliberately remind the programmer of accessing elements in an array in their respective syntaxes. (The `Dictionary<K,V>` type in the `System.Collections.Generic` namespace is one such class.)

In F#, creating an indexer can take one of several forms.

To duplicate the classic C# form in which the property can be accessed via the square-bracket syntax, define a property named `Item`, which is the conventional name for the indexer property across the CLR, and use this slightly altered form of the property syntax:

```fsharp
[<Class>]
type Person(fn : string, ln : string, a : int) =
    let mutable age = a
    let fullName = fn + " " + ln
    new () as this = Person("", "",0) then
        System.Console.WriteLine(this)
    new (fn,ln) as this = Person(fn, ln, 0) then
        System.Console.WriteLine(this)
    member p.IsPerson = true
    member p.FirstName = fn
    member p.LastName = ln
    member p.Age
        with get() = age
        and set(newAge) =
            match newAge with
            | newAge when newAge > 0 ->
                age <- newAge
            | _ ->
                failwith "Age cannot be 0 or less"
    member p.FullName with get() = fullName
    member p.NameAndAge
        with get() =
            System.String.Format("{0} ({1} years old)",
                p.FullName, p.Age)
    member p.AgeGracefully() =
        System.Console.WriteLine("I feel wiser!")
        p.Age <- p.Age + 1
    member p.Item
        with get(organ) =
            match organ with
            | "Heart" -> "Ba-dump"
            | "Stomach" -> "Growl"
            | "Mouth" -> "Chomp chomp swallow"
            | "Brain" -> "Crackle crackle"
            | _ -> ""
```

*Code snippet Class.fs*

When accessing the indexer, the F# form looks just slightly different than that of C#, in that the square-bracket form is still considered a member of the class, and so must be dot-prefixed, as any other member access must be:

```fsharp
System.Console.WriteLine("{0}'s heart says {1}",
    p1.FullName, p1.["Heart"])
```

Just as properties can be defined either as read-only or read-write, indexer properties can also be defined either as read-only (such as the preceding code), read-write, or, rarely, write-only. In the event that a writable indexer property is defined, its set clause must be defined as returning unit.

Multiple indexer properties may be defined, so long as the parameters to the get (and/or set) of the indexer are different in either type or number.

Alternatively, if the indexer needs only be accessible from F# (or from another language that allows access to indexed properties, such as Visual Basic), then any name can be used for the property name:

```
[<Class>]
type Person(fn : string, ln : string, a : int) =
    let mutable age = a
    let fullName = fn + " " + ln
    new () as this = Person("", "",0) then
        System.Console.WriteLine(this)
    new (fn,ln) as this = Person(fn, ln, 0) then
        System.Console.WriteLine(this)
    member p.IsPerson = true
    member p.FirstName = fn
    member p.LastName = ln
    member p.Age
        with get() = age
        and set(newAge) =
            match newAge with
            | newAge when newAge > 0 ->
                age <- newAge
            | _ ->
                failwith "Age cannot be 0 or less"
    member p.FullName with get() = fullName
    member p.NameAndAge
        with get() =
            System.String.Format("{0} ({1} years old)",
                p.FullName, p.Age)
    member p.AgeGracefully() =
        System.Console.WriteLine("I feel wiser!")
        p.Age <- p.Age + 1
    member p.Item
        with get(organ) =
            match organ with
            | "Heart" -> "Ba-dump"
            | "Stomach" -> "Growl"
            | "Mouth" -> "Chomp chomp swallow"
            | "Brain" -> "Crackle crackle"
            | _ -> ""
    member p.Organ
        with get(name) =
            match name with
            | "Heart" -> "Ba-dump"
            | "Stomach" -> "Growl"
            | "Mouth" -> "Chomp chomp swallow"
            | "Brain" -> "Crackle crackle"
            | _ -> ""
```

*Code snippet Class.fs*

Using this named indexer property looks a bit awkward for those used to the square-bracket style of indexer, because now the property name must take a parameter, which makes it look more like a method call:

```
let p1 = new Person("Jason", "Mauer")
System.Console.WriteLine("{0}'s heart says {1}",
    p1.FullName, p1.Organ("Heart"))
```

As with any indexed property, named indexer properties can also be defined either as read-only (such as the preceding code), read-write, or, rarely, write-only. Named indexer properties can also be overloaded, so long as the parameters to the indexer property differ in either number and/or in type:

```
[<Class>]
type Person(fn : string, ln : string, a : int) =
    let mutable age = a
    let fullName = fn + " " + ln
    new () as this = Person("", "",0) then
        System.Console.WriteLine(this)
    new (fn,ln) as this = Person(fn, ln, 0) then
        System.Console.WriteLine(this)
    member p.IsPerson = true
    member p.FirstName = fn
    member p.LastName = ln
    member p.Age
        with get() = age
        and set(newAge) =
            match newAge with
            | newAge when newAge > 0 ->
                age <- newAge
            | _ ->
                failwith "Age cannot be 0 or less"
    member p.FullName with get() = fullName
    member p.NameAndAge
        with get() =
            System.String.Format("{0} ({1} years old)",
                p.FullName, p.Age)
    member p.AgeGracefully() =
        System.Console.WriteLine("I feel wiser!")
        p.Age <- p.Age + 1
    member p.Item
        with get(organ) =
            match organ with
            | "Heart" -> "Ba-dump"
            | "Stomach" -> "Growl"
            | "Mouth" -> "Chomp chomp swallow"
            | "Brain" -> "Crackle crackle"
            | _ -> ""
    member p.Organ
        with get(name) =
            match name with
            | "Heart" -> "Ba-dump"
            | "Stomach" -> "Growl"
            | "Mouth" -> "Chomp chomp swallow"
            | "Brain" -> "Crackle crackle"
            | _ -> ""
    member p.Organ
```

```
with get(id) =
    match id with
    | 1 -> "Ba-dump"
    | 2 -> "Growl"
    | 3 -> "Chomp chomp swallow"
    | 4 -> "Crackle crackle"
    | _ -> ""
```

*Code snippet Class.fs*

Note that for any given indexer property, named or otherwise, the `get`/`set` clauses must specify matching parameter lists for any given definition; in other words, the `get` clause parameter list must match that of the `set` clause.

## Methods

Conceptually, a method is not all that different from a function (see Chapter 13), in that both model some kind of behavior, and frequently the two are interchangeable. As working definitions, we define "behavior defined as part of a class" as a method, and "behavior defined outside of a class" as a function, though these definitions aren't ironclad. In the interests of full disclosure, though, be aware that despite the conceptual similarities to a function and a method — both model behavior, both accept some number of parameters and yield a value, and so on — the F# language does treat the two as quite different creatures at times, so although both are frequently interchangeable, this isn't always the case, and there are number of things a function can do that a method can't, and vice versa.

The definition of a method on a class can take two forms: If the method is intended as an internal-only definition, it can be introduced via a `let` binding, whereas if it is intended as a public-facing definition, it is typically done via a `member` definition.

Defining a `member` method is not significantly different from defining a property, save that the parameters to the method are captured in an argument list in parentheses immediately after the method name, similar to the style seen in C#:

```
[<Class>]
type Person(fn : string, ln : string, a : int) =
    let mutable age = a
    let fullName = fn + " " + ln
    member p.FullName with get() = fullName
    member p.Greet(otherPerson : Person, message) =
        System.Console.WriteLine("{0} says {1} to {2}",
            p.FullName, message, otherPerson.FullName)
```

*Code snippet Class.fs*

Calling a method looks much like it does in any other .NET language, using the object reference, the dot-qualified name of the method, and the list of values to pass as arguments to the method:

```
p1.Greet(p2, "Howdy!")
```

The parameters in the method's parameter list can either be inferred or specified explicitly with type annotations, or a mix of both, as shown. The return type of the method is inferred from the last expression defined in the body of the method, without any explicit return type declared:

```
[<Class>]
type Person(fn : string, ln : string, a : int) =
    let mutable age = a
    let fullName = fn + " " + ln
    member p.FullName with get() = fullName
    member p.Greet(otherPerson : Person, message) =
        System.Console.WriteLine("{0} says {1} to {2}",
            p.FullName, message, otherPerson.FullName)
    member p.CreateGreeting(otherPerson : Person, message) =
        System.String.Format("{0} says {1} to {2}",
            p.FullName, message, otherPerson.FullName)
```

*Code snippet Class.fs*

So far, methods aren't all that different from their C# cousins.

However, methods may also be written in what F# refers to as "curried" form (because the format looks like what curried functions will look like when we discuss them in Chapter 13), where the arguments after the method may be listed after the method name without parentheses:

```
[<Class>]
type Person(fn : string, ln : string, a : int) =
    let mutable age = a
    let fullName = fn + " " + ln
    member p.FullName with get() = fullName
    member p.Greet(otherPerson : Person, message) =
        System.Console.WriteLine("{0} says {1} to {2}",
            p.FullName, message, otherPerson.FullName)
    member p.CreateGreeting(otherPerson : Person, message) =
        System.String.Format("{0} says {1} to {2}",
            p.FullName, message, otherPerson.FullName)
    member p.CurriedGreet target message =
        System.Console.WriteLine("{0} says {1} to {2}",
            p.FullName, message, target)
```

*Code snippet Class.fs*

This is only accepted when the parameters are inferred; type descriptors cannot be present when working with this style. Stylistically, lots of F# methods are written this way, particularly because when done this way, methods can be curried just as functions can, whereas using the parenthesized style requires the complete set of parameters (excepting those marked as optional).

Because of the similarity of syntax between F# tuples and C# methods, it's important to point out that these two methods are legal overloads because they represent two entirely different method signatures:

```
member p.Greet(target : Person, message) =
    System.Console.WriteLine("{0} says {1} to {2}",
        p.FullName, message, target.FullName)
// . . .
member p.Greet(target : Person) (message : string) =
    System.Console.WriteLine("{0} says {1} to {2}",
        p.FullName, message, target.FullName)
```

*Code snippet Class.fs*

The first is a method taking a single argument, a two-argument tuple (of `Person * string`). The second is a method taking two arguments, one of `Person` and the other of `string`. In most direct invocation cases, F# can silently "convert" or accept either syntax, but it's important to realize that the two are different: only the first form will be curryable, whereas the second form will support method overloading (because the types of the tuple argument will be different). As a result, mixing the two styles inside of a single class is highly discouraged.

*The above paragraph is slightly deceptive. While the F# language allows the developer to define overloaded methods that use both curried and tupled arguments, calling them is another matter. Attempts to write* `p1.Greet(p2)`, *assuming* `p1` *and* `p2` *are* `Person` *objects, will result in the compiler disallowing the call, citing "One or more of the overloads of this method has curried arguments. Consider redesigning these members to take arguments in tupled form." So, again, while it is theoretically possible to overload based on curried-vs-tupled style arguments, it's really, really strongly discouraged.*

## Overloaded Methods

Just as with other .NET languages, the F# environment supports overloaded methods: methods with the same name, whose signature differs either in the number of arguments (the *arity* of the method), the parameter types of the arguments, or both:

```
[<Class>]
type Person(fn : string, ln : string, a : int) =
    let mutable age = a
    let fullName = fn + " " + ln
    member p.FullName with get() = fullName
    member p.Greet(otherPerson : Person, message) =
        System.Console.WriteLine("{0} says {1} to {2}",
            p.FullName, message, otherPerson.FullName)
    member p.Greet(otherPerson : Person) =
        System.Console.WriteLine("{0} says 'Howdy!' to {1}",
```

```
                p.FullName, otherPerson.FullName)
    member p.CreateGreeting(otherPerson : Person, message) =
        System.String.Format("{0} says {1} to {2}",
            p.FullName, message, otherPerson.FullName)
```

*Code snippet Class.fs*

Just as with C# or Visual Basic, F# does not permit overloading based on return type — the argument list to the overloaded method must somehow be different so that the right one can be selected based on what arguments are passed in the method invocation. In addition, F# has an extremely difficult time with overloaded methods and curried-style methods; so as a general rule, choose either the curried style for a given method name, or an overload style, but not both.

Because F# doesn't do as many implicit conversions (such as automatically widening an int to a float or double) as C# or Visual Basic does, F# developers looking to avoid having to do explicit widening casts will find overloading methods to be useful. However, in general, community F# code to date doesn't create quite as many overloaded methods as seen in C# or Visual Basic code, so new F# developers should exercise caution when creating lots of overloaded methods.

## Named Parameters

At the point of invocation, F# permits method parameters to be specified in an out-of-order style using named parameters, much as Visual Basic supports, for those methods where the order of the parameter invocation can be hard to remember:

**Available for download on Wrox.com**

```
[<Class>]
type Person(fn : string, ln : string, a : int) =
    let mutable age = a
    let fullName = fn + " " + ln
    member p.FullName with get() = fullName
    member p.Greet(otherPerson : Person, message) =
        System.Console.WriteLine("{0} says {1} to {2}",
            p.FullName, message, otherPerson.FullName)
    member p.Greet(otherPerson : Person) =
        System.Console.WriteLine("{0} says 'Howdy!' to {1}",
            p.FullName, otherPerson.FullName)
    member p.CreateGreeting(otherPerson : Person, message) =
        System.String.Format("{0} says {1} to {2}",
            p.FullName, message, otherPerson.FullName)
    member p.WhoWhatWhereWhenWhy(what,
                                where,
                                whenn : System.DateTime,
                                why) =
        System.String.Format("{0} is doing {1} at {2} on {3} " +
            "because {4}",
            p.FullName, what, where, whenn, why)
```

*Code snippet Class.fs*

Notice that the declaration of the method is no different than any other method on the class; the F# compiler will effectively "reorder" the order of parameter invocation to line up correctly with the method being invoked:

```
let p1 = new Person("Meredith", "Solomon", 28)
let wwwww =
    p1.WhoWhatWhereWhenWhy(
        whenn=System.DateTime.Now,
        where="in the sitting room",
        what="relaxing",
        why="because I'm tired")
System.Console.WriteLine(wwwww)
```

The method being invoked need not be written in F#; any method written in any .NET language can be invoked using named parameters:

```
System.Console.WriteLine(arg=[||], format="This is a message")
```

This facility is available to any .NET assembly called by F# because the CLR requires languages to capture the parameter names as part of the compilation information and store them in the assembly for later use. This is particularly useful when invoking methods on assemblies written to assume a named-argument language facility, such as that provided in Visual Basic. (By far, the most common scenario for this is when invoking Microsoft Office assemblies, which were written to assume a Visual Basic client.)

## Optional Parameters

Some methods may have a varying "set" of parameters that can be passed individually, in groups, or as a complete set; in other words, a given method may have up to four potential parameters, and if F# supported only method overloading, 24 different method overloads would need to be written to support all of the possible permutations.

Because F# recognizes that sometimes a method simply doesn't need some or all the parameters to a method, F# allows method arguments to be marked in their definitions as optional, using the ?:

```
[<Class>]
type Person(fn : string, ln : string, a : int) =
    let mutable age = a
    let fullName = fn + " " + ln
    member p.FullName with get() = fullName
    member p.Greet(otherPerson : Person, message) =
        System.Console.WriteLine("{0} says {1} to {2}",
            p.FullName, message, otherPerson.FullName)
    member p.Greet(otherPerson : Person) =
        System.Console.WriteLine("{0} says 'Howdy!' to {1}",
            p.FullName, otherPerson.FullName)
    member p.CreateGreeting(otherPerson : Person, message) =
        System.String.Format("{0} says {1} to {2}",
            p.FullName, message, otherPerson.FullName)
    member p.WhoWhatWhereWhenWhy(what,
                                 where,
```

```
                                     whenn : System.DateTime,
                                     why) =
               System.String.Format("{0} is doing {1} at {2} on {3} " +
                   "because {4}",
                   p.FullName, what, where, whenn, why)
           member p.Alibi(?what : string,
                          ?where : string,
                          ?whenn : System.DateTime,
                          ?why : string) =
               ()
```

*Code snippet Class.fs*

When a parameter is marked this way, it changes its type declaration slightly, to an Option instance of the declared or inferred type. Thus, in the preceding example, each of the string parameters is now implicitly declared as a string option, and the same is true of the DateTime instance.

Calling the method can be done using either traditional placement syntax, or named-argument syntax, or even a combination of the two:

```
   let alibi1 = p1.Alibi("relaxing", "in the sitting room",
                    System.DateTime.Now, "because I'm tired")
   let alibi2 = p1.Alibi("relaxing", "in the sitting room",
                    why="because I'm tired",
                    whenn=System.DateTime.Now)
```

Because of all the Option instances, implementing the body of this method can be tricky using traditional if/else constructs; by the way, this is another place where pattern-matching can be incredibly useful:

```
   member p.Alibi(?what : string,
                  ?where : string,
                  ?whenn : System.DateTime,
                  ?why : string) =
       match (what, where, whenn, why) with
       | (Some(wht), Some(whr), Some(whn), Some(why)) ->
           System.String.Format("{0} did {1} {2} on {3} because {4}",
               p.FullName, wht, whr, whn, why)
       | (None, None, None, None) ->
           System.String.Format("{0} has no alibi at all",
               p.FullName)
       | (_, _, _, _) ->
           System.String.Format("{0} has no alibi at all",
               p.FullName)
```

See Chapter 6 for more details on pattern-matching.

Optional arguments must come after any nonoptional arguments in the parameter list. Optional arguments are also only available to members, not functions declared via let bindings inside the class.

F# does not provide for any sort of default parameter value, such as we find in languages such as C++, but much the same effect can be had via the use of a `defaultArg` function defined somewhere where the member method can find it:

```
member p.AnotherAlibi(?what : string, ?where : string,
                      ?whenn : System.DateTime,
                      ?why : string) =
    let defaultArg x y = match x with None -> y | Some(v) -> v
    let wht = defaultArg what "nothing"
    let whr = defaultArg where "noplace"
    let whn = defaultArg whenn System.DateTime.Now
    let why = defaultArg why "of no reason"
    System.String.Format("{0} did '{1}' '{2}' because '{3}'",
        p.FullName, wht, whr, why)
```

*Code snippet Class.fs*

When invoking optional arguments by name, the `Option` value (`Some(x)` or `None`) can be explicitly passed by prefixing the named optional argument with a `?`, just as it is declared:

```
let alibi3 = p1.Alibi("relaxing", "in the sitting room",
                ?why=Some("because I'm tired"),
                whenn=System.DateTime.Now)
```

Note that, of course, method parameters can also be explicitly declared as `Option` types, without resorting to the preceding syntax. In general, F# developers will again want to choose one of the two syntaxes and be consistent, at least within a single class, module, or assembly.

## STATIC MEMBERS

Declaring a member to be static (that is, a member that is not associated with any particular instance of that type) is strikingly similar to how it is done in other languages: a modifier, `static`, appears before the member definition. No self-identifier prefix is placed on the member definition, because the member is not associated with an instance of the type and therefore needs no identification.

Properties can be declared as `static`, as can methods:

```
[<Class>]
type Skynet() =
    static member CreateTerminator() =
        new Person("T", "800", 0)
    static member AfterJudgmentDay
        with get() =
            let jd = new System.DateTime(1997, 8, 29)
            System.DateTime.Now.ToBinary() > jd.ToBinary()
```

Accessing a `static` property is just as it is for most other .NET languages, prefixing the method or property with the type name:

```
let T800 =
    if Skynet.AfterJudgmentDay then
        Skynet.CreateTerminator()
```

```
        else
            new Person("Arnold", "Schwarzenegger", 50)
```

Fields can also be declared as `static`, using `val`-based syntax similar to that seen for instance fields, with all the usual dire warnings about shared state and recommendations to avoid it:

```
[<Class>]
type Skynet() =
    [<DefaultValue>]
    static val mutable private terminatorsBuilt : int64
    static member CreateTerminator() =
        Skynet.terminatorsBuilt <- Skynet.terminatorsBuilt+1L
        new Person("T", "800", 0)
    static member AfterJudgmentDay
        with get() =
            let jd = new System.DateTime(1997, 8, 29)
            System.DateTime.Now.ToBinary() > jd.ToBinary()
```

`Static` fields can also be introduced via `let` declarations:

```
[<Class>]
type Skynet() =
    [<DefaultValue>]
    static val mutable private terminatorsBuilt : int64
    static member CreateTerminator() =
        Skynet.terminatorsBuilt <- Skynet.terminatorsBuilt+1L
        new Person("T", "800", 0)
    static member AfterJudgmentDay
        with get() =
            let jd = new System.DateTime(1997, 8, 29)
            System.DateTime.Now.ToBinary() > jd.ToBinary()
    static let humansKilled = 3000000000L
```

*Code snippet Class.fs*

The static `let` creates an immutable, private field, unless prefixed with the mutable keyword, as described in the discussion about `let`-declared fields earlier in this chapter. Note that just as with the `val`-declared static field, `let`-declared fields also need to be prefixed with the type name when referenced, even within the type itself.

## Operator Overloading

F# permits the definition of methods whose name is actually a set of non-alphanumeric symbols, frequently known as operator overloading in other languages. Technically, that term is inappropriate here, because F# not only allows the definition of methods whose name matches that of traditional operators (+, –, and so on) but also to define new operators that have never been defined before.

Defining an operator is similar to defining a static method, except that the operator symbol is used instead of an alphanumeric name and wrapped in parentheses:

```
[<Class>]
type Munchkin() =
    let mutable lv = 1
    let mutable armor : Item =
```

```
        new Item("Clothes of Ineptitude", "Armor", 0)
    member m.Level
        with get() = lv
    member m.Armor
        with get() = armor
        and set(i) = armor <- i
    member m.GoUpALevel() =
        lv <- lv + 1
    member m.TotalBonus =
        lv + armor.Bonus
    static member (<<==) (m : Munchkin, mi: MunchkinItem) =
        m.Armor <- mi
        m
```

*Code snippet Class.fs*

This then implicitly allows for using the method in an infix style notation, rather than the explicit dot-name style normally used for method invocation:

```
let ted = new Munchkin()
let coolArmor = new Item("Functional Plate","Armor",5)
ted <<== coolArmor
```

When compiled, the operator method will either be compiled using a normal .NET operator method name (such as `op_Greater` for the F# method (>)), or mangled into a method name prefixed with `op_` in the standard .NET convention, as described in the F# specification. The preceding method, for example, will be converted into a static method named `op_LessLessEqualsEquals`.

Normally, operators shouldn't change the value of the objects they operate on, but instead return new objects with the changed value, such as the following:

**Available for download on Wrox.com**

```
[<Class>]
type Complex(r : int32, i : int32) =
    member c.R = r
    member c.I = i
    static member (+) (c1 : Complex, c2 : Complex) =
        new Complex(c1.R + c2.R, c1.I + c2.I)
    static member (-) (c1 : Complex, c2 : Complex) =
        new Complex(c1.R - c2.R, c1.I - c2.I)
```

*Code snippet Class.fs*

In addition to being more functionally stylistic, the second example has no concurrency or mutable state concerns.

As written, the operators defined are *binary* operators, meaning they require two arguments to process; if the operator wants to be *unary*, meaning it takes only a single argument (like the negation operator that takes a positive number and makes it negative, or vice versa), then the operator name must be prefixed with a ~ in its definition:

**Available for download on Wrox.com**

```
[<Class>]
type Complex(r : int32, i : int32) =
    member c.R = r
    member c.I = i
    static member (+) (c1 : Complex, c2 : Complex) =
```

```
        new Complex(c1.R + c2.R, c1.I + c2.I)
    static member (-) (c1 : Complex, c2 : Complex) =
        new Complex(c1.R - c2.R, c1.I - c2.I)
    static member (~-) (c : Complex) =
        new Complex(-(c.R), c.I)
```

*Code snippet Class.fs*

Although the usual warnings about trying to get too tricky or cute with operators applies, because we can define new operators for given types, it offers an opportunity to create terse code that still avoids the "accidental overloading of meaning" that frequently accompanied attempts to do operator overloading in C++. For example, if Persons are frequently being compared against one another using the IComparable.CompareTo() interface method, we can define an operator that performs that comparison tersely:

```
    static member (<==>) (lhs : Person, rhs: Person) =
        match (lhs.FullName.CompareTo(rhs.FullName)) with
        | x when x > 0 || x < 0 -> x
        | _ -> lhs.Age.CompareTo(rhs.Age)
```

This then allows us to do CompareTo() comparisons in traditional infix-style notation:

```
    let compare = p1 <==> p2
```

Some developers claim that this code is too cryptic, but clearly there is no predefined notation of an <==> operator, which then neatly disposes of the principal traditional criticism of operator overloading (that of confused semantics). In any event, as with all features of the language, F# developers are not required to use this, but much of the existing language is defined using these constructs, and it will likely be necessary to at least understand this syntax.

## DELEGATES AND EVENTS

Delegates — in essence, managed function pointers — trace a history back to the earliest days of programming, when C programmers would pass pointers-to-procedures to other routines to allow those routines to "call back" without having predetermined knowledge of what procedures to call. This technique was used for a number of years to allow for a primitive form of higher-order programming (such as is discussed in Chapter 13) and to promote a notification mechanism while still maintaining a decoupling between components. The latter approach is how most delegates are used in .NET, typically in close cooperation with events, though this is changing as functional programming styles begin to permeate through the ecosystem.

Events in F# classes come in two flavors. The first is the basic flavor of event as expressed in other .NET languages, the delegate-centric event, in which clients interested in receiving notifications about an event register a delegate instance (obeying all the traditional laws of delegates, of course) into a language-managed list of delegates via the implicit add and remove methods generated by a language keyword. The other approach, however, is a more powerful mechanism that F# programs can take advantage of some of the core capabilities of the F# language, such as event filtering and lambda expressions, while still offering the same delegate-based functionality to other .NET languages looking to use the F# type.

## Subscribing

The easiest way in which to interact with an event is to register with an existing event, such as those exposed by various parts of the .NET Framework Class Library — one such event is the ProcessExit event, on the AppDomain type, which is fired whenever the process in which the AppDomain is being hosted exits. (For more on AppDomains and their relationship to processes, see http://msdn.microsoft.com/en-us/library/system.appdomain.aspx.)

Obtaining the AppDomain is a no more difficult than calling the appropriate static property on the AppDomain class:

```
let ad = System.AppDomain.CurrentDomain
```

When the AppDomain has been retrieved, however, registering with the ProcessExit requires a delegate instance — one which wraps a method that takes an object and an EventArgs as parameters and returns nothing, in particular. This means that somehow F# has to take an F# method and wrap it into a delegate instance.

Normally, the F# developer will not need explicit delegates, for two reasons. First, because the F# language supports functions as first-class citizens (as is shown in Chapter 13), less need arises to wrap a method up in a delegate to pass it around, as is commonly seen in idiomatic C# and Visual Basic. Second and more important, however, because the F# language was created to have full fidelity and awareness of the underlying CLR platform, the F# compiler will often automatically handle the conversion from an F# function or method to a .NET delegate silently and without explicit programmer intervention. So, for example, if an F# type has a method that satisfies the parameter requirements of the ProcessExit event, it can be passed directly to the event without any further modification:

```
type Watcher() =
    static member GoingAway(args : System.EventArgs) =
        System.Console.WriteLine("Going away now....")

let ad = System.AppDomain.CurrentDomain
ad.ProcessExit.Add(Watcher.GoingAway)
```

In truth, many additional things are happening "under the hood" in the preceding code, but for the vast majority of .NET FCL events, this will be sufficient. Deeper understanding, however, requires a deeper exploration of delegates before the F# support around delegates and events can be appreciated.

## Delegates

Formally, a delegate instance is an instance of the type System.Delegate, or as is most often the case, of its subtype System.MulticastDelegate. Delegate instances are most often constructed by the C# or Visual Basic compiler "behind the scenes," in response to the developer using a language keyword (such as delegate) indicating that a delegate is wanted. Delegates must be created to be of a particular declared delegate type, again typically declared using a keyword and a syntax that looks much like a method or procedure declaration.

At first glance, F#'s delegate support is not much different than its sister languages' support. Declaring an explicit delegate type, for example, uses the `delegate` keyword and an explicit function signature:

```
type Notify = delegate of string -> string
```

In .NET parlance, this creates a class that inherits from `System.MulticastDelegate`, just as if it had been declared in C# or Visual Basic. This means, among other things, that it has the implicit `Invoke` and `BeginInvoke`/`EndInvoke` methods present on delegate types declared from those languages and can be used just as any other delegate instance can.

And, in keeping with the delegate spirit, creating an instance of this delegate type occurs just as it does in other .NET languages — the object is `new`'ed, passing a reference to the method or function to wrap when the delegate is invoked:

```
type Child() =
    member this.Respond(msg : string) =
        System.Console.WriteLine("You want me to {0}? No!", msg)
        "No!"

let c = new Child()
let np = new Notify(c.Respond)
let response = np.Invoke("Clean your room!")
System.Console.WriteLine(response)
```

*Code snippet Class.fs*

Notice, however, that where C# or Visual Basic makes the invocation of the delegate occur "just as if" it were a method or function, F# requires the explicit method call to `Invoke` to invoke the delegate's wrapped method.

Because this is an instance of `MulticastDelegate`, all the operations and behaviors familiar to .NET developers — chaining them via the `Combine` method, invoking them asynchronously via the `BeginInvoke`/`EndInvoke` pair, and so on — are equally supported. Anything the C#-declared delegate can do, the F#-declared delegate can also do.

It is important to note, however, that if the F#-declared delegate is intended to be used from other languages, the exact declaration of the delegate type is crucial. In particular, F# developers must pay close attention to the difference between curried-argument and tupled-argument forms of delegates:

```
type CurriedDelegate = delegate of int * int -> int
type TupledDelegate = delegate of (int * int) -> int
type DelegateTarget() =
    member this.CurriedAdd (x : int) (y : int) = x + y
    member this.TupledAdd (x : int, y : int) = x + y
```

*Code snippet Class.fs*

And attempting to use a method declared in one form with a delegate declared in the other form will result in an error — curried-argument methods can only be used in curried-argument delegates and ditto for tupled-argument methods and delegates:

```
let dt = new DelegateTarget()
let cd1 = new CurriedDelegate(dt.CurriedAdd)
//let cd2 = new CurriedDelegate(dt.TupledAdd)
      // will not compile
let td1 = new TupledDelegate(dt.TupledAdd)
//let td2 = new TupledDelegate(dt.CurriedAdd)
      // will not compile
```

The F# compiler will quickly disabuse any developer trying to use one for the other, however, so in practice this turns out to be less of a concern than it might seem at first. For the C# and Visual Basic developer, these two delegate types will be night-and-day different, and no confusion will be apparent. (Which form is easier to use from C# or Visual Basic is a subject of some debate and probably will remain so.)

## DelegateEvents

Creating a delegate-based event on an F# type requires the F# developer to create a member of DelegateEvent type, which (because this is a generic) requires a type parameter describing the kind of delegate to use as the event notification callback. So, for example, if an F# type, such as the following, modeling a rock band:

```
type RockBand(name : string) =
    member rb.Name = name
    member rb.HoldConcert(city : string) =
        System.Console.WriteLine("Rockin' {0}!")
```

*Code snippet Class.fs*

wants to notify its fan club:

```
type Fan(home : string) =
    member f.FavoriteBandComingToTown(city : string) =
        if home = city then
            System.Console.WriteLine("I'm SO going!")
        else
            System.Console.WriteLine("Darn")
```

*Code snippet Class.fs*

when it tours a particular city, it must expose an event of type ConcertHandler:

```
type ConcertHandler = delegate of obj * string -> unit
type RockBand(name : string) =
    let concertEvent = new DelegateEvent<ConcertHandler>()

    member rb.Name = name

    [<CLIEvent>]
```

```
member rb.OnConcert = concertEvent.Publish
member rb.HoldConcert(city : string) =
    concertEvent.Trigger( [| rb; city |] )
    System.Console.WriteLine("Rockin' {0}!", city)
```

so that the `Fan` can register with the `RockBand` and receive those updates:

```
type Fan(home : string, favBand : RockBand) as f =
    do
        favBand.OnConcert.AddHandler(ConcertHandler(
            f.FavoriteBandComingToTown))
    member f.FavoriteBandComingToTown (_: obj) (city : string) =
        if home = city then
            System.Console.WriteLine("I'm SO going!")
        else
            System.Console.WriteLine("Darn")
```

Such that now, creating a `RockBand` and a few `Fans`:

```
let rb = new RockBand("The Functional Ya-Yas")
let f1 = new Fan("Detroit", rb)
let f2 = new Fan("Cleveland", rb)
let f3 = new Fan("Detroit", rb)
rb.HoldConcert("Detroit")
```

when the `RockBand` goes on tour, the `Fans` will be notified appropriately.

Of course, experienced .NET developers will find that the delegate type behind this event-handling example to be of an inferior and older style — the preferred style, starting in .NET 2.0, is to use the FCL-declared `EventHandler` type, which (were it to be declared in F#) looks like this:

```
type EventHandler = delegate of obj * System.EventArgs -> unit
```

Where the first parameter is the "sender" of the event (the `RockBand`) and the second parameter is an `EventArgs`-derived class that serves as a collection of data elements describing the event. So, adjusting to this more appropriate style, the preceding code transforms into something more .NET-ecosystem-friendly:

```
type ConcertEventArgs(city : string) =
    inherit System.EventArgs()
    member cea.City = city
    override cea.ToString() =
        System.String.Format("city:{0}", city)

type RockBand(name : string) =
    let concertEvent = new DelegateEvent<System.EventHandler>()

    member rb.Name = name

    [<CLIEvent>]
    member rb.OnConcert = concertEvent.Publish
    member rb.HoldConcert(city : string) =
        concertEvent.Trigger([| rb;
            new ConcertEventArgs(city) |])
```

```
            System.Console.WriteLine("Rockin' {0}!", city)

    type Fan(home : string, favBand : RockBand) as f =
        do
            favBand.OnConcert.AddHandler(
                System.EventHandler(f.FavoriteBandComingToTown))
        member f.FavoriteBandComingToTown
                (_ : obj)
                (args : System.EventArgs) =
            let cea = args :?> ConcertEventArgs
            if home = cea.City then
                System.Console.WriteLine("I'm SO going!")
            else
                System.Console.WriteLine("Darn")
```

*Code snippet Class.fs*

The "_" in the `FavoriteBandComingToTown` method is the placeholder argument name, indicating the method never uses it and therefore feels no need to give it a name, and the `:?>` in the method body is the dynamic downcast operator, as described more in Chapter 9, to convert the passed parameter to a `ConcertEventArgs` type.

Stylistically, the event handler in the `Fan` class will often be an anonymous function, written like so:

```
    type Fan(home : string, favBand : RockBand) as f =
        do
            favBand.OnConcert.AddHandler(
                fun (_ : obj) (args : System.EventArgs) ->
                    let cea = args :?> ConcertEventArgs
                    if home = cea.City then
                        System.Console.WriteLine("I'm SO going!")
                    else
                        System.Console.WriteLine("Darn")
                )
```

There is no structural difference between the two approaches (anonymous event handler vs. named method), so developers should choose whichever appeals more to their sense of aesthetics.

## Beyond DelegateEvents: Events

As it stands, the support for events in F# demonstrated thus far is somewhat lukewarm — a good argument could be made that the support for events found in C# or Visual Basic rivals or even surpasses this. However, F# also adds additional support for handling events in a more functional style via the `Event` module, such as processing events in a stream using pipelines and filters. (Currying is covered in Chapter 13, and pipelining is covered in Chapter 17.)

For example, the `Event.add` function will take a function (member or otherwise) and register it on the exposed event, and `Event.filter` will take a function yielding a Boolean result, and only pass the event on if the filter function returns `true`:

```
    rb.OnConcert
        |> Event.filter
            (fun evArgs ->
                let cea = evArgs :?> ConcertEventArgs
```

```
                            if cea.City = "Sacramento" then false
                                // Sacramento is dead to rock bands
                            else true)
            |> Event.add
                (fun evArgs ->
                    let cea = evArgs :?> ConcertEventArgs
                    System.Console.WriteLine("{0} is rockin' {1}",
                        rb.Name, cea.City))
```

*Code snippet Class.fs*

This can create powerful event-handling effects, particularly given the various functions found in the `Event` module. F# developers doing event-handling would be well-advised to experiment with the functions found there before writing significant amounts of event-handler code.

Events can also be exposed to F#-only code by constructing an instance of the `Event<>` type and registering functions to be called when the event is triggered (via the event's `Trigger` method) by calling `Event.add`, in much the same way that `DelegateEvent` operates. The `Event` object has the advantage that it is simply an object, and not a keyword or special language element, but has the disadvantage that it works only with other F# code.

## ACCESS MODIFIERS

Access modifiers are used to control the visibility of members within a type, ranging from "accessible to any element in the CLR process space" (`public`), to "accessible to elements only within this same type" (`private`). As has already been seen, however, normally the F# compiler infers an appropriate default access modifier for most members, making the need for an explicit access modifier unnecessary.

When more control over the access control of a particular member is wanted, an access modifier can appear on the member declaration, after the `member` keyword but before the member name (and self-identifier prefix, if this is an instance member):

```
[<Class>]
type Sport(name) =
    member private p.Rules
        with get() = ""
```

The available access control modifiers are more or less synonymous with the list of modifiers found in the C# and Visual Basic languages:

➤ `public`: No restrictions on access; any other .NET program element can find and use this element.

➤ `private`: Access is permitted only from the enclosing type (or module or namespace).

➤ `internal`: Access is permitted only from the assembly in which this element is defined.

In addition, the F# language implementers have already earmarked the keyword `protected`, presumably to introduce it into a future version of F# to serve as an access modifier similar to its C# cousin (access permitted only from the enclosing type or one of its derived types).

F# permits access modifiers on a variety of different parts of the type, including methods, properties (both `get` and `set` clauses, which may not need be set at the same level of accessibility), constructors (except the primary constructor), or fields. F# requires that any `let` bindings inside the class must always be `internal`, so no access modifier is ever allowed on these.

There are a few syntactic restrictions in certain places. In the case of constructors, the access modifier appears before the `new` keyword. When used on a `val`-declared field, the access modifier must appear after the "mutable" keyword (if present).

F# also permits types to be decorated with access modifiers, in much the same way that individual members of a type can be decorated. In the case of a type, the access modifier appears after the `type` keyword but before its name:

```
[<Class>]
type internal Sport(name) =
    member p.Rules
        with get() = ""
```

In the case of a "private" type, the type will not be visible outside of the file in which it is declared; the reason for this will be made clearer in Chapter 11 when we talk about modules and namespaces. In addition, the primary constructor of a type will be granted the same visibility as that of the type itself, because it's exceedingly rare that a type would want a primary constructor's accessibility to be different than the type's.

The default accessibility of declared elements in an F# class is as follows:

```
[<Class>]
type (* public *) ExampleClass(field1 : string) =
    [<DefaultValue>]
    val mutable (* private *) valField : string

    // Always private
    let mutable mutField2 = "Changeable"
    let helper = field1 + ", helped"

    (* public *)
    new () =
        ExampleClass("")

    member (* public *) e.Property
        with (* public *) get() = field1
    member (* public *) e.ReadWriteProp
        with (* public *) get() = mutField2
        and (* public *) set(value) = mutField2 <- value
```

*Code snippet Class.fs*

In general, as mentioned, given that `member`-declared elements are marked public by default and `let` bindings as internal (that is, assemblywide accessible) by default, most F# developers find that they will not be reaching for access modifiers nearly as often as their C# or Visual Basic brethren.

Although unusual, it is possible to define private constructors on types, even the primary constructor, using the following syntax:

```
[<Class>]
type PrivatePerson private(fn, ln, a) =
    private new() = PrivatePerson("", "", 0)
    static member Create(fn, ln, a) = new PrivatePerson(fn, ln, a)
    static member Create() = new PrivatePerson()
```

Typically, the private constructor is used to prevent direct construction and instead defer construction through a "factory method," such as that defined in the preceding example.

## TYPE EXTENSIONS

Historically, object-oriented developers have found themselves caught on the horns of dilemma: To make it easiest to maintain code, it's best to encapsulate details about the class, but frequently that same maintenance requires extending a class in ways the class creator never intended and therefore never provided easy access to. As a result, some developers have taken to such drastic (and counterintuitive) actions such as declaring all fields and methods as "protected" at the least, so as to allow maintainers to extend a class and have full access to the internals of that class. Unfortunately, such actions have historically led to unmaintainable code over time, because now the guarantees that encapsulation was supposed to provide (reassurance that all the code that modifies a given field is contained inside one class) are now broken.

With the introduction of C# 3.0, Microsoft changed the game somewhat, introducing *extension methods*, static methods defined on a third-party class that can appear as if they were declared on the original class, without requiring an inheritance relationship. F# provides a similar feature, known as *type extensions*, to do much the same kind of thing, but in a slightly simpler manner and with greater capability.

Assume an F# developer has found necessary reason to extend a class defined like this:

```
[<Class>]
type Student(name : string, subject : string) =
    member s.Name = name
    member s.Subject = subject
```

If the code is being extended within the same namespace or module as the original definition, then the extension is called an *intrinsic extension* (because the code extension is intrinsic to the same unit where it is being defined), and basically the compiler will stitch together the definitions into a single type in much the same way it does for partial type definitions in C# or Visual Basic. Otherwise, the extension code must be in a module (see Chapter 11 for a discussion on the differences between namespaces and modules), and it is called an *extension member*. When the module containing an extension member is opened, that member becomes available as if it were an instance or static method defined on the type originally, again much like the C# 3.0 extension method facility.

Syntactically, defining a type extension looks something like a type definition, with some restrictions:

```
type Student with
    member s.FullDescription = s.Name + " " + s.Subject
```

Because the compiler is playing some syntactic games here, and not changing the basic definition of the type's internals, no new fields may be added to the type, whether as `val` declarations or `let` declarations.

Type extensions can add constructors:

```
type Student with
    new() = Student("", "")
    member s.FullDescription = s.Name + " " + s.Subject
```

And although it doesn't make much sense to do so without the ability to define fields, it's possible to introduce constructors that take additional parameters beyond the constructors defined on the original type:

**Available for download on Wrox.com**

```
type Student with
    new() = Student("", "")
    new(name, subject, school) =
        Student(name, subject)
    member s.FullDescription = s.Name + " " + s.Subject
```

*Code snippet Class.fs*

Static members (and, by extension, "operators") are also fair game, as are instance and static methods.

Because type extensions are not part of the type, the type extension has no additional access to private members as any other method or function of any other type would have — that is to say, it has none and attempts to reference private members will generate a compile-time error.

Because this functionality is effectively a product of the compiler, type extensions can operate on any type defined in the .NET environment, including those defined in the Base Class Library:

```
type System.String with
    member s.IsUpper =
        s.ToUpper() = s
```

However, in general, type extensions should be treated with care, because now functionality relating to a class is being "spread out" over several different locations, which contradicts the basic point of object-oriented development, to gather up all the concerns relating to a given idea into a single location (the class). As with many language features, when used judiciously, type extensions can simplify code significantly, but when flagrantly tossed around, type extensions can render otherwise well-written code into a mess that not even a mother would love (or could read).

# SUMMARY

F# supports a full range of object-oriented features for defining traditional class design, and a few new ideas that either are missing entirely from its siblings in the Visual Studio environment or are just being introduced. However, our romp through the object-oriented world of F# is not yet complete because F# also supports inheritance, and no discussion of object-orientation would be complete without it.

# 9

# Inheritance

**WHAT'S IN THIS CHAPTER?**

➤ Understanding inheritance in F#

➤ Understanding field and constructor invocation

➤ Using casts

➤ Defining and using interfaces

➤ Applying object expressions

Within the object-oriented parlance, inheritance is frequently used to mean implementation inheritance, where a given type can express a relationship to another type, effectively importing all the data and behavior of that parent type. Originally thought (in Smalltalk and C++) to be a staple of the object-oriented design process, then later criticized and revamped to split into implementation and interface inheritance in languages such as Java and C#, inheritance nonetheless represents a powerful and useful technique for not only expressing relationships between types, but also in ensuring that behavior relating to a group of types remains defined in precisely one place. As a full-fledged member of the object-oriented family of languages, F# offers full support for inheritance between types, with the additional "twists" that come with a new language.

## BASICS

Assume that there is a base type defined in F# (or, if wanted, in another .NET language), something along the lines of:

**Available for download on Wrox.com**

```
[<Class>]
type Person(fn, ln, a) =
    member p.FirstName = fn
    member p.LastName = ln
    member p.Age = a
```

*Code snippet Inheritance.fs*

We can define a new type that inherits from this base type by referencing it in the opening lines of the derived type definition:

```
[<Class>]
type Student(fn, ln, a, sub, sch) =
    inherit Person(fn, ln, a)
    member p.Subject = sub
    member p.School = sch
```

*Code snippet Inheritance.fs*

This establishes an IS-A relationship between the derived type and the base type, such that any members defined on the base type are also accessible in the derived type, in addition to those members defined on the derived type, as expected:

```
let s = new Student("Ted", "Pattison", 50, "Beer",
                    "DevelopMentor")
System.Console.WriteLine("{0} {1} attends {2} and studies {3}",
        s.FirstName, s.LastName, s.School, s.Subject)
```

By default, as is the norm for any language running on top of the .NET framework, if a class does not explicitly define an inheritance relationship, it inherits from the ultimate base class, System. Object. This means that every type in F#, like every type defined in C# or Visual Basic, ultimately extends that core base type, either directly or indirectly through its parent type.

Any type that derives from a base type can be passed where a base type is expected, and this serves as the basis for classic object-oriented polymorphism. Normally, F# type inference can make this less obvious than what is seen in other object-oriented languages, but type descriptors can make this relationship obvious:

```
[<Class>]
type Person(fn, ln, a) =
    member p.FirstName = fn
    member p.LastName = ln
    member p.Age = a
    member p.Greet(other : Person) =
        System.Console.WriteLine("Howdy, {0}, from {1}!",
            other.FirstName, p.FirstName)
```

*Code snippet Inheritance.fs*

Passing a Student in for the expected Person works as expected:

```
let s = new Student("Ted", "Pattison", 50, "Beer",
                    "DevelopMentor")
let p = new Person("Ted", "Neward", 38)
p.Greet(s)
```

Note that, as previously mentioned, the base type could easily be one defined in C# or Visual Basic and the derived type in F#, or vice versa. With little restriction, inheritance is free to operate across language lines on the CLR.

## Fields and Constructors

Frequently, a derived type introduces not only new methods and properties, but also new data elements to be stored within the object instance. In F#, because the data elements are often introduced via the primary constructor, the syntax for introducing new data elements on the derived type is remarkably simple, as shown here:

```
[<Class>]
type Person(fn, ln, a) =
    member p.FirstName = fn
    member p.LastName = ln
    member p.Age = a
    member p.Greet(other : Person) =
        System.Console.WriteLine("Howdy, {0}, from {1}!",
            other.FirstName, p.FirstName)

[<Class>]
type Student(fn, ln, a, sub, sch) =
    inherit Person(fn, ln, a)
    member p.Subject = sub
    member p.School = sch
```

*Code snippet Inheritance.fs*

Just as the primary constructor in the base class silently introduces fields to hold those constructor values throughout the lifetime of the object instance, the primary constructor in the derived class also introduces fields. However, for those data elements that are passed up to the base class constructor through the `inherit` clause, the F# compiler is smart enough not to re-introduce the same fields twice; in other words, in the preceding example, the F# compiler knows that the first three parameters are destined for the base class, and as a result the `Student` type has two fields defined within it, rather than five.

However, if the derived type references any of the parameters defined in the constructor, the story changes:

```
[<Class>]
type Student(fn, ln, a, sub, sch) =
    inherit Person(fn, ln, a)
    member s.FormalName = fn + " " + " of " + sch
    member s.Subject = sub
    member s.School = sch
```

*Code snippet Inheritance.fs*

Here, because a data element defined in the primary constructor is directly referenced within the definition of the derived class, the F# compiler creates a new field in the derived class to hold that data. This means that now the data is being duplicated — once in a field in the base part of the object, and once in a field in the derived part of the object.

To avoid this, the derived class can use the property defined on the base class:

```
[<Class>]
type Student(fn, ln, a, sub, sch) =
    inherit Person(fn, ln, a)
    member s.FormalName = s.FirstName + " " + " of " + sch
    member s.Subject = sub
    member s.School = sch
```

This will also have the nice effect of ensuring that any additional logic around the field defined in the property-get clause is being invoked, such as any calculation, lazy-resolution, or caching behavior.

As with any inheritance relationship in .NET, the derived class must invoke a base class constructor, but any such constructor is fair game:

**Available for download on Wrox.com**

```
[<Class>]
type Person(fn, ln, a) =
    new() = Person("", "", 0)
    member p.FirstName = fn
    member p.LastName = ln
    member p.Age = a
    member p.Greet(other : Person) =
        System.Console.WriteLine("Howdy, {0}, from {1}!",
            other.FirstName, p.FirstName)

[<Class>]
type Student(fn, ln, a, sub, sch) =
    inherit Person()
    member s.FormalName = s.FirstName + " " + " of " + sch
    member s.Subject = sub
    member s.School = sch
```

*Code snippet Inheritance.fs*

And of course, the derived type is free to define its own constructors beyond the primary constructor, delegating to the primary constructor of the derived type (which then defers to the base type constructor, and so on up the inheritance chain):

**Available for download on Wrox.com**

```
[<Class>]
type Student(fn, ln, a, sub, sch) =
    inherit Person()
    new() = Student("", "", 0, "", "")
    new(fn, ln, a) = Student(fn, ln, a, "", "")
    member s.FormalName = s.FirstName + " " + " of " + sch
    member s.Subject = sub
    member s.School = sch
```

*Code snippet Inheritance.fs*

If the derived type wants any private `let`-bindings or `do` expressions, they appear after the `inherit` clause but before any member declarations:

**Available for download on Wrox.com**

```
[<Class>]
type Student(fn, ln, a, sub, sch) =
    inherit Person()
    let gpa = 0.0
    do System.Console.WriteLine("Whoo-hoo! College!")
```

```
new() = Student("", "", 0, "", "")
new(fn, ln, a) = Student(fn, ln, a, "", "")
member s.FormalName = s.FirstName + " " + " of " + sch
member s.Subject = sub
member s.School = sch
```

*Code snippet Inheritance.fs*

If the derived type provides a primary constructor, there is no way for a derived type constructor to directly invoke a base type constructor — all invocation must be done through the primary constructor on the derived type, which then defers to the base constructor of choice.

But in cases where a primary constructor is missing or left out for the derived type, the derived type must specify in its own constructor which base type constructor to invoke:

**Available for download on Wrox.com**

```
[<Class>]
type Person2 =
    val firstName : string
    val lastName : string
    val age : int32
    new(fn, ln, a) = { firstName=fn; lastName=ln; age=a }
    new() = { firstName = ""; lastName = ""; age = 0 }
    member p.FirstName = p.firstName
    member p.LastName = p.lastName
    member p.Age = p.age

[<Class>]
type Student2 =
    inherit Person2
    val subject : string
    val school : string
    new(fn, ln, a, subj, sch) =
        { inherit Person2(fn, ln, a); subject = subj; school = sch}
    member s.Subject = s.subject
    member s.School = s.school
```

*Code snippet Inheritance.fs*

Note that the presence or absence of a primary constructor in the base type makes no difference to the derived type:

**Available for download on Wrox.com**

```
[<Class>]
type Person2(fn, ln, a) =
    let firstName = fn
    let lastName = ln
    let age = a
    new() = Person2("", "", 0)
    member p.FirstName = firstName
    member p.LastName = lastName
    member p.Age = age

[<Class>]
type Student2 =
    inherit Person2
    val subject : string
```

```
val school : string
new(fn, ln, a, subj, sch) =
    { inherit Person2(fn, ln, a); subject = subj; school = sch}
new() =
    { inherit Person2(); subject = ""; school = "" }
member s.Subject = s.subject
member s.School = s.school
```

*Code snippet Inheritance.fs*

However, given the prevalence and usefulness of primary constructors, it's not likely that F# developers will see this form used a great deal.

## OVERRIDING

As previously mentioned, when a type inherits from a base type, it picks up all the behavior of that base type. For example, every type defined in F# will automatically inherit the `ToString()` method (among others) from the `System.Object` base type, because every class in the .NET ecosystem ultimately inherits from `System.Object`. However, the default behavior of `ToString()` leaves something to be desired for most types, as it usually just prints out the type name:

```
let p = new Person("Ken", "Sipe", 40)
let p_str = p.ToString()
System.Console.WriteLine(p_str)
    // prints "Inheritance+Person"
```

This behavior, although nice to have picked up without requiring any additional work on our part, is not nice enough to keep.

Fortunately, as most C# or Visual Basic developers already know, the .NET environment allows derived classes to override (replace) the behavior of a base type method by defining the same method on the derived type, and F# is no different:

```
[<Class>]
type Person(fn, ln, a) =
    new() = Person("", "", 0)
    member p.FirstName = fn
    member p.LastName = ln
    member p.Age = a
    member p.Greet(other : Person) =
        System.Console.WriteLine("Howdy, {0}, from {1}!",
            other.FirstName, p.FirstName)
    override p.ToString() =
        System.String.Format("[Person: {0} {1} {2}]",
            fn, ln, a)
```

*Code snippet Inheritance.fs*

The key difference to a method attempting to override a base type method and defining a new method member is the use of the keyword `override` in place of `member`. The compiler then ensures that the method name and its signature are exactly identical to a method defined as overridable in the base type, and if not, it will signal an error.

*Note that it is still possible to introduce a new method of the same name and signature, but doing so "hides" the base type method of that name and generates a warning from the compiler. This is sometimes desirable behavior, referred to as shadowing, but usually means the developer didn't realize said method already exists. As a general practice shadowing should be avoided.*

If the overriding method body wants to invoke the base type method body, it can do so using the predefined keyword `base` to refer to the base type:

```
[<Class>]
type Person(fn, ln, a) =
    new() = Person("", "", 0)
    member p.FirstName = fn
    member p.LastName = ln
    member p.Age = a
    member p.Greet(other : Person) =
        System.Console.WriteLine("Howdy, {0}, from {1}!",
            other.FirstName, p.FirstName)
    override p.ToString() =
        let typename = base.ToString()
        System.String.Format("[{3}: {0} {1} {2}]",
            fn, ln, a, "")
```

However, doing so is an error unless the type has an explicit `inherit` clause; in other words, the preceding example is an error until it is modified to read:

```
[<Class>]
type Person(fn, ln, a) =
    inherit System.Object()
    new() = Person("", "", 0)
    member p.FirstName = fn
    member p.LastName = ln
    member p.Age = a
    member p.Greet(other : Person) =
        System.Console.WriteLine("Howdy, {0}, from {1}!",
            other.FirstName, p.FirstName)
    override p.ToString() =
        let typename = base.ToString()
        System.String.Format("[{3}: {0} {1} {2}]",
            fn, ln, a, "")
```

*Code snippet Inheritance.fs*

Note that other members, namely properties, can also be overridden, just as methods can. The syntax for doing so remains identical to that shown here. (That is, instead of using `member`, use `override`.)

# Abstract Members

Frequently, a base type want to ensure that derived types create custom behavior specific to them — in F#, this is done via the `abstract` keyword, and requires a slightly different syntax than has been seen thus far. Specifically, designating a member as `abstract` requires that the type descriptor of the member be provided, which in the case of a method is its method signature:

```
[<Class>]
type Person(fn, ln, a) =
    inherit System.Object()
    new() = Person("", "", 0)
    member p.FirstName = fn
    member p.LastName = ln
    member p.Age = a
    member p.Greet(other : Person) =
        System.Console.WriteLine("Howdy, {0}, from {1}!",
            other.FirstName, p.FirstName)
    override p.ToString() =
        let typename = base.ToString()
        System.String.Format("[{3}: {0} {1} {2}]",
            fn, ln, a, "")
    abstract Work : unit -> unit
```

*Code snippet Inheritance.fs*

The syntax for a method signature is slightly different than might be expected — as with most languages, it describes the parameters and return type of the method, but instead of comma-separated lists of parameters wrapped by parentheses (such as is seen in C#), F# uses an arrow-based notation, with each parameter separated by a right-arrow and the return type appearing at the end of the notation.

> *This arrow-based notation is in keeping with F#'s historical roots, namely that of the ML language. Interested readers can either read Ullman's* The ML Programming Language *for why this syntax makes sense, or flip forward to the discussion on curried methods in Chapter 13.*

If the type defines an abstract method, such as the previous example, then the type itself must be marked with the `AbstractClass` attribute instead of the `Class` attribute. In addition to marking the class with an `abstract` modifier at the CLR level, the F# compiler and .NET runtime prevent direct instantiation of this type, and derived types must provide an overridden method implementation of all abstract methods before they can be instantiated:

```
[<AbstractClass>]
type Person(fn, ln, a) =
    inherit System.Object()
//    new() = Person("", "", 0)
    member p.FirstName = fn
    member p.LastName = ln
    member p.Age = a
    member p.Greet(other : Person) =
```

```
                System.Console.WriteLine("Howdy, {0}, from {1}!",
                    other.FirstName, p.FirstName)
        override p.ToString() =
            let typename = base.ToString()
            System.String.Format("[{3}: {0} {1} {2}]",
                fn, ln, a, "")
        abstract Work : unit -> unit

    [<Class>]
    type Student(fn, ln, a, sub, sch) =
        inherit Person(fn, ln, a)
        let gpa = 0.0
        do System.Console.WriteLine("Whoo-hoo! College!")
        new() = Student("", "", 0, "", "")
        new(fn, ln, a) = Student(fn, ln, a, "", "")
        member s.FormalName = s.FirstName + " " + " of " + sch
        member s.Subject = sub
        member s.School = sch
        override s.Work() =
            System.Console.WriteLine("Studying!")
```

*Code snippet Inheritance.fs*

Note that the second constructor defined in the preceding base type must now be commented out, because the base type is defined as abstract and therefore cannot be instantiated. The primary constructor, on the other hand, remains unaffected.

## Default

If a type wants to provide opportunity for derived types to customize a method, yet still provide an implementation that derived types can use as is without customization, F# allows the type to define a "default" member to go along with the abstract member declaration. This pair of actions corresponds to the `virtual` keyword in C# or the `Overridable` keyword in Visual Basic:

```
    [<Class>]
    type Person(fn, ln, a) =
        inherit System.Object()
        new() = Person("", "", 0)
        member p.FirstName = fn
        member p.LastName = ln
        member p.Age = a
        member p.Greet(other : Person) =
            System.Console.WriteLine("Howdy, {0}, from {1}!",
                other.FirstName, p.FirstName)
        override p.ToString() =
            let typename = base.ToString()
            System.String.Format("[{3}: {0} {1} {2}]",
                fn, ln, a, "")
        abstract Work : unit -> unit
        default p.Work() =
            System.Console.WriteLine("Working!")
```

*Code snippet Inheritance.fs*

Both the `abstract` declaration and the `default` implementation are required to mark this as an overridable method. Omitting the `abstract` declaration will cause the compiler to complain about not finding an abstract member to override with the default implementation, and omitting the default implementation will require the type to be marked as `AbstractClass` to avoid an error.

As previously mentioned, any member (method or property) can be marked as abstract, and similarly, any member can be implemented with a default implementation:

```
[<Class>]
type Person(fn, ln, a) =
    inherit System.Object()
    new() = Person("", "", 0)
    member p.FirstName = fn
    member p.LastName = ln
    member p.Age = a
    member p.Greet(other : Person) =
        System.Console.WriteLine("Howdy, {0}, from {1}!",
            other.FirstName, p.FirstName)
    override p.ToString() =
        let typename = base.ToString()
        System.String.Format("[{3}: {0} {1} {2}]",
            fn, ln, a, "")
    abstract Work : unit -> unit
    default p.Work() =
        System.Console.WriteLine("Working!")
    abstract Salary : int32 with get
    default p.Salary
        with get() = 0
```

Property members, as always, can be specified as `get`, `set`, or both and can even be "split" across types, one implemented on the base type and one on the derived:

**Available for download on Wrox.com**

```
[<AbstractClass>]
type Person(fn, ln, a) =
    inherit System.Object()
    member p.FirstName = fn
    member p.LastName = ln
    member p.Age = a
    member p.Greet(other : Person) =
        System.Console.WriteLine("Howdy, {0}, from {1}!",
            other.FirstName, p.FirstName)
    override p.ToString() =
        let typename = base.ToString()
        System.String.Format("[{3}: {0} {1} {2}]",
            fn, ln, a, "")
    abstract Work : unit -> unit
    default p.Work() =
        System.Console.WriteLine("Working!")
    abstract Salary : int32 with get, set
    default p.Salary
        with get() = 0

[<Class>]
type Student(fn, ln, a, sub, sch) =
```

```
inherit Person(fn, ln, a)
let gpa = 0.0
do System.Console.WriteLine("Whoo-hoo! College!")
new() = Student("", "", 0, "", "")
new(fn, ln, a) = Student(fn, ln, a, "", "")
member s.FormalName = s.FirstName + " " + " of " + sch
member s.Subject = sub
member s.School = sch
override s.Work() =
    System.Console.WriteLine("Studying!")
override s.Salary
    with set(v) = System.Console.WriteLine(v)
```

*Code snippet Inheritance.fs*

It's not often that splitting up the behavior of a property is necessary, but it's always comforting to know that such a solution is possible for those odd situations where it is needed.

 *For the CLR-trivia-minded, the CLR actually supports an even deeper "split," in that IL allows for the definition of a property where a* get *is abstract/virtual and a* set *is not, or vice versa. Earlier versions of F# accidentally supported this, but this was removed in Beta 2.*

## CASTING

Frequently, when using inheritance, it's important to know whether a given object instance is of a particular derived type; remember, in the .NET environment, a reference to an object isn't always pointing to the object of that derived type, because, as described earlier, a derived type object can be passed anywhere a base type is expected:

```
[<Class>]
type Person(fn, ln, a) =
    // . . . as above

[<Class>]
type Student(fn, ln, a, sub, sch) =
    // . . . as above

let s = new Student("Ted", "Pattison", 50, "Beer",
                    "DevelopMentor")
let p = new Person("Ted", "Neward", 38)
p.Greet(s)
```

In this particular example, the method defined has no real idea what kind of object is passed in, other than that at some point in its inheritance chain, Person is involved. To discover more about the actual object passed in, F# permits several different kinds of casting operations, using different cast operators, depending on the exact kind of cast desired.

## Upcasting

Normally, in an object-oriented language, casting an object to a base type reference is not necessary, because the language can do that kind of conversion automatically, just as it does with `ints` to `longs`, for example. And, normally, in a type-inferenced language, the compiler can be trusted to infer the right kind of reference when an object is used or created.

Occasionally, however, it's necessary to work with a reference of a base type, and because F# doesn't do any implicit conversion, problems can emerge. For example, simply trying to create a reference to a base type and point it to a derived type object will fail:

```
// This will NOT compile
let p : Person = new Student("Ken", "Sipe", 40)
```

Despite that `Student` inherits from `Person`, F# will not allow this to compile. Technically, this is an illegal statement in any language — because `Person` and `Student` are not the same type, it shouldn't compile. For the most part, developers have never seen this as an error only because C# and Visual Basic allow for an implicit conversion — the upcast from `Student` to `Person`.

Because F# doesn't do any implicit conversion, an explicit upcast is necessary. Doing this in F# uses an operator (`:>`) and the type to convert to, like this:

```
let p = new Student("Ken", "Sipe", 40) :> Person
```

Like almost all other language bits in F#, use of the `:>` is an expression — it returns a reference of the type described on the right side. The left operand is the object or reference upon which to perform the cast, and the right operand is the type to which to cast. The correctness of this cast is checked at compile-time, because the compiler should have all the information by which to ensure that this is a legal operation, so this cast will either succeed or fail to compile.

Although not as commonly used, the `:>` operator can also be replaced by `upcast`, whose syntax looks somewhat similar to that of the operator:

```
let p2 : Person = upcast new Student("Ken", "Sipe", 40)
```

In this case, however, the type to which the reference is being converted is inferred from the left side of the expression, making `upcast` slightly more terse than the operator equivalent. However, in practice, `:>` shows up more often in F# code, because the type often cannot be inferred correctly when using upcast.

## Downcasting

The opposite of the upcast, of course, is the familiar `downcast`, known and loved (and hated) by millions of developers, wherein the language attempts to take an object of a derived type being referenced by a base type and produce a reference to the derived type. In F#, this is done again with an operator, the `:?>` operator:

```
let p : Person = new Student("Ken", "Sipe", 40) :> Person
let s : Student = p :?> Student
```

Because the legitimacy of this cast cannot be known until runtime, F# programmers should put the same kind of defensiveness around this operation as C# and Visual Basic developers do around any casts performed there. In the event the downcast fails, the usual .NET `ClassCastException` is thrown.

To avoid the potential `ClassCastException`, an object can be tested to see if it will be successfully castable using the `:?` operator. It's used much the same way as the `downcast` operator, except that it returns a bool value indicating whether the cast is successful.

Like upcasting, downcasts can also be written in a keyword-like form using `downcast`:

```
let p2 : Person = upcast new Student("Ken", "Sipe", 40)
let s2 : Student = downcast p2
```

Again, as with upcast, the use of downcast is relatively rare and is only useful in those situations where the type to which to cast is easily inferable from the left side of the expression, which usually acts enough of a restriction to make the `:?>` operator preferable.

## Flexible Types

Because upcasting is automatically done in most of the other languages running on the .NET platform, much of the .NET Framework makes heavy use of base-type parameters in its methods. In many cases, F# developers will want to create classes and methods that allow for similar kinds of functionality, but the need to explicitly perform the `upcast` will feel tedious and annoying after a short while.

Fortunately, F# supports a special kind of reference type designation known as the *flexible type constraint*. In code, it is abbreviated as `#Person` and indicates that any type that inherits from `Person` is acceptable as a parameter:

```
type Printer() =
    member this.PrintName(p : #Person) =
        System.Console.WriteLine("{0}", p.FirstName)
```

This then allows the use of any object that has the type in its pedigree or is of the exact type specified:

```
// using "p" and "s" from earlier...
let printer = new Printer()
printer.PrintName(p)
printer.PrintName(s)
```

(Formally, when declaring the reference, the F# language is actually declaring the reference as a generic parameter with a type constraint using the `upcast` operator, à la:

```
type Printer() =
    member this.PrintName(p : #Person) =
        System.Console.WriteLine("{0}", p.FirstName)
    member this.GenericPrintName(p : 'a when 'a :> Person) =
        System.Console.WriteLine("{0}", p.FirstName)
```

Generics are covered in more detail in Chapter 10.)

# Boxing and Unboxing

One of the novel features of the CLR was its use of a unified type system tree, meaning all types through the CLR inherit from a single base class (System.Object, also known as obj in F#), including all primitive types. Given that Object has a number of methods on it, requiring some kind of method dispatch table and an object "sync lock," implying overhead per object, and that primitive types don't want to carry any additional overhead, the CLR had to come up with some particular magic to make the unified type system work well in the majority of cases.

The solution, as well-read C# and Visual Basic developers already know, was to create two instructions in the CLR, box and unbox, which convert a value type (the CLR term for types that should act as primitive types do — see Chapter 3 for details) into an object reference when necessary, and vice versa. Normally, these instructions are automatically inserted into the compiled code by the C# or Visual Basic compilers, because both of those languages support automatic implicit conversions. Because F# doesn't support automatic implicit conversions, F# developers will sometimes find the need at times to do the boxing or unboxing "by hand," which is done using the F# language keywords box and unbox, respectively:

```
let oi = box 42
System.Console.WriteLine("oi's type is {0}", oi.GetType())
let i : int32 = unbox oi
System.Console.WriteLine("i's type is {0}", i.GetType())
```

Like the downcast instruction, the unbox call infers the type to which to unbox from the left side of the expression, in this case an int32.

## Equality, Hashing, and Comparison

Because all types in the CLR ultimately inherit from the System.Object base type, and because two of the four methods defined on that type deal with object comparison (Equals and GetHashCode), the .NET programmer is frequently presented with the requirement to define appropriate implementations of these methods on their custom type definitions. Because of the ubiquity of defining these methods, F# provides some additional support to make it easier to define them.

Naturally, the F# developer is always free to define overridden implementations of the two methods directly (with some restrictions, as described here), but F# also provides several custom attributes to let the F# developer tell the compiler exactly what kind of equality and comparison semantics this type is supposed to have:

> ➤ Microsoft.FSharp.Core.ReferenceEquality

> ➤ Microsoft.FSharp.Core.StructuralEquality

> ➤ Microsoft.FSharp.Core.CustomEquality

> ➤ Microsoft.FSharp.Core.NoEquality

> ➤ Microsoft.FSharp.Core.StructuralComparison

> ➤ Microsoft.FSharp.Core.CustomComparison

> ➤ Microsoft.FSharp.Core.NoComparison

At the heart of this discussion is whether the type being defined should be treated as an object — meaning it has an explicit sense of identity, and users will want to differentiate between two objects even if they have the same contents — or as a value — meaning only the contents of the instance are important, and if two objects have the same contents, then they are equivalent even if they are separate objects. Normally, developers use custom overrides of Object.Equals to define some kind of structural equivalence and/or comparison and rely on the default behavior of Object.Equals (or the static method Object.ReferenceEquals) to provide identity equality tests. But F#'s introduction of tuple types and discriminated unions throws that somewhat akimbo — if developers create a discriminated union, for example, they may want more control over how the F# language treats it for comparison and/or equality purposes.

The first two generate Equals() methods that will provide equality implementations similar to what .NET developers are used to for reference types (those that inherit from System.Object directly) and value types (those that inherit from System.ValueType, such as types using struct in C# or Structure in Visual Basic), respectively.

In other words, ReferenceEquality will generate an Equals method that will return true only if the two references point to the same object. (In fact, ReferenceEquality generates no new methods for Equals or GetHashCode, defaulting to those inherited from System.Object.)

Using StructuralEquality will force the F# compiler to generate an Equals method that will compare each of the fields in the type for equality, which implies that each of those fields must also have StructuralEquality semantics. If StructuralEquality is placed on a nonvalue type definition, the F# compiler will reject it.

If CustomEquality is used, then the compiler will enforce the presence of an Equals method on that type. If the F# developer provides a custom Equals method, implements the System.IEquatable or the System.Collections.IStructuralEquatable interfaces, the F# compiler will insist on having the CustomEquality attribute defined on that type.

NoEquality, as might be inferred, does nothing, but the compiler also takes note of this and fails the use of this type anywhere an "equality" type constraint is required. (Type constraints are described in more detail in Chapter 10.)

StructuralComparison, as its name infers, will generate an implementation of System .IComparable that "does the right thing," meaning it compares each of the fields and returns –1, 0, or 1 based on the greater-or-lesser comparison of each of those fields, so that (for example) two tuples, when compared, behave as would be expected:

```
let t1 = (1, 1)
let t2 = (1, 1)
let t3 = (1, 2)
System.Console.WriteLine("{0}", (t1 = t2)) // true
System.Console.WriteLine("{0}", (t1 < t3)) // true
System.Console.WriteLine("{0}", (t3 < t1)) // false
```

NoComparison generates nothing, and CustomComparison assumes (and enforces) that a custom implementation of the System.IComparable interface will be defined on the type.

Because of the particular restrictions around CLR value and reference types, and the various assumptions about how equality and comparison works, this means that these attributes can be used only in particular combinations on particular types:

➤   Nothing

➤   `[<NoComparison>]`

➤   `[<NoEquality; NoComparison>]`

➤   `[<CustomEquality; NoComparison>]` on a structural type

➤   `[<ReferenceEquality>]` on a non-`Struct` structural type

➤   `[<ReferenceEquality; NoComparison>]` on a non-`Struct` structural type

➤   `[<StructuralEquality; NoComparison>]` on a structural type

➤   `[<CustomEquality; CustomComparison>]` on a structural type

➤   `[<StructuralEquality; CustomComparison>]` on a structural type

➤   `[<StructuralEquality; StructuralComparison>]` on a structural type

As can be seen, these attributes are mostly useful only for structural types, not "class" types. More details can be found in the F# Specification.

In practice, for the definition of reference types, F# provides some built-in functions that make it nearly trivial to calculate the hash or do a generic comparison of any two types: `hash` and `compare`. Their usage is shown here:

```
[<AbstractClass>]
type Person(fn, ln, a) =
    inherit System.Object()
    override this.GetHashCode() =
        hash (fn, ln, a)  // convert to tuple, then take hash
    override this.Equals(other) =
        compare this (other :?> Person) = 0
```

 *If you are diligently typing in the examples as you read this book, you will notice that the compiler generates an error for both this and the following examples, complaining that the type* Person *doesn't support the* System.IComparable *interface. Hold that thought, as you fix the problem in the very next section, once interfaces are introduced.*

Because `compare` requires the two objects being compared to be of the same type, and the `Object.Equals` method describes its parameter as an `Object`, the downcast is necessary. In practice, developers will want to test this downcast before making the blind assumption (unless they are OK with the default behavior of throwing an exception should the cast fail).

These two functions can make the definition of custom relational operators (<, >, and so on) almost trivial:

```
[<AbstractClass>]
type Person(fn, ln, a) =
    inherit System.Object()
    override this.GetHashCode() =
        hash (fn, ln, a)
    override this.Equals(other) =
        compare this (other :?> Person) = 0
    member p.FirstName = fn
    member p.LastName = ln
    member p.Age = a
    static member op_Equality (l, r) = (compare l r) = 0
    static member op_LessThan (l, r) = (compare l r) < 0
    static member op_GreaterThan (l, r) = (compare l r) > 0
```

However, the definition of those operators (op_Equality, op_LessThan, and op_GreaterThan) are only necessary if this type is to be consumed from languages other than F#; so long as the type implements the IComparable interface, F# knows how to use it via standard operator definitions defined for =, <, >, and their brethren.

## INTERFACES

As developers familiar with C# and Visual Basic will already know, interfaces define a set of behavior (methods, properties, and so on) that any implementing class must provide or else be considered abstract and therefore uninstantiable. Within the .NET environment, interfaces are used to allow a type to belong to a group of related types without having to use up the (single) implementation inheritance slot because a type may inherit from any number of interfaces.

F# permits both interface implementation, meaning an F# type can incorporate an interface as part of its definition, and interface definition, meaning F# can define new interface types. The syntax for doing so is remarkably consistent with the definition of types, to the point where the F# developer can often ignore the details between classes and interfaces when defining them. Again, this is in keeping with F#'s desire to let developers focus on the problem rather than the physical details of how code should be laid out. However, it can seem entirely too subtle to developers used to having full control over those details; fortunately, for those developers who want to have full control, F# again provides some constructs to make the design and implementation of interfaces more explicit.

### Implementation

Implementing an interface on an F# type is not much different from inheriting from a base class, though the syntax is slightly different. The results of implementing an interface, however, are strikingly different.

Assuming the interface already exists somewhere (predefined in the CLR Framework Class Library, or in an assembly against which the F# compiler is compiling), implementing an interface in F# looks like:

```
[<AbstractClass>]
type Person(fn, ln, a) =
    inherit System.Object()
    override this.GetHashCode() =
        hash (fn, ln, a)  // convert to tuple, then take hash
    override this.Equals(other) =
        compare this (other :?> Person) = 0
    interface System.IComparable with
        member this.CompareTo(other) =
            let other = other :?> Person
            let tln : string = this.LastName
            let ln = tln.CompareTo(other.LastName)
            if ln <> 0 then
                let tfn : string = this.FirstName
                let fn = tfn.CompareTo(other.FirstName)
                if fn <> 0 then
                    let ta : int = this.Age
                    ta.CompareTo(other.Age)
                else
                    fn
            else
                ln

    member p.FirstName = fn
    member p.LastName = ln
    member p.Age = a
```

Syntactically, to implement an interface, the type uses the keyword `interface`, the interface type to implement, and the keyword `with`, and then gives definitions for each of the members in that interface. If there are multiple interfaces that the type wants to implement, they simply appear in their own `interface` block, in any order the developer wants:

```
[<AbstractClass>]
type Person(fn, ln, a) =
    inherit System.Object()
    interface System.IComparable with
        member this.CompareTo(other) =
            let other = other :?> Person
            let tln : string = this.LastName
            let ln = tln.CompareTo(other.LastName)
            if ln <> 0 then
                let tfn : string= this.FirstName
                let fn = tfn.CompareTo(other.FirstName)
                if fn <> 0 then
                    let ta : int = this.Age
                    ta.CompareTo(other.Age)
                else
                    fn
            else
```

```
                    ln
interface System.IFormattable with
    member this.ToString(s : string,
                         fp : System.IFormatProvider) : string=
        "Not interesting enough to implement yet"

member p.FirstName = fn
member p.LastName = ln
member p.Age = a
```

 *Note that this code (without the definition of* `Equals()` *or* `GetHashCode()`, *unlike the prior example) generates a warning from the F# compiler — it recognizes the* `IComparable` *interface and notices that the type doesn't provide an override of* `Object.Equals()`, *which usually goes hand-in-hand with* `IComparable`. *As a result, it automatically generates an override implementation of* `Object.Equals()` *defined in terms of* `IComparable` *but suggests that the developer provide one explicitly.*

F# requires that all interface members must be defined when implementing an interface — it is not possible, in the current language definition, to leave a member undefined and force a class derived from this one to provide that definition. However, in the odd case where that behavior is the exact behavior wanted (such as the case where the developer wants to ensure that classes that derive from `Person` are cloneable via the `ICloneable` interface, but doesn't want to define a default behavior for it), not all is lost:

```
[<AbstractClass>]
type Person(fn, ln, a) =
    inherit System.Object()
    interface System.ICloneable with
        member this.Clone() : obj =
            this.DoTheCloneThing()
    abstract DoTheCloneThing : unit -> obj
```

Now the base type `Person IS-A ICloneable`, whose `Clone()` method calls over to the abstract method `DoTheCloneThing`, thus must be implemented in derived types.

## Calling Interface Methods

F# differs significantly from C# or Visual Basic in that the methods defined when implementing an interface are known as explicit interface method definitions. This means that the usual C# or Visual Basic trick of calling the interface method on the object type is no longer valid, which can throw many experienced .NET developers for a loop when first discovering this.

For example, consider this F# example:

```
let p = new Student("Rachel", "Reese", 28,
                    "Silverlight", "Agilitrain")
let pclone = p.Clone() // will NOT compile
```

Despite the fact that Student inherits from Person, which in turn implements the ICloneable interface, the second line in this example will not compile — F# doesn't recognize the Clone method on the Student type. To invoke the Clone method, F# requires the call to be through an ICloneable reference:

```
let pclone = (p :> System.ICloneable).Clone()
```

Although this may seem awkward to the C# and Visual Basic developer used to the automatic implicit conversion, in practice F#'s type inference can often make this explicit upcast unnecessary, particularly where flexible type constraints are used.

## Definition

Defining an interface is actually quite trivial in F#, in that the syntax for defining an interface is strikingly similar to that of defining a class type — the annotation changes from Class to Interface, and all members must be abstract, but other than that, everything stays the same:

```
[<Interface>]
type IDrinker =
    abstract Drink : unit -> unit
    abstract FavoriteDrink : string
```

As with classes, interfaces can define methods or properties that must then be implemented on the implementing type. If the type fails to implement all the members of the interface, the implementing type must be marked abstract, just as with classes that fail to implement all base type members.

Implementing an F#-defined interface is no different than implementing an interface defined in the FCL:

```
[<Class>]
type Student(fn, ln, a, sub, sch) =
    inherit Person(fn, ln, a)
    let gpa = 0.0
    do System.Console.WriteLine("Whoo-hoo! College!")
    new() = Student("", "", 0, "", "")
    new(fn, ln, a) = Student(fn, ln, a, "", "")
    interface IDrinker with
        member this.Drink() =
            System.Console.WriteLine("Chug! Chug! Chug!")
        member this.FavoriteDrink = "Keystone Light"
    member s.FormalName = s.FirstName + " " + " of " + sch
    member s.Subject = sub
    member s.School = sch
```

In some cases, an interface may want to extend another interface, providing some additional members for implementing types to define:

```
[<Interface>]
type IEater =
    abstract Eat : unit -> unit
    abstract FavoriteFood : string

[<Interface>]
```

```
type IGlutton =
    inherit IDrinker
    inherit IEater
    abstract EatAndDrink : unit -> unit
```

Any type that implements the IGlutton interface must now provide definitions for the members of IDrinker, IEater, and the new method introduced in IGlutton.

## OBJECT EXPRESSIONS

At times, an F# developer wants to create an implementation of an interface or derived type, but the implementation of this type is used so rarely its definition doesn't seem worth creating a named type for it. In those scenarios, F# permits the creation of an *object expression*, essentially an anonymously named type that implements a given interface or inherits from a base class and provides, at the point of its creation, the necessary implementation:

```
let p = { new IDrinker with
            member this.Drink() =
                System.Console.WriteLine("Sip")
            member this.FavoriteDrink =
                "Macallan 25" }
p.Drink()
```

The reference returned from an object expression is the type specified after the new keyword. Object expressions can also work with any type, abstract or otherwise:

```
let p2 = { new Person("Ted", "Neward", 38) with
            member this.DoTheCloneThing() = null
            member this.Work() =
                System.Console.WriteLine("Writing a book!") }
p2.Work()
```

As demonstrated, any constructor parameters to the object expression follow the typename, as with any other construction statement. The curly-braces around the expression are also required; they cannot be omitted.

## SUMMARY

As has already been noted, F# supports the full range of object-oriented features, meaning that F# can do everything that any other object-oriented language can do, including implementation inheritance and the ability to define and consume interfaces. F# is a "fully-loaded" object-oriented language.

But at times the desire isn't to add variability through inheritance. Instead, the necessary design stroke is to create classes that can vary a particular type or set of types used throughout the class definition. This is known as parametric polymorphism, and more colloquially as generics, and is the subject of the next chapter.

# 10

# Generics

**WHAT'S IN THIS CHAPTER?**

➤ Understanding generics in F#

➤ Using generic types

➤ Applying type constraints

➤ Working with statically resolved types

For the experienced C# or Visual Basic developer, this chapter will likely be simultaneously similar and yet maddeningly different from what's familiar in those languages. Generics have always played a key part in functional languages, thanks in large part due to the type inferenced nature of those languages, and as a result generics will be used far more often when writing F# code. This represents both a blessing and a curse: A blessing, in that code will often "silently" be more reusable and extensible than the C# or Visual Basic developer originally intended, but also a curse, in that some of the deeper and darker corners of generics and type systems, safely ignorable when writing object-oriented code, must now be confronted and programmers' demons slain.

## BASICS

Normally, when developers write code, they use placeholders that will eventually contain values and manipulate those values in particular ways; we call those placeholders "variables" and, if those variables are part of a class instance, "fields." Generics, also known as parametric types, provide the ability for developers to write code using placeholders for the types of those variables or fields. Generics allow the compiler to continue to exercise full static type-checking, yet write classes that can be used with a variety of different types, all statically checked at compile-time.

In languages like C# and Visual Basic, writing genericized code for anything but the simplest of cases becomes frustrating and difficult, because those languages require explicit type descriptors that must be used anywhere a type is used. For example, a generic "queue" class, a first-in-first-out (FIFO) data structure that maintains an order of items pushed into it, would look something like this in C#:

```
public class Queue<T>
{
    public void Clear();
    public bool Contains(T t);
    public int Count { get; }
    public T Dequeue();
    public void Enqueue(T o);
    public T Peek();
}
```

Its cousin written in Visual Basic would look not much simpler, but with different punctuation marks:

```
Class Queue(Of T)
    Public Overridable Sub Clear()
    Public Overridable Function Contains(t As T) As Boolean
    Public Overridable ReadOnly Property Count As Integer
    Public Overridable Function Dequeue() As T
    Public Overridable Sub Enqueue(t As T)
    Public Overridable Function Peek() As T
End Class
```

Later, the developer may want to take that Queue and put a bunch of Person objects into it, which, because the Queue is instantiated with a Person type at its construction, means the compiler can ensure that only Person objects are put into the Queue. Any attempt to put a non-Person object into that Queue will fail at compile-time and thus prevent a bug from occurring.

```
Queue<Person> line = new Queue<Person>();
Line.Enqueue(new String("Will this fail?"));
```

For most C# and VB developers, the story around generics more or less ends here: Parameterized types provide type-safe collections, and beyond that, they get awkward and hard to use and thus rarely show up. For example, any attempt to put a Student (which derives from Person) into a Person-only Queue would work, but attempts to pass a Queue of Students where a Queue of Persons was expected would not, driving O-O developers mad.

Parameterized types have had a long, rich history in functional programming languages, and, thanks to type inference, often far exceed the O-O community in their usage. Because the compiler can infer generic types in some cases, sometimes the only thing to say about parameterized types is that they're there, and the developer need not worry about it beyond that.

But in many cases, F# code will want or need to make the parameterization more explicit, and the F# language provides some simple rules to do so.

## Type Parameters

Creating a generic type is remarkably easy, and syntactically similar to what the C# developer already uses. To create the classic "stack" (LIFO) using generics, the type parameter is placed inside angle brackets after the type name declaration, and that parameter name can be used as a type substitute throughout the remainder:

```
type Stack<'T>() =
    let mutable data = []
    member this.Push(elem : 'T) =
        data <- elem :: data
    member this.Pop() =
        let temp = data.Head
        data <- data.Tail
        temp
    member this.Length() =
        data.Length
```

*Code snippet MeasurementLog.xaml*

 *Note that this is hardly the most efficient implementation, but it serves for a demonstration.*

Notice that the type parameter is prefixed with a single-quote; this is a non-negotiable part of the type parameter. Historically (dating back to its OCaml days), just as C# prefers type parameters named "T" and "U", and so on, F# prefers type parameters named 'a and 'b, so idiomatically, the preceding code should be rewritten as:

```
type Stack<'a>() =
    let mutable data = []
    member this.Push(elem : 'a) =
        data <- elem :: data
    member this.Pop() =
        let temp = data.Head
        data <- data.Tail
        temp
    member this.Length() =
        data.Length
```

More than one parameter can appear in the type declaration, as long as they are separated by a comma:

```
type TwoArgGeneric<'a, 'b>(a : 'a, b : 'b) =
    let vA = a
    let vB = b
    override tag.ToString() =
        System.String.Format("TwoArgGeneric({0},{1})", a, b)
```

Creating an instance of the generic type is straightforward, using similar syntax as creating a nongeneric object instance, but passing a type argument in brackets:

```
let s1 = new Stack<System.String>()
```

In (almost) any expression where a type is expected, a type parameter can be used. Thus, for example, the type parameter can be used in a `typeof` expression to obtain the `Type` object for the type it represents:

```
type Reflector<'a>() =
    member r.GetMembers() =
        let ty = typeof<'a>
        ty.GetMembers()
```

Of course, genericizing the entire type here is a bit unnecessary, because the type itself is only used inside the `GetMembers()` method. In this case, the type parameter can be localized to the method itself, making it a method type parameter.

## Member Type Parameters

Member type parameters are localized uses of generics, limiting the scope of the type parameter's use to the method on which it is declared:

```
type Reflector2() =
    static member GetMembers<'a>() =
        typeof<'a>.GetMembers()
```

Typical use of generic methods often require no special syntax, because type inference can often pick up the correct type to use from its context, but in those cases when an explicit type needs to be given (such as in the preceding code), put the bracketed type parameter between the method name and the argument list (if any):

```
let stringMembers = Reflector2.GetMembers<System.String>()
```

Of course, a type can have (different) type parameters at both the type scope and method scope, if wanted.

# TYPE CONSTRAINTS

One thing the compiler has to be careful about is making promises it can't keep. For example, in the following code (which will not compile), the compiler can't be sure that this will work:

```
type InterestingType<'a>(data : 'a) =
    member it.DoIt() =
        data.DoSomething()
```

Specifically, because `DoSomething()` isn't a method that is guaranteed to appear on whatever type happens to be passed in for `'a` when the `InterestingType` instance is created, the compiler can't be certain that the call will work. As a result, it fails to compile this code, complaining that "Lookup on Object of Indeterminate Type Based on Information Prior to This Program Point."

Several solutions present themselves. One is to eliminate the generic entirely and use traditional O-O techniques to handle this, by creating an interface that declares the DoSomething method, and force any types that are passed in to the InterestingType constructor to be instances of that interface:

```
[<Interface>]
type IDoSomething =
    abstract DoSomething : unit -> unit

type OOInterestingType(data : IDoSomething) =
    member it.DoIt() =
        data.DoSomething()
```

Doing this has some drawbacks, however, stemming from the fact that the type isn't known at compile-time — only a part of the type is known (it inherits from the IDoSomething interface). Although this is sufficient in this simple demo, it won't always do.

The second approach is to use a *type constraint*, which is a declaration, enforceable by the compiler, that must be met when used:

```
[<Interface>]
type IDoSomething =
    abstract DoSomething : unit -> unit

type InterestingType<'a when 'a :> IDoSomething>(data : 'a) =
    member it.DoIt() =
        data.DoSomething()
```

The when clause in the type parameter declaration tells the compiler that whatever type is passed in for this parameter must meet the requirement, which in this case, given the :> syntax, means that the 'a type must inherit from the named type (IDoSomething).

The following sections explore the many other kinds of type constraints that are enforced by the F# compiler.

## Type Constraint

A type constraint, shown in the previous text, requires that the type argument inherit from the type specified, or if the type specified is an interface, that the type argument implement that interface.

## Equality Constraint

The equality constraint insists that the type has the capability to be compared against other values of its type for equality:

```
type MustBeEquallable<'a when 'a : equality>(data : 'a) =
    member it.Equal(other : 'a) =
        data = other
```

This is a commonly used constraint, along with the comparison constraint, next.

## Comparison Constraint

The comparison constraint insists that the type has support for doing comparison operations:

```
type MustBeComparable<'a when 'a : comparison>(data : 'a) =
    member it.Greater(other : 'a) =
        data > other
    member it.Lesser(other : 'a) =
        data < other
```

How the type implements its less-than or greater-than support is, of course, entirely up to the type in question, so long as it satisfies the basic signature of the two operations.

## Null Constraint

A null constraint simply lists `null` in the constraint clause:

```
type MustBeNullable<'a when 'a : null>(data : 'a) =
    class
    end
```

When used, this tells the compiler that the type parameter must be "nullable," meaning the constant value `null` is an acceptable value for it. In .NET 4.0, this means every type (thanks to nullable types introduced in .NET 2.0) is acceptable; the only exceptions are the F# list, tuple, function, class, record, or union types.

## Constructor Constraint

A constructor constraint, as its name implies, requires that a given constructor member be present and accessible:

```
type MustBeConstructible<'a when 'a : (new : unit -> 'a)> =
    member it.NewIt() =
        new 'a()
```

This will be particularly useful in situations where a given component needs to be instantiated within a particular context — rather than use Reflection to invoke a constructor, the constructor can be directly called with confidence (and better performance), because the compiler has ensured it is present.

## Value Type and Reference Type Constraints

At times, it will be necessary to restrict acceptable types to either the set of value types or reference types:

```
type MustBeStruct<'a when 'a : struct>() =
    class
    end
type MustBeClass<'a when 'a : not struct>() =
    class
    end
```

Note that the not is not a general "reverse" of the type constraint but is a formal part of the reference type constraint. That is, we cannot write "not null" to create a "not-nullable" type constraint.

## Other Constraints

Other constraint types (enumeration type constraints, delegate constraints, and unmanaged constraints) are available, but are marked by the F# documentation as Not Intended for Common Use. The explicit member constraint is also labeled as such, but its use has shown up enough in F# code and samples that knowing how to read it is a good idea, even if it's not recommended for casual use.

# STATICALLY RESOLVED TYPE PARAMETERS

In certain cases, the F# compiler can eliminate the generic type parameter entirely and simply replace the type parameter with the actual type at compile time. These kinds of type parameters are indicated with the caret symbol (^) instead of the single-quote character when declaring the type parameter, and they are most commonly used with the type constraints listed in the previous section. In particular, they are used frequently within the F# library and for that reason should at least be readable by F# developers.

As the name implies, the major difference between statically resolved type parameters and "regular" type parameters is that statically resolved type parameters are replaced at compile time (much as C++ template parameters are), rather than used at runtime to instantiate the generic type, as "classic" .NET generics are. As a result, there are a few differences between "regular" generics and statically resolved type parameter generics.

For starters, statically resolved type parameters cannot be used on types — only methods and functions (described in Part III, "Functional Programming") can have statically resolved type parameters. So, for example, it is possible to write a generic function that does some odd or highly specialized math:

```
let inline (+@) (x : ^a) (y : ^a) =
    x + x * y

let result = 1 +@ 2
System.Console.WriteLine("result = {0}", result)
```

In addition, as the preceding example demonstrates, statically resolved type parameters can be used on inline functions, where "regular" generic parameters cannot. (Functions and inline functions are described more in Chapter 13.)

Because statically resolved type parameters are compile-time resolved, they allow for an additional generic constraint type.

## Explicit Member Constraint

An explicit member constraint tells the compiler to ensure that a given member is present on the type, such as a method or property:

```
type MustBeDoItable<'a when 'a : (member DoIt : unit -> unit)>() =
    class
    end
```

This would be a possible replacement for the inheritance-based constraint used earlier, assuming the compile-time replacement was acceptable (instead of runtime replacement). In general, however, if there are multiple members that need to be specified, it's going to be easier to put those members into an interface and use that as the constraint.

## SUMMARY

F#'s support for parameterized types is rich and powerful, particularly when combined with constraints and statically resolved type parameters, and makes writing reusable code just that much more powerful. But just writing reusable code is only part of the reusability story; the code must be packaged into a form that promotes reusability and reduces name conflicts, which is the subject of the next chapter.

# 11

# Packaging

**WHAT'S IN THIS CHAPTER?**

➤ Understanding modules and namespaces

➤ Defining assemblies in F#

Although it would be nice to imagine that when classes are written they can stand alone, the truth of the modern development environment makes it clear that a class stands among thousands, if not hundreds of thousands, of other classes, and only so many combinations of characters produce meaningful names. For classes to avoid verbose monikers like `OurCompanysGenericLinkedList`, some kind of higher packaging and syntactic partitioning system needs to be in place. In the .NET universe, this packaging system is called the assembly, and the syntactic partitioning is the namespace. As a CLR language, F# supports both but also adds a new mechanism from its functional heritage, the module, into the mix.

## NAMESPACES

.NET supports a system of lexical scoping, allowing different types of the same name to be neatly sectioned away from one another, known as namespaces. At its heart, a namespace is just a prefix to the typename, one which can be (usually) avoided in practical use via some kind of namespace-inclusion statement, such as `using` in C# or `Imports` in Visual Basic. Namespaces have almost no runtime component to them — the CLR references every type internally by its fully qualified name. Namespaces, then, are purely a programmer convenience.

### Referencing a Namespace

In F# code, to include the list of types in a namespace in the list of top-level accessible names, use the `open` keyword followed by the namespace name:

```
open System
open System.Diagnostics
open System.Reflection
```

You can use the open statement at a variety of scopes, though because the effects of the statement are felt only after its point of use, some idiomatic F# use holds that all such open statements should appear at the top of the F# source file or script.

As with most .NET languages, when a namespace has been referenced via the open statement, the namespace prefix can be left off the typenames when used:

```
Console.WriteLine("Much shorter, thank you")
```

Like many of the other .NET languages, F# auto-opens use a number of different namespaces on behalf of the F# programmer, because the types in those namespaces are considered to be so common that requiring F# programmers to open them manually would be a nuisance. As a result, every F# file has a "silent" list of opens at the top of the file, as if the developer had written:

```
open Microsoft.FSharp
open Microsoft.FSharp.Core
open Microsoft.FSharp.Core.LanguagePrimitives
open Microsoft.FSharp.Core.Operators
open Microsoft.FSharp.Text
open Microsoft.FSharp.Collections
open Microsoft.FSharp.Core.ExtraTopLevelOperators
```

Most obviously missing from this list are any of the common .NET Framework Class Library namespaces, such as System.

## Defining a Namespace

Because namespaces serve as a mechanism for partitioning similarly named classes away from one another and preventing accidental name conflicts, it's important for the F# developer to also define namespaces in which to define their own types. Doing so in F# is surprisingly easy — namespace followed by the namespace desired opens a new namespace, and that namespace remains open until replaced by a new namespace declaration. (The lack of a namespace declaration does not imply that the code is defined in the "empty" namespace, however — more on this in a moment.)

Thus, defining a type Person in the namespace Examples would look like:

**Available for download on Wrox.com**

```
namespace Examples

open System

type Person(fn : string, ln : string, a : int) =
    member this.FirstName = fn
    member this.LastName = ln
    member this.Age = a
    override this.ToString() =
        String.Format("{0} {1} is {2} years old",
            this.FirstName, this.LastName, this.Age)

namespace MoreExamples

type Student() =
    override this.ToString() = "Student"
```

*Code snippet Packaging.fs*

This defines two types, one formally named `Examples.Person`, and the other formally named `MoreExamples.Student`. Nesting of namespaces is not allowed in F#; to create a "nested" namespace, such as `Examples.Cool`, the full "nested" name must be given in the namespace declaration.

Note that F# will not permit any code before the first `namespace` declaration in an F# file, so general F# coding idiom will have the first line denote the namespace used, or else no namespace is used throughout the file.

## MODULES

Modules come to F# from its functional roots, through its inheritance of the OCaml programming language. Traditionally, functional languages have needed a way to partition functions away from other potentially similarly named functions but haven't wanted to "lose" that name-container prefix the way .NET developers have casually tossed aside namespaces. For example, `add` could mean one of many different things, which `List.add` clarified.

Further complicating the F# story is that, as previously mentioned, namespaces in the CLR are essentially an abstraction of the languages on top of the platform and not something the CLR recognizes as a formal construct. Thus, the functional style of a namespace "owning" top-level functions could prove to be problematic particularly when interoperating with other .NET languages. As a result, F# chose to incorporate another mechanism, the module, which on the surface of things seems to clash directly with namespaces. However, modules and namespaces have significantly different behavior and serve different purposes.

### Referencing a Module

To use a module, F# reuses the `open` keyword again to much the same effect — opening a module makes the functions and types declared inside that module available without requiring the fully qualified name. At this level, there is little difference between a namespace and a module, and most F# programmers will not even know the difference when using them.

### Defining a Module

Defining a module is relatively straightforward, just as the namespace is: The `module` keyword followed by a legitimate identifier name begins a module definition, and that module declaration is in scope until it is replaced by a new one:

**Available for download on Wrox.com**

```
module Examples

module Examples =

    open System

    type Person(fn : string, ln : string, a : int) =
        member this.FirstName = fn
        member this.LastName = ln
        member this.Age = a
        override this.ToString() =
            String.Format("{0} {1} is {2} years old",
```

```
                this.FirstName, this.LastName, this.Age)

    module MoreExamples =

        type Student() =
            override this.ToString() = "Student"
```

However, something subtle and slightly different is happening here: the first `module` declaration is establishing an overall container for all subsequent declarations, so the formal name of the `Person` type in the preceding example will be `Examples.Examples.Person`. This is reinforced because every subsequent module declaration is a kind of `type` definition inside the "top-level" declaration, as evidenced because the second declaration requires an `=` and its contents must be indented, just as a type definition requires.

The F# compiler automatically assigns a default module/namespace name to every given F# source file, defining it to be the same as the source file itself (minus the extension). However, this rule applies only in single-file F# applications or scripts; multi-file applications or libraries must have a first-line `namespace` or `module` declaration, so it's good habit to provide one even when unnecessary.

Note that namespaces can (and frequently will) contain `modules`, like so:

```
namespace Packaging

module Examples =

    open System

    type Person(fn : string, ln : string, a : int) =
        member this.FirstName = fn
        member this.LastName = ln
        member this.Age = a
        override this.ToString() =
            String.Format("{0} {1} is {2} years old",
                this.FirstName, this.LastName, this.Age)

    module MoreExamples =

        type Student() =
            override this.ToString() = "Student"
```

Much of the F# library is written in this style.

Where modules and namespaces differ wildly is in their definition and, more strikingly, in their contents: Whereas a namespace can only have types defined within it, a module can have types and/or functions and/or values (see Chapter 13) defined within it:

```
module Packaging

open System

module FunctionalExample =
    let doSomething() =
        Console.WriteLine("I did something!")
    let aValue = 5
```

The object-oriented mindset might see the F# module as a file-sized class that automatically contains all the top-level-declared elements within it, and that would not be far off the mark — at the IL level, absent any other module or namespace declarations, the module is compiled as a class, the module-level functions as static methods, and the module-level values as properties.

This, then, raises the ugly question of whether the F# developer should prefer modules or types with static members, and no clear answer presents itself. In general, it seems that popular opinion falls on the side of how the code will be used — if the code will be used from other F# programs, a module is preferred (as is the case for much of the F# library), but if the code is intended for consumption by other .NET languages, then classes-with-static-members is likely to be a better approach to take. In particular, if the goal is to create the moral equivalent to the `static class` from C# 2.0, then the F# module is the right thing to use.

## SUMMARY

F#'s support for both namespaces and modules is a new wrinkle in the traditional "name game" around types. In general, the F# developer can find the best mileage to be that of using namespaces to declare the "high-level" names (such as the company name), and modules to group closely related functions and values together in a construct that offers similar — but not exact — kinds of capability as a class.

# 12

# Custom Attributes

**WHAT'S IN THIS CHAPTER?**

➤   Understanding attribute syntax in F#

➤   Defining new custom attributes

➤   Applying custom attributes

Custom attributes form a core part of the .NET platform, and as a fully fledged, card-carrying member of the Microsoft family of languages, F# uses and supports custom attributes just as easily and as much as C# or Visual Basic do.

## USING CUSTOM ATTRIBUTES

F#, like most .NET languages, uses a variety of BCL-defined attributes to help describe how code should be compiled and consumed not only by other programs written in F#, but also by other .NET programs written in other .NET languages.

Like custom attributes defined in other languages, a custom attribute can appear just about anywhere F# defines a linguistic atom, so custom attributes can appear (among other places) on fields, method, or types, in a manner highly reminiscent of the C# and Visual Basic custom attribute syntax combined, using both square brackets and angle brackets:

```
open System

[<Serializable>]
type Person(FirstName : string, LastName : string, Age : int) =
    override p.ToString() =
        String.Format("[Person: {0} {1} {2}",
            FirstName, LastName, Age)
```

As could probably be inferred, this defines a class, `Person`, that has the BCL-defined `Serializable` attribute annotated on it, indicating that this class can be serialized using the standard BCL serialization classes and methods.

If the attribute defines or requires additional information (such as the optional message to be displayed when compiling against a deprecated method or class annotated with the `Obsolete` attribute), those parameters are passed either in order or as name-value pairs, depending on how the attribute is defined. More details on the differences between in order parameters and name-value pair parameters is given in the "Creating and Consuming" section.

However, because F# offers a few additional syntactical elements that neither C# nor Visual Basic offer, such as module-level functions and bindings (see Part III, "Functional Programming," for more details on functions, and Chapter 11 for more details on modules), F# also permits custom attributes to be defined at the function level:

```
[<EntryPoint>]
let Main args =
    // ...
```

As is described in more detail in Chapter 18, this defines the custom attribute on a static element (property or method) defined by that name-value binding and can later be discovered, often either via Reflection or via some other form of metadata consumer (such as the unmanaged metadata COM interfaces that many of the Visual Studio tools use). In this particular case, as described next, the `EntryPoint` attribute tells the F# compiler where the entry point in this application is defined, instead of simply assuming the last file to be compiled in this assembly as the entry point.

Following is a list of custom attributes defined by the .NET environment and/or the F# language, and the effects that attribute has during compilation and/or execution.

## EntryPoint

This attribute is defined by the F# language to help the programmer define the entry point (the first line of code) to be executed in the program; it has no effect in F# Class Library projects.

Normally, without this attribute, F# compiles the last module (file) in the project to be the entry point and the sequence of module-level definitions to be the lines of code to be executed; this is what allows F# to write one-liner programs like:

```
Console.WriteLine("Hello, world!")
```

as full-fledged .NET applications. However, in certain cases, F# developers may want (or need) to take a more C#-ish or Visual Basic-ish approach to the entry point of the application and define the entry point as a member method of a class:

```
type App() =
    [<EntryPoint>]
    let Main(args) =
        System.Console.WriteLine("Hello world!")
        0
```

Although this will compile, at runtime an exception will be thrown, claiming that the method annotated with `EntryPoint` must be static. When a static method annotated with `EntryPoint` is defined, however, the F# compiler finally reveals (through a warning) the idiomatic manner in which F# wants `EntryPoint` to be used: on a module-level function:

```
type App() =
    member public a.Main(args) =
        System.Console.WriteLine("Hello world!")
        0

[<EntryPoint>]
let Main(args) =
    let app = new App()
    app.Main(args)
```

Alternatively, the method in `App` could be static, although the common .NET idiom holds that having a singleton `App` object instance can be a useful place to hold singleton data and settings.

Note that the F# compiler will enforce that the method marked with `EntryPoint` takes an argument (a string array representing the command-line arguments passed to the application) and implicitly returns `int` (the "exit code" of the application).

Of course, as with all .NET applications, the command-line arguments can always be retrieved via the `System.Environment` method `GetCommandLineArgs()`, and the exit code can be set before termination via the `System.Environment.ExitCode` property, or the `System.Environment.Exit()` method call, so an explicit `EntryPoint` is not necessary.

## Obsolete

The `System.Obsolete` attribute, when defined on a type, method, namespace, module, or other F# element, can generate a warning when code (whether F# or otherwise) uses that element:

```
open System

type ObsoleteExperiment() =
    [<Obsolete>]
    member e.TestMethod() =
        System.Console.WriteLine("Don't use this!")

let e = new ObsoleteExperiment()
e.TestMethod()
```

When compiled, the call to `TestMethod()` generates a warning from the F# compiler: "This construct is deprecated". Because this is a BCL-level attribute, more importantly, other compilers (such as the C# or Visual Basic compilers) also honor the attribute and emit similar or identical warnings.

If the author of the deprecated functionality wants, a message can also be communicated to the client indicating why this particular construct should not be used:

```
type ObsoleteExperiment() =
    [<Obsolete("This method really just sucks")>]
    member e.AnotherMethod() =
        null.ToString()s
```

This message then appear in the compiler warning, right after the standard "This construct is deprecated" text.

As might be expected, this attribute should be used only during code refactoring to indicate to clients that this construct may eventually be dropped (and will break client code when it does). Practically speaking, Obsolete has one other interesting side effect: Obsolete-annotated methods do not appear in the Visual Studio IntelliSense drop-down list as an attempt to minimize its use in new or refactored client code.

## Conditional

The System.Diagnostics.Conditional attribute marks code as conditionally compiled, depending on whether a compiler-defined string (typically "DEBUG", the compiler-defined string indicating a Debug build) is specified as being "on" during compilation. If said string is not present during compile, then the call to the Conditional-annotated method simply does not happen.

For example, consider this class:

```
open System
open System.Diagnostics

type ConditionalDemo(data : string, count : int) =
    [<Conditional("DEBUG")>]
    member c.DumpInternals() =
        Console.WriteLine("data: {0}, count: {1}",
            data, count)
    override c.ToString() =
        String.Format("ConditionalDemo()")
```

The DumpInternals method will actually be executed only during debug builds, because the method call compilation will happen only on the condition that the "DEBUG" string is passed as a compiler flag:

```
let cd = new ConditionalDemo("password", 5)
Console.WriteLine(cd.ToString())
cd.DumpInternals()
```

Thus, the final preceding line (the call to DumpInternals) will appear only in Debug builds.

This attribute is intended to save .NET developers from having to bracket debug or diagnostic code with #if/#endif tokens to keep it out of Release builds.

## ParamArray

The System.ParamArray attribute, when defined on the last argument in a list of method (or function) arguments, tells the .NET environment to treat this as a variable-arguments method:

```
open System

type ParamArrayExperiment() =
    member e.TestMethod( [<ParamArray>] args : obj array) =
        for o in args do
            System.Console.WriteLine(o.ToString())

let e = new ParamArrayExperiment()
e.TestMethod("one", 2, 3.0)
```

```
e.TestMethod("This is just one argument")
e.TestMethod() // No arguments, empty array
```

The `ParamArray` attribute must appear on the last parameter in the argument list, and any parameters prior to the `ParamArray` argument must still be present when called for the method call to compile correctly.

F# also allows application of this attribute on the parameters passed to a function, as well:

```
let varargsFunction([<ParamArray>] args : obj array) =
    for o in args do
        System.Console.WriteLine(o.ToString())
```

However, just because we can put the attribute on the function doesn't mean F# allows functions to be called using a variable-argument style:

```
varargsFunction("one", 2, 3.0)
// error: This expression was expected to have type obj array
// but here has type 'a * 'b * 'c
```

The problem here is that syntactically, F# wants to see the comma-separated list as a tuple type instance that forms a single argument passed to the function, rather than collecting them into an array for passing. As a result, idiomatically, `ParamArray` will be used only on methods of classes.

 *Note that other .NET languages that call into the function may treat it as a variable-arguments array, depending on the details of the language; see Chapter 18 for more details.*

## Struct, Class, AbstractClass, Interface, Literal, and Measure

These attributes are F#-specific and are used to describe how the F# type should be mapped to the underlying CLR (in the case of `Struct`, `Class`, `AbstractClass` or `Interface`), how the F# type should be compiled (in the case of `Literal`), or how the F# type should be viewed with respect to other F# types (in the case of `Measure`).

`Struct` is described in Chapter 7, `Class` and `AbstractClass` in Chapter 8, and `Interface` in Chapter 9. `Literal` and `Measure` are described in Chapter 3.

## Assembly Attributes

The various `Assembly` attributes are used to configure the assembly-level manifest metadata that F# will emit into the compiled assembly during compilation. These are the same attributes that the Visual Studio compiler generates for Visual C# and Visual Basic projects from the Properties page, but given F#'s recent newcomer status to the Visual Studio family, F# developers looking to set these values should assume they have to do so "by hand," by specifying these attributes with the `assembly` prefix in one .fs file in the project. For example, to mark an assembly as version 1.0.0.0, owned by Neward and Associates, an .fs file should include:

```
open System.Reflection

[<assembly:AssemblyVersion("1.0.0.0")>]
[<assembly:AssemblyCopyright("(c) 2010 Neward & Associates")>]
do
    ()
```

Note that to "attach" the attribute to something not at a type or function level, the F# compiler requires all assembly-level attributes to be attached to a do block declared at the top-level of the file. In general, it's most often going to be easiest to put these attributes into the same file that contains the program's entry point, if one is specified.

These attributes (`AssemblyFileVersion`, `AssemblyDescription`, `AssemblyTitle`, `AssemblyCopyright`, `AssemblyTrademark`, `AssemblyCompany`, `AssemblyKeyFile`, and so on) are described in more detail in the MSDN documentation in the `System.Reflection` namespace — aside from the F# syntax, they are exactly identical to examples described in C# or Visual Basic.

## DefaultMember

This attribute, when used on a type, indicates the default member for that type, which is often used in other .NET languages as a shorthand way of accessing an indexer property.

## Serializable, NonSerialized

The `Serializable` attribute is used to mark a type as being eligible for serialization, a process by which an object instance can be reduced to a stream of bytes, then brought back into existence from that same stream of bytes, and contains the same field data as it contained at the time of serialization. The `NotSerializable` attribute is used to mark a field as being exempt from this serialization process in a `Serializable`-marked type.

For more details on `Serializable` and `NotSerialized`, see the MSDN documentation and the namespace `System.Runtime.Serialization`.

## AutoOpen

This is an F#-only attribute applicable at the assembly level. When used, it takes a string as a parameter, indicating a namespace or module name. When this assembly is referenced, the namespace or module specified in this attribute is automatically opened, as if the F# programmer had typed open <namespace> in the script or source file referencing the assembly.

It has no meaning outside of F#.

## Other Attributes

The .NET BCL is chock-full of other attributes used in a variety of tech-specific settings, such as the custom attributes used in Windows Communication Foundation (WCF) code to indicate communication bindings for services and clients. Use of these attributes follows the same patterns as the previous attributes, and deeper coverage of those attributes accompanies the appropriate text in Part IV, "Applications."

Of course, at any point, F# developers are free to create their own custom attributes, as described in the next section. For the most part, however, unless F# developers build a library or tool such as something similar to the Entity Framework, WCF, or some other infrastructure-oriented idea, most custom attributes will simply be used, rather than created.

## CREATION AND CONSUMPTION

As a CLI Producer (meaning the language can produce types suitable for consumption by other CLR languages), F# is just as capable of producing custom attributes as C# or Visual Basic is.

## Creation

Any C# or Visual Basic developer versed in creating a custom attribute in either of those languages will find the process of creating a custom attribute in F# to be strikingly similar. This is not an accident, thanks to the hybrid nature of F# as both a functional and object-oriented language.

Fundamentally, creating a custom attribute type in F# consists of defining a new type that inherits from the System.Attribute base class and adorning the new type with an attribute (AttributeUsage) that describes where the new type can be used as an attribute, and ensuring that the new type can be found by other .NET (F# or otherwise) assemblies. Then, to use F# or other languages, simply reference the assembly containing the custom attribute and use the attribute where wanted. (This presumes that somebody — compiler, library, or runtime environment — will use Reflection in some way to discover the attribute, which we cover in the next section.)

For example, imagine a requirement: If an exception is thrown, a customer demands that the programmer or group responsible for the exception-generating code be identified (probably so that they can fire them or at least threaten to take away their video-game privileges). Because the Exception base class defines a member that provides Reflective access to the member that generated the exception (TargetSite), when the exception is caught, we can interrogate the source of the exception to see if it has our custom attribute, and if it does, display the miscreant who wrote the code and his pitiful justification.

First, the custom attribute needs be defined. A custom attribute is, at heart, just a class that inherits from the System.Attribute base class:

```
type BlameAttribute() =
    inherit System.Attribute()
```

At this point, it is a fully fledged member of the attribute family and can be used in code:

```
[<Blame>]
let faultyMethod() =
    null.ToString()
```

Sharp-eyed readers will note that the class is defined as BlameAttribute, but used as Blame; this is a .NET convention dating back to the earliest days of .NET, and one that is honored across all .NET languages to date. It is entirely syntactically possible to define a custom attribute without the "Attribute" suffix, but doing so is likely to be frowned upon in code reviews and earn the odious "Donut Purchaser" responsibilities at the next team meeting.

This custom attribute, however, needs to carry some additional data with it, as per the requirement previously described, namely, the programmer who last touched this faulty code and an optional reason for why this code is so bad. From a usage standpoint, this means we want to use it like this:

```
[<Blame("Aaron Erickson")>]
let faultyMethod() =
    null.ToString()
```

or if he wants to provide an excuse, like so:

```
[<Blame("Aaron Erickson", Reason="I told it's not done!")>]
let faultyMethod() =
    null.ToString()
```

Translated, this means the attribute needs to have one required and one optional parameter. For attributes, this means that the class must have one constructor parameter (the required parameter) and one read/write field or property (the optional parameter). As is described in Chapter 8, this means the attribute must look like this:

```
open System

type BlameAttribute(owner : string) =
    inherit Attribute()

    let mutable reason = ""

    member public b.Owner
        with get() = owner
    member public b.Reason
        with get() = reason
        and set(value) = reason <- value

    override b.ToString() =
        String.Format("Blame {0}{1}",
            b.Owner,
            if b.Reason = ""
                then ", just because!"
                else ", because " + b.Reason)
```

It might be helpful to restrict the kinds of places that the `BlameAttribute` can be used — for example, it doesn't make sense to define `Blame` on method parameters — which is done using another attribute, the `AttributeUsage` attribute, on `BlameAttribute` itself:

```
[<AttributeUsage(AttributeTargets.Assembly |||
                 AttributeTargets.Class |||
                 AttributeTargets.Constructor |||
                 AttributeTargets.Enum |||
                 AttributeTargets.Field |||
                 AttributeTargets.Interface |||
                 AttributeTargets.Method |||
                 AttributeTargets.Module |||
                 AttributeTargets.Struct)>]
type BlameAttribute(owner : string) =
    // . . .
```

This gives the compiler the necessary support to ensure that `Blame` can only be placed on assemblies, modules, classes, enums, interfaces, structs, constructors, fields, or methods.

At this point, the attribute is good for use; actually digging it out at runtime, however, requires a bit more code, not within the attribute itself but within the code that wants to use the attribute.

## Consumption

Consuming the custom attribute requires the use of .NET's Reflection API, which provides access to the full-fidelity metadata contained within a .NET assembly. A full discussion of the .NET Reflection API is beyond the scope of this particular problem, but fortunately, the `Exception` class provides an easy escape: Because the `TargetSite` property of the `Exception` object provides the Reflective element that generated the exception, it's relatively trivial to use that to find the offending party, if a `Blame` attribute is attached to it.

Of course, first the exception must be caught:

```
try
    faultyMethod() |> ignore
with
| ex ->
    Console.WriteLine("Bam!")
```

Each Reflection object (whether it represents a method, field, property, class, or some other Reflective element) has a method defined on it, `GetCustomAttributes()`, that returns an array of objects containing any custom attributes defined on that Reflective element. So, for example, when the preceding faulty code is invoked, the Exception object's `TargetSite` will point to a `System.Reflection.MethodInfo` object that represents the `faultyMethod` method. When `GetCustomAttributes()` is called on it, it will return any custom attributes defined on `faultyMethod`, of which there is currently only one.

However, because a given Reflective element can have zero-to-many custom attributes on it, `GetCustomAttributes()` has an easy way to filter out all the custom attributes except the one type that holds interest, by passing in the `System.Type` of the attribute.

`GetCustomAttributes()` also takes a Boolean parameter, indicating whether the search for a custom attribute should take into account parent-defined versions of the element — for example, if the method in question is an overridden member of a derived class, should it search on base-class-defined versions of that method to see if custom attributes appear there, as well?

Thus, digging out the `Blame` attribute looks like this:

```
try
    faultyMethod() |> ignore
with
| ex ->
    let tgt = ex.TargetSite
    let custAttrs =
        tgt.GetCustomAttributes(typeof<BlameAttribute>, true)
    if custAttrs.Length > 0 then
        Console.WriteLine("Aha! {0}", custAttrs.[0])
    else
        Console.WriteLine("Nobody to blame, sorry!")
```

Note that the returned array of custom attributes from `GetCustomAttributes()` is an `obj` array, and if the particular properties from `BlameAttribute` need to be accessed, it will require a downcast:

```
try
    faultyMethod() |> ignore
with
| ex ->
    let tgt = ex.TargetSite
    let custAttrs =
        tgt.GetCustomAttributes(typeof<BlameAttribute>, true)
    if custAttrs.Length > 0 then
        let blame = (custAttrs.[0]) :?> BlameAttribute
        Console.WriteLine("Aha! {0} did it!", blame.Owner)
    else
        Console.WriteLine("Nobody to blame, sorry!")
```

Bad programmer. No pizza.

Of course, this same technique could be used to provide runtime-accessible documentation for types and members, similar to what dynamic languages such as Ruby or Python provide so that F# developers using the F# REPL can discover both the types and their accompanying documentation during REPL development. And custom attributes can also be applied to any of a dozen other scenarios, limited only by the .NET developer's imagination.

## SUMMARY

As any good .NET citizen does, F# provides full-fidelity access to the metadata required by the CLR, and at least part of this access is through the definition, application, and consumption of custom attributes. The syntax is remarkably similar — yet in many ways terser — than that used by C# or Visual Basic, and as such shouldn't be any kind of hurdle for the experienced .NET developer coming to F#.

# PART III
# Functional Programming

▶ **CHAPTER 13:** Functions

▶ **CHAPTER 14:** Immutable Data

▶ **CHAPTER 15:** Data Types

▶ **CHAPTER 16:** List Processing

▶ **CHAPTER 17:** Pipelining and Composition

# 13

# Functions

**WHAT'S IN THIS CHAPTER?**

➤ Reasoning about Functions

➤ Understanding Type Restriction

➤ Using First Class Functions

➤ Partially Applying Functions

The way you think about functions is one of the things that most strongly differentiates F# from the other .NET languages. This doesn't come down to how functions are represented under the hood. Instead, it has more to do with the way functions are used conceptually.

When programming in F#'s functional style, functions are thought of as just another data type much like any object. They are frequently both passed into and returned from other functions. They also often have data stored inside of them through partial application or closures.

Although this can be done in other languages, it's not a frequently used feature and can take some getting used to. However, in time you will see that by leveraging these functional features more often, you can bring much to the table in terms of code succinctness and clarity. Indeed, much of F#'s power comes from this style of avoiding objects and focusing on functions.

## TRADITIONAL FUNCTION CALLS

Traditionally, in mainstream imperative languages like C, C++, and C#, we treat functions as something completely different than the data that flows through our programs. They take a set of data, do some work on or with that data, and, most likely, change the state of our program in some way. They are like the channels through which the execution of our program flows, changing various data states along the way.

Unfortunately, this approach makes it difficult to build reusable components. Without the ability to pass functions, it is difficult to compose new structures at runtime, swap out components for testing or have a subcomponent communicate back to its parent. Over the years various techniques have emerged to mitigate this.

One of the first was to use function pointers (aka delegates). Function pointers allow us to pass the location of functions in memory so that they can be called later. However, these are cumbersome to define and often lack type safety. Also, because languages that use this technique often have only compile-time type checking, ad-hoc runtime type systems often need to be constructed.

Another common technique is to use abstract inheritance. The general concept of this technique is that you define an abstract class that requires certain member functions are filled in. You then pass your function in terms of a concrete implementation of this abstract class. However, this approach requires quite a lot of additional code and, as the inheriting class may have hidden private variables, dependencies on unspecified behavior emerge.

Yet another is Eventing. Events allow us to easily inject callbacks into our existing code via a special mechanism for calling sets of function pointers. However, in addition to the runtime type problems inherent in using function pointers, it has a whole slew of others issues due to the dependence on subscribers. How can we be sure the correct subscribers are being called? How can we be sure our subscribers are unsubscribing correctly? Also, ordering often cannot be guaranteed, especially when many asynchronous calls are being made. The combination of these factors can make event-driven programming a tangled mess of dependencies.

As you'll find out in Chapter 14, many of the problems in using these constructs stem from compile-time-only type systems or the use of shared state. However, even ignoring these, we find that much additional code must be written even for a single additional composable call to be used. For this reason, imperative programmers often avoid these language features as they can add a significant amount of bulk to their program. Instead they opt to write rigid code and use cut and paste as their primary form of code reuse.

## MATHEMATICAL FUNCTIONS

In functional programming, functions are considered first-class language constructs. Like in mathematics, functions can be partially filled in and assigned to variables. Functions can be passed into or returned from other functions. They can even be written inline inside of other functions sharing parents' input variables.

This makes writing code in F# much more like math than other languages. Frequently you compose functions out of other functions at runtime. You then can push your data through the resulting function to obtain your result.

Instead of designing in terms of the behavior of your object, which has been composed of other objects, you design in terms of the behavior of your function that has been composed of other functions. These ideas are fundamentally quite similar, but without having to constantly define objects, you generate much less structural code. The other main difference is, unlike objects, functions have immutable internal state. Given the same set of arguments, they always have the same behavior. This makes them much easier to test and significantly more likely to do exactly what you intended.

## COMING FROM C#

If you are deeply familiar with C# lambda expressions, you are way ahead of the game. C# lambda expressions are arguably first-class language citizens. They are capture in-scope variables. They even grant some limited type inference. F# functions (and lambda expressions) support all these features and more.

First, they have much better type inference. Only rarely will you find yourself needing to define the input and output types of an F# function. This is because the F# compiler uses the powerful Hindley-Milner type inference algorithm (http://www.codecommit.com/blog/scala/what-is-hindley-milner-and-why-is-it-cool). This alone greatly reduces code size.

This means there is no need to build intermediate objects to move data between functions. That is, they can have arguments passed in one at a time and return sets of multiple data types. This means there is no need to define intermediate classes used simply to move data between functions.

Third, F# functions support tail recursion optimization. This means that, if written so that the recursive call always occurs as the final step before returning, F# functions will not overflow the stack. This allows you to leverage recursion in many more cases and be confident that your recursive functions will execute as expected.

Perhaps the biggest feature over C# lambda expressions is that F# functions do not need to be contained within an explicit class. Using F#'s interactive window, you can compose your program one function at a time, playing with different ideas. This makes development much faster because a stiff object-oriented design doesn't need to be in place in order to simply try a new idea. Object-oriented architecture can be applied at a later time, once the underlying ideas of the program have solidified. One of the biggest benefits in this style of writing software is that tests end up being function level and so don't need to constantly be rewritten for architecture changes.

## FUNCTION ARGUMENTS AND RETURN VALUES

Function arguments and return values are a bit different in F# than in other .NET languages. They have a different syntax and use type inference by default. Both of these features come directly from F#'s ML heritage.

However, as F# compiles to IL just like C# or VB, it also is ultimately limited to the same underlying type representations. More than in any other .NET platform language, it is important to understand this type system and the limits of its capability to both generalize and restrict. Similarly, learning to transcend these limitations by leveraging F#'s *inline* keyword to enhance type generalization and restriction can be a great boon.

### Automatic Generalization and Restriction

In F# the type of each function argument is automatically resolved for you through context whenever possible. The compiler examines how the arguments are used and attempts to provide a type that satisfies the most general case allowed by the underlying CLR type system. This process is called automatic generalization.

Consider this function which simply returns the minimum of two arguments:

```
> let min arg1 arg2 = if arg1 < arg2 then arg1 else arg2;;

val min : 'a -> 'a -> 'a when 'a : comparison
```

Here the type inference engine saw that `arg1` and `arg2` were compared with the less-than operator inside of the `min` function and so inferred that the arguments to `min` must have the same restrictions as the arguments to less-than. That is, they both must be the same type and have the comparison constraint. The less-than operator could just as well be another function. In that case the argument types would be inferred based on the signature of that other function.

There are a few important caveats to this. The first is that numerical operators are resolved to `int` if not observed being used in another context. For example, if you define a simple `add` function without any context you might expect it to generalize to all of the potential inputs of the plus operator. This is not the case; instead it will take and return integers by default.

```
> let add a b = a + b;;

val add : int -> int -> int
```

If you give the compiler an external context for this function, it will resolve the arguments in terms of that context.

```
> let add a b = a + b
add 2.0 3.0;;

val add : float -> float -> float
```

However, as the function signature has now been solidified to take two `float`s and returns another, if you now attempt to use this function with the `int` type, it will fail.

```
> add 2 3;;

  add 2 3;;
  ----^

C:\Users\Rick\AppData\Local\Temp\stdin(6,5): error FS0001: This expression
was expected to have type
    float
but here has type
    int
```

Of course, this is less than ideal. Why should you need to write a specific version of our `add` function for each basic data type? Thankfully, you don't. There is a solution to this problem: the `inline` keyword and statically resolved type parameters.

## The inline Keyword

Much like in other languages supporting this keyword, when a function is defined with `inline` the resulting function is injected directly into the locations from which it is called at compile-time. In older languages this was done for the sake of execution speed. In a tight loop, function calls can have significant overhead.

However, with modern processors this has become much less of an issue. These days our processors are often sitting idle, starved for information. The cost of a function call is usually a small drop in the overall bucket. Also, modern compilers are much better at optimization and will often do automatic inlining when appropriate. For these reasons the C# and VB.NET languages opted to not include this feature.

In F#, `inline` is mainly used for its effect on type inference. An inlined function supports much more robust type inference as it is not bound to the rules of the CLR as tightly. It can infer arguments in terms of statically resolved type parameters.

So, whereas in the previous section we saw that our `add` function was being automatically restricted to only accept a single type of input parameter, if we define the same function as `inline` it can now accept either.

```
> let inline add a b = a + b;;

val inline add :
   ^a ->  ^b ->  ^c
      when ( ^a or  ^b) : (static member ( + ) :  ^a *  ^b ->  ^c)

> add 2.0 3.0;;
val it : float = 5.0

> add 2 3;;
val it : int = 5
```

In this case the compiler is generalizing on the plus operator even though it is not generic. As long as the passed arguments support a plus operator that takes the other type, it will resolve correctly. The only caveat is that this type of inference can only happen at compile-time. Functions defined as `inline` will not be usable from other .NET languages.

## Type Annotations

It is sometimes necessary to explicitly describe your type parameters in F#. Most often type inference works incorrectly due to a bug elsewhere in your program. However, occasionally the compiler cannot determine the type of your parameter for you or will infer a type you don't expect. Whatever the case may be, understanding type annotations is essential to writing F# effectively.

Basic type annotation syntax is simple; you just wrap the argument in parentheses, add a colon after the argument name and express the type after it.

```
> let plusOne (x: int) = x + 1;;

val plusOne : int -> int
```

In this example we are annotating x but the return type is still inferred. To annotate the return type, place a colon after the argument list and follow it with the to-be-returned type.

```
> let plusOne x : int = x + 1;;

val plusOne : int -> int
```

The return type, as well as each argument, may or may not be annotated individually.

```
> let plus x (y: double) = x + y;;

val plus : double -> double -> double
```

It is often necessary to only annotate one argument to ensure type inference works correctly or to find that pesky bug causing your program to fail compilation. It ends up working quite a lot like dominos. When one type is correctly identified, many others fall into place as well. Once the types around it are resolved, incorrect code will stand out like a sore thumb.

## Generics and Type Constraints

F#'s type system isn't limited to just basic types. It supports the full range of generics and type constraints as other .NET languages. In fact, its type system can infer most of these automatically.

For example if you were to write a function that compares two arguments with the equals operator, the arguments automatically generalize to a generic type with the equality comparison constraint.

```
> let areEqual arg1 arg2 =
    arg1 = arg2;;

val areEqual : 'a -> 'a -> bool when 'a : equality
```

However, it is also possible to explicitly mandate these constraints when making type annotations. This can be done through application of the when keyword.

```
> let areEqual<'a when 'a : equality> (arg1: 'a) (arg2: 'a) =
    arg1 = arg2;;

val areEqual : 'a -> 'a -> bool when 'a : equality
```

In some cases you may want to have multiple constraints on a type. To do this, separate each constraint with the and keyword.

```
> let isNull<'a when 'a : equality and 'a : null> (arg: 'a) =
    arg = null;;

val isNull : 'a -> bool when 'a : equality and 'a : null
```

A list of commonly used generic type constraints follows.

| CONSTRAINT | EXAMPLE |
| --- | --- |
| Type (or Parent) | `<'a when 'a :> Object>` |
| Nullable | `<'a when 'a : null>` |
| New() | `<'a when 'a : ( new: unit -> 'a )>` |
| Value Type | `<'a when 'a : struct>` |
| Reference Type | `<'a when 'a : not struct>` |
| Comparison | `<'a when 'a : comparison>` |
| Equality | `<'a when 'a : equality>` |

## Statically Resolved Type Parameters

As mentioned in the previous section on the `inline` keyword, F# also supports a much richer set of compile-time-only type constraints. To use them you must trade in generic type parameters for something called statically resolved type parameters. Parameters defined in this way are only available to F# functions marked as `inline`.

One particularly useful example is the member restriction type constraint. This constraint allows you to generalize a type on methods, properties, and even operators.

```
type PresentFromTheGods(isGood) =
    member x.IsGood : bool = isGood

let inline IsItGood< ^a when ^a : (member IsGood : bool)> (container: ^a)  =
    let isgood = (^a : (member IsGood : bool ) container)
    isgood
```

In this example the `IsItGood` function may take any object that has a gettable `IsGood` property that returns a `bool`. When passed an argument of a type defined by the member restriction statically resolved type parameter, some special syntax must be used to extract the value of that member. Here the value of the `container`'s `IsGood` member is extracted into the `isgood` variable and then returned.

```
> IsItGood (new PresentFromTheGods(true));;
val it : bool = true
```

At compile time inline code will be generated in place of the function call. This allows for shared code that is fast and has liberal constraints.

However, as you can see from this example, statically resolved type parameters have syntax that is quite esoteric. In most cases it's best to stick with a combination of inline inference and CLR supported type constraints. This way, you can be sure that they will hold at runtime and that your functions will be available when calling F# assemblies from other languages.

## PARTIAL APPLICATION

In this example only one of `add`'s two arguments is passed in. After the value 1 is applied, the `x` argument is fixed to 1. The result of this is a new function which adds one to any integer passed in.

Partial application is the passing in of only some arguments to a function. This allows the arguments to be stored within the function and passed around implicitly with it. The remaining arguments can be then applied later when they are available or when you want the function to be executed.

```
> let add x y = x + y
let addOne = add 1;;

val add : int -> int -> int
val addOne : (int -> int)

> addOne 5;;
val it : int = 6
```

Partial application has many benefits. As you'll see in Chapter 17, it allows functions to be composed much more readily. Also, you no longer need to pass around a separate set of arguments along with your function. You can bake the repeatedly used arguments right inside and just pass the partially applied function around. This reduces the size of your code by making it unnecessary to build container classes that contain only the repeatedly used inputs of a given function or class.

## Currying

In F#, partial application is done through a process called currying. A curried function is a function that internally has been broken down into a series of one parameter functions. When a parameter is passed in, another function is returned whose argument is the next parameter. This occurs until all parameters are filled in and the function is executed. This is done automatically for you in F#, but let's take a look at what it looks like conceptually.

```
> let explicitCurryAddTwoNumbers x =
    function y -> x + y

val explicitCurryAddTwoNumbers : int -> int -> int
```

Here we have a function which takes a single argument, x, and returns another function of a different argument, y. This returned function has x captured inside of it, ready for use later. This capturing of variables bound in a parent is called a closure.

```
> let plusOne = explicitCurryAddTwoNumbers 1;;
val plusOne : (int -> int)
> plusOne 2;;
val it : int = 3
```

After passing a value into the function, the internal function is returned with x bound. This function can then have another argument applied to it. This ends up being functionally equivalent to the implicit currying in F#.

```
> let addTwoNumbers x y = x + y
let plusOne = addTwoNumbers 1;;

val addTwoNumbers : int -> int -> int
val plusOne : (int -> int)
> plusOne 2;;
val it : int = 3
```

As you can see by comparing the two examples above, explicit currying requires an additional nested function for each parameter. For example, three arguments would require two nested functions.

```
> let explicitCurryAddThreeNumbers x =
    function y -> function z -> (x + y + z);;

val explicitCurryAddThreeNumbers : int -> int -> (int -> int)
```

Although this is possible to do in languages that don't support currying, simulating it with closures becomes tedious quickly. You need to explicitly nest each function, and each time a function is called, you are restricted to passing in only a single argument at a time. F# supports currying by default, so neither of these steps are necessary.

# Restrictions on Functions and Methods

As useful as they are, for the sake of efficiency and interoperability F# has imposed a few restrictions on functions and curried methods. Not knowing about these beforehand can cause quite a bit of difficulty because they are somewhat nonintuitive.

First, functions defined outside the scope of a class cannot be overloaded. This makes sense because conceptually a free floating function is bound to a name that does not include its full type signature.

```
> let square x: int = x * x
let square x: double = x * x;;
error FS0037: Duplicate definition of value 'square'
```

Just as with data values, you cannot have multiple instances that have the same name within the same scope. However, you can bind a function to an existing name in a subscope as long as the type signature is exactly the same. Neither of these restrictions applies to class methods. As in other .NET languages, class methods may be overloaded.

```
> type SquareHelper =
    static member square (x: int) = x * x
    static member square (x: double) = x * x;;

type SquareHelper =
  class
    static member square : x:int -> int
    static member square : x:double -> double
  end
```

However, curried class methods cannot be overloaded. And any member of more than a single argument will be curried by default.

```
> type BadMultHelper =
    static member multiply (x: int) (y: int) = x * y
    static member multiply (x: double) (y: double) = x * y;;

    static member multiply (x: int) (y: int) = x * y;
    -------------------^^^^^^^^
```

```
The method 'multiply' has curried arguments but has the same name as another
method in this type. Methods with curried arguments cannot be overloaded.
Consider using a method taking tupled arguments.
```

The currying of class methods can be prevented by using tuple syntax for function arguments.

```
> type GoodMultHelper =
    static member multiply (x: int, y: int) = x * y
    static member multiply (x: double, y: double) = x * y;;

type GoodMultHelper =
  class
    static member multiply : x:int * y:int -> int
    static member multiply : x:double * y:double -> double
  end
```

Don't be concerned about the possible performance impact in potentially creating a tuple just to pass in. In actuality, F# tupled arguments turn into normal .NET calls with discrete arguments under the hood. Both types of functions will look the same from other .NET languages. The only real difference is in how they are used in the F# language syntax.

## FUNCTIONS AS FIRST CLASS

According to *Structure and Interpretation of Computer Programs* (`http://mitpress.mit.edu/sicp/full-text/book/book.html`), a language construct is considered to be first class if it has no more restrictions than other constructs of that language. In particular, the following properties are listed:

➤ It can be passed as a parameter.

➤ It can be returned as a result.

➤ It can be stored in variables and data structures.

If you consider function pointers, then you might say even humble C fulfills most of these requirements. However, like most imperative languages that inherit syntax from it, C lacks the capability to create new functions at runtime. Functions cannot be composed or partially applied. In this way they are clearly inferior to even a `struct` data type.

With the introduction of anonymous delegates in 2.0, C# functions also have all the properties previously listed and while somewhat cumbersome to use, may be considered first-class language constructs. The main difference with F# is that treating functions as first-class is simple to do, requires little syntax, and is leveraged just about everywhere when writing in the idiomatic language style.

## Recursive Functions

Much as a data type can have a reference to itself, a true first class function should be able to as well. In fact, it should be able to call itself using that reference just as it might any other function. A function that does this is called a recursive function and the process of using recursive functions is called recursion.

To write recursive functions in F#, you must define the function with the `rec` keyword. This keyword binds the function in such a way as to be visible to itself.

```
let rec pow x n = if n <> 0
                  then x * pow (x) (n - 1)
                  else 1.0
```

This `pow` function raises its argument x to the nth power. It does this by calling itself repeatedly, each time reducing the value of its n parameter by one and multiplying x by the result of the last call to `pow`. However, in F# this is a poor implementation of `pow`.

To understand why, you first need to understand how this function will execute at runtime. Each time `pow` calls itself, another stack frame is generated. In the ideal case, n eventually becomes zero and `pow` will return 1 instead of calling itself again. Each layered call will then return, and the result will be multiplied by x. Finally, the result of all of those multiplications will be returned.

However, each function call takes up additional stack memory, and the stack is only a finite size. If n is too large, eventually your program will run out of stack memory and throw a StackOverFlowException.

```
> pow 2.0 100000;;
Process is terminated due to StackOverflowException.
```

This, combined with the overhead of each additional function call, makes for a convincing argument against recursion in other .NET languages. However, F# supports two features that make it very good at recursion. First, F# has been heavily optimized to allow for deep recursion.

```
> pow 2.0 1000;;
val it : float = 1.071508607e+301
```

Second, it has a feature called tail call optimization that allows the compiler to turn some recursive calls into fast loops under the hood. The caveat to this is that it only applies to recursive functions whose final call leaves no work left to be done. If after calling itself the function has to do anything other than return, it can't be optimized. This may sound like it might make tail call recursion all but useless, but as you'll see here and in following chapters, it is profoundly important for both speed and safety.

To make the above example tail recursive, you need to define the same problem in a way that does not cause any work to be done after the recursive call is made. This is most easily done by introducing a new argument to hold whatever it was you were relying on the stack to hold previously. A function argument used solely to pass itself data while performing recursion is called an accumulator.

```
let rec tailpow x n r = if n <> 0
                        then tailpow (r * x) (n - 1) r
                        else r
```

In this better example r acts as the accumulator. It holds the result of the previous computation. Instead of performing the computation lazily as the recursive calls return, they are performed at each step and the result is passed into r. Finally, when n is equal to zero, the result is returned.

It might seem as though having the additional parameter is a big problem. However, it's a simple matter to embed this function inside another and so hide the accumulator.

```
let pow x n =
    let rec tailpow (x:float) n r = if n <> 0
                                    then tailpow x (n - 1) (r * x)
                                    else r
    tailpow x n 1.0
```

In fact, using techniques mentioned in the "Creating Functions at Runtime" section make this even easier and opens up even more possibilities for recursion.

## Higher Order Functions

Higher order functions are functions that use one particular property of a first class function. That is, they take and/or return other functions. As an example, take a look at a simple function that takes another function of no arguments.

```
> let square x = x * x
let performAndAddOne func = func() + 1;;

val square : int -> int
val performAndAddOne : (unit -> int) -> int

> performAndAddOne (fun () -> square 2);;
val it : int = 5
```

The function we pass in takes no arguments and returns the square of 2. When this is passed in to performAndAddOne it is executed, 4 is returned and 1 is added to it. What is interesting about this is not what is being done, but how. The passed in function, as well as the function it is passed in to, could just as well manipulate complex binary data.

Another slightly more advanced example of this from the .NET framework would be List<T>'s generic ForEach function. ForEach takes a function and applies it to each member in a data set. Popular functional examples include map, reduce, and fold, which are discussed in Chapter 16.

Beyond the simple idea of what higher order functions are, is the much more complex idea of what they enable. Ultimately, they allow the programmer to define a program in terms of a series of discrete data transformations instead of a series of state changes. Indeed, this idea is at the core of functional programming.

In languages without higher order functions, while, do-while, for, and foreach must be implemented in the compiler. The same would go for a generalized map, reduce, and fold. Even when using a somewhat imperative style, higher order functions enable you to write these on your own.

```
> let rec forEach (func: 'a -> unit) (collection: list<'a>) =
    if (Seq.isEmpty collection) then
        ()
    else
        func (List.head collection)
        forEach func (List.tail collection)

let printNum num = printfn "%i" num

let testList = [ 0; 1; 2; 3; 4 ];;

val forEach : ('a -> unit) -> 'a list -> unit
val printNum : int -> unit
val testList : int list = [0; 1; 2; 3; 4]

> forEach printNum testList;;
0
1
2
3
4
val it : unit = ()
```

Without some of the more advanced constructs like recursion, higher order functions provide little value other than syntactic sugar. Truly, it is the whole of the ideas presented in this part of the book that when used together make functional programming so useful.

One important idea to take away from this is that, like many functional programming constructs, higher order functions enable language-oriented programming. By leveraging them you can now accomplish much of what you would have previously needed a new compiler to do.

## Storing Functions

Although it is possible to do a great deal with only the ability to pass and return functions from other functions, storing functions in the same way as other data types grants even more power. For example, this technique is often leveraged to reuse a partially applied function over and over within the same scope.

```
> let processEachDataset (data1, data2, data3) =
    let transform = getDataTransform()
    let newData1 = transform data1
    let newData2 = transform data2
    let newData3 = transform data3
    (newData1, newData2, newData3);;

val processEachDataset : 'a * 'a * 'a -> 'a * 'a * 'a
```

It is also possible to perform some work with a set of functions that you have previously accumulated.

```
> let processDatasetWithCurrentTransforms data =
    let transforms = getDataTransforms()
    let rec applyTransforms data transforms =
        match transforms with
        | [] -> data
        | thisTransform :: otherTransforms ->
            applyTransforms (thisTransform data) otherTransforms
    applyTransforms data transforms;;

val processDatasetWithCurrentTransforms : 'a -> 'a
```

One particularly strong example of this is F#'s asynchronous workflows. Using the Async module you can take a collection of functions and send them off to separate threads to execute with little code. Without the ability to put functions into collections, powerful constructs like this would be impossible.

## Creating Functions at Runtime

The ability to pass and return functions from other functions is powerful alone. Greatly enhancing this is the ability to create new functions at runtime.

In F# this can be accomplished in a number of ways that are each useful for a wide range of practical applications. Closures provide the ability to bind variables out of the scope in which a function is defined. First-class functional composition is used to build new functions out of others.

## Closures

Lexical closures are by far the easiest way to create new functions at runtime. Simply put, when a function is defined within another, it binds the values that are defined before it in the parent function's scope. This can be done with any first-class language construct: values, objects, and functions.

Think back to school and the approximate derivative of a function. You might recall that it can be expressed in terms of f(x + dx) – f(x – dx) / (2 * dx) where dx is a number close to zero. Without higher order functions, this is quite difficult to calculate in a nonspecific way. Given higher order functions, it's possible to calculate the derivative of a function for a single value of x in the following way:

```
let approxDerivative f dx x = (f(x + dx) - f(x - dx)) / 2 * dx;;
```

However, without a way to create a function, this can only find values of the derivative at certain points. With closures you can create a function that creates the approximate derivative function of a given function.

```
let approxDerivative f dx =
    let derivative x = (f(x + dx) - f(x - dx)) / 2.0 * dx in
    derivative
```

In this example the function and dx values are passed into the parent function and are captured by the derivative function. This new function can now be returned containing these bound values.

The simplest implication of this is that, when repeatedly calling the same function, you no longer have the need to pass the same arguments again and again. Instead, you can simply create an embedded function that closes over the unchanging arguments and call it. This is quite a boon, especially when dealing with mutable variables. You no longer need to consider that they might change the bound function's behavior. Once bound, values will not change unless mutated by reference.

## Lambda Expressions

A lambda expression is simply special syntax for a function without a name. It can be defined completely inline. It can also still be curried and close over variables just like any other function. It can even be assigned to a variable. However, it need not be.

Lambda expression syntax is simple, just use the `fun` keyword followed by a list of arguments and then the function contents. Going back again to the derivative example, we can make the closure version look much cleaner if we use a lambda expression:

```
let lamdbaDerivative f dx = fun x -> (f(x + dx) - f(x - dx)) / 2.0 * dx
```

In this example the function is returned directly without any need for intermediate constructs. The syntax is clean and easy to understand, ideal for passing to or returning from other functions.

This feature is particularly useful when calling the many F# library functions that take another function as a parameter. The resulting code reads much more easily than a separate function definition when written in this way.

However, do be careful when using multiline lambda expressions. They can easily get out of hand and be difficult to differentiate from their surrounding context. They are also difficult to write tests against. For these reasons, if your lambda expression is longer than one or two lines, it is often better to define it in a separate function instead.

## Composition with Partial Application

As previously discussed, currying allows you to partially compose functions by applying only some of the parameters a function requires. In the case of the derivative example, you can use partial application to build a derivative function without using closures. Consider the initial example:

```
let calcApproxDerivative f dx x = (f(x + dx) - f(x - dx)) / 2.0 * dx
```

Given that this function already exists, we can use partial application to build a specific derivative function quite easily.

```
let square (x: float) = x * x
let derivativeOfSquare = calcApproxDerivative square 0.001;;
```

So, while not quite as flexible as closures, in many cases it is possible to leverage partial application to do the same thing.

# SUMMARY

Your first task in getting acclimated to F# is to get a handle on the type inference system. It's not difficult; you just have to learn how the type inference system makes the decisions it does. When things go wrong, use Visual Studio to mouse over your value and check out its inferred type. It will soon be obvious where type annotations are needed.

Next, try playing with closures, partial application, and lambda expressions. Although entirely avoidable in C# and VB.NET, one of the most important steps in getting familiar with F# is becoming used to treating functions as first-class language citizens.

These ideas are much different than what you have been used to in idiomatic C#. Becoming adept at leveraging these constructs primarily requires practice. Don't be afraid to try things out in the interactive window and see what happens.

# 14

# Immutable Data

## WHAT'S IN THIS CHAPTER?

➤ Understanding Why Immutability Is Good

➤ Managing State and Mutation Responsibly

➤ Passing References

➤ Enhancing Performance

The term functional is similar to object oriented in that it represents a collection of language design choices and associated design methodologies. In this chapter, you'll explore the data side of functional programming in F# through a combination of language features and methodology. When you arrive on the other side, you'll know why immutable data structures are so important and have ways of handling mutation in a safe way.

## THE PROBLEM WITH STATE

For years, the vast majority of programmers have combined data in mutable form and operations on that data in constructs known as classes. Along with the numerous advantages of this methodology come a number of disadvantages that are not often discussed. Most of these disadvantages stem from the use of these classes as black boxes that each encapsulate some part of the state of your program. This state is hidden by a mess of unspecified behavior, implicit in the method definitions of the classes.

When consuming these classes, you find yourself unable to directly understand their implementation. The same call to a class method may produce different results, and often does. This problem is not restricted to a single class because many classes mutate each other or are interlinked with complex networks of events. A single method call can cause a ripple effect of state changes throughout your program.

The foundation of your reasoning about these programs is unsound. As the number of possible state changes per call increases, so does the number of potential bugs. A single change to a class can cause bugs to appear in a completely different part of the program. This problem is compounded to a large degree by asynchronous, parallel, or event-driven programming.

If you have attempted to build a test harness for a large legacy class, you have likely experienced this firsthand. A precise model of behavior can be difficult to nail down when that behavior is defined by a large number of stateful constructs. Modern testing and design methodologies have been invented to help mitigate some of these problems, but little has been done to combat the source.

The good news is that by taking a functional approach you can eliminate the vast majority of these errors. By changing your thinking to be in terms of immutable data and transformations of that data, most of these problems simply evaporate. As all inputs and outputs are exposed, you can be sure that calls are doing only what you expect. Intermediate program states are not exposed because data is immutable and changes are made primarily through atomic reference swapping.

## STATE SAFETY

Bar none, the biggest problem with modern object-oriented languages is that they make it near impossible to guarantee any kind of state safety. This single problem is responsible for everything from the modern concurrency nightmare to the epidemic of difficult-to-test code. Many sets of best practices have arisen to help. However, they come at a heavy cost in terms of both performance and code size because they lack language support.

### Programwide State Safety

When data and operations on that data are inextricably intertwined, several problems arise. First, object graphs are subject to simultaneous and conflicting state changes. Second, it cannot be ensured that data is in the correct state for a call to complete successfully. Third, changes in seemingly unrelated objects may affect the output of a call. To understand these problems better, it is necessary to examine them in more detail and see how having immutable data prevents these types of error from occurring.

Errors arising from simultaneous operations on a stateful object graph are one of the primary reasons for the great interest in functional programming. An unfortunate side effect of classes being considered black boxes is that without examining the content of the class you're using you can never be sure that it was written in a thread-safe way.

```
type UnsafeAccessClass() =
    let mutable i = 0
    member this.IncrementTenAndGetResult() =
        i <- i + 10
        i
```

As you can see when multiple calls to `UnsafeAccessClass.IncrementTen ()` occur in separate threads, the output will vary depending on the order of thread execution. To explore what can happen, take a look at this small framework that views the possible outputs based on discrete timings by breaking this class into calls for each line.

```
open System
open System.Threading

type UnsafeAccessClass() =
    let mutable i = 0
    member this.IncrementTen() =
        i <- i + 10
        this
    member this.GetResult() = i

let asyncExecuteClass (ac: UnsafeAccessClass) (firstSleep: int, secondSleep: int) =
    async {
        Thread.Sleep( firstSleep*firstSleep*20 )
        let incremented = ac.IncrementTen()
        Thread.Sleep( secondSleep*secondSleep*20 )
        let result = incremented.GetResult()
        return result, DateTime.Now.Ticks
    }

let compareUnsafeExecution firstThreadSleeps secondThreadSleeps =
    let ac = new UnsafeAccessClass()
    let threadWork = [ asyncExecuteClass ac firstThreadSleeps;
                       asyncExecuteClass ac secondThreadSleeps]
    let results = Async.RunSynchronously (Async.Parallel threadWork)
    if snd results.[0] < snd results.[1] then
        [ "1st", (fst results.[0]); "2nd", (fst results.[1]) ]
    else
        [ "2nd", (fst results.[1]); "1st", (fst results.[0]) ]
```

Let's examine each of the possible output cases.

```
//Execution Order: 1,1,2,2
let case1 = compareUnsafeExecution (1, 2) (3, 4)
//Execution Order: 2,2,1,1
let case2 = compareUnsafeExecution (3, 4) (1, 2)
//Execution Order: 1,2,1,2
let case3 = compareUnsafeExecution (1, 3) (2, 4)
//Execution Order: 2,1,2,1
let case4 = compareUnsafeExecution (2, 4) (1, 3)
//Execution Order: 1,2,2,1
let case5 = compareUnsafeExecution (1, 4) (2, 3)
//Execution Order: 2,1,1,2
let case6 = compareUnsafeExecution (2, 3) (1, 4)

val case1 : (string * int) list = [("1st", 10); ("2nd", 20)]
val case2 : (string * int) list = [("2nd", 10); ("1st", 20)]
val case3 : (string * int) list = [("1st", 20); ("2nd", 20)]
val case4 : (string * int) list = [("2nd", 20); ("1st", 20)]
val case5 : (string * int) list = [("2nd", 20); ("1st", 20)]
val case6 : (string * int) list = [("1st", 20); ("2nd", 20)]
```

*Code snippet ThreadDataTesstMutable.fs*

Notice that given just this simple example with a single mutated variable and two threads, there are six possible execution orderings. The result of this is two possible return values and two possible return orderings. The number of orderings will explode exponentially with the number of threads. Even worse, the number of different possible results has an exponential relationship with both the number of mutations and the number of threads.

Now, let's examine the possible outputs given an immutable class.

```
type SafeAccessClass(i) =
    new() = SafeAccessClass (0)
    member this.IncrementTen() = new SafeAccessClass(i + 10)
    member this.GetResult() = i

val case1 : (string * int) list = [("1st", 10); ("2nd", 10)]
val case2 : (string * int) list = [("2nd", 10); ("1st", 10)]
val case3 : (string * int) list = [("1st", 10); ("2nd", 10)]
val case4 : (string * int) list = [("2nd", 10); ("1st", 10)]
val case5 : (string * int) list = [("2nd", 10); ("1st", 10)]
val case6 : (string * int) list = [("1st", 10); ("2nd", 10)]
```

*Code snippet ThreadTestImmutable.fs*

Note that the return ordering cannot be guaranteed. However, the combination of immutability and F#'s asynchronous workflows make this a nonissue.

Almost all the `System.Drawing` namespace works in a similar way, and extensive steps must be taken to ensure calls to `Clone()` are performed in the correct places. Often consumers of these classes make underlying assumptions about the state of internal class data with disastrous results. When using immutable data, considerations of this type become completely unnecessary.

This leads to the problem of ensuring data is in the correct state before a call is made. Method calls may require a particular ordering for internal data structures to be properly initialized, or assumptions may be made about the state of method inputs. This results in the need for explicit preconditions to verify that these assumptions are `true`. Preconditions that when violated, can result in runtime failures.

Let's take a quick look at an example of implicitly required ordering of method calls with a common pattern that is often used in C#:

```
exception NotInitialized

type InitializeClass() =
  let mutable initialized = false;
  member this.Initialize() =
    initialized <- true
  member this.Perform() =
    if not initialized then raise NotInitialized
```

The problems generated by the need for preconditions are two-fold. First, if the programmer forgets about even one precondition, the data may be in a bad state and cause an exception of an unhandled type to be thrown. Second, it is much better to correct program flow issues of this type at compile-time. As discussed in the previous chapter, it is possible to prevent the need for most of these preconditions by effectively leveraging the F# type system. Immutability also helps here immensely by ensuring that the contents of class fields do not change after construction. These two features alone eliminate the need for most precondition checks.

Finally, there is the issue of seemingly unrelated objects affecting each other in unexpected ways. As classes often hold shared or bidirectional references, a change in one class may cause unexpected behavior in another. As an example of this, take a look at a simple settings class and the classes that reference it.

```
type ListGenerationManager() =
    let mutable GenerateInstances = 0
    member this.InstancesToGenerate
        with get () = GenerateInstances
        and set (value) = GenerateInstances <- value
    member this.GetIntegerGenerator() = new IntegerListGenerator(this)
    member this.GetFloatGenerator() = new FloatListGenerator(this)

and IntegerListGenerator(manager: ListGenerationManager) =
    member this.GenerateInstances() =
        List.init manager.InstancesToGenerate (fun i -> int i)

and FloatListGenerator(manager: ListGenerationManager) =
    member this.GenerateInstances() =
        List.init manager.InstancesToGenerate (fun i -> float i)
```

*Code snippet ListGenerationManager.fs*

In cases where invisible shared state is present, attempting to fix a bug without cataloging everywhere the classes sharing that state are constructed or used is extremely difficult. Without full knowledge of their context, it is impossible to correctly reason about their behavior. Furthermore, attempting to change the referenced class may cause unexpected behavioral changes to pop up in its consumers. Just as the runtime state changes ripple through these objects, so do the effects of behavioral changes.

With immutable data you can be confident that these types of situations do not occur as changes to the internal state of the object will always be accompanied by the construction of a new object. This prevents interobject behavioral dependencies from being created in the first place.

These common problems are all easy to avoid when programming with immutable data. Given the same input set, your functions will reliably produce the same output. Data is transformed and passed around, instead of being encapsulated and kept around. As you might expect, this greatly reduces the number of state-related bugs in a given program. As your data is unable to change, you can rest assured that these types of unexpected conditions will not occur.

## Local Data State Safety

A big problem with mutable data is that it can be difficult or impossible to reason about what the contents of a variable will be after a call is made. This is part of the reason extensive debugging tools are needed when programming in most modern object-oriented languages. Will a passed-in list be kept in the same order? Will the data transform you gave as input still contain the same values? Worse, even after spotting a bug caused by the unexpected mutation of data, it can be time-consuming to find exactly where that mutation took place. Changes can occur anywhere the object is passed or held.

When classes are designed this way, it creates a situation where the ordering of calls and handling of data becomes very important. Without extreme care brittle code is the result. A great example of this is the .NET List class. Any call that uses this class can potentially cause its contents to change.

```
type ListData =
    struct
      val mutable Number: int
      val mutable Name: string
      new( number, name ) = { Number = number; Name = name }
      override this.ToString() =
          String.Format( "Number: {0}, Name: {1}", this.Number, this.Name )
    end

let clrList = new List<ListData>( [| new ListData(1, "Johnny");
                                     new ListData(5, "Lisa");
                                     new ListData(3, "Mark") |]);

> clrList.ToArray();;
val it : ListData [] =
  [|Number: 1, Name: Johnny; Number: 5, Name: Lisa; Number: 3, Name: Mark|]

let sortedClrList =
    let ListDataComparison (d1:ListData) (d2:ListData) =
        d1.Number - d2.Number in
        clrList.Sort( ListDataComparison )
    clrList

> sortedClrList.ToArray();;
val it : ListData [] =
  [|Number: 1, Name: Johnny; Number: 3, Name: Mark; Number: 5, Name: Lisa|]

> clrList.ToArray();;
val it : ListData [] =
  [|Number: 1, Name: Johnny; Number: 3, Name: Mark; Number: 5, Name: Lisa|]

let reversedClrList =
    clrList.Reverse()
    clrList

> reversedClrList.ToArray();;
val it : ListData [] =
  [|Number: 5, Name: Lisa; Number: 3, Name: Mark; Number: 1, Name: Johnny|]

> sortedClrList.ToArray();;
val it : ListData [] =
  [|Number: 5, Name: Lisa; Number: 3, Name: Mark; Number: 1, Name: Johnny|]

> clrList.ToArray();;
val it : ListData [] =
  [|Number: 5, Name: Lisa; Number: 3, Name: Mark; Number: 1, Name: Johnny|]
```

One commonly used method of avoiding data mutation is to explicitly clone the class each time it is passed. This adds extra code to your program and makes it slower, but at least it allows some semblance of safety.

```
let clrList = new List<ListData>( [| new ListData(1, "Johnny");
                                      new ListData(5, "Lisa");
                                      new ListData(3, "Mark") |]);
let sortedClrList =
    let newList = new List<ListData>(clrList)
    let ListDataComparison (d1:ListData) (d2:ListData) =
        d1.Number - d2.Number in
        newList.Sort( ListDataComparison )
    newList

> sortedClrList.ToArray();;
val it : ListData [] =
  [|Number: 1, Name: Johnny; Number: 3, Name: Mark; Number: 5, Name: Lisa|]

> clrList.ToArray();;
val it : ListData [] =
  [|Number: 1, Name: Johnny; Number: 5, Name: Lisa; Number: 3, Name: Mark|]
```

F# does all it can to prevent you from unexpectedly mutating the contents of a list, and it does so at compile time. In fact, even if the members of `ListData` are marked mutable, the following sample will not compile. The immutable property is maintained for the data structure and its contents.

```
> let incrementedClrList =
    clrList.ForEach( (fun data -> data.Number <- data.Number + 1) )
    clrList

error FS0256: A value must be mutable in order to mutate the contents or take the
address of a value type, e.g. 'let mutable x = ...'
```

Unfortunately, other .NET languages don't make such guarantees. In these languages, great pains must be taken and great inefficiencies must be incurred to avoid mutation. The following C# example compiles and can be used without any errors being raised.

```
public static List<ListData> IncrementAllInList(List<ListData> list)
{
    list.ForEach((data => data.Number += 1));
    return list;
}
```

Therefore, when using these languages, it is often wise to do a deep clone before passing your list into another part of your program. This is the only way you can be confident that neither the order nor the content of the elements will change. This process is often very resource-intensive and can be painful to implement.

An alternative to this is to build a read-only version of a .NET list by using `List.AsReadOnly`. However, this returns an `IList` and so can't be used in places where a standard list is taken. Also, using a read-only list may protect against reordering, element addition, and element removal, but it won't stop a consumer from directly modifying the elements themselves. Unless you have control over the entire API, `AsReadOnly` and the `IList` it returns are little more than a bandage on a gaping wound.

Now, in C# you would wisely implement `ICloneable` and a generic `List<T>`. `DeepClone()` extension method to make this easier on yourself. However, the vast majority of the .NET framework is composed of `structs` and sealed classes that do not implement `ICloneable`. For this reason, separate deep clone extension methods for each `List-DataType` combination must be created.

```
let deepCloneList (list: List<ListData>) =
    let newList = new List<ListData>()
    list.ForEach( (fun data ->
        newList.Add( new ListData( data.Number, data.Name ) ) ) )
    newList
```

Thankfully, F# comes with a number of immutable data structures that, when used, eliminate these problems. Now, take a look at similar code that uses F# lists instead (for more information on F# lists see Chapter 5).

```
> let initialList = [ new ListData(1, "Johnny");
                      new ListData(5, "Lisa");
                      new ListData(3, "Mark") ];

val initialList : ListData list =
  [Number: 1, Name: Johnny; Number: 5, Name: Lisa; Number: 3, Name: Mark]

> let sortedList =
    let numberSelector (d: ListData) = d.Number in
        List.sortBy numberSelector initialList

val sortedList : ListData list =
  [Number: 1, Name: Johnny; Number: 3, Name: Mark; Number: 5, Name: Lisa]

> let reversedList = List.rev initialList

val reversedList : ListData list =
  [Number: 3, Name: Mark; Number: 5, Name: Lisa; Number: 1, Name: Johnny]
```

Notice that, after being constructed, you can always be confident about the contents of an F# list instance. It will never be unexpectedly changed by a call. Coupled with immutable list members, this makes it easy to reason about exactly what your code will do even before writing a test or walking through it in a debugger.

To further this ability to reason about code, functional programs are constructed with a different approach than those that are object oriented. As you may have noticed, instead of using classes to create black boxes, you are using immutable data structures and functions that return new data. This practice ensures that when viewing code it is easy to tell exactly what is being done and exactly where those effects are applied, even in the face of out-of-scope code changes.

## DATA MUTATION

One of the advantages of F# is that, although it encourages immutability, it is not a pure functional programming language. That is, F# allows for the mutation of data. This difference frees programmers to use the most expressive paradigm for the algorithm they are implementing, instead of being forced to use convoluted or inefficient code.

However, this puts the responsibility for state safety solely in your hands. Although pure functional languages force the programmer to behave, it is entirely possible to build F# programs with all the problems discussed in the previous two sections. For this reason, it is important to carefully consider the patterns you use to make state changes in your program.

## Avoiding Mutation

An important part of becoming an effective F# programmer is learning to avoid the mutable keyword whenever possible. Once you get the hang of the language constructs you'll see that in the vast majority of cases data mutation is completely unnecessary. It is usually only when you begin to use imperative .NET framework classes, such as WinForms, that you need to start using a significant amount of mutable data.

As an example, consider putting numbers into buckets according to their least factor. Using mutable data this task might be accomplished in the following way:

**Available for download on Wrox.com**

```
let leastFactor n =
    let max = int (sqrt (float n))
    let mutable lastTried = 1
    let mutable keepLooping = true
    while keepLooping do
        lastTried <- lastTried + 1
        if n % lastTried = 0 || lastTried > max
        then keepLooping <- false
    if lastTried > max then n else lastTried

let bucketByLeastFactors numbers =
    let mutable buckets = Array.create (1 + List.max numbers) []
    for number in numbers do
        let lf = leastFactor number
        buckets.[lf] <- [number] @ buckets.[lf]
    buckets

let printFactorBuckets factorBuckets =
    for i in 0 .. (Array.length factorBuckets) - 1 do
        let factoredList = factorBuckets.[i]
        if not (List.isEmpty factoredList) then
            printfn "%d -> %A" i factoredList

let factorBuckets = bucketByLeastFactors [ 0 .. 25 ]
```

*FactorBucketsMutable.fs*

```
> printFactorBuckets factorBuckets;;

0 -> [0]
1 -> [1]
2 -> [24; 22; 20; 18; 16; 14; 12; 10; 8; 6; 4; 2]
3 -> [21; 15; 9; 3]
5 -> [25; 5]
7 -> [7]
11 -> [11]
```

```
13 -> [13]
17 -> [17]
19 -> [19]
23 -> [23]
```

It may look like employing mutable data here is your only option as, at the very least, it seems like you need a place to accumulate your primes into buckets. However, if you restructure the flow of data, you will see that it is unnecessary in all cases.

```
let leastFactor n =
    let maxFactor = int (sqrt (float n))
    let rec factorTest = function
        | i when i > maxFactor -> n
        | i when n % i = 0 -> i
        | i -> factorTest (i + 1)
    factorTest 2

let bucketByLeastFactors (numbers: int list) =
    let rec addToBucket bucketIndex n bucketsList =
        let neededBuckets = bucketIndex - List.length bucketsList
        if neededBuckets >= 0 then
            addToBucket bucketIndex n
                (bucketsList @ [ for i in 0 .. neededBuckets -> [] ])
        else
            List.mapi
                (fun i bucket ->
                    if bucketIndex = i then ([n] @ bucket)
                    else bucket)
                bucketsList
    List.fold
        (fun bucketsList n -> (addToBucket (leastFactor n) n bucketsList))
        List.empty
        numbers

let printFactorBuckets factorBuckets =
    List.iteri
        (fun i factored ->
            if List.length factored > 0
            then printfn "%d -> %A" i factored)
        factorBuckets

let factorBuckets = bucketByLeastFactors [ 0 .. 25 ]
```

*FactorBucketsImmutable.fs*

```
> printFactorBuckets factorBuckets

0 -> [0]
1 -> [1]
2 -> [24; 22; 20; 18; 16; 14; 12; 10; 8; 6; 4; 2]
3 -> [21; 15; 9; 3]
5 -> [25; 5]
7 -> [7]
```

```
11 -> [11]
13 -> [13]
17 -> [17]
19 -> [19]
23 -> [23]
```

First, compare the leastFactor functions. The mutable iterative sample has been changed into a tail recursive iterative function by breaking it into subcases. It still effectively iterates from 2 to the maxFactor but instead of directly looping and mutating the variable, in each iteration the factorTest function is called with the possible factor incremented by one.

The changes to bucketByLeastFactors are significantly more extensive. Because the goal is to build a list of lists, you must thread this data structure through each of your numbers to be factored. After each number is visited, a new bucketsList is returned. In effect, this is what List.fold does.

After generating the least factor with the (leastFactor n) call, the result is passed, along with the current number and the current bucketsList, into the addToBucket function. This function takes a bucketList and returns a new bucketList with the passed-in number appended to the bucket at the index of the least factor.

This is done by first checking to make sure the appropriate bucket exists; if it doesn't then enough buckets are appended to ensure that it does and recursively calls itself with the freshly expanded bucketList. If it does, a new list of lists is created via the List.mapi function. The only difference between the lists being that the bucket at the least factor index has the newly factored number appended to the front. This bucketList is then returned and used in the next iteration of List.fold.

Getting the hang of this can be a bit difficult at first. This example contains two recursion patterns and two List module functions. F# provides quite a few constructs that help reduce the burden of immutability. The first step in becoming adept at F# is learning these patterns and constructs so that you can program effectively with immutable data. With a little practice they become as familiar as the design patterns and loops you have used for years in object-oriented programming.

When first starting out with F#, the prospect of learning all this can be quite intimidating. The most important thing to keep in mind is isolating mutable data within the confines of a single function. This practice provides most of the safety of immutability but without needing deep knowledge of functional patterns and immutable data structures.

## Bubble and Assign

One technique for relatively safe state mutation, which is easy to begin with, is bubble and assign. When possible, you should always bubble your changes up the call stack and do your variable assignment within the same scope.

```
let simulationLoop () =
    let worldState = getInitialWorldStateArray()
    while simulationIsRunning() do
        let changes = getWorldStateChanges(worldState)
        for change in changes do
            let i, j, newValue = change
            worldState.[i].[j] <- newValue
        updateUI(worldState)
```

*This is a structural example and does not compile.*

By simply returning changes to the current scope and then applying them, state changes can be isolated to this single function. Each iteration of the getWorldStateChanges function returns a set of unapplied changes to the worldState array. These changes are then applied to the array one at a time in a very controlled way.

This simple technique is easy to understand and effective in many cases. It keeps state changes within the scope in which the mutable data is defined and is generally low overhead. The trade-off is that you are limited in terms of where your data can be accessed from and the types of data that can be easily used.

## Reference Cells

You will often find the bubble and assign technique too constraining. In these cases, reference cells are usually the easiest solution. With reference cells your state mutations are made with an atomic reference assignment operation. This replaces an entire data instance with a new one. As your state is enclosed in a heap allocated reference, you can now mutate it from within closures or other functions.

The most common way to do reference swapping is via a reference cell. To do this, define a reference cell with the ref keyword, assign it with the reference assignment operator and retrieve its underlying value with the dereference operator.

```
> let refInt = ref 10;;
val refInt : int ref = {contents = 10;}

> refInt := 20;;
> refInt;;
val it : int ref = {contents = 20;}

> let normalInt = ! refInt;;
val normalInt : int = 20
```

Because using a reference cell effectively boxes your type within a reference type, it is now possible to mutate it from anywhere it or any closures that contain it are accessible. For this reason it is important to carefully consider the implications of both where the reference cell is located and where it is accessed from. It is well known that even judicious use of global variables can lead to major problems with parallelization, code reuse, and the ability to reason about what is happening. However, global variables are just the worst possible case of a larger domain of antipatterns. Any widely accessible mutable data will have these same characteristics, albeit to a lesser degree.

```
let gameLoop actors display input =
    let mutable gameIsRunning = true
    let worldState = ref (getInitialWorldStateArray())
    let applyChanges changes =
        for (i,j,value) in changes do
```

```
        (!worldState).[i].[j] <- value
while gameIsRunning do
    for actor in actors do
        applyChanges (actor.getChanges !worldState)
    applyChanges (input.getChanges !worldState)
    display.update !worldState
    gameIsRunning <- not input.quit
```

 *This is a structural example and does not compile.*

Note that in the preceding example, all the state changes are confined to this one function. As a general rule of thumb, it is best to limit assignment and passing of mutable data to as small of a scope as possible.

Now, consider the following worst-case example:

```
let gameIsRunning = ref true
let worldState: option< option<int> array array > ref = ref None

let initializeWorldStateArray () =
    worldState := Some(getInitialWorldStateArray())

let updateGameStateFromActors () =
    for actor in !actors do
        actor.updateWorldState worldState

let updateGameStateFromUserInput () =
    userInput.updateWorldState worldState
    gameIsRunning := not userInput.quit

let updateUI () = ui.update worldState

let gameLoop () =
    initializeWorldStateArray()
    while !gameIsRunning do
        updateGameStateFromActors()
        updateUI()
        updateGameStateFromUserInput()
```

 *This is a structural example and does not compile.*

This is effectively a bunch of mutable variables and functions that transparently operate on those variables. As you do not even require function wrappers to access or change the data, the state of this program can be changed anywhere silently and is all but impossible to debug. Code constructed in this way is also notoriously difficult to reuse or parallelize.

If instead, you swap close to your reference by moving the mutable reference declaration down the stack and push the needed changes up the stack, the negative effects of mutability are isolated to a small portion of your overall code. It is always best to keep your mutable data access and assignments limited to as small of a scope as possible.

## Passing by Reference

Although often overlooked, passing by reference is a very effective way to perform mutation. As only those functions granted special access can manipulate the reference, you can be confident that hidden mutations are not happening elsewhere. Passing by reference requires three steps be taken. First, the variable must be marked as mutable. Second, you must wrap the value in a reference cell with the in boxing operator. Third, the function must be annotated to take its argument as a reference with the byref keyword.

```
> let mutable number = 10
let doubleNumber (number: int byref) = number <- 2 * number
doubleNumber (&number);;

> number;;
val it : int = 20
```

By using the byref keyword, calls that perform mutation stand out as they now require a boxing operator to be applied.

```
let gameLoop actors display input =
    let mutable gameIsRunning = true
    let mutable worldState = getInitialWorldStateArray()
    let applyChanges changes (worldState: 'a option [] [] byref) =
        List.iter
            (fun (i,j,value) -> (worldState).[i].[j] <- value)
            changes
    while gameIsRunning do
        for actor in actors do
            applyChanges (actor.getChanges worldState) (&worldState)
        applyChanges (input.getChanges worldState) (&worldState)
        display.update worldState
        gameIsRunning <- not input.quit
```

 *This is a structural example and does not compile.*

Effectively, the byref keyword makes a contract between the caller and the callee that states that it has permission to mutate the reference. For this reason it is the safest way to perform direct mutation.

## Message Passing

A very effective way to enhance the safety of state mutation is through message passing. This entails using discriminated union subtypes (see Chapter 7, "Complex Composite Types") as the enumeration of possible messages along with the data corresponding to that message. Simply put, the type name, the message, describes the change to be made while the type itself contains the data necessary to complete that change. Message passing is most commonly used when describing programming with mailboxes. However, as you'll see in the Data and State Flow subsection of Chapter 15, "Data Types," mailboxes are not necessary to gain the safety benefits of message passing.

# PERFORMANCE CONSIDERATIONS

As you saw in the Data Safety section, the mutable nature of .NET constructs can make it difficult to reason about code. This can be alleviated somewhat by judicious copying, but this practice has significant performance implications. This is why F#'s immutable data structures are designed in such a way as to minimize the number of objects that must be collected.

For example, when changes to a list are made, only the parts of it that are affected by the change are replaced in the new instance. In practice, this use of intelligent implementations under the hood largely mitigates the performance cost of immutability. These, and other optimizations, are why it is always important to avoid making assumptions about performance when using F#.

One important trick to know is that you can enable timing in the F# interactive window. This is a fast way to check out the performance of new code without the need for a profiler or timing harness.

```
> #time;;

--> Timing now on

> let l = [0 .. 1000000];;
Real: 00:00:00.390, CPU: 00:00:00.390, GC gen0: 5, gen1: 2, gen2: 0
```

To turn it off, simply type the command again.

```
> #time;;

--> Timing now off
```

However, as not all optimizations are available to F# interactive, it is always best to ultimately use a profiler on Release mode generated assemblies to find areas of slow performance. At best, the `#time` feature can give you a general idea.

As testing every line of code written in this way would be tedious and time-consuming, it is important to understand the underlying implementation and performance characteristics of each of the basic F# data structures. For the sake of convenience, I'll expand upon what was previously stated in Chapter 7.

## Lists

F# lists are immutable singly linked lists and so are designed for left-to-right access. Head and iterative access are always $O(1)$. However, indexing to a particular element is $O(n)$, where n is the index of the node in the list. For this reason, large F# Lists are best used with forward iterative operations only. Thankfully, functional programming is largely oriented toward the iterative processing of data and, due to their immutability and data sharing, lists are often your best choice.

Due to the `O(n)` element access of linked lists, when using them it is important to carefully consider the performance characteristics of your implementation. When appending two lists, it is best to place the longer of the two on the right whenever possible. This allows the entire structure of the right list to be shared with the newly created list.

```
> let smallList = [0 .. 100]
let bigList = [0 .. 10000000];;

> smallList @ bigList;;
Real: 00:00:00.000, CPU: 00:00:00.000, GC gen0: 0, gen1: 0, gen2: 0

> bigList @ smallList;;
Real: 00:00:02.214, CPU: 00:00:02.215, GC gen0: 29, gen1: 17, gen2: 0
```

Both ordering and operator use are important considerations when generating lists with recursive functions. If your recursive function appends to the right side of a list, the append will grow slower with every recursive call. However, it is also important to remember that if you have a recursive call on the left side of a list operation, your function cannot take advantage of tail recursion optimization and will both execute more slowly and be at risk of stack overflow. For these reasons, in most cases it is best to generate lists iteratively with accumulators, list comprehensions, or `List.init`.

A simple example of this is the reversal of a list. The following naive implementation will give `O(n^2)` performance.

```
let rec badReverse list =
    if List.isEmpty list then []
    else badReverse list.Tail @ [list.Head]
```

Looking at this example, two flags should immediately pop up in your mind. First, `list.Head`, a single element, occurs on the right side of the append operator, which means it will be quite slow.

```
> badReverse [0 .. 10000];;
Real: 00:00:05.105, CPU: 00:00:05.101, GC gen0: 396, gen1: 90, gen2: 1
val it : int list =
  [10000; 9999; 9998; 9997; 9996; 9995; 9994; 9993; 9992; 9991; 9990; 9989;
   9988; 9987; 9986; 9985; 9984; 9983; 9982; 9981; 9980; 9979; …]
```

Second, the recursive call is on the left side and so tail recursion optimization will not be used. This means you are at risk of a stack overflow.

```
> badReverse [0 .. 100000];;

Process is terminated due to StackOverflowException.
```

If you instead thread an accumulator through your list reversal, you can perform the operation in `O(n)` time and without the risk of a stack overflow. Generally, the phrase threading an accumulator simply means to pass yourself intermediate values with each recursion. This topic is discussed in further depth in Chapter 16.

```
let appendReverse list =
    let rec recReverse rest reversed =
        if List.isEmpty rest then reversed
        else recReverse rest.Tail ([rest.Head] @ reversed)
```

```
    recReverse list []

> appendReverse [0 .. 100000];;

Real: 00:00:00.033, CPU: 00:00:00.031, GC gen0: 1, gen1: 0, gen2: 0
val it : int list =
  [100000; 99999; 99998; 99997; 99996; 99995; 99994; 99993; 99992; 99991;
   99990; 99989; 99988; 99987; 99986; 99985; 99984; 99983; 99982; 99981; …]
```

There's also a third issue here. A single element is repeatedly added, but append is used instead of cons. Whenever repeatedly adding a single element to a list, it's better to use the cons operator instead of creating a new list and appending it; cons simply creates a single new list node while append contains quite a lot of logic to ensure all possible states of both lists are covered. With lists up to 100,000 elements, the impact is negligible. However, when you have millions of elements the impact becomes quite significant.

```
let consReverse list =
    let rec recReverse rest reversed =
        if List.isEmpty rest then reversed
        else recReverse rest.Tail (rest.Head :: reversed)
    recReverse list []

> let list = [0 .. 1000000];;
Real: 00:00:00.291, CPU: 00:00:00.296, GC gen0: 7, gen1: 7, gen2: 2

> appendReverse list;;
Real: 00:00:00.345, CPU: 00:00:00.343, GC gen0: 6, gen1: 4, gen2: 1

> consReverse list;;
Real: 00:00:00.064, CPU: 00:00:00.062, GC gen0: 2, gen1: 2, gen2: 0
```

To simplify things further, you can use pattern matching syntax. This makes the two recursive cases stand out apart from each other better.

```
let patternMatchingReverse list =
    let rec recReverse rest reversed =
        match rest with
        | [] -> reversed
        | head::tail -> recReverse tail (head::reversed)
    recReverse list []
```

However, as in most cases, the best solution is to use the built-in list module operators as they are concise, safe, and designed with performance in mind.

```
> List.rev [0 .. 100000];;

Real: 00:00:00.015, CPU: 00:00:00.015, GC gen0: 0, gen1: 0, gen2: 0
```

When using these operators, you can be confident that the underlying implementation has been done in an intelligent way and that your code will be easy for others to understand. Also, if you take a glimpse at the F# source code, you will see that library list operations are almost all implemented via pattern matching. When no existing list operation fits your need, pattern matching is most often the best choice.

## Arrays

F# arrays are in all ways traditional .NET arrays. They are contiguous in memory, and just as in other .NET languages, indexing is always `O(1)`. Also, as arrays are themselves a special class of CLR reference type, they are by far the most efficient way to store and operate on sets of other value types in memory. However, appending to, or otherwise changing the structure of arrays will often require a completely new allocation. For this reason when managing large datasets, which don't need random access, lists are the better choice.

It is also important to note that F# does not enforce immutability for arrays.

```
> let a = [|0 .. 5|];;
val a : int [] = [|0; 1; 2; 3; 4; 5|]

> a.[0] <- 1;;
val it : unit = ()

> a;;
val it : int [] = [|1; 1; 2; 3; 4; 5|]
```

When using arrays in F#, you must always keep in mind that their contents may change, especially in the case where they are passed in to a standard .NET library. Of course, this is not quite as much of a problem when you completely control access to the array. F# assignment requires a special operator that is easy to spot. Also, when designing for fast concurrency with shared mutable datasets, arrays are often the ideal choice.

However, as discussed in the data mutation section, it's best to choose the scope of your mutable data carefully. Do think carefully before using globally shared mutable arrays.

## Sequences

F# `Seqs` are simply instances of the `IEnumerable` interface. Similar to lists, sequence indexing is `O(n)`, where n is the cost of evaluating the contents of each prior element. The benefits of using sequences are that they are evaluated when called and are simple to manage. However, this delayed evaluation can come at a high performance cost if you are not careful. For example, while `Seqs` cost very little to allocate, if repeatedly iterated over performance can be very slow.

```
> let simpleSeq = seq { for i in 0 .. 1000000 do yield i }
Real: 00:00:00.000, CPU: 00:00:00.000, GC gen0: 0, gen1: 0, gen2: 0

> for i in 0 .. 10 do Seq.iter (fun i -> ()) simpleSeq
Real: 00:00:01.241, CPU: 00:00:01.232, GC gen0: 0, gen1: 0, gen2: 0
```

One way to mitigate this somewhat is to use `Seq.cache`. This function will generate a sequence that caches each value of its output when generated. The next time the sequence is used, already visited elements won't need to be evaluated. However, `Seq.cache` is only fast for expensive element computations. It does not remove the overhead in `IEnumerable` itself.

```
> let cachedSeq = Seq.cache simpleSeq;;
Real: 00:00:00.000, CPU: 00:00:00.000, GC gen0: 0, gen1: 0, gen2: 0

> for i in 0 .. 10 do Seq.iter (fun i -> ()) cachedSeq;;
Real: 00:00:00.688, CPU: 00:00:00.686, GC gen0: 73, gen1: 0, gen2: 0
```

Often a better approach for repeatedly iterated-over sequences is to convert them into a list at the first available opportunity. While conversion will carry the same cost as the initial sequence traversal, additional iterations will be much cheaper.

```
> let listFromSeq = Seq.toList simpleSeq
Real: 00:00:00.313, CPU: 00:00:00.312, GC gen0: 7, gen1: 2, gen2: 1

> for i in 0 .. 10 do List.iter (fun i -> ()) listFromSeq
Real: 00:00:00.031, CPU: 00:00:00.031, GC gen0: 0, gen1: 0, gen2: 0
```

In this particular case, due to the large number of elements, the creation of the list is rather expensive. However, with only ten iterations, the conversion to a list is well worth the initial cost as it is nearly twice as fast.

Of course, this technique is not applicable when using sequences that are evaluated based on a function that references mutable data. However, this style of using sequences should usually be avoided for the same reasons described above in the State Safety section.

## Tuples

Perhaps second only to lists, tuples are one of the most frequently used data structures in F#. Most frequently, they are used to conveniently bind together sets of function inputs and outputs and make for much more readable functional code. In .NET 4.0 and later, F# tuples are .NET tuple types in the System namespace.

Although some were concerned with the design decision to implement tuples as reference types, after much testing it was found that this made little or no difference for the vast majority of applications and broadly increased tuple interoperability.[*] In cases where performance is paramount, such as number crunching in a tight loop, using a predefined `struct` in the place of a tuple may grant a small performance improvement.

## Records

Records are similar to C# anonymous types and are used in much the same way. They allow you to quickly generate data-only classes with named fields for data processing. Similarly to tuples, the fact that records are immutable reference types may cause a small amount of additional overhead. In some cases you may find using a `struct` in their place grants a performance improvement.

## structs

Fundamentally, F# `structs` are no different from those in any other .NET language. As they are value types, they have significantly different performance characteristics than classes; `structs`

---

[*]http://msdn.microsoft.com/en-us/magazine/dd942829.aspx

are best used only in cases where the use of many small objects creates significant performance or memory overhead.

Because `structs` are value types, they can be allocated on the execution stack instead of the heap and do not need to be garbage collected; `structs` also have much smaller memory footprints than classes. However, it is also important to note that each time a value type is passed, it is copied. For this reason, haphazard use of `structs` can actually reduce the performance of your program.

One example of a case where `structs` can be beneficial is when repeatedly creating a large number of small data instances, such as in image processing.

```
type StructData =
    struct
        val R: byte
        val G: byte
        val B: byte
        new( r, g, b ) = { R = r; G = g; B = b }
    end

type RecordData = { R: byte; G: byte; B: byte }

let pixels = 1920 * 1200
> let structArray = [| for i in 0 .. pixels do
                          yield new StructData( 0uy, 0uy, 0uy ) |]
Real: 00:00:00.387, CPU: 00:00:00.390, GC gen0: 0, gen1: 0, gen2: 0

> let recordArray = [| for i in 0 .. pixels do
                          yield { R = 0uy; G = 0uy; B = 0uy } |]
Real: 00:00:00.846, CPU: 00:00:00.780, GC gen0: 5, gen1: 2, gen2: 0
```

For the best possible performance in these situations it is best to use only a combination of arrays and value types, that is `structs`, `enums`, and `primitives`. When exclusively value types are used, the entire data structure can be laid out contiguously in memory. This is ideal for fast member access and caching.

One of the few differences with `structs` in F# is that members are immutable by default. This is done via automatic property generation. As `structs` are primarily used to enhance performance, and the added call needed when accessing a property does take a small amount of additional time, it is useful to know that when `struct` members are defined as `mutable` they are instead generated as publicly accessible fields.

```
type MutableStructData =
    struct
        val mutable R: byte
        val mutable G: byte
        val mutable B: byte
        new( r, g, b ) = { R = r; G = g; B = b }
    end
```

As always when dealing with mutable data, it is important to consider the data safety ramifications of this design decision before making this optimization. In the vast majority of cases, you'll find the improvement in removing one call is negligible. Even with each iteration accessing every RGB value in every pixel in the equivalent of a 20MP image, my tests saw only a 10% performance improvement. Also, it's important to always keep in mind that value types are copied when passed unless they are inside of an array or another reference type. This means that when you mutate them the changes will not show up in any parent function or method.

## SUMMARY

As you saw in this chapter, F# gives you the tools to mitigate many of the problems inherent in objected-oriented programming by providing a set of useful data constructs. Data immutability helps make your programs safe, parallelizable, and easy to understand.

However, F# neither enforces your use of immutable data structures nor good mutation practices. Without proper application F# code can be just as buggy, rigid, and difficult to maintain as any other language. This especially goes for the optimizations mentioned in the performance considerations section of this chapter. As the benefits only rarely outweigh the risks, it is best to always optimize only after your profiler has shown a problem. If you take only one thing away from this chapter, make it the careful consideration of all variables mutable.

# 15

# Data Types

WHAT'S IN THIS CHAPTER?

➤ Understanding ambiguously defined data

➤ Encapsulating state in types

➤ Leveraging discriminated unions

➤ Defining recursive data types

Specifying types is often thought of as merely a way to tell your computer how to handle the contents of some location in memory. However, as time has progressed, it has been discovered that data types actually can do much more. Beyond telling the compiler which operations to perform on binary data, types can provide a powerful way to label the conceptual meaning of your data. In effect, they become contracts about the semantic meaning of that data. Both data and functions labeled in this way are easier to reason about and can help to ensure the correctness of your code.

## AMBIGUOUSLY TYPED DATA

A problem rife in current mainstream design methodologies is the frequent use of ambiguously typed data. A bool, a double, an exception and a null are all very general. They each carry no meaning other than that which is given to them by their surrounding context. The compiler can do nothing to check if your method inputs, and their internal uses are valid.

What is stopping you from passing a double that represents a probability into a method that wants a specific scalar measurement? Even NASA, with its legendary software QA, has experienced defects of this type. One of these failures has even caused the failure of a very expensive mission. You may be surprised to learn that null references and mishandled exceptions are exactly the same class of defect. They are both caused by inadequately constrained inputs and outputs. They both also cost countless hours in wasted bug-fixing time each year.

To combat this, F# has two features: units of measure (See Chapter 3, "Primitive Types") and discriminated unions (See Chapter 7, "Complex Composite Types"). Units of measure allow you to give semantic meaning to basic types and ensure that they are not allowed in places they don't belong. Discriminated unions allow you to do the same but for any type of function inputs and outputs. In leveraging these constructs you can greatly reduce the number of bugs in your programs.

## FAILING FAST

The fail fast methodology applies well to all types of programming. When a program is designed to fail fast, computation isn't wasted, incorrect state changes are not made, and you are left in a better situation to correctly compensate for the specific type of failure right when it happens.

In using object-oriented design, you often think of failing fast as most important because incorrect state changes must be avoided at all costs. However, in statically checked functional programming, you think of failing fast to prevent incorrect programs from ever executing in the first place. Compile time is the fastest type of failure, the easiest to correct, and has the least impact on your users. The more classes of error that your compiler can protect you from, the more likely your code is to be correct after the first successful compilation.

## SPECIFICITY

As mentioned in the chapter overview, using runtime preconditions to constrain data is a less than ideal solution. This practice greatly increases the chance of runtime failure from untested edge cases or errors introduced by the modification of code. If instead you can encode the specific meaning and constraints implied by that meaning into your types, you can easily avoid most of these types of errors. F#'s powerful type system allows you to do just that, and without a significant increase in the size of your code, a decrease in its performance or an increased maintenance cost.

In the data safety section of Chapter 14, "Immutable Data," you saw how immutability can help enhance your ability to reason about code. However, although it is easier to reason about the state of an immutable list, immutability in no way constrains its contents. That is, you can still pass an unordered list into a function that requires an ordered one.

```
let nLargestNumbers n sortedNumbers =
    let rec nFirstElements n list =
        match n with
        | 0 -> []
        | _ -> match list with
               | [] -> []
               | h::t -> [h] @ nFirstElements (n - 1) t
    nFirstElements n sortedNumbers
```

*Code snippet nLargestNumbers.fs*

In some cases, your first inclination might be to check the order of that list as a precondition. However, ensuring the correct ordering of a list is an `O(n)` operation. As previously shown, you could just order the list each time the function is called, but this is an `O(nLog(n))` operation. Wouldn't it be better if you could somehow encode the ordering of the list in its type?

As you'll see in this section, by leveraging discriminated unions you can both enforce these states for function inputs and label the state of your function outputs.

## Option as an Example

A great place to start when thinking about the F# type system is the option type. As discussed in Chapter 5, "Composite Types," the option type allows you to encode the lack of a value in a much more type safe way than null. The reason the option type is such a great place to start is that this same idea of encoding meaning in the type system can be used in many other ways.

```
let getFormattedWebData url =
    let webData = getWebData url
    match webData with
    | Some(data) -> formatData data
    | None -> None
```

Option wraps another type and must be explicitly unwrapped later to be used. The returned information about the state must be dealt with before the data can be touched. As `Option<T>` must be explicitly checked before being opened, you are forced to verify its contents before trying to perform any computation with it. The great value in this is that when you have instances of types that aren't options, you can be sure that they contain a value. This is in contrast with null, which may always be present and so must repeatedly be checked for, thus littering your code with frequent precondition checks and potentially causing unexpected runtime null reference exceptions.

Now, it is important to know that when dealing with standard CLR libraries you may still encounter null in F#. In these cases it is always best to wrap these calls to return an option type immediately. However, when using with the F# specific libraries, the option type is used by default and this need not be a consideration.

## Encapsulating State in Types

You just learned about how the option type gives you the advantage of no longer having to perform runtime precondition null checks on data's state as your checks are instead being enforced by the type system. This same idea can be extended beyond simply replacing null. In actuality, it can be used to encode and enforce any discretely identifiable piece of state information.

As a trivial example, consider an ordered list. With some algorithms the difference between having an appropriately ordered data set or an unordered data set can be the difference between `O(n)` and possible `O(n^2)` performance. Others, which are written to depend on ordering, will not function at all.

One example of the later is the removal of duplicates. With a sorted list this is a simple `O(n)` operation. Without ordering, this process requires a completely different, and much more complex, algorithm.

```
let removeDupesFromOrdered orderedList =
    List.foldBack (fun element noDupes ->
        match noDupes with
        | [] -> [element]
        | (h::_) -> if element = h then noDupes
                    else [element] @ noDupes)
        orderedList []

> removeDupesFromOrdered [0; 1; 1; 2; 3; 4; 5; 5; 6];;
val it : int list = [0; 1; 2; 3; 4; 5; 6]
```

What if you want to ensure that only a sorted list could be passed in to your function? In C# this would likely mean inheriting from `ReadOnlyCollection` and perhaps adding an extension method to list which returned a new sorted instance. However, this would mean writing a significant amount of code and, as constructors are not inherited, potentially updating that code with each additional .NET framework release.

However, in F# you can leverage the discriminated union feature and do the same thing with significantly less code, in a similar way to how the option type is implemented.

```
type OrderedList<'a> = | OrderedList of 'a list

let toOrderedList list = OrderedList(List.sort list)

let toList (OrderedList orderedList) = orderedList


let removeDuplicatesFromOrderedList (orderedList: OrderedList<'a>) =
    let removeDupes list =
        List.foldBack (fun element noDupes ->
            match noDupes with
            | [] -> [element]
            | (h::_) -> if element = h then noDupes
                        else element :: noDupes)
            list []
    match orderedList with
    | OrderedList list -> OrderedList(removeDupes list)
```

*Code snippet OrderedList.fs*

As you can see here, you can no longer use normal lists with this version of the `removeDuplicates`.

```
removeDuplicatesFromOrderedList [0; 1; 1; 2; 2; 3]
error FS0001: This expression was expected to have type
    OrderedPropertyList<'a>
but here has type
    'b list
```

To use this function you now must wrap your list to encode in the type system that it is ordered.

```
> let orderedList = toOrderedList [0; 1; 1; 2; 2; 3]
val orderedList : OrderedList<int> = OrderedList [0; 1; 1; 2; 2; 3]

> removeDuplicatesFromOrderedList orderedList
val it : OrderedList<int> = OrderedList [0; 1; 2; 3]
```

Even more interesting, you can encode several different possible data states into one discriminated union type. This allows your functions to take or return many different information states and, in so doing, behave in the best possible way for every possible situation.

```
type PropertyList<'a> =
    | Normal of 'a list
    | Ordered of 'a list
    | NoDuplicates of 'a list

let CreateNoDuplicatesListFromPropertyList list =
    function
    | NoDuplicates(_) -> list
    | Normal(noProperty) ->
        NoDuplicates (noProperty |> Set.ofList |> List.ofSeq)
    | Ordered(ordered) ->
        NoDuplicates (List.foldBack (fun element noDupes ->
            match noDupes with
            | [] -> [element]
            | (h::_) -> if element = h then noDupes
                        else element :: noDupes) ordered [])
```

*Code snippet PropertyList.fs*

By taking information that would have been implicit in the ordering of your calls and using a type wrapper to make this assumption explicit, you are moving contextual constraints into the type system. This will increase the compile-time safety of your code by ensuring that your data will only go into the correct functions. This also allows you to verify things that would otherwise be time consuming to explicitly verify with preconditions or class wrappers, such as the internal state of a list.

## Avoiding Exceptions

One significant enhancement that comes from the wrapping of state in a type is the lack of need for exceptions. Exceptions are both costly in terms of performance and dangerous in terms of behavior. Also, the need for many `try` blocks detracts significantly from the readability of your code.

In most cases, exceptions are not all that exceptional and so need not behave differently than a normal function return value. In the vast majority of cases, they are simply a way of having multiple function output types in languages that lack discriminated unions.

In F#, instead of frequently using exceptions, it is better to encode your various return states within discriminated unions. In cases where you might be tempted to return null, you use the option type as previously described. However, when you want to create your own set of return types, you need to define your own discriminated union.

```
type UriOutput =
    | Uri of System.Uri
    | Malformed of string

let buildUri stringUri =
    try Uri( new System.Uri(stringUri) )
    with | _ -> Malformed(stringUri)
```

As in this example, it is often advantageous to wrap existing .NET method calls in functions that return discriminated unions. In this way, you can greatly increase code readability. In F#, exceptions, along with their unseemly `try-with` blocks, are no longer necessary in most cases. When every state is enumerated explicitly, your code is much easier to maintain and is significantly easier to read.

## Data and State Flow

Just as you saw with exceptions, discriminated unions allow you to encode many different data states directly into your type and so ensure that they are properly handled. Designing systems to behave in this way is a simple four-step process. As an example, consider a `WebClient` interface that takes either a `Uri` or a `String` and returns the correct data structure for the type of data found.

First, enumerate your input states with a discriminated union type.

```
type WebClientInput =
    | StringInput of String
    | UriInput of System.Uri
```

*Code snippet DownloadWithWebClient.fs*

Second, do the same for your possible output states.

```
type WebClientOutput =
    | MalformedUri of string
    | TextContent of string
    | BinaryContent of byte []
    | NoContent
    | WebClientException of System.Net.WebException
```

*Code snippet DownloadWithWebClient.fs*

Third, you must build your function to return each of these states in the appropriate situation.

```
let downloadWithWebClient (inputUri: WebClientInput) =
    let downloadFromUri (uri: System.Uri) =
        try
            use client = new System.Net.WebClient()
            let dlData = client.DownloadData(uri)
            if dlData.Length = 0 then NoContent
            else if (client.ResponseHeaders.["content-type"]
                            .StartsWith(@"text/"))
                then
                    let dlText =
                        System.Text.Encoding.Default.GetString(dlData)
                    TextContent(dlText)
                else
                    BinaryContent(dlData)
        with
            | :? System.Net.WebException as e -> WebClientException(e)
    match inputUri with
    | UriInput(classUri) -> downloadFromUri classUri
    | StringInput(stringUri) ->
```

```
match buildUri stringUri with
| Uri(s) -> downloadFromUri s
| Malformed(s) -> MalformedUri(s)
```

Finally, consume and appropriately handle your expected return states.

```
let printWebClientOutput clientOutput =
    match clientOutput with
    | MalformedUri(uri) -> printfn "Input Uri was malformed: %s" uri
    | TextContent(content) -> printfn "Page Content: %s" content
    | BinaryContent(content) -> printfn "Binary Data: %d" content.Length
    | NoContent -> printfn "No content was found."
    | WebClientException(e) -> printsn "Exception: %s" (e.ToString())
```

The F# compiler issue warnings when not all returned states are handled. This provides a much safer style of data handling than exceptions that are in no way encoded in the function signature. Also, as `match` statements support wildcards, you need to consider only the relevant states to your current context.

```
open System.IO

let downloadToFile (inputUri: WebClientInput) outputLocation =
    match downloadWithWebClient inputUri with
    | TextContent(text) -> File.WriteAllText( outputLocation, text )
    | BinaryContent(binary) -> File.WriteAllBytes( outputLocation, binary )
    | _ -> printfn "Download Failed"
```

It is important to keep in mind that when using wildcards you will no longer receive compiler warnings when some states are not covered in your `match` statement. For this reason, it is usually best to explicitly match all states in production code. This ensures that potentially relevant states will not be missed with future code changes.

In this example, all your possible inputs and outputs are discretely defined. The beauty in this is that you can now handle these cases in an explicit and elegant way. If you wanted to add an additional input type, you would need only extend `WebClientInput` and add another case to your `match` statement. Similarly, if you wanted to add another `output` case, you simply extend `WebClientOutput` and add that case as a new return value of your function. This makes it simple to add new `input` types and `output` states as the need arises.

## Recursively Defined Data Types

Beyond their use in increasing type safety, discriminated unions may also be used to define complex data structures through recursive type definitions. Recursive type definitions are discriminated unions in which some subtypes leverage either themselves or a child type in its definition. One simple example of this would be a binary tree.

```
type BinaryTree<'a> =
    | Node of BinaryTree<'a> * BinaryTree<'a>
    | Leaf of 'a
```

*Code snippet BinaryTree.fs*

In this case, a node may either be a leaf or contain a tuple of two more binary trees. This technique can be leveraged to quickly build data structures that would have taken orders of magnitude more code in other languages.

One might argue that, although the definition is simplified, it may be more difficult to implement functionality for this data structure based on the nodes themselves not containing any methods. As you'll see in the following depth-first search example, this is not the case. It is a simple matter to externalize what would have previously been object-oriented code.

```
let rec dfs tree leafData =
    match tree with
    | Leaf(l) -> if l = leafData then Some(l) else None
    | Node(a,b) -> let dfsA = dfs a leafData in
                    if Option.isSome dfsA then dfsA
                    else dfs b leafData

let binaryTree =
    Node(
        Node( Leaf(1), Leaf(2) ),
        Node( Leaf(3), Node( Leaf(4), Leaf(5) ) ) );;
val binaryTree : BinaryTree<int> =
  Node (Node (Leaf 1,Leaf 2),Node (Leaf 3,Node (Leaf 4,Leaf 5)))

dfs binaryTree 5;;
val it : int option = Some 5

dfs binaryTree 33;
val it : int option = None
```

*Code snippet BinaryTree.fs*

As you can see here, recursive data type definitions are quite powerful constructs. When combined with recursive functions, they can be leveraged to build what would otherwise be complex data and difficult to maintain structures with very little code.

Although perhaps a bit intimidating at first, with a little practice it's a trivial matter to go from a definition in which an object calls its children to one in which a function recurses on each data structure node. In most cases, this can be done by replacing what would have been the `this` construct with the object operated on. Getting your head around this is one of many paradigm shifts necessary to become effective at F# when coming from an imperative language.

## SUMMARY

Although it may seem more difficult to think carefully about the best way to type your data, it is not significantly different than spending time thinking about how you might structure your classes in object-oriented programming. A little bit of time spent upfront thinking conceptually about your data can give great benefits in terms of clarity and safety.

By making the compiler work for you, you can catch many more kinds of bugs at compile-time without having to hope that your tests check for those particular types of edge cases. In many cases, you can completely avoid using exceptions and do not need to deal with the extra conceptual overhead they introduce into your code. This all adds up to less technical debt and higher quality code. It's a big win for both the programmer writing the code and those who must maintain it later.

# 16

# List Processing

**WHAT'S IN THIS CHAPTER?**

➤ Understanding collection processing abstractions

➤ Subsetting collections

➤ Transforming collections

➤ Understanding accumulators

➤ Leveraging scanning and folding

Functional programming in F# really shines when dealing with the processing of linear data structures. A linear data structure is any in which traversal of every node is linear in nature. That is, each element of the data structure can be visited sequentially in terms a previous element. Lists and sequences fit into this category. Arrays do partially as they are often accessed in this way.

The reason F# is particularly suited to this is primarily the great number of constructs provided by the language framework. F# provides a copious number of functions for the manipulation and analysis of each of its data structures. Although large in number, the elegance and simplicity provided by these functions is one of the fundamental reasons F# excels at list processing.

## COLLECTION ABSTRACTIONS

There are many ways to think about processing the elements of the list. You might even view much of the history of programming to be the history of linear data set processing. First, consider the lineage of imperative list iteration.

At the lowest level there is the humble JMP instruction from which you must construct your list from scratch; in higher level languages this is analogous to the `goto` statement. At a slightly higher level of abstraction there is the `while` statement which, in exchange for some flexibility in where you jump to, expresses the idea of repeatedly doing something until a condition is met much more clearly. This concept is also the most basic idea behind iteration. Furthering this exchange of flexibility for clarity there is the `for` statement that gives us a direct way to express iteration.

Then, at the highest level of imperative iteration, there is the `foreach` statement. The `foreach` statement is clear and concise but lacks much of what `for` can do. In fact, the difficulty in using `foreach` for things other than explicit iteration is what makes it so much clearer. You sacrifice the ability to determine ordering and skip elements to glance at a small chunk of very expressive code and immediately understand what it does.

So, imperative languages offer a one-dimensional and increasingly restrictive set of options for controlling execution flow. On one side of the spectrum, there is the liberal `goto` statement, and on the other the restrictive `foreach` statement.

On the other hand, functional programming offers a much richer set of tools. On one side of the progression sits recursion, and on the other a profusion of higher order functions project outward. These functions have names like `filter`, `map`, `reduce`, and `fold`. Although similar to `foreach` in clarity of expression, each is used to elegantly express different ideas.

## MODULE FUNCTIONS

Unlike in the .NET libraries, where modification of data structures is most often performed by calling class methods on a specific data structure instance, F# provides static modules for each data structure. In the vast majority of cases these module functions do not modify their parameters; instead, they return a fresh data structure to which the modification has been performed.

In this chapter, many of the collection module functions will be discussed. It is important to note that not every `construct` discussed here applies to and works exactly the same way with every data structure. For example, the `Seq` module will delay work while `List` and `Array` will perform operations immediately.

The goal is less to give you a comprehensive guide to module functions and more to give you the knowledge necessary for understanding the classes of problems they solve, how to use them to solve these problems, and an understanding of the jargon used in the language documentation.

## COLLECTION SUBSETS

Subset functions are used to find the parts of an existing collection that satisfy some predicate. A predicate is simply a function that takes an instance of some type and returns `true` or `false` based on some criteria. In these cases, the predicate function must take the same type as the elements of the collection. Because of their simplicity, they are an ideal place to start when learning about list processing with higher order functions.

# filter

filter takes a collection, and a predicate of that collection's contained type. It then returns a collection containing only the elements for which that predicate returns true.

```
> let names = ["Sally"; "Donny"; "Johnny"; "Josephine"; "Jose"; "Al"];;

val names : string list = ["Sally"; "Donny"; "Johnny"; "Josephine";
                           "Jose"; "Al"]

> let joNames =
    List.filter
        (fun (name: string) -> "Jo" = name.Substring(0,2) )
        names;;

val joNames : string list = ["Johnny"; "Josephine"; "Jose"]
```

As with almost the entirety of F#'s list processing functions, filter does not modify the original collection. Instead, it returns a completely new collection containing the operation's output. In this case the type inside of the filter lambda must be qualified with an annotation; this can be avoided by using the forward pipelining operator as discussed in Chapter 17.

The usefulness of filter might seem obvious. Think of it as the F# version of a SQL WHERE clause. It is used to cut your collection down into the subset of elements needed for your remaining computations or desired output.

# partition

partition is similar to filter; the function you pass into it has exactly the same signature. The difference between them is that, although filter returns only the elements for which your function returned true, partition also returns the elements for which false was returned in a second collection.

```
> let numbers = [1 .. 10];;

val numbers : int list = [1; 2; 3; 4; 5; 6; 7; 8; 9; 10]

> let even, odd = List.partition (fun x -> x % 2 = 0) numbers;;

val odd : int list = [1; 3; 5; 7; 9]
val even : int list = [2; 4; 6; 8; 10]
```

In this example the elements of the first list are partitioned into odd and even subsets. As partition returns a tuple of the two lists, the tuple assignment syntax is used to bind the results to two separate variables.

At first glance, it seems that the primary benefit of partition is that it allows you to cut your dataset into two parts with only a single pass. However, as an additional benefit to doing a multipass filter, there is no need to worry about dropped or duplicate elements. The resulting collections can be processed and then recombined later to produce a complete set. With `partition`, you can be sure that the two resulting collections will contain nonoverlapping subsets of the original collection.

# ELEMENT TRANSFORMATIONS

Element transformations perform a given function on each element of a collection independently. In all cases, the result is a new collection that maintains the element ordering of the initial collection. The defining characteristic of these functions is that each element's transformation has no dependencies on the result for other elements. One benefit to this is that they can often be done in parallel for significant performance benefit. Another is that they are easy to think about because you need to consider only what is happening on a per-element basis.

## map

In its most basic form, `map` takes a single collection and a transformation function. This function is applied to each element and creates a corresponding new element in the resulting collection. This is useful for a great number of things from element type conversions to calculations across a large data set.

```
> let friends = ["Sally"; "Donny"; "Jay"; "Josephine"];;

val friends : string list = ["Sally"; "Donny"; "Jay"; "Josephine"]

> let lowercaseFriends =
    List.map
        (fun (str: string) -> str.ToLower())
        friends;;

val lowercaseFriends : string list = ["sally"; "donny"; "jay"; "josephine"]
```

In this example the names in the friends list are normalized by converting them to lowercase. This is done by calling `ToLower()` on each element. Note that each transformation is independent, needing no information from other nodes in the list.

There are also a few slightly more complex variations of `map`. Consider combining datasets of equal length where the ordering of those datasets represents some type of meaning correspondence between the elements of those datasets. `mapn` (where n is a number) allows you to map across multiple data structures at once. If the collections are of unequal length, the remaining elements in the longer collection will be ignored.

For example, you may have a list of names and a list of birthdays where the index in those lists represents the same unique person. You can use `map2` to combine those birthdays with the person.

```
> let birthdays = ["August 20th"; "April 10th"; "December 31st"; "October 3rd"];;

val birthdays : string list =
  ["August 20th"; "April 10th"; "December 31st"; "October 3rd"]

> let friendsWithBirthdays =
    List.map2
```

```
        (fun name birthday -> sprintf "%s was born on %s" name birthday)
        friends birthdays;;

val friendsWithBirthdays : string list =
    ["Sally was born on August 20th"; "Donny was born on April 10th";
     "Jay was born on December 31st"; "Josephine was born on October 3rd"]
```

Similarly, map3 allows you to do this with three collections. It's just like map2 except it takes three lists and a function of three elements.

```
> let places = ["Hartford, CT"; "Los Angeles, CA"; "Tokyo, Japan";
  "Munich, Germany"];;

val places : string list =
    ["Hartford, CT"; "Los Angeles, CA"; "Tokyo, Japan"; "Munich, Germany"]

> let friendsBirthdaysAndLocation =
    List.map3
        (fun name birthday loc ->
            sprintf "%s was born on %s and lives in %s" name birthday loc)
        friends birthdays places;;

val friendsBirthdaysAndLocation : string list =
    ["Sally was born on August 20th and lives in Hartford, CT";
     "Donny was born on April 10th and lives in Los Angeles, CA";
     "Jay was born on December 31st and lives in Tokyo, Japan";
     "Josephine was born on October 3rd and lives in Munich, Germany"]
```

As elements might already have a meaning prescribed in their ordering, it is often useful to know the index of the element we are currently mapping. This is where mapi comes into play. It's just like map, except that it gives your function the current index in the collection as the first argument.

```
> let users = ["Sally"; "Donny"; "Johnny"; "Josephine"; "Jose"];;

val users : string list = ["Sally"; "Donny"; "Johnny"; "Josephine"; "Jose"]

> let usersWithUniqueNumber = List.mapi (fun i user -> (i, user)) users;;

val usersWithUniqueNumber : (int * string) list =
    [(0, "Sally"); (1, "Donny"); (2, "Johnny"); (3, "Josephine"); (4, "Jose")]
```

mapi is useful when ordering is important. It can have similar utility to the id in a database table. It might be used to inspect neighbor elements or to preserve initial ordering. For example, you might want to give each element an id before using partition so that you might recombine them later.

mapi2 is simply the combination of mapi and map2. It takes two collections and a function. It then gives your function one element from each of these collections at a time and their index.

```
> let lastnames = ["Struthers"; "Osmond"; "Depp";
                   "de Beauharnais"; "Canseco"];;

val lastnames : string list =
    ["Struthers"; "Osmond"; "Depp"; "de Beauharnais"; "Canseco"]
```

```
> let usersWithLastnamesAndUniqueNumbers =
    List.mapi2
        (fun i first last -> (i, sprintf "%s %s" first last))
        users lastnames;;

val usersWithLastnamesAndUniqueNumbers : (int * string) list =
  [(0, "Sally Struthers"); (1, "Donny Osmond"); (2, "Johnny Depp");
   (3, "Josephine de Beauharnais"); (4, "Jose Canseco")]
```

In all cases, the underlying idea in using map remains consistent. It is used to map the meaning of each element in a collection to a single element of a new collection, a transformation from one or more collections to another of equal length and ordering.

## choose

Choose is effectively a combination of map and filter. The difference in thinking about how to use this function lies in that with choose the return type of each function application must be an option type. Return values wrapped in Some are included in the result collection whereas None signifies that the current computation should not be included in the result.

```
> let friends = ["Sally"; "Donny"; "Jay"; "Johnny";
                 "Josephine"; "Jose"];;

val friends : string list =
  ["Sally"; "Donny"; "Jay"; "Johnny"; "Josephine"; "Jose"]

> let lowercaseShortNames =
    List.choose
        (fun (x: string) ->
            match x with
            | x when x.Length > 5 -> None
            | x -> Some(x.ToLower()))
        friends;;

val lowercaseShortNames : string list = ["sally"; "donny"; "jay"; "jose"]
```

In this example, names longer than five characters have been filtered by returning None when they are encountered. Shorter names are converted to lowercase and wrapped with Some to signify that they should be included in the result.

By electing to use choose instead of a separate map and filter, you can save the time associated with the wasted map computations and a second iteration through the collection. Also, in many cases it can be clearer what the purpose of an operation is when it is done in a single step.

## collect

Collect is a variation on map in which the evaluation of each element is expected to return a new collection. These collections are then assembled to produce a single result collection.

```
> let partiallyParsedNames = ["Thomas; Richard"; "Derk; Kant; Kafka";
                              "Captain Crunch; Mister Rogers"];;
```

```
  val partiallyParsedNames : string list =
    ["Thomas; Richard"; "Derk; Kant; Kafka"; "Captain Crunch; Mister Rogers"]

> let parsedNames =
    List.collect
        (fun (field: string) ->
            Array.toList (
                field.Split( [|"; "|], System.StringSplitOptions.None )))
        partiallyParsedNames;;

  val parsedNames : string list =
    ["Thomas"; "Richard"; "Derk"; "Kant"; "Kafka"; "Captain Crunch";
     "Mister Rogers"]
```

Interestingly, `collect` can produce the same filtering behavior as `choose`. When you want an element to be excluded, simply return an empty list.

```
> let friends = ["Sally"; "Donny"; "Jay"; "Johnny";
                 "Josephine"; "Jose"];;

  val friends : string list =
    ["Sally"; "Donny"; "Jay"; "Johnny"; "Josephine"; "Jose"]

> let lowercaseShortNames =
    List.collect
        (fun (x: string) ->
            match x with
            | x when x.Length > 5 -> []
            | x -> [ x.ToLower() ])
        friends;;

  val lowercaseShortNames : string list = ["sally"; "donny"; "jay"; "jose"]
```

Most commonly, `collect` is useful when you want to flatten a collection of collections. It can also be used to break single complex elements into new collection subsections on-the-fly. One example of where this can be exceptionally useful is when grooming large amounts of text data that may be incorrectly delimited.

## ACCUMULATORS

Before continuing, it is important to understand the idea of an accumulator and what "threading an accumulator through the computation" means. Thinking back to the idea of a standard `foreach` loop, an accumulator would be a variable defined outside of that loop that is used to hold state between each iteration. Accumulators are useful in functional programming for exactly the same reasons that loop external variables are in imperative programming.

Because in functional programming the mutation of variables is avoided, instead of updating an external value, you return what you would have wanted the contents of that external variable to be after the evaluation of the current element. This accumulated value is passed to your function each time an element is evaluated from the previous to the current application. This is what is meant by "threading an accumulator."

## reduce

At the heart of `reduce` is a simple idea: take a collection of elements and boil it down to a single instance of the same type. Among other things, it is quite useful for comparing or summing collection elements.

Application of `reduce` is done by passing in a reduction function and a collection. For the initial element evaluation, the first two collection elements are passed into the reduction function. After that, the current element and the accumulator are passed. This is done in left-to-right order over the entire collection. When all elements have been visited, the accumulator is returned.

```
> let friends = ["Sally"; "Donny"; "Jay"; "Johnny";
                 "Josephine"; "Jose"];;

val friends : string list =
  ["Sally"; "Donny"; "Jay"; "Johnny"; "Josephine"; "Jose"]

> let longestName =
    List.reduce
        (fun (longest: string) (this:string) ->
            if longest.Length >= this.Length then longest else this)
        friends;;

val longestName : string = "Josephine"
```

In this example, the accumulator is the longest name found so far. For each element, the length of the current longest name is compared with the length of the current element, and the larger of the two is then returned. Each element in the collection is tested in this way. After all elements have been tested, the accumulator will contain the longest string in the list. This accumulator is what is finally returned.

In some cases it is beneficial to perform your reduce starting with the right side of the collection instead of the left. In these cases you can use `reduceBack`. This is a variation on reduce that performs the same operation except in the reverse order. Functionally, it is the equivalent of first reversing your collection and then performing a normal reduce.

```
> let longestName =
    List.reduceBack
        (fun (this: string) (longest:string) ->
            if longest.Length >= this.Length then longest else this)
        friends;;

val longestName : string = "Josephine"
```

Note that with `reduceBack` the order of the reduction function is reversed. The second argument is the accumulator and not the first. This difference is to reflect the order in which you are traversing the collection.

Several of the more simple collection functions can be implemented quite simply in terms of `reduce`. Some that come to mind are `average`, `max`, `min`, `count`, `countby`, and `sum`. Each of these operate on a collection and return a single instance that is the same type as what the collection contains. To be sure you have a firm understanding of how accumulators work, I suggest trying to implement each of these functions in terms of `reduce`.

# fold

Conceptually, `fold` is much like `reduce`, although significantly more general. The differences stem from the fact that `fold` can have an accumulator that is of a different type than that of its input collection's elements. Because of this, `fold` requires that an initial value for the accumulator be passed in.

Application of `fold` is done by passing in a folding function, a collection and an initial accumulator value. When complete, the final accumulator value is returned. `fold` visits each element once, applying the given function to the current element and the accumulator. Much like `reduce` this is done in left-to-right order over the contents of the collection.

```
> let strings = ["The"; "quick"; "brown"; "fox"; "jumps";
                 "over"; "the"; "lazy"; "dog"];;

val strings : string list =
  ["The"; "quick"; "brown"; "fox"; "jumps"; "over"; "the"; "lazy"; "dog"]

> let totalLength =
    List.fold
        (fun acc (str: string) -> acc + str.Length)
        0
        strings;;

val totalLength : int = 35
```

In this example, the accumulator is the combined length of all `strings` measured so far. For each element, the accumulator is added to the length of the current list and that value is returned as the next value. As you can see, the initial value of the accumulator is given as zero.

Also much like `reduce`, `fold` has a right-to-left version named `foldBack`. One case where this is particularly useful is when folding over a list to build another list.

```
> let spacedStrings =
    List.foldBack
        (fun str acc ->
            if List.isEmpty acc then [str] @ acc
            else [str] @ [" "] @ acc)
        strings
        [];;

val spacedStrings : string list =
  ["The"; " "; "quick"; " "; "brown"; " "; "fox"; " "; "jumps"; " "; "over";
   " "; "the"; " "; "lazy"; " "; "dog"]
```

In this example, the list being empty on the first iteration allows the correct insertion of spaces. As the rightmost element is the first visited, the accumulator is empty when the folding function is applied.

Were you to use `fold` instead of `foldBack`, this simple operation would be quite expensive for long lists. As discussed in the optimization section of Chapter 14, appending to the tail of a list requires destroying that list and building an entirely new one. By folding backward, you can simply append to the head of the accumulator list while maintaining the initial ordering and preserving the existing list structure. In effect, you are building a new list right to left while visiting the initial list in the same order.

Both `fold` and `foldBack` have implementations that allow you to fold over two collections at the same time. These are named `fold2` and `foldBack2`. Like `map2`, both collections may contain different types. However unlike `map2`, `fold2` and `foldBack2` require the input lists to be the same length.

```
> let punctuation = [" "; " "; " "; " "; " ";
                     " "; " "; " "; "."];;

val punctuation : string list = [" "; " "; " "; " "; " "; " "; " "; "."]

> let totalLengthWithPunctuation =
    List.fold2
        (fun acc (str: string) (punc:string) ->
            acc + str.Length + punc.Length)
        0
        strings
        punctuation;;

val totalLengthWithPunctuation : int = 44
```

Here, the sentence punctuation has been kept in a separate list. To get a full count of the number of characters, `fold2` is used to thread an accumulator over both lists at the same time and add up the total length of the `strings` inside.

Because the accumulator need not be the same type as the contents of the collection, `fold` ends up being one of the most dynamic list processing `constructs`. In fact, almost any other function on a list can be written in terms of `fold` or `foldBack`. This includes `filter`, `map`, and `reduce`. For example, to implement `map` you simply make the accumulator the same type as the collection and build up your result as you walk across the collection.

## scan

Much like `fold` is an extension of `reduce`, `scan` is an extension of `fold`. While `fold` returns only the result of the final computation, `scan` returns a collection of all intermediate results. In this way, `scan` is like a combination of `fold` and `map`.

Application of `scan` is exactly the same as `fold`: you pass it a collection, a scanning function, and an initial accumulator value. The scanning function takes an element of that collection and the previous accumulator, returning the next accumulator value. Each element is visited once, and the given function is applied to the current element and the accumulator. When finished, a collection of all accumulator values is returned.

```
> let wordOffset =
    List.scan
        (fun acc (str: string) -> acc + str.Length)
        0
        strings;;

val wordOffset : int list = [0; 3; 8; 13; 16; 21; 25; 28; 32; 35]
```

By applying the same function as used in the previous `fold` example, you can create an offset index were the strings to be concatenated. The only difference in this case is that `scan` returns each intermediate value of the accumulator instead of just the final one.

Like most other accumulator based functions, `scan` also has a right-to-left version named `scanBack`.

```
> let backwardWordOffset =
    List.scanBack
        (fun (str: string) acc -> acc + str.Length)
        strings
        0;;

val backwardWordOffset : int list = [35; 32; 27; 22; 19; 14; 10; 7; 3; 0]
```

Here the same function is applied, and we instead get the distance of each word from the end of the sentence. Note that just like in other right-to-left accumulator functions, both the `scanning` function and `scanBack` take arguments in reverse order.

## SUMMARY

Getting the hang of F#'s vast array of list processing functions may seem an overwhelming task. Fortunately, most are just variations on the same few ideas. A good place to start is with just `filter`, `map`, and `fold`. If you can get to the point of applying just these three functions with confidence, the rest will come easily when needed.

If while reading this you were thinking some of the more complex functions, such as `scan`, might not be all that useful you probably would be correct. It is always best to use the least complex construct possible. This means `fold` should be favored over `scan` and `filter`, `reduce` or `map` over `fold`. However, for calculating prior-dependant transformations of sequences, complex functions such as `scan` are fantastic tools to have.

# 17

# Pipelining and Composition

**WHAT'S IN THIS CHAPTER?**

➤ Understanding pipelining operators

➤ Understanding composition operators

➤ Getting started with pipelining function composition

➤ Using advanced function composition

What is it about functional languages that make them so powerful for data structure processing? One answer to this is composability. Instead of being a built-in language construct such as `for` or `foreach`, functional abstractions like `map` and `reduce` are themselves functions. They are first-class language citizens, no different than any function you might write yourself. This means that they are much more flexible because they can be built one argument at a time, passed around, and even combined with other functions.

Out of this composability comes a data-oriented programming technique called pipelining. In pipelining, functions are combined or chained together with special operators. This allows you to pass the results of one function directly and unambiguously into the next. In this way, programs can be constructed as a series of discrete data transformations. As you will see, this approach produces short and expressive data processing programs.

## BASIC COMPOSITION AND PIPELINING

When writing code using composition and pipelining, there are four primary operators. Each of these is a combination of two ideas, performing an operation to the left or right and either pipelining data or composing functions. When combined, they provide a powerful set of tools that allow you to write concise and visually appealing code.

# Pipelining

When pipelining, the result of each function call is passed directly into the next. Data passes through this series of pipes undergoing conversions, filters, and normalizations. Eventually, when the data reaches the other side, you have the results you need as explained by a simple set of steps.

Although programming in this style has long been considered controversial in imperative-object oriented programming languages, functional languages provide you with the tools to do this in a safe and readable way. The end result is very concise and easy-to-maintain code. LINQ is a great example of this. Although initially designed to facilitate SQL-style querying, it also can be extended quite dramatically for declarative and transformation based programming in C# and VB.NET. However, even what LINQ offers can't come close to the flexibility provided by native functional composition.

## Forward Pipe (|>)

The forward pipe operator is used to pass arguments to a function from the left side or the previous line. For example, given a data set like the following:

```
type Place = { Name: string; Population: int }

let places = [ { Name = "New York"; Population = 9000000; }
               { Name = "Los Angeles"; Population = 4000000; }
               { Name = "Frankfurt"; Population = 700000; }
               { Name = "Tokyo"; Population = 13000000;} ]
```

It's a simple matter to build a query that finds the cities with a population more than 5 million and then normalize the names of those cities by converting them to uppercase.

```
> let over5MilUppercase =
    places
    |> List.filter (fun p -> p.Population > 5000000)
    |> List.map (fun p -> p.Name.ToUpper() );;

val over5MilUppercase : string list = ["NEW YORK"; "TOKYO"]
```

Don't let the fact that operators look like pure syntax fool you; just like most other constructs in F#, under the hood they are functions. This becomes obvious if we inspect the operator in the F# interactive window.

```
> (|>);;

val it : ('a -> ('a -> 'b) -> 'b) = <fun:it@1>
```

The only difference between this and a normal function is that binary operators (operators that take two arguments) pull arguments from their left and right sides and are evaluated with low precedence.

Looking at the type signature, you can see it's not all that complicated. On the left side it takes a value of one type (`'a`) and on the right a function (`'a -> 'b`). It then returns a value of the same

type as its function argument (`b`). The passed in function is used to convert the `input` type into the
`output` type. Were we to write this function ourselves, it would look like the following:

```
> let pf input func = func(input);;

val pf : 'a -> ('a -> 'b) -> 'b

> (pf);;

val it : ('a -> ('a -> 'b) -> 'b) = <fun:clo@3>
```

So, in the preceding example, places is on the left side of the first pipe operator and so corresponds
to the first (`'a`) in the function type signature. On the right side something slightly more complex
is going on; `filter` is first evaluated with only one of its arguments using a language feature called
partial application. This feature is discussed thoroughly in Chapter 13.

```
> List.filter (fun p -> p.Population > 5000000);;

val it : (Place list -> Place list) = <fun:it@4-13>
```

The partially applied representation of `filter` takes a `Place list` and returns a `Place list`,
fitting nicely into the right side (`'a -> 'b`) of the forward pipe operator's type signature. The
operator grabs this partially applied `filter` function from its right side and applies the places value
to it from the (`'a`). Just as if the filter had been called directly with the list of places, another list is
returned (`'b`).

```
> places
    |> List.filter (fun p -> p.Population > 5000000);;

val it : Place list = [{Name = "New York"; Population = 9000000;};
                       {Name = "Tokyo"; Population = 13000000;}]
```

This same process is repeated each time the pipe operator is used. On the next line, the newly filtered list of places is taken from the right and a partially applied map is taken from the right. The
result of applying this list of places to the mapping function is then returned.

That's it. The forward pipe operator simply changes the order you specify function and argument. The
secret is in that the operator takes the value first (from its left side) and the function second (from its
right). This allows the result of the previous line to be applied to a function on the current line.

This operator is one of the most commonly used in F#. As the F# compiler is single pass, having the
primary argument on the previous line also means that its type can be evaluated before the function
it is applied to. This greatly improves type inference and so eliminates the need for type annotations
in many cases.

## Backward Pipe (<|)

The backward pipe operator is used to pass arguments in to a function from the right side or next
line. It is much the same as forward, except that the order of its arguments is reversed. It takes
`input` on its right side and applies it to a function on its left.

Take a look at the example where the cities were filtered to populations under five million and then converted to uppercase using the backward pipe operator.

```
> let over5MilUppercase =
    List.map (fun (p: Place) -> p.Name.ToUpper() )
    <| (List.filter (fun (p: Place) -> p.Population > 5000000)
        <| places);;


val over5MilUppercase : string list = ["NEW YORK"; "TOKYO"]
```

Here, the list of places is backward piped into the filter function. In turn, the result of that is then backward piped into map. The primary difference here, other than the reversed ordering, is that additional parentheses are needed to ensure correct order of operation. This is because F# evaluates everything with the same precedence in the function contents from top to bottom and left to right. Without the parentheses, the compiler would try to pipe filter directly into the partially applied map function on the previous line and compilation would fail.

Under the hood, the backward pipe operator's underlying function is exactly the same as the forward operator, except the order of arguments is reversed.

```
> (<|);;

val it : (('a -> 'b) -> 'a -> 'b) = <fun:it@5-2>

> let pb func input = func(input);;

val pb : ('a -> 'b) -> 'a -> 'b

> (pb);;

val it : (('a -> 'b) -> 'a -> 'b) = <fun:clo@7-3>
```

Here you see ('a -> 'b) corresponding to the function taken from the left, 'a corresponding to the value taken from the right, and 'b corresponding to the result. The ('a ->'b) function is used to convert 'a into 'b.

Although it is much less commonly used than the forward pipelining operator for line displacement, the backward pipelining operator is often used for avoiding parentheses around subexpressions on the same line.

```
Seq.map (fun x -> x * 2) (Seq.init 10 (fun i -> i * 2))

Seq.map (fun x -> x * 2) <| Seq.init 10 (fun i -> i * 2)
```

Both of these examples are equivalent. However, the second is arguably more readable because it has fewer parentheses. This improvement in readability can be particularly great in cases where many small operations are performed on the same line to fill the arguments of a function.

## Composition

Consider the case where you would want to apply a series of operations to a data set. In object-oriented languages, you might build a series of classes based on an interface, or functions that match some delegate, and then add them to a generic collection defined to take their shared underlying type. You could then loop over this collection, applying each of these transformations to the result of the previous in turn.

The great benefit in this approach is that a series of operations can be defined dynamically at runtime. However, this methodology has a serious limitation. With this approach, each transformation must take and return the same type. A single change in type means that the processing class or delegate can't be added to your collection.

Another approach might be to perform operations as you previously saw with pipelining. The result of each function call is passed directly into the next, which eventually ends up providing you with the result you need. The equivalent to this in object-oriented languages would be chaining the result of many static method calls.

With this approach, you've solved the problem of composing operations of different types. However, as each pipelining step or static method call is compiled into place and can't be changed, you've given up the ability to define which operations are used at runtime.

In F#, you can have both of these properties through a feature known as function composition. The composition operators allow you to combine any two functions with compatible type signatures into one without executing either. Among many other things, this allows you to both build up a large collection of data transforming functions at runtime and use many different intermediate types.

## Forward Composition (>>)

The forward composition operator takes two functions and composes them into a single function in which the left is applied to the input first and then the right is applied to the result of that. Although simple conceptually, this operator can profoundly change what your code can do.

Take a look at how forward composition can be used in the example from forward pipelining.

```
> let findNamesOfPlacesOver5MilInUppercase =
    List.filter (fun p -> p.Population > 5000000)
    >> List.map (fun p -> p.Name.ToUpper());;

val findNamesOfPlacesOver5MilInUppercase : (Place list -> string list)

> findNamesOfPlacesOver5MilInUppercase places;;

val it : string list = ["NEW YORK"; "TOKYO"]
```

Taking a deeper look at the actual composition, you see the partially applied `filter` and `map` functions are combined into a single function that takes the type of the first function as input and returns the type of the second.

```
> List.filter (fun p -> p.Population > 5000000);;

val it : (Place list -> Place list) = <fun:it@16-8>

> List.map (fun p -> p.Name.ToUpper());;

val it : (Place list -> string list) = <fun:it@17-10>
```

```
> List.filter (fun p -> p.Population > 5000000)
  >> List.map (fun p -> p.Name.ToUpper());;

val it : (Place list -> string list) = <fun:it@18-15>
```

Although powerful, the forward composition operator is actually just a simple function under the hood.

```
> (>>);;

val it : (('a -> 'b) -> ('b -> 'c) -> 'a -> 'c) = <fun:it@26-16>
```

The forward composition operator takes one function on the left of type ('a -> 'b) and another on the right of ('b -> 'c). It then returns another function ('a -> 'c) that takes the same type as the first function but returns the same type as the second.

```
> let fc fun1 fun2 input = fun2( fun1( input ) );;

val fc : ('a -> 'b) -> ('b -> 'c) -> 'a -> 'c

> (fc);;

val it : (('a -> 'b) -> ('b -> 'c) -> 'a -> 'c) = <fun:clo@28>
```

Internally, these two functions are combined by simply calling one inside the other. When the operator is used, the argument functions are partially applied but the input variable remains free. This allows the resulting function to be called with the expected input type at any later time.

## Backward Composition (<<)

The backward composition operator takes two functions and composes them into a single function in which the right is first applied to the input and then the left is applied to the result of that. As you might have expected, this is exactly the same as forward composition except with reversed arguments.

Take a look at how the backward composition operator can be used to make a functionally equivalent example to one shown in forward pipelining.

```
> let findNamesOfPlacesOver5MilInUppercase =
  List.map (fun (p: Place) -> p.Name.ToUpper() )
  << List.filter (fun (p: Place) -> p.Population > 5000000);;

val findNamesOfPlacesOver5MilInUppercase : (Place list -> string list)

> findNamesOfPlacesOver5MilInUppercase places;;

val it : string list = ["NEW YORK"; "TOKYO"]
```

The partially applied `filter` and `map` functions are composed together. This is just as in the version from forward composition, except the argument ordering is reversed. The list of places is then passed in to this composed function and the result is returned.

As you might have suspected, the backward composition operator's signature is the same as the forward version except with reversed arguments.

```
> (<<);;

val it : (('a -> 'b) -> ('c -> 'a) -> 'c -> 'b) = <fun:it@7>
```

Just the opposite of forward composition, the left side takes a function on the left of type (`'a -> 'b`) and on the right of (`'c -> 'a`). These are combined to form a new function of type (`'c -> 'b`) where `'c` is the input type of the function on the right side, and `'b` the output type of the function on the left.

```
> let fb fun1 fun2 input = fun1( fun2( input ) );;

val fb : ('a -> 'b) -> ('c -> 'a) -> 'c -> 'b

> (fb);;

val it : (('a -> 'b) -> ('c -> 'a) -> 'c -> 'b) = <fun:clo@9>
```

This is done in exactly the same way as with forward composition. The input functions on the left and right are partially applied to the operator's internal function, which is then returned. When evaluated, the input will first be applied to the function taken from the right and then the result of that will be applied to the function from the left.

## APPLYING PIPELINING AND COMPOSITION

The most important thing to keep in mind when building data pipelines is the input and output types of the functions involved. When data is pipelined into a function, that data must have the same signature as that function expects. Similarly, when composing two functions, the output type of the first function must match the input type of the second.

If you understand the C# or VB.NET type system, this should make perfect sense to you. You can't fit a square peg into a round hole, as they say. However, unlike in other .NET languages, F# will never automatically convert your data to a different type. This applies even to classes written in other languages. Both the upcasting and downcasting of class instances must always be explicitly stated. In addition, the different numeric types such as `int` and `float` must be explicitly converted to each other. Keeping this in mind is useful when writing any programs in F# but particularly important when using composition and pipelining.

# From Loops to Pipelining

Coming from the imperative programming world, it takes some change in perspective to move from thinking in terms of mutations in a loop to transformations in a function pipeline. The shift in perspective is one of focusing on what you want done in discrete steps instead of how you want to do it all at the same time.

Take a look at this simple example where you are trying to decide among several vacation spots.

```
type VacationLocation =
    { Name: string; Pop: int; Density: int; Nightlife: int }

let destinations =
    [ { Name = "New York"; Pop = 9000000; Density = 27000; Nightlife = 9 }
      { Name = "Munich"; Pop = 1300000; Density = 4300; Nightlife = 7 }
      { Name = "Tokyo"; Pop = 13000000; Density = 15000; Nightlife = 3 }
      { Name = "Rome"; Pop =  2700000; Density = 5500; Nightlife = 5 } ]

let findVacationImperitive data =
    let mutable outputList = []
    for i = List.length data - 1 downto 0 do
        let current = data.[i]
        let size = current.Pop / current.Density
        if current.Nightlife >= 5 &&
           size >= 200 &&
           current.Density <= 8000
        then
            outputList <- List.Cons(current.Name, outputList)
    outputList;;
```

*Code snippet FindVacationImperitive.fs*

```
> findVacationImperitive destinations;;
val it : string list = ["Munich"; "Rome"]
```

In this imperative version, the data set is passed in, and if it passes a set of predicates, the name value of the record is added to a list. There's a lot going on here that you shouldn't need to think about. First, you need to explicitly build and maintain a data structure to store data in. Second, program flow must be explicitly controlled via a backward loop and an `if` statement. Third, all this logic is tangled together and difficult to extract in a meaningful way. If all you want to do is find the name of a city that meets some criteria, why must the movement of every chunk of data be explicitly stated? It ends up being a tangled mess.

This example is much clearer when pipelining is used. To convert to pipelining, each of the predicates in the `if` statement is changed into a `filter` statement. After being filtered we perform the conversion to just the city name with a map. Everything else in the example can be thrown away.

```
let findVacationPipeline data =
    data
    |> List.filter (fun x -> x.Nightlife >= 5)
    |> List.filter (fun x -> x.Pop / x.Density >= 200)
```

```
|> List.filter (fun x -> x.Density <= 8000)
|> List.map (fun x -> x.Name);;
```

*Code snippet FindVacationPipeline.fs*

```
> findVacationPipeline destinations;;

val it : string list = ["Munich"; "Rome"]
```

The collection of records is simply passed through a series of filters and converted to an output format. Each step is explicit about the action it performs and can be changed or removed easily. The programmer need not spend much time thinking about exactly how each of these steps is being done.

## From Pipelining to Composition

Now, what if you were building this into a website that can help millions of people find the best vacation destination? One flexible way to approach this would be to dynamically build a set of `filter` functions defined by values given by the user.

```
> let getSimpleVacationPipeline nightlifeMin sizeMin densityMax =
    List.filter (fun x -> x.Nightlife >= nightlifeMin)
    >> List.filter (fun x -> x.Pop / x.Density >= sizeMin)
    >> List.filter (fun x -> x.Density <= densityMax);;

val getSimpleVacationPipeline :
    int -> int -> int -> (VacationLocation list -> VacationLocation list)
```

You can just call the `getSimpleVacationPipeline` function with the values for each of the given filters. When called, the lambda expressions given for each filter acts as a closure over the parameter value it uses. These filter functions are then composed into a single function that is returned. You can take this composite `filter` function and use it to perform your filtering step at a later time.

```
> let myPipeline = getSimpleVacationPipeline 5 200 8000;;

val myPipeline : (VacationLocation list -> VacationLocation list)

> let applyVacationPipeline data filterPipeline =
    data
    |> filterPipeline
    |> List.map (fun x -> x.Name);;

val applyVacationPipeline :
    'a -> ('a -> VacationLocation list) -> string list

> applyVacationPipeline destinations myPipeline;;

val it : string list = ["Munich"; "Rome"]
```

In this example, `myPipeline` is the composite filter function returned by the call to `getSimpleVacationPipeline`. This composite filter is then passed into the `applyVacationPipeline` function along with the data set. This function pushes the data into the composite filter and then performs the same simple map as was used in the pure pipelining example.

## Advanced Composition

Although interesting, the static set of filters in the previous example is insufficient for our use case. Any reasonable web interface would allow the user to toggle filters on and off. To gain the needed functionality, you need to go one step further and leverage a combination of option types and the identity function.

The option type has been discussed in Chapter 15, "Data Types." It simply provides a way to say a value may or may not exist. It's quite like the idea of null, but much safer. The identity function is similarly quite simple. It's just a predefined function that takes a value and immediately returns it. Consider it as a kind of a no-op used to make the dynamic gluing of transformation functions a smoother process. In F#, the identity function is given the name id.

By making each argument to your pipeline building function an option type, you can specify if each corresponding function should be added to the filter pipeline by simply selecting if the input value is some value or none.

```
> let getVacationPipeline nightlifeMin sizeMin densityMax searchName =
    match nightlifeMin with
    | Some(n) -> List.filter (fun x -> x.Nightlife >= n)
    | None -> id
    >> match sizeMin with
        | Some(s) -> List.filter (fun x -> x.Pop / x.Density >= s)
        | None -> id
    >> match densityMax with
        | Some(d) -> List.filter (fun x -> x.Density <= d)
        | None -> id
    >> match searchName with
        | Some(sn) -> List.filter (fun x -> x.Name.Contains(sn))
        | None -> id;;
```

*Code snippet GetVacationPipeline.fs*

```
val getVacationPipeline :
  int option ->
    int option ->
      int option ->
        string option -> (VacationLocation list -> VacationLocation list)
```

Now that each of the input arguments is an option type, we can specify them as Some or None to toggle each filter on or off. When a value is passed in as None, the identity function is returned instead of a filter. Notice that a new name searching filter was added in this example as a place to demonstrate passing in none.

```
> let myPipeline = getVacationPipeline (Some 5) (Some 200) (Some 8000) None;;

val myPipeline : (VacationLocation list -> VacationLocation list)

> applyVacationPipeline destinations myPipeline;;

val it : string list = ["Munich"; "Rome"]
```

So, as values were passed in for the first three filters, they were each included in the composition. The name searching `filter` was left out as `None` was passed in for its parameter. The result is a `filter` exactly the same as the previous example but composed based on the availability of `input`.

You might have noticed that this version of `getVacationPipeline` was already a bit large and had a significant amount of repeated code. As a final step, the repeated code can be factored out in to a single function. This step is rather advanced but will make adding new filters in the future much easier.

**Available for download on Wrox.com**

```
> let getVacationPipeline nightlifeMin sizeMin densityMax searchName =
    let getFilter filter some =
        match some with
        | Some(v) -> List.filter (filter v)
        | None -> id
    getFilter (fun nlMax x -> x.Nightlife >= nlMax) nightlifeMin
    >> getFilter (fun sMax x -> x.Pop / x.Density >= sMax) sizeMin
    >> getFilter (fun dMin x -> x.Density < dMin) densityMax
    >> getFilter (fun sName x -> x.Name.Contains(sName)) searchName;;
```

*Code snippet GetVacationPipelineRefactored.fs*

```
val getVacationPipeline :
  int option ->
    int option ->
      int option ->
        string option -> (VacationLocation list -> VacationLocation list)
```

In this example, all the repeated code has been refactored into one function named `getFilter`. This function takes a filtering function of two arguments and an `option` type. The new argument to each of the `filter` functions is a place where the value of the `option` type will be filled in if it exists. You can see this step inside `getFilter` as `(filter v)`. After the missing value is filled in, the `filter` function is passed as an argument to `List.filter`. Just as in each example leading up to this, the partially composed `List.filter` is returned and combined with its neighbors via the function composition operator.

Although succinct and usable, the example is by no means as far as this can be taken in F#. You might imagine representing a set of possible filters as a list and their corresponding optional inputs as another. These lists could be folded over with the forward composition operator and a function similar to `getFilter`. However, that is only one of many possible directions to take this. When functions are just another type of data, the possibilities are virtually limitless.

## SUMMARY

The ability to treat functions as data, when combined with F#'s large library of data manipulation constructs, gives you a language in which you can build very powerful data manipulation programs but which are also short and easy to read. This is one of F#'s core strengths. To leverage this strength you first need to understand the composition and pipelining operations well. Next, spend time playing with the various list manipulation functions. In very little time, you'll gain full enough intuition to build composition helper functions and possibly your own data structures. The key to this is practice.

# PART IV
# Applications

▶ **CHAPTER 18:** C#

▶ **CHAPTER 19:** Databases

▶ **CHAPTER 20:** XML

▶ **CHAPTER 21:** ASP.NET MVC

▶ **CHAPTER 22:** Silverlight

▶ **CHAPTER 23:** Services

# 18

## C#

**WHAT'S IN THIS CHAPTER?**

➤ Calling C# libraries from F#

➤ Exploring the complexities of C# libraries

➤ Calling F# libraries from C#

➤ Structuring F# libraries for C# consumption

➤ Avoiding common pitfalls

While F# is definitely useful on its own, if it were unable to leverage programs written in other languages such as C#, it would be far less practical for general use than it could be. And C# programs greatly benefit from using new F# programs. This chapter explains how these two languages can interoperate together and provides some tips to make that interoperation easier.

## OVERVIEW

One of the most significant reasons why F# is a compelling functional language is that it is best positioned for broad usage among software developers on the .NET platform. It isn't the only functional language in that it not only can leverage the .NET framework but there are also many others — including implementations of Clojure and Scheme. What sets F# apart is not only "inclusion in the box" as part of Visual Studio, but also the downstream implications of that, meaning it will be available to a broader pool of developers, which leads to broader skill availability, which helps build a talent base that makes organizations more likely to consider using the language.

Of course, none of this would be possible if these more risk-averse organizations could leverage existing investments in C# in their F# programs. Although it would be nice to live in an "ideal programmer world" where one picks and chooses the legacy code base one gets to program to, reality is that no language will ever get significant usage if it can't build on work that has already been done.

## CALLING C# LIBRARIES FROM F#

Given a great deal of the code written on the .NET platform is written in C#, it would be almost impossible to write a meaningful F# program without calling C# code at some point. This section covers the simple cases, and more interestingly, some of the more complex cases that tend to be hard to handle from the F# side.

## Simple Method Calling Scenarios

The vast majority of F# to C# integration scenarios is intuitive. Consider the following somewhat trivial C# class:

```csharp
namespace CSharpLibrary
{
    public class CSharpLibraryUsedWithFSharp
    {
        public int SomeMutableProperty { get; set; }
        public int AnotherMutableProperty { get; set; }

        public CSharpLibraryUsedWithFSharp()
        {

        }

        public bool SomeFunction(int firstParam, int secondParam)
        {
            return true;
        }
    }
}
```

*Code snippet CSharpLibraryUsedWithFSharp.cs*

If this class is in a project called CSharpLibrary that compiles to a class library, after referencing the library from your F# project, the following could be written to call SomeFunction:

```fsharp
module FSharpCallingCSharp
open System
open CSharpLibrary
//typical call to C#
let newCSharpObject = new CSharpLibraryUsedWithFSharp()
let someResult = newCSharpObject.SomeFunction(42,69)
```

*Code snippet FSharpCallingCSharp.fs*

The semantics of dealing with C# objects in F# is not all that different from how you would deal with dealing with C# objects in C#. The last two lines in C# barely look any different at all:

```
var newCSharpObject = new CSharpLibraryUsedWithFSharp();
var someResult = newCSharpObject.SomeFunction(42,69);
```

At this level, moving from C# to F# is a simple matter of replacing `var` with `let` and removing the semicolons. You might wonder what all the fuss is about! As might be expected, however, there is much more just a little bit behind the scenes. This gets put into sharp relief when attempting to call C# methods using F# pipeline syntax:

**Available for download on Wrox.com**

```
//this works
let anotherResult = (42,69) |> newCSharpObject.SomeFunction
//but you can't do this stuff
let wontWork = newCSharpObject.SomeFunction 42 69
let alsoWontWork = 69 |> 42 |> newCSharpObject.SomeFunction
let neitherWillThisAttemptedCurryingExample = 69 |> newCSharpObject.SomeFunction
```

*Code snippet FSharpCallingCSharp.fs*

What becomes more clear when looking at this in pipeline form is that from F#, a method with multiple parameters is actually a method with a single parameter that is presented from F# in the form of a tuple. As a result of this, when using C# functions in F#, the same options around function composition will generally not be available. Consider the following common F# currying example:

```
let someFSharpFunction a b = a + b
let curriedFunction = 42 |> someFSharpFunction
let actualResult = 69 |> curriedFunction
```

Although the preceding is a simple exercise in F#, doing so with methods defined in C# is not possible in a way that most people would consider elegant, if it is possible at all.

## C# Object Construction

Constructing C# objects in F# is mostly trivial:

```
let newCSharpObject = new CSharpLibraryUsedWithFSharp()
```

The `new` facility in F# works mostly how a C# developer would expect it would. Construction with arguments takes the familiar form as well:

```
let paramsOnly = new CSharpLibraryUsedWithFSharp(11,22)
```

In C# 3.0, a new feature, object initializers, were introduced, which allow for provision of the initial property values of (usually) mutable properties. Property initialization in F# is not all that different:

```
let initializersOnly =
  new CSharpLibraryUsedWithFSharp(
    SomeMutableProperty = 55,
    AnotherMutableProperty = 56)
```

The key difference on the F# side is that parentheses are used, not braces, as you would in C#. If you want to mix explicit constructor parameters with property initializers, the explicit parameters come first:

```
let paramsAndInitializers =
    new CSharpLibraryUsedWithFSharp(
        11,
        22,
        SomeMutableProperty = 55,
        AnotherMutableProperty = 56)
```

## F#, C#, and null

Idiomatic F# code avoids the use of `null` as much as possible, in favor of option types for situations where the goal is to express lack of a value. However, there are situations where you may be calling C# code that does, in fact, need to provide a proper C# style null parameter:

```
//this works
let shouldBeTrue = String.IsNullOrEmpty(null)
//this does not work
let doesNotCompile = String.IsNullOrEmpty(None)
```

It is important to note that in the world of F#, nulls are to be avoided most of the time. When calling C# code that might return a `null`, it is often far safer to check for that condition and contain it at the source of the issue, like this:

```
//pretend this is your normal null spewing C# function
let someRandomStrangeFunctionThatMightReturnNull =
    match DateTime.Now.Day with
    | 31 -> "This is a 31st Day in a 31 Day Month, Yipee"
    | _ -> null

//this is how you will protect against such functions in your F# code
let wontBeNull =
    match someRandomStrangeFunctionThatMightReturnNull with
    | null -> None
    | v -> Some(v)
```

*Code snippet FSharpCallingCSharp.fs*

In the preceding example, `someRandomStrangeFunctionThatMightReturnNull` represents a prototypical C# function that breaks out F# rules about avoiding nulls. This function is not idiomatic F# but helps us illustrate what C# programs sometimes return to us. The `wontBeNull` value calls that function but does so in a `match` statement, which converts the `null` to a `None` if `null` is returned, otherwise, producing a `Some` with the embedded value if such a value exists. This pattern should be used around calls to non F# libraries, including C# programs, that either:

**a.**   Are known to return null in certain cases

**b.**   Are from an outside API that might return null — or is unknown about its status as to whether null is returned

A savvy C# programmer may notice that an option with a simple type, such as Some(42), is actually similar to a Nullable<int> in C#. In fact, they are similar in some ways. However, in F#, Some(x) allows x to be any type of object, which allows a programmer to not only be more explicit when stating intent for "lack of an object," but also allows generic functions that deal with both nonobjects and objects to consistently use the same kind of structure to differentiate between Some(T) and None.

## F# and C# Methods that Expect Delegates

Calling C# methods that expect delegate parameters, although not hard, is also not entirely obvious. There is no automatic conversion from an F# function to a particular delegate signature in C#. Consider the following C# code:

```csharp
public class CSharpLibraryUsedWithFSharp
{
    public int SomeMutableProperty { get; set; }
    public int AnotherMutableProperty { get; set; }

    public delegate int BinaryIntegerMathOp(int op1, int op2);

    public CSharpLibraryUsedWithFSharp()
    {

    }

    public int PerformMathOnMyProperties(BinaryIntegerMathOp op)
    {
        return op(SomeMutableProperty, AnotherMutableProperty);
    }
}
```

*Code snippet CSharpLibraryUsedWithFSharp.cs*

A delegate type has been declared called BinaryIntegerMathOp, which takes two integers and converts them into a single integer. The method PerformAMathOperationOnMyProperties takes a BinaryIntegerMathOp as a parameter and returns the result of the operation.

The following is a way a C# programmer would likely first approach the problem when using F#:

```fsharp
let delegateExample = new CSharpLibraryUsedWithFSharp(
  SomeMutableProperty = 55,
  AnotherMutableProperty = 56)
let addNumbersAsDelegate =
  new CSharpLibraryUsedWithFSharp.BinaryIntegerMathOp(
    fun x y -> x + y
  )
let subNumbersAsDelegate =
  new CSharpLibraryUsedWithFSharp.BinaryIntegerMathOp(
    fun x y -> x - y
  )
let shouldBe111 =
```

```
    delegateExample.PerformMathOnMyProperties(addNumbersAsDelegate)
let shouldBeMinusOne =
    delegateExample.PerformMathOnMyProperties(subNumbersAsDelegate)
```

In this example, specific delegate types are declared and used. This kind of convention may be needed in cases where a method has multiple overloads that take delegates that have the same parameters and return types, to disambiguate which method is to be called. However, if that is not the case, the following simpler and more F# idiomatic syntax may be used:

```
let simplerForm
    = delegateExample.PerformMathOnMyProperties(fun x y -> x+ y)
let subSimplerForm
    = delegateExample.PerformMathOnMyProperties(fun x y -> x - y)
```

## F# and C# Events

Working with events in C# classes is fairly straightforward. Consider the following class that publishes an event:

```
public class CSharpLibraryUsedWithFSharp
{
    public delegate void BeerFinishingHandler(string nameOfBeer);
    public event BeerFinishingHandler FinishedABeer;

    public void HaveADrinkingBinge()
    {
        if (FinishedABeer != null)
        {
            FinishedABeer("Belgian Trappist");
            FinishedABeer("Three Philosophers");
            FinishedABeer("Red Hook");
            FinishedABeer("Stella");
            FinishedABeer("Another Stella");
            //as time goes by, standards get lower
            FinishedABeer("Pabst Blue Ribbon");
            FinishedABeer("Schlitz");
            //throw a type mismatch exception?
            FinishedABeer("Zima");
        }
    }
}
```

In F#, subscribing to events is not unlike one would do in C#, though the syntax is arguably a bit cleaner:

```
let eventExample = new CSharpLibraryUsedWithFSharp()
eventExample.add_FinishedABeer( fun s -> printfn "Drank a %s" s )
do eventExample.HaveADrinkingBinge()
```

Subscribing to events is very similar to a typical case of delegate passing, as the preceding code demonstrates with the call to add_FinishedABeer. The method add_FinishedABeer is automatically generated when C# has a public event, comparable to what the += event assignment operator does in C#.

Of course, there are times when you may want to unsubscribe to an event. At first glance, the exposed method remove_FinishedABeer looks promising:

```
//wont remove the event, since it is a different function instance
eventExample.remove_FinishedABeer( fun s -> printfn "Drank a %s" s )
```

The problem, of course, is that the remove method needs a means to know what it is removing, because there can be many subscribers to a given event. The preceding code won't create an exception, but because fun s -> printfn "Drank a %s" s gets converted into a different instance of the delegate than the one passed into the add_FinishedABeer method we originally called, it does nothing because the new delegate we create by passing a simple F# function won't be found.

To remove a subscription, we must keep a reference to the original delegate that was passed in to handle the event:

**Available for download on Wrox.com**

```
let anotherEventExample = new CSharpLibraryUsedWithFSharp()
let handleMyBeer = new CSharpLibraryUsedWithFSharp.BeerFinishingHandler(
  fun s -> printfn "Drank a %s" s )
anotherEventExample.add_FinishedABeer( handleMyBeer )
//this remove will work, since it is the same delegate instance
anotherEventExample.remove_FinishedABeer( handleMyBeer )
```

*Code snippet FSharpCallingCSharp.fs*

In this example, an explicit reference to the delegate is created. This works because remove uses reference equality of the delegate to indicate which to remove. The same instance must be used in the remove that was used in the corresponding add for the remove to actually work.

## F# to C# Summary

Although F# calling C# is straightforward most of the time, there are some cases where it is not exactly clear how the C# concept translates into F# code that may want to leverage the feature. This is particularly true in areas such as passing around functions, delegates, dealing with events, and dealing with concepts like null that are not mainstream F#. Things get more interesting, however, when you switch to making use of F# libraries in C#.

## CALLING F# LIBRARIES FROM C#

A very compelling use case for F#, as organizations start to adapt it, is to integrate specialized modules that do calculation and math that are written in F# into existing C# programs. For the most part, using F# programs from C# code is simple. However, there are certain things that can be done that make F# libraries easier for outside programs to understand, whether they are written in C#, other CLR languages, or even other F# programs.

## Basics of Calling F#

Much interaction that occurs when C# calls F# works exactly how you would expect it to. Consider the following type definition in F#:

```
namespace FSharpLibraryUsedWithCSharp
open System
type FSharpLibrary() =

    member this.MethodCallNoParameters() =
        42
    member this.NoParamsMakesAReadOnlyProperty =
        "I am a property result"
    member this.MethodCallWithParameters x y =
        x + y
    member this.MethodCallWithTupleFormParameters(x,y) =
        x * y
```

*Code snippet FSharpCallingCSharp.fs*

The preceding type and function, as defined in F#, represents various ways that a given F# type may define members. From the C# side, a call to `MethodCallNoParameters` will look as follows:

```
var someFSharpObject = new FSharpLibrary();
var simpleFunction = someFSharpObject.MethodCallNoParameters();
```

The most significant thing to notice is that if the desired signature is to be a `zero parameter` method, rather than as a property, an empty set of parentheses should be suffixed on the member name in F#. Without the parentheses, the member will take the form of a read-only property:

```
var withoutParmsIAmAProperty = someFSharpObject.NoParamsMakesAReadOnlyProperty;
```

Calling members with parameters, whether those parameters are defined in F# in tuple form, operate like normal parameters in C#:

```
var withParameters = someFSharpObject.MethodCallWithParameters(1, 2);
var withParametersTupleForm =
    someFSharpObject.MethodCallWithTupleFormParameters(1, 2);
```

It is worth noting that even though internal to an F# program, tuple form would be passed to `MethodCallWithTupleFormParameters`, doing so from a C# program does not work:

```
//worth mentioning that this does *not* compile
var passingATupleAsParameters
        = someFSharpObject
                .MethodCallWithTupleFormParameters(new Tuple<int, int>(1, 2));
```

## F# Tuples in C# Programs

Although the practice of using `Tuples` as external return values in an external API is not recommended, in the event that a `Tuple` is returned from a function in F# to a C# program, it will take the form of a the new `Tuple` type in .NET 4.0. Consider the following F# member on the type defined in the previous section:

```
member this.MemberThatReturnsATuple() =
    ("Aaron","Erickson",37,new DateTime(2010,3,1))
```

From the point of view of a C# programmer, this member will return an object of type `Tuple<string, string, int, DateTime>`.

```
var someTuple = someFSharpObject.MemberThatReturnsATuple();
var firstValue = someTuple.Item1;
var secondValue = someTuple.Item2;
var thirdValue = someTuple.Item3;
var lastValue = someTuple.Item4;
```

Tuples are very useful, but from the standpoint of C# programs, they are not terribly descriptive, especially outside the context of where they are used, as the names of the items of Item1, 2, 3, and so forth do not really describe much.

## Dealing with F# Records from C#

F# records generally come to C# as buckets that hold read-only properties. Consider the following simple record type defined in F#, and a member in `FSharpLibrary` that returns an instance of the record:

```
type PersonRecord = {FirstName:string;LastName:string;Age:int}

type FSharpLibrary() =
  member this.MemberReturnsARecord() =
    {FirstName="Aaron";LastName="Erickson";Age=37}
```

This is a common way for an F# program to return information to a C# program. This is especially true in the sense that it is not as common for F# to deal in objects, and hence, something that would be considered bad practice, the ever vilified "anemic domain" object, is just fine for moving information over an integration seam such as an F# API.

From the perspective of C#, the code is hardly unusual:

```
var someRecord = someFSharpObject.MemberReturnsARecord();
var firstName = someRecord.FirstName;
var lastName = someRecord.LastName;
var age = someRecord.Age;
```

Each of the properties in the record type works as expected. As we would expect, the properties of the F# object are immutable, just as they are on the F# side of the fence.

Creation of F# records from C# is simple as well:

```
//creation of a record (notice the generated ctor)
var aPerson = new PersonRecord("Matthew", "Erickson", 8);
```

It is notable that when F# compiles a record, it generates the appropriate constructor that does the initial population of the immutable values within the record. Records, used in this way, are not bad things to pass through an API seam, especially for things that would take the role in C# of a data transfer object.

## Passing Functions to F# Functions

As understood from previous chapters where function composition is discussed, it is common for F# programs to accept functions as parameters. Consider the following F# member:

```
member this.MemberThatTakesAFunction a b func =
    func a b
```

This member is a simplistic member that applies `func` to `a` and `b`. Simple enough in F#, but this kind of thing becomes painful to use from C#:

```
//calling a member that takes a function as a parameter
var uglyFunc = FuncConvert.ToFSharpFunc<int, FSharpFunc<int, int>>(
  a => FuncConvert.ToFSharpFunc<int,int>(b => a + b)
);
var operationResult = someFSharpObject.MemberThatTakesAFunction(2, 2, uglyFunc);
```

In the preceding example, few would disagree that the preceding `uglyFunc`, is misnamed. Not only does it require a reference to `FSharp.Core` to make the code at all (almost always a bad sign), but it also forces construction of the function in an unintuitive manner. Although it does reveal how the F# composes functions, there is no simple mapping from a more intuitive `Func<int, int, int>` you would use in C# to the `int->int->int` that F# is expecting. As a result, it forces the programmer to go through the F# mechanics of composition in C#, and as a result, writing a lot of unidiomatic and confusing C# code in the process.

A better way to allow C# to pass functions to F# code is to use the `Func<>` or `Action<>` types, as appropriate:

```
member this.IsBetterForCSharpInterop(a,b,func:Func<int,int,int>) =
    func.Invoke(a, b)
```

which can be called from C# and other .NET languages more idiomatically:

```
var betterResult
    = someFSharpObject.IsBetterForCSharpInterop(2, 2, (a, b) => a + b);
```

As a general rule, you should use natural F# functions when operating with other F# code, but when designing an API that will likely be called from other CLR languages, use `Func<>` or `Action<>` with those outside APIs.

## Dealing with F# Discriminated Unions from C#

Discriminated unions, from the standpoint of the C# programmer, have the appearance of Enums, but do not quite match up with them. As a result of this, it is not terribly common for F# programmers to expose discriminated unions in APIs. However, if an API returns such a discriminated union, it is helpful to have a sense of what will happen. Consider the following:

```
type CoolColors = Green | Blue | Purple

type FSharpLibrary() =
  member this.ReturnADiscriminatedUnion() =
    Blue
```

The preceding code is simple F# code that returns `CoolColors.Blue`, which is part of the `CoolColors` discriminated union. The following is perfectly good C# code that utilizes this:

```
var shouldBeBlue = someFSharpObject.ReturnADiscriminatedUnion();
var shouldBeTrue = shouldBeBlue == CoolColors.Blue;
```

As can be seen, it is almost like working with an enumeration. However, unlike an enumeration, there is no ability to use the discriminated union in a switch statement, or do anything nearly as powerful as an F# match construct. One of the reasons discriminated unions are not recommended for use in APIs is that they tend to cause a number of ugly constructs in languages that are not suited for using them, such as:

**Available for download on Wrox.com**

```
if (shouldBeBlue == CoolColors.Blue)
{
    //do blue stuff
}
else if (shouldBeBlue == CoolColors.Green)
{
    //do green stuff
}
else if (shouldBeBlue == CoolColors.Plaid)
{
    //do crazy stuff
}
```

*Code snippet CSharpLibraryUsedWithFSharp.cs*

The preceding example is exactly the kind of C# code that most programmers want to get away from, especially given that anything that is making a decision like that in C# code based on a discriminated union could probably do so with much more clarity inside the F# library. Although it may be necessary in a case where you deal with third-party libraries, it is generally better to deal with discriminated unions in the world of F# rather than in C#.

## Working with F# Option Types from C#

F# option types are another one of those cases that may sometimes leak outside of the F# world but probably should remain in the F# world at least until there is a clean mapping in the CLR from F# to the rest of the CLR languages. Consider an API written in F# containing something like the following that uses an `option int` as a return value:

```
member this.ReturnAnOption() =
  if DateTime.Now.Hour = 6 then
    Some(6)
  else
    None
```

The poor C# user who uses this API is going to need to not only reference FSharp.Core (which has the type definition for options), but will also need to do something like the following to convert the option into a more appropriate type for C#:

```
//getting back an option
var mightHaveSomething = someFSharpObject.ReturnAnOption();
var someNullable =
  mightHaveSomething == FSharpOption<int>.None
  ? new int?()
  : mightHaveSomething.Value;
```

Of course, there are some key differences between Nullable and F# options. Nullable applies only to structs, whereas FSharpOption applies to any kind of object. The FSharpOption is also more explicit in that it can differentiate between a null object and None — though truth be told, in practice, most of the time null and None have the same semantic meaning from the perspective of the C# programmer.

## RULES OF THUMB FOR WRITING F# APIS

In this chapter so far, various means of dealing with what C# programmers might call "F# oddities" have been covered. Over time, it is likely that many of these concepts from F# that are not easily expressed in the CLR will find their way in, much like Tuple<T> has become a core part of the .NET framework. However, until something is in that core, it is far safer to write APIs that conform to things that map easily to other languages as they are currently defined.

To help write APIs that will interoperate nicely with other languages, consider the following rules of thumb:

➤ **Avoid using Tuple as return types from APIs.** Even though the concepts are supported in C# and other CLR languages in .NET 4.0, code that works with Tuple<T> is often hard to read outside the context where the Tuple is defined.

➤ **Avoid FSharpOption unless you are confident your API consumer can take a dependency on FSharp.Core.** The FSharpOption<T> type is, arguably, a better Nullable than Nullable, something that can help C# programmers move away from using null as a sentinel value meaning None. However, the drawback of forcing the direct dependency to FSharp.Core is an important consideration, as is the complexity of dealing with a legacy codebase where Nullable and FSharpOption might end up getting mixed together, creating even more confusion than you started with.

➤ **Record types are all good — use them at will.** F# Record types allow a programmer to do in one line of F# code what often takes many lines of C#, expressing the concept of an immutable holder of data (that is, for transfer between systems) very cleanly.

➤ **Avoid use of discriminated unions in public APIs.** These are great for internal F# code, but to C# code, the language constructs for dealing with them in a way idiomatic to good C# simply are not present.

➤ **Do not use F# native functions as parameter types in public APIs.** Prefer `Func<>` and `Action<>` over native F# functions in APIs that pass functions around, as there is a great deal of pain involved for languages other than F# to create proper F# functional constructs.

➤ **Use each language for its purpose.** For the same reason C# is likely better than F# for expressing hardcore OO concepts, F# is better than C# for doing things like functional composition. Within those areas of strength, it is best to stick with the language at hand. Don't try to use F# to compose functions written in C#, and don't try to use F# in some elaborate C# inheritance chain. In an API where one interoperates with the other, select concepts that are cleanly expressed in both languages when working over the seam.

## SUMMARY

There are great reasons for being a polyglot — that is, proficient in multiple languages in a manner that allows the programmer to use each language where it is best suited. Many enterprise solutions have aspects that are best expressed in functions, such as business intelligence and complex calculations, where other aspects are best expressed in objects. By knowing not only how to use both languages, but also how to use them together, the .NET programmer is well suited to not only get the best of both worlds, but also to do so in a way that does not make both F# and C# code bases difficult to maintain.

# 19

# Databases

**WHAT'S IN THIS CHAPTER?**

➤ Implementing basic CRUD operations

➤ Understanding how ORMs and F# interact

➤ Creating your own mapping layer

➤ Implementing DDL functionality

There are few, if any, interesting applications that do not use data in one way, shape, or form. If we are to write interesting programs in F#, at some point, it is likely a database will be involved. This chapter explains how databases can be accessed using F# and walks through an example framework for dealing with data in F#.

## OVERVIEW

One of the core strengths of F# is processing large sets of data and doing interesting things with it. Most examples where F# was used early on were around things like computation of XBox 360 TrueSkill (http://blogs.technet.com/apg/archive/2008/06/16/trueskill-in-f.aspx). This case, which involves taking a great deal of information gathered from players of Xbox 360 consoles and using said information to produce rankings that allow for smarter matching of players when engaging in multiplayer games, is a canonical use case where F# shines. These cases — where lots of incoming raw information can be processed by complex algorithms to generate business value — are well suited to the F# language.

One thing you might start to notice are the similarities between some of the declarative properties of F# and the declarative nature of the primary languages used for database inter-action, Structured Query Language. For example, the `select` construct in SQL is quite similar to the `Seq.map` construct in F#. The same can be said for (no pun intended) mapping the concept of where to Seq.filter, and various other constructs based on Seq. F#, when examined closely, is ideally situated as a functional language that has all the power of what you would do with SQL, with the added bonus that it is easily leveraged on the .NET framework. It allows separation of code that works with data (using F#), from code that retrieves data (using SQL).

In this chapter, various ways to work with F# will be demonstrated. It covers core fundamentals using core ADO.net libraries, what happens when you introduce an ORM into the mix, and then explores some possibilities around more F#-friendly ways to work with data.

## RETRIEVING DATA USING ADO.NET

There is little you can do without at least fundamentally getting some data in the first place. Thankfully, there are a multitude of means by which you can retrieve data on the .NET framework. The most fundamental way, however, is to simply use ADO.NET primitives to accomplish this task. Assume the following exist:

➤   A local instance of Microsoft SQL Server 2008

➤   Integrated security, with the current user having administrative access to the local server

➤   A local database called DemoData

## Creating a Database Connection

Under those assumptions, a database connection can be created with the following code:

**Available for download on Wrox.com**

```
module RawADOExample
open System.Data
open System.Data.SqlClient

//raw ADO example
let readPeople =
  use connection =
    new SqlConnection(
      "Server=localhost;Integrated security=SSPI;database=DemoData")
```

*Code snippet RawADOExample.fs*

Most people familiar with other .NET languages will not find the preceding line of code that different than a similar line of code in C# that accomplishes the same thing. Of course, it is important to note that like many other objects that use external resources and implement IDisposable to have a means to release said resources, it is important to use the use binding when instantiating them. This is analogous to putting code in a using block in C#.

Creating connections to other data sources is a matter of finding other concrete classes that support the IDbConnection interface, of which there are a robust number of options if you prefer to work with something other than MS SQL Server.

# Reading Data

Of course, a connection alone is not going to do much all by itself. Performing a query requires a command object that holds the query. The query itself is SQL code, which for this example, can be used in string form:

```
module RawADOExample
open System.Data
open System.Data.SqlClient

//raw ADO example
let readPeople =
  use connection = new SqlConnection(
    "Server=localhost;Integrated security=SSPI;database=DemoData")
  use command = new SqlCommand("select firstname, lastname from person",connection)
```

*Code snippet RawADOExample.fs*

Again, this is not that different than code you would write in any other .NET language for reaching a database. Nothing really interesting has yet been done, however. If the desire is to retrieve some actual data, then the command is going to need to be executed. If an assumption is made that the firstname and lastname columns of the person table can be read as strings (that is, varchar, char, or something like that), the following record type can be used as a container:

```
type Person = {Id:int;FirstName:string;LastName:string}
```

The next step is to actually run the query, take the results, and populate a list of Person records:

```
module RawADOExample
open System.Data
open System.Data.SqlClient

type Person = {Id:int;FirstName:string;LastName:string}
//raw ADO example
let readPeople =
  use connection =
   new SqlConnection("Server=localhost;Integrated security=SSPI;database=DemoData")
  connection.Open()
  use command = new SqlCommand("select firstname, lastname from person",connection)
  use rawResult = command.ExecuteReader()
  let people = seq {
      while rawResult.Read() do
        yield {
          Id = rawResult.["FirstName"] :?> int;
          FirstName = rawResult.["FirstName"] :?> string;
          LastName = rawResult.["LastName"] :?> string
        }
      }
  people |> Seq.toList
```

*Code snippet RawADOExample.fs*

For those familiar with how ADO.NET works, this is a familiar pattern. A call to `command.ExecuteReader()` is made, which provides a `SqlDataReader` through which data can be accessed. In the example, there is an F# spin on the old `while-Read()`-next loop. In this case, the result is compiled into a sequence expression that specifies how the loop can be iterated through and reads the results into `Person` records. It is important to note that, like all sequence definitions, nothing has actually happened yet — this code merely *specifies* how the sequence is to be read. It does not actually read it until the next line, `people |> Seq.toList`, which iterates through the `people` sequence and materializes an actual list of `Person` records.

## Filtering Data

As simple as it may seem to simply do a `Seq.filter` operation on the result of selecting for all the records in a given table at once, such operations do not scale for anything but very small data sets. As a result, when working with larger databases, the need to let the database do some of the work of filtering data right at the source will present itself. This is, of course, what databases do best, and it would be pretty silly not to let the database help in the task of querying data.

For this sample, it is going to be assumed that the goal is to implement a query for people based on the `FirstName` column in the database. Such code needs to add a parameter object into the query that specifies which first name is to be queried for:

```
let retrievePeopleNamed firstName =
  use connection =
   new SqlConnection("Server=localhost;Integrated security=SSPI;database=DemoData")
  connection.Open()
  use command =
    new SqlCommand("select firstname, lastname from person where firstname =
@firstname",connection)
  let parameter = new SqlParameter("firstName",firstName)
  do command.Parameters.Add parameter |> ignore
  let rawResult = command.ExecuteReader()
  let people = seq {
        while rawResult.Read() do
          yield {
            Id = rawResult.["FirstName"] :?> int;
            FirstName = rawResult.["FirstName"] :?> string;
            LastName = rawResult.["LastName"] :?> string
          }
      }
  people |> Seq.toList
```

*Code snippet RawADOExample.fs*

The first key difference is the inclusion of the `@firstname` literal within the string used to build the command:

```
use command =
  new SqlCommand("select firstname, lastname from person where
firstname = @firstname",connection)
```

The `@firstname` literal is a placeholder for where the parameter will go. This approach of using parameters is important because without them, SQL injection bugs are almost always introduced:

```
use command = new SqlCommand("select firstname, lastname from person where
firstname = " + firstName, connection)
```

If a user decides to be clever and submit a `firstName` of `'; drop database`, it is not an understatement to imagine that there could be some serious issues!

When there is a query and placeholder in place, parameters can be added:

```
let parameter = new SqlParameter("firstName",firstName)
do command.Parameters.Add parameter |> ignore
```

## Insert, Update, and Delete

Using the same concept of commands and parameters, the next step is to implement the other three main database operations. The following code demonstrates how, on the vast majority of databases, we might do those operations:

**Available for download on Wrox.com**

```
let doCreateUpdateDelete() =
  use connection =
   new SqlConnection("Server=localhost;Integrated security=SSPI;database=DemoData")
  connection.Open()

  //create
  use createCommand =
    new SqlCommand("insert into person (firstname,lastname) values
(@firstname,@lastname)",connection)
   let firstNameParameterCreate = new SqlParameter("firstName","Aaron")
   let lastNameParameterCreate = new SqlParameter("lastName","Erickson")
   do createCommand.Parameters.Add firstNameParameterCreate |> ignore
   do createCommand.Parameters.Add lastNameParameterCreate |> ignore
   do createCommand.ExecuteNonQuery() |> ignore

  //update
  use updateCommand =
    new SqlCommand("update person set firstname=@firstname, lastname=@lastname
where id=@id", connection)
   let firstNameParameterUpdate = new SqlParameter("firstName","Not")
   let lastNameParameterUpdate = new SqlParameter("lastName","Sure")
   let idParameterUpdate = new SqlParameter("id",42)
   do updateCommand.Parameters.Add firstNameParameterUpdate |> ignore
   do updateCommand.Parameters.Add lastNameParameterUpdate |> ignore
   do updateCommand.Parameters.Add idParameterUpdate |> ignore
   do updateCommand.ExecuteNonQuery() |> ignore

  //delete
  use deleteCommand = new SqlCommand("delete person where id=@id", connection)
   let idParameterDelete = new SqlParameter("id","42")
   do deleteCommand.Parameters.Add idParameterDelete |> ignore
   do deleteCommand.ExecuteNonQuery() |> ignore
```

*Code snippet RawADOExample.fs*

The only difference between the read examples and these are the use of `.ExecuteNonQuery()`, which is the standard way to perform operations that do not return records from a database using ADO.NET. Outside of that, the exact same techniques for inserting parameters into standard SQL queries apply.

One striking thing, however, about using raw ADO.net in any language, F# included, is the raw volume of code required to do, what are in essence, really simple tasks. When one considers that the entire code base of the Microsoft TrueSkill system is around 100 lines of F# code, having 15 lines of code to do three simple operations seems excessive. Thankfully, there are frameworks built on top of ADO.net to help deal with this complexity.

## F# AND OBJECT RELATIONAL MAPPING

The first place someone who is frustrated with the verbosity of raw ADO.NET might look to get some relief is to the many Object/Relational Mapping layers out there, such as `NHibernate` or the Microsoft Entity Framework. Despite the general conclusion in Ted Neward's Famous Essay, "The Vietnam of Computer Science" (http://blogs.tedneward.com/2006/06/26/ The+Vietnam+Of+Computer+Science.aspx), for many cases, ORMs are a great solution for many types of problems.

You need to remember what the 'O' in ORM stands for — namely that it expects objects. Objects, of course, tend to have a state that is typically assumed to be mutable. Further, most ORMs require that properties be virtual so that their implementation can be overridden to do things like lazy loading.

The following is a typical implementation of the `Person` record from the previous examples in this chapter if you were going to use it with `NHibernate`:

```
type NHPerson() = class
  let mutable _id : int = 0
  let mutable _firstName : string = ""
  let mutable _lastName : string = ""

  abstract Id : int with get, set
  default x.Id with get() = _id and set(v) = _id <- v

  abstract FirstName : string with get, set
  default x.FirstName with get() = _firstName and set(v) = _firstName <- v

  abstract LastName : string with get, set
  default x.LastName with get() = _lastName and set(v) = _lastName <- v
end
```

*Code snippet NHibernateExample.fs*

The situation in Entity Framework v4 (the first version to support POCO objects) is quite similar, with the only important difference being the lack of a need for doing the abstract declarations for properties that are not going to be lazy loaded. Nearly all ORMs have a "special thing" of one type or another that need to be done to objects to work with the ORM.

In either case there are problems. Most ORM systems depend on mutability. The internal mechanism of ORM systems for object construction tends to be something like:

**1.** Create object, usually through a parameterless constructor.

**2.** Set properties based on a configuration file mapping — or perhaps a `fluent` convention based mapping à la `FluentNHibernate`.

**3.** Use a dynamic proxy mechanism that will intercept access to lazily loaded properties, submitting additional queries to load said properties.

As has been covered before, F# programs generally avoid mutability. This is especially true if the reason that mutability is allowed is solely to support an ORM. If one of the reasons we consider F# is to move away from mutability, having to introduce it to make an ORM work is actually a step backward. Generally speaking, unless there is an externally defined requirement to use an ORM, we recommend that software developers avoid using ORM technologies with F#.

## INTRODUCING F# ACTIVE RECORD (FAR)

F# Active Record (FAR) is an Open Source Project I founded that makes it possible to get ORM-like features, but in a way that uses convention over configuration, while embracing an approach more idiomatic to F#.

The idea with FAR is to make mapping from rows in a database to records in F# drop-dead easy, while retaining a functional style of programming. It is not designed to cover everything that we might ever want to do with a database. In fact, it is biased toward simplicity, leaving out edge case features in favor of making the *included* functionality very robust and predictable.

## Reading Data

For example, consider the following `Person` record definition:

```
type Person = {Id:int;FirstName:string;LastName:string;Age:int}
```

Code for populating a sequence of `Person` objects should look something like this:

```
use context = new ForSqlContext("SomeConnectionString")
let people = context.SequenceFrom<Person>()
```

In this case, `people` is now a `seq<Person>` that further F# code can do work with. It is assumed that there is a table name in the targeted database that matches the type name of `Person`, and that there are columns in said table that correspond to the record properties of `Id`, `FirstName`, `LastName`, and `Age`. This approach works so long as a convention that type names match table names, and property names match column names, holds true. Although this obviously can't work in all situations, there are a great number of cases where it does. It is those situations where the convention can be maintained where this kind of approach can result in a drastic drop in the amount of mapping code in the system.

For more on convention over configuration, please see http://en.wikipedia.org/wiki/ Convention_over_configuration.

In a case where the `Person` table has a smaller number of rows, this approach works particularly well. Filtering on a small set is a matter of applying `Seq.filter` with an appropriate predicate to the following result.

A *predicate* is a function that returns `true` or `false`. A filtering predicate in this context needs to start with one parameter of the type we are filtering and resolve to a Boolean value:

```
let me = people |> Seq.filter( fun p -> p.FirstName = "Aaron" )
```

This, however, is not an approach that will scale. If `people` is something more like the list of people in the United States Social Security database, rather than the list of employees in a small company, bringing that sequence out of the database and into memory to analyze it is not the most scalable approach.

## Querying Data

To not have to bring all the records into memory, a need will exist for a way to easily tell the system that the predicate — the part where it is specified `p -> p.FirstName = "Aaron"` — should be analyzed in the database. Using FAR, the technique for doing so looks like this:

```
use context = new ForSqlContext("SomeConnectionString")
let me = context.SequenceFrom<Person>( <@ fun p -> p.FirstName = "Aaron" @>  )
```

Notice two key differences in this version compared to the previous one. The first one is that the predicate is being passed to the `SequenceFrom` method of the context object. This method's purpose is to analyze the predicate passed in, convert that predicate to the appropriate raw SQL code that will be used for the query on the database management system, and retrieve the result in a manner similar to the version of `SequenceFrom` that has no parameters and simply returns everything.

The other key difference is that the predicate was quoted (using `<@ @>` syntax). Quoting the predicate is necessary in this case, as the `SequenceFrom` method needs to analyze the predicate to evaluate it and generate a database query that will ultimately run against the database. Remember, one of the key reasons for quotation is to execute code "by other means." In a case like this, the desire is to execute the predicate against the data. For that to happen, the predicate has to be converted to a form that is useful where the query will occur, which happens to be in the database, not in F#.

## Adding Data

Creating new records in the database is nearly as simple as reading them:

```
type Person = {Id:int;FirstName:string;LastName:string;Age:int}
type Cat = {PetName:string;Color:string;IsCute:bool;IsMean:bool}

[<Test>]
static member TestReadPeopleAndPets =

    use context = new ForDataContext("SomeConnectionString")
    do context.Create {Id=1;FirstName="Aaron";LastName="Erickson";Age=37} |> ignore
    do context.Create {Id=2;FirstName="Erin";LastName="Erickson";Age=34} |> ignore
    do context.Create {Id=3;FirstName="Adriana";LastName="Erickson";Age=13} |> ignore
    do context.Create {Id=4;FirstName="Matthew";LastName="Erickson";Age=8} |> ignore
```

```
let people =
  context.SequenceFrom<Person>( <@ fun p -> p.LastName = "Erickson" @> )
    |> Seq.toArray

Assert.AreEqual(people.Length,4)

do context.Create {PetName="Puppy Cat";Color="Ginger";IsCute=true;IsMean=false}
  |> ignore
do context.Create {PetName="Dmitry";Color="Blue-Gray";IsCute=true;IsMean=true}
  |> ignore

let theCats =
  context.SequenceFrom<Cat>()  |> Seq.toArray

Assert.AreEqual(theCats.Length,2)
```

*Code snippet DALTestDriver.fs*

In this example, the `Person` and `Cat` types are declared using simple F# record types. Using the `ForDataContext` that is created for when you want to read data, the `Create` method can be used to add rows to the database.

The `Create` method is generic, in that it can detect the type of record passed to it and use that record's type to determine which table it should insert the record to. The `Create` method returns a number of rows affected, which in most operations where you are creating a row, should tend to resolve to 1. In the preceding example, because the result is not needed for further processing, it is simply passed to ignore, and the next record is added.

## Updating Data

Update, like create, uses a convention-based minimalist approach:

```
do context.Update {Id=3;FirstName="Adriana";LastName="Erickson";Age=13} |> ignore
```

Update uses a convention that the first property that ends in `Id` is expected to be, for database purposes, the identity upon which the update will be based. It would roughly translate to the following SQL code:

```
update person set firstname='Adriana', lastname='Erickson', age=13 where id=3
```

If the `Id` column in the database were `personid`, rather than simply `id`, so long as `personid` is the first field that ends in `id` in the record, the following would also work:

```
do context.Update {PersonId=3;FirstName="Adriana";LastName="Erickson";Age=13}
  |> ignore
```

## Deleting Data

As you might expect, deletion does not stray from our simplistic formula:

```
do context.Delete {Id=4;FirstName="Matthew";LastName="Erickson";Age=8} |> ignore
```

The preceding code specifies a query that, in this case would roughly translate to:

```
delete from person where id=4
```

Technically, for `delete`, only the `Id` field is needed. However, because the record type defines the table, and the record does not allow `null` values in the other fields, the rest of the record is specified in the example.

## What Isn't Supported

One of the reasons the library can remain as simple as it does is that it is explicitly stateless. There is no change tracking, no concept of attach/detach, and no pretense that the library is something other than a means to act as either a producer or consumer of F# record types. Other things that make more traditional ORM systems complex, such as configuration files, mappings, and base classes to inherit from, are also avoided in favor of simplicity and predictability in terms of how it works.

## Coming Soon

At the time of this writing, there are some features that have yet to be implemented but should be complete by the time of publication. Support for stored procedures, inner joins, and a broader set of predicate types are in the works. Progress on this project can be followed at `http://github.com/ericksoa/FAR`.

## HOW FAR WORKS

One of the principles of being a good software developer is to have at least some level of understanding about how the libraries work. As such, this section explores the internals of the FAR library.

## Dependencies

To do our decomposition of a query, .NET reflection will be used, as well as various elements of `Microsoft.FSharp.Quotations`. As well, `System.Data.SqlClient` will be used so that the appropriate connections and commands can be created. Although future versions may refactor this by extracting out database specific concerns from parsing concerns, for now, it will be assumed that the target database is Microsoft SQL Server:

```
module FSharpActiveRecord
open System
open System.Reflection
open System.Data.SqlClient
open Microsoft.FSharp.Quotations
open Microsoft.FSharp.Quotations.DerivedPatterns
```

*Code snippet FSharpDAL.fs*

# Utility Routines

The next two routines provide a wrapper behind creation of typical ADO.NET primitives that will be used across various specific methods in the library:

```
let MakeConnection connectionString =
    new SqlConnection(connectionString)

let MakeCommand commandText connection =
    new SqlCommand(commandText, connection)
```

These functions provide a means for various routines within the system that need connections without having to; at least in the method itself, depend on `System.Data.SqlClient` specifics.

The next routine is an important utility that allows you to take a sequence of strings and return a comma-separated list:

```
//ConvertToCommaSeparatedString courtesy of Mark Needham, ThoughtWorks
let ConvertToCommaSeparatedString (value:seq<string>) =
    let rec convert (innerVal:List<string>) acc =
        match innerVal with
            | [] -> acc
            | hd::[] -> convert [] (acc + hd)
            | hd::tl -> convert tl (acc + hd + ",")
    convert (Seq.toList value) ""
```

*Code snippet FSharpDAL.fs*

When generating SQL, a frequent need is to generate comma-separated lists of things such as column names and parameters. Because this list should not have a comma at the end of the list, something is needed that distinguishes between the last item and everything else when generating the list. This routine fits the bill rather nicely.

The next thing that is needed, if you generate a lot of SQL, is something that converts primitive F# types to strings that reflect their SQL counterparts:

```
let FSharpTypeToSqlType fSharpType size =
    match fSharpType, size with
        | t, Some(s) when t = typeof<string> -> sprintf "varchar(%i)" s
        | t, _ when t = typeof<string> -> "varchar(255)"
        | t, _ when t = typeof<int> -> "int"
        | t, _ when t = typeof<bool> -> "bit"
        | t, _ when t = typeof<DateTime> -> "datetime"
        | _, _ -> raise( new NotSupportedException() )
```

*Code snippet FSharpDAL.fs*

This routine takes a `type` (as a .NET Type object) and a `size` as an `int option`. Based on combinations of type and size, it generates a SQL type signature. This type of routine is especially useful in cases where we need to drive SQL types from .NET types, as is done in the creation of tables in a database.

## Table Creation

This is especially useful for cases when the desire is to create a table based on a record type:

```
let private CreateTable tableName columns connectionString =
  let columnList =
    columns
    |> Seq.map (fun (name, colType, size) ->
       sprintf "%s %s" name (FSharpTypeToSqlType colType size))
    |> ConvertToCommaSeparatedString
  let query = sprintf "create table %s (%s)" tableName columnList
  use connection = connectionString |> MakeConnection
  use createCommand = MakeCommand query connection
  do connection.Open() |> ignore
  do createCommand.ExecuteNonQuery() |> ignore

let CreateTableFor<'a> connectionString =
  let tableName = typeof<'a>.Name
  let columnSpecSelector (p:PropertyInfo) = (p.Name,p.PropertyType,None)
  let columnSpecs = typeof<'a>.GetProperties() |> Seq.map columnSpecSelector
  do CreateTable tableName columnSpecs connectionString
```

*Code snippet FSharpDAL.fs*

CreateTableFor is a generic function that takes a record type that will be used as a template for creating a table and a connection string used to reach an actual database. Using .NET reflection, it uses Seq.map to create a set of (type * name * size) tuples (columnSpecs). It passes the tableName (from the generic type), the columnSpecs, and the connection string to a private CreateTable method that does the work to convert things into a SQL create table script that can be executed against a database.

The job of generating SQL is made easy by some of the utility functions that are already in place. The column list part of the create script, usually taking the form of something like somename sometype somesize, anothername anothertype anothersize is handled by mapping the tuples through FSharpToSqlType and formatting them using sprintf.

From there, the next step is to format the rest of the SQL, putting together the table and columnList and then do typical ADO.NET work of creating a connection and command needed to run the actual query.

The FAR library contains many routines such as CreateTable that simplify database creation, destruction, and other similar tasks that are especially important in setup and teardown of integration tests. Please see the book's sample code or the FAR library website for more details on these routines.

## Query Processing

The real useful part of this library is the conversion of idiomatic F# code to SQL. However, for this to work, the following is needed:

```
let makeSimpleSelect table fields =
    let commaSeperatedFields = fields |> ConvertToCommaSeparatedString
    sprintf "select %s from %s" commaSeperatedFields table
```

This first routine takes a table name and a seq<string> that represents database fields. It then generates a typical SQL query that we would use against a single table. For example, passing Person and [FirstName,LastName] would generate:

```
select firstname,lastname from person
```

This is a good start, but far more needs to be done if you want the ability for more complex predicates to be passed along with a record type. More complex queries require that an expression be parsed and tree structure be built that represents it so it can be converted to SQL. Start by defining the following tree structure in the form of a discriminated union:

```
type ParseNode =
    | EqualNode of Type list * Expr list
    | AndNode of ParseNode option * ParseNode option
    | OrNode of ParseNode option * ParseNode option
//other nodes as needed
```

The preceding example is a simplistic version of what can represent a parse tree. It will start with equality tests as terminal nodes in the tree, which can be combined with various combinations of the terms and or or. For example p.FirstName = "Aaron" and (p.LastName = "Erickson" or p.LastName="Burr") might look like:

```
---------AndNode-------
    |                 |
EqualNode         OrNode-------------------
p.FirstName = "Aaron"     |                 |
                    p.LastName = "Erickson"  p.LastName = "Burr"
```

Two routines will use this tree. One has to take an F# quoted predicate and generate the tree; the other will recursively walk the tree to generate equivalent SQL code.

### Generating the Parse Tree

Start by declaring a context from which we will run queries that contain the connection object:

```
type ForDataContext =
    val connection : SqlConnection
    new(connectionString) = { connection = connectionString |> MakeConnection }
    with
        interface IDisposable with
            member disposable.Dispose() =
                disposable.connection.Close()
```

Within this type, members are created that depend on this common context. The first is the routine that generates the parse tree:

```
//takes a predicate and generates a tuple composed of
//  parameterized sql * parameters
static member private ParseCriteria<'a> (criteria:Expr<'a -> bool>) =

   let rec predicateParser expr =
     match expr with
       | SpecificCall <@ (=) @> (optionExpr, types, exprs)
         -> Some(EqualNode(types,exprs))
       | SpecificCall <@ (&&) @> (optionExpr, types, exprs)
         -> Some(AndNode(predicateParser(exprs.[0]),predicateParser(exprs.[1])))
       | SpecificCall <@ (||) @> (optionExpr, types, exprs)
         -> Some(OrNode(predicateParser(exprs.[0]),predicateParser(exprs.[1])))
       | Patterns.IfThenElse (left, middle, right)
         -> match middle with
              | Patterns.Call(optionExpr, types, exprs)
                -> Some(AndNode(predicateParser(left), predicateParser(middle)))
              | Patterns.Value(value, valueType)
                -> Some(OrNode(predicateParser(left), predicateParser(right)))
              | _ -> None
       | _ -> None
```

*Code snippet FSharpDAL.fs*

Our overall goal with `ParseCriteria` is to take a quoted predicate and generate a SQL string and a series of ordered parameters that will be applied to that string to perform a query. This parsing is made much simpler by inclusion of the `Microsoft.FSharp.Quotations` and `Microsoft.FSharp.Quotations .DerivedPatterns` namespaces. Most of the work is done by the recursive `predicateParser` routine, which recursively walks the provided predicate, mapping the expression tree to something we can more easily consume.

`SpecificCall` is an active pattern that matches a given quoted expression (such as `<@ (=) @>` ) against what the tree contains. In F#, this works very well for the `EqualNode` type, which when matched, emits an `EqualNode` that contains a pair of expressions and types that can be used for generating an equals SQL expression.

The other instances of `SpecificCall` work in certain circumstances where one would expect them to, and if they are present, will emit the appropriate `AndNode` or `OrNode`. `AndNode` and `OrNode` both take two arguments, for their left and right side, which will be provided by recursive calls to `predicateParser` on the respective left and right sides of the provided expression tree.

Of course, there is a special case, which is that sometimes optimizations get applied to the tree. If the quoted `and` or quoted `or` get converted for some reason into `IfThenElse` calls in the predicate, those need to be handled as well. `IfThenElse` is another active pattern that can be used to match against for that case. `And` and `Or` both get converted to `IfThenElse` in certain ways that are recognizable. If the middle node in `IfThenElse` is a `Call`, it can be deduced that it was converted from `(&&)`, and be handled accordingly. If it is a `Value`, it can be deduced it was converted from `(||)`.

The result of all this, provided that the expression matches the rules, is a tree that we can much more cleanly generate SQL from, as the following demonstrates:

```
let paramEnumerator =
  let paramNames = 1
    |> Seq.unfold (fun i -> Some(i+1,i))
    |> Seq.map( fun i -> sprintf "param%i" i)
  paramNames.GetEnumerator()

let nextParam() =
  paramEnumerator.MoveNext() |> ignore
  paramEnumerator.Current

let paramList = new System.Collections.Generic.List<string * obj>()

let rec queryString (treeNode:ParseNode option) =
  match treeNode with
  | Some(node) ->
    match node with
    | EqualNode (left,right) ->
      match (right.[0],right.[1]) with
      | (Patterns.PropertyGet (option,property,someList),
          Patterns.Value(value, valueType)) ->
        let p = nextParam()
        do (p,value) |> paramList.Add
        sprintf "%s = @%s" property.Name p
      | _ -> raise(new InvalidOperationException())
    | AndNode (left,right)
        -> sprintf "(%s and %s)" (queryString left) (queryString right)
    | OrNode (left,right)
        -> sprintf "(%s or %s)" (queryString left) (queryString right)
  | None -> ""
```

*Code snippet FSharpDAL.fs*

There are a couple of things that need to be done here. The first step is to generate SQL that will be transformed into the `where` clause at the end of the overall SQL query. The next step is to generate a set of parameter objects that will be used with the ADO.NET command object to thread the query parameters together.

To do the parameter list, it will be necessary to use a mutable list structure that can be added to and that holds the parameter names and values. Also needed will be something that generates unique parameter names. These parameters need to be generated on an on-demand basis while parsing is taking place. The `paramEnumerator` is a utility that can be used to act as something of a dispenser for parameters that are guaranteed to be unique to the query. The `nextParam()` function executes this generator, as is used by `queryString` as it is doing its work. `paramList` is then used to accumulate these parameters as `queryString` does its work.

The real work of `queryString` is to handle the various node cases, and either just generate SQL (in the case of an `EqualNode`), or — in the case of `AndNode` or `OrNode` — take the result of recursive `queryString` calls and compound the results together into the appropriate syntax.

This is all brought together in the full implementation of `ParseCriteria`:

```
//takes a predicate and generates a tuple composed of
//  parameterized sql * parameters
static member private ParseCriteria<'a> (criteria:Expr<'a -> bool>) =

    let rec predicateParser expr =
      match expr with
        | SpecificCall <@ (=) @> (optionExpr, types, exprs)
          -> Some(EqualNode(types,exprs))
        | SpecificCall <@ (&&) @> (optionExpr, types, exprs)
          -> Some(AndNode(predicateParser(exprs.[0]),predicateParser(exprs.[1])))
        | SpecificCall <@ (||) @> (optionExpr, types, exprs)
          -> Some(OrNode(predicateParser(exprs.[0]),predicateParser(exprs.[1])))
        | Patterns.IfThenElse (left, middle, right)
          -> match middle with
              | Patterns.Call(optionExpr, types, exprs)
                -> Some(AndNode(predicateParser(left), predicateParser(middle)))
              | Patterns.Value(value, valueType)
                -> Some(OrNode(predicateParser(left), predicateParser(right)))
              | _ -> None
        | _ -> None

    let parsedResult =
      match criteria with
        | Patterns.Lambda(var,lambda) -> predicateParser lambda
        | _ -> None

    let paramEnumerator =
      let paramNames = 1
        |> Seq.unfold (fun i -> Some(i+1,i)) |> Seq.map( fun i
            -> sprintf "param%i" i)
      paramNames.GetEnumerator()

    let nextParam() =
      paramEnumerator.MoveNext() |> ignore
      paramEnumerator.Current

    let paramList = new System.Collections.Generic.List<string * obj>()

    let rec queryString (treeNode:ParseNode option) =
      match treeNode with
      | Some(node) ->
        match node with
        | EqualNode (left,right) ->
          match (right.[0],right.[1]) with
          | (Patterns.PropertyGet (option,property,someList),
              Patterns.Value(value, valueType)) ->
            let p = nextParam()
            do (p,value) |> paramList.Add
            sprintf "%s = @%s" property.Name p
          | _ -> raise(new InvalidOperationException())
        | AndNode (left,right)
            -> sprintf "(%s and %s)" (queryString left) (queryString right)
        | OrNode (left,right)
```

```
                -> sprintf "(%s or %s)" (queryString left) (queryString right)
      | None -> ""

  queryString parsedResult, paramList.ToArray()
```

Of course, a couple more utility functions are needed to make the context work. A connection needs to be opened if it isn't open yet. (Remember, we can run multiple queries from the same context.) Also needed is a way to easily take the SQL and command objects and execute them:

```
member private context.OpenConnectionIfNeeded() =
  if (context.connection.State <> Data.ConnectionState.Open)
    then context.connection.Open()

//core routine that takes sql + parameters and yields readers that
//  eventually get composed into records we want to work with
member private context.DoQuery query (rawParameters:array<string * #obj>) =
  use command = MakeCommand query context.connection
  do rawParameters
     |> Array.map( fun r -> new SqlParameter(fst r,snd r) )
     |> Array.iter( fun p -> command.Parameters.Add p |> ignore )
  do context.OpenConnectionIfNeeded()
  let reader = command.ExecuteReader()
  seq { while reader.Read() do yield reader }

member private context.DoCommand command (rawParameters:array<string * #obj>) =
  use command = MakeCommand command context.connection
  do rawParameters
     |> Array.map( fun r -> new SqlParameter(fst r,snd r) )
     |> Array.iter( fun p -> command.Parameters.Add p |> ignore )
  do context.OpenConnectionIfNeeded()
  command.ExecuteNonQuery()
```

These methods use similar techniques that were used when doing raw ADO for creating and using connections and commands. The only difference is they do so in a much more generic fashion. With these utility methods in place, the next step is to go forth and implement the query interface:

```
//core routine that composes and executes the query
member private context.SequenceFrom<'a>
  ((whereClause:string),(parameters:array<string * #obj>)) =
  let tableName = typeof<'a>.Name
  let memberNameSelector (m:#MemberInfo) = m.Name
  let propertyNames = typeof<'a>.GetProperties() |> Seq.map memberNameSelector
  let query = (makeSimpleSelect tableName propertyNames) + " " + whereClause
  let creator = Reflection.FSharpValue.PreComputeRecordConstructor(
    typeof<'a>,BindingFlags.Public)
  let data = context.DoQuery query parameters
  let readObjectsFromReaderByField (reader:SqlDataReader) (keys:seq<string>) =
    keys |> Seq.map( fun(k) -> reader.[k] ) |> Seq.toArray
  data |> Seq.map(
```

```
          fun r -> creator(readObjectsFromReaderByField r propertyNames) :?> 'a )

//Performs queries where you have (for now) simple object.Property = someValue
member context.SequenceFrom<'a> (criteria:Expr<'a -> bool>) =
  let queryAndParams = criteria |> ForDataContext.ParseCriteria
  context.SequenceFrom<'a> (
    (sprintf "where %s" (fst queryAndParams)),(snd queryAndParams))
```

*Code snippet FSharpDAL.fs*

The public version takes the quoted predicate *criteria*, generates a SQL query and parameter set, and calls the private `SequenceFrom`, which expects a `where` clause in string form, as well as an array of parameter name and object tuples that will be used for parameters.

In the private overload of `SequenceFrom`, the rest of the query will be built. F# reflection is used to build a mechanism (`creator`, in the preceding example) for creating F# records based on results we get returned from the `SqlDataReader`.

When a creator is set up, the next step is to call `context.DoQuery` that yields a `DataReader` that, when iterated, advances through the records. What is returned is a sequence iterator that converts each state of the `SqlDataReader` into the appropriate record type. What is notable about this is that it returns a `seq<'a>` for a reason. A user of the library could choose to take only the top five elements, and in doing so, will use the built in forward-only cursor functionality of MS SQL Server to avoid taking the entire set of rows over the wire for only the top five elements.

Wrapping up, for the convenience of people who want to read all the records, this overload is added:

```
        //simple case where we are getting all the rows from a table
member context.SequenceFrom<'a>() =
  context.SequenceFrom<'a>(String.Empty,Array.empty)
```

## Implementation of Other FOR Operations

Other operations are, thankfully, much simpler to implement. Take create for example:

```
member context.Create someObject =
  let tableName = someObject.GetType().Name
  let columnsAndValues =
    someObject.GetType().GetProperties() |> Seq.map(
      fun p -> (p.Name,p.GetValue(someObject,Array.empty)))
  let columnNames columnsValuePair =
    columnsValuePair
    |> Seq.map( fun pair -> fst pair)
    |> ConvertToCommaSeparatedString
  let convertToValueParameterBucket columnsValuePair =
    columnsValuePair
    |> Seq.map( fun pair -> sprintf "@%s" (fst pair))
    |> ConvertToCommaSeparatedString
  let query =
    sprintf
      "insert into %s (%s) values (%s)"
      tableName
```

```
      (columnsAndValues |> columnNames)
      (columnsAndValues |> convertToValueParameterBucket)
  let parameters = columnsAndValues |> Seq.toArray
  context.DoCommand query parameters
```

*Code snippet FSharpDAL.fs*

The common pattern for nonquery operations where a parse tree need not be analyzed is simply to do some reflection over the generic type, read the values from the provided record in some manner that matches a convention, construct a SQL command, and execute it. The implementations of delete and update differ only by the SQL that is generated; nearly everything else is the same.

### The Use Case for F# Active Record

FAR, as a library, is meant to be a simple, minimalist, and illustrative implementation that covers a large, but not exhaustive, set of cases for how F# applications might access data. It does so in a manner that allows the library to be independent of the domain, avoiding inheritance or any other special "things" that need to be done to make a record work with FAR. If you have a record, and you have a table and columns that match up, FAR can work.

## SUMMARY

In this chapter, we covered ways for F# programs to interact with data, particular in ways that will feel idiomatic to F# developers. You may choose to use raw ADO.NET, use F# Active Record, or use one of the more object-oriented frameworks. What is important, across all of these, is to minimize the amount of plumbing code you write, so you can focus on doing something with data, rather than simply gathering it.

# 20

# XML

WHAT'S IN THIS CHAPTER?

➤  Making F# work with XML

➤  Using Linq to XML with F#

➤  Understanding how F# and DOM work together

➤  Applying active patterns for XML parsing

XML is a fact of life for most software developers, regardless of language. It is found everywhere, from configuration files holding nothing but a small number of settings, to the giant stores of weather data provided in XML format by the National Oceanic and Atmospheric Administration of the United States. Although history will judge whether having all this XML was a good idea, the fact remains that it's there. Love it or hate it, developers have to deal with it.

In this chapter, you learn how to use F# with XML processing tools such as those found in the `System.Xml` namespace in the .NET framework. This chapter covers techniques that simplify most XML processing tasks. Special attention is provided to demonstrate how you can use things such as XPath and active patterns to simplify the task of processing and transforming XML.

## OVERVIEW

Boiled down to its essence, most things that deal with XML do the following:

➤  Read XML, typically to store it in some sort of language representation

➤  Query the XML, often again to extract parts of it into some sort of language representation

➤ Process the XML, sometimes to produce more XML or to generate some side effect

➤ Persist the XML, so that other programs can join in the fun of working with XML

For more details on the various W3C standards that make up the XML grammar and suite of specifications, we recommend the W3C website.

# F# AND LINQ-TO-XML

Of the various means to read and process XML, LINQ-to-XML, introduced in .NET 3.5, is likely the simplest way to query and process XML in F#.

## Reading

Imagine writing an application that reads a weather forecast from the Internet and presents an average expected temperature to the user. When using the weather service in the Yahoo developer API to read the weather report, you might request the response from the Yahoo API URL http://weather.yahooapis.com/forecastrss?w=2484280. The request that results from that call reads as follows:

```
<?xml version="1.0" encoding="UTF-8" standalone="yes" ?>
<rss version="2.0" xmlns:yweather="http://xml.weather.yahoo.com/ns/rss/1.0"
xmlns:geo="http://www.w3.org/2003/01/geo/wgs84_pos#">
<channel>

<title>Yahoo! Weather - Romeoville, IL</title>
<link>http://us.rd.yahoo.com/dailynews/rss/weather/Romeoville__IL/
*http://weather.yahoo.com/forecast/USIL1019_f.html</link>
<description>Yahoo! Weather for Romeoville, IL</description>
<language>en-us</language>
<lastBuildDate>Sun, 20 Dec 2009 4:44 pm CST</lastBuildDate>
<ttl>60</ttl>
<yweather:location city="Romeoville" region="IL"   country="United States"/>

<yweather:units temperature="F" distance="mi" pressure="in" speed="mph"/>
<yweather:wind chill="27"   direction="0"   speed="0" />
<yweather:atmosphere humidity="83"  visibility="5"  pressure="30.07"  rising="1" />
<yweather:astronomy sunrise="7:15 am"   sunset="4:24 pm"/>
<image>
<title>Yahoo! Weather</title>
<width>142</width>
<height>18</height>
<link>http://weather.yahoo.com</link>
<url>http://l.yimg.com/a/i/us/nws/th/main_142b.gif</url>
</image>
<item>

<title>Conditions for Romeoville, IL at 4:44 pm CST</title>
<geo:lat>41.64</geo:lat>
<geo:long>-88.08</geo:long>
<link>http://us.rd.yahoo.com/dailynews/rss/weather/Romeoville__IL/
```

```
*http://weather.yahoo.com/forecast/USIL1019_f.html</link>
<pubDate>Sun, 20 Dec 2009 4:44 pm CST</pubDate>
<yweather:condition  text="Cloudy"  code="26"  temp="27"  date="Sun, 20 Dec 2009
4:44 pm CST" />
<description><![CDATA[
<img src="http://l.yimg.com/a/i/us/we/52/26.gif"/><br />
<b>Current Conditions:</b><br />
Cloudy, 27 F<BR />
<BR /><b>Forecast:</b><BR />
Sun - Light Snow Early. High: 29 Low: 23<br />
Mon - Cloudy. High: 28 Low: 25<br />
<br />
<a href="http://us.rd.yahoo.com/dailynews/rss/weather/Romeoville__IL/
*http://weather.yahoo.com/forecast/USIL1019_f.html">Full Forecast at Yahoo!
Weather</a><BR/><BR/>
(provided by <a href="http://www.weather.com" >The Weather Channel</a>)<br/>
]]></description>
<yweather:forecast day="Sun" date="20 Dec 2009" low="23" high="29"
text="Light Snow Early" code="14" />
<yweather:forecast day="Mon" date="21 Dec 2009" low="25" high="28"
text="Cloudy" code="26" />
<guid isPermaLink="false">USIL1019_2009_12_20_16_44_CST</guid>
</item>

</channel>
</rss><!-- api6.weather.ac4.yahoo.com compressed/chunked Sun Dec 20 15:02:47 PST
2009 -->
```

Although reading this whole request manually and parsing it might be an interesting exercise, Linq to XML with F# provide us a much simpler means to perform this task. Start off by reading the result of the URL into an XDocument, from Linq to XML:

```
let weatherXml =
    "http://weather.yahooapis.com/forecastrss?w=2484280" |>
    XDocument.Load
```

The simplest way to start reading XML when you have a valid XDocument reference is to simply inspect the elements and do something with them:

```
let readTheElements =
    weatherXml.Elements() |>
    Seq.iter ( fun(e) -> do printfn "%s" e.Value )
```

The preceding function takes all the Elements at the root of the document (in this case, a single element of an RSS feed at the top level) and prints them out to standard output (in this case, the console). This includes not just those elements at the top level of the document, but all elements, regardless of level. The sequence of elements is passed to Seq.iter, which applies the function to each XElement in the sequence. The function being applied to each element takes the element, prints it to the screen, and returns unit.

Of course, the question frequently comes up about what the order of the elements will be when doing queries against XML in this manner. In the aforementioned example, order is not relevant to the task, so it is not specified. That said, because the XML order is usually controlled by implementation-specific factors at the site that produces the XML, it is usually a bad idea to depend on implicit order from the document. Should we want to control the order of processing, the preferred approach is to take the sequence that results from Elements() and process the results through Seq.orderBy with the appropriate explicit ordering function.

Although we can certainly do a lot of interesting work simply reading XML and processing it somehow, the real power of LINQ to XML is in the query capability. In fact, if you are simply reading XML and doing your own queries using for loops and if statements, you are not really leveraging the power of F# or LINQ to XML to make your code more readable and efficient.

## Querying

LINQ-to-XML was built to make code that queries XML documents more readable. Recall the previous short snippet of F# that accesses the URL that contains an upcoming weather forecast and then parses it into an XML document for further use:

```
let weatherXml =
    "http://weather.yahooapis.com/forecastrss?w=2484280" |>
    XDocument.Load
```

The preceding statement creates a weatherXml function that returns an XDocument representing a weather forecast for Romeoville, Illinois. XDocument is the root of most LINQ-to-XML operations and has factory methods to create an XDocument instance from a variety of different sources:

| METHOD | PURPOSE |
| --- | --- |
| XDocument.Load | Create an XDocument based on a URI, TextReader, XmlReader, or stream. |
| XDocument.Parse | Create an XDocument based on a string of XML content. |

The resulting XDocument provides a base from which further queries can be performed. For example, to produce a sequence of all elements that have forecast as the element name in the local namespace, we apply a filter to the descendant XElements of the XDocument, using the Seq.filter higher-order function:

```
let weatherXml =
    "http://weather.yahooapis.com/forecastrss?w=2484280" |>
    XDocument.Load
let forecastElements =
    weatherXml.Descendants()
    |> Seq.filter( fun(e) -> e.Name.LocalName = "forecast" )
```

*Code snippet XmlDemo.fs*

The Descendants() method on the object returned from weatherXml returns a sequence of all the XElements below that given element. When called on an XDocument, the sequence represents all the XElements in the particular XDocument.

If we then assume that we want to find all the attributes of all the forecast elements, this is done easily by pipelining two more lines of code:

```
let weatherXml =
    "http://weather.yahooapis.com/forecastrss?w=2484280" |>
    XDocument.Load
let allForecastAttributes  =
    weatherXml.Descendants()
    |> Seq.filter( fun(e) -> e.Name.LocalName = "forecast" )
    |> Seq.collect ( fun(e) -> e.Attributes() )
```

*Code snippet XmlDemo.fs*

The `Seq.map` gathers the attributes from each element, which yields a result of a sequence of sequences with all the attributes of various forecast elements. A good way to think about the result of that line is to imagine a series of piles of attributes, each pile relating to an element from which it came. The next line, `Seq.concat`, puts all the attributes into a single sequence of attributes, stacking all the separate "piles" into a single stack of attributes.

From here, we may be interested only in attributes that relate to a low or high temperature in a forecast. To gather those attributes, we add the following:

```
let weatherXml =
    "http://weather.yahooapis.com/forecastrss?w=2484280" |>
    XDocument.Load
let allHighAndLowAttributes =
    weatherXml.Descendants()
    |> Seq.filter( fun(e) -> e.Name.LocalName = "forecast" )
    |> Seq.collect ( fun(e) -> e.Attributes() )
    |> Seq.filter( fun(a) -> a.Name.LocalName = "high" ||
                             a.Name.LocalName = "low" )
```

*Code snippet XmlDemo.fs*

The function `allHighAndLowAttributes` returns a sequence of `XAttribute` objects, namely, attributes named `"high"` and `"low"`, for computing the expected average temperature over all the forecasts provided by the Yahoo weather service. From here, if we want to compute the average, we simply need to take the values from string into double and then compute the average:

```
let weatherXml =
    "http://weather.yahooapis.com/forecastrss?w=2484280" |>
    XDocument.Load
let averageForecastTemp =
    weatherXml.Descendants()
    |> Seq.filter( fun(e) -> e.Name.LocalName = "forecast" )
    |> Seq.collect ( fun(e) -> e.Attributes() )
    |> Seq.filter( fun(a) -> a.Name.LocalName = "high" ||
                             a.Name.LocalName = "low" )
    |> Seq.map ( fun(a) -> a.Value |> Double.Parse )
    |> Seq.average
```

*Code snippet XmlDemo.fs*

Two statements are added here. First, the `Seq.map` statement takes the `Value` property of each attribute and parses it into a `double`. Note that there is an assumption here that the attribute value is numeric for the sake of clarity; we could also use `Double.TryParse` to filter out any attributes with a non-numeric value.

The second statement added takes the resulting `double`s and produces the average using `Seq.average`.

Of course, the readability and reusability of this leaves much to be desired, so a quick refactoring where the functions are more properly named and where the magic number in the URI is removed reads as follows:

```fsharp
let getYahooWeather id =
  let weatherXml =
    sprintf "http://weather.yahooapis.com/forecastrss?w=%d" id |>
    XDocument.Load
  let byForecastElements (e:XElement) =
    e.Name.LocalName = "forecast"
  let elementToAttributes (e:XElement) =
    e.Attributes()
  let byHighAndLowAttributes (a:XAttribute) =
    a.Name.LocalName = "high" || a.Name.LocalName = "low"
  let attributeValueToDouble (a:XAttribute) =
    a.Value |> Double.Parse

  let averageForecastTemp =
    weatherXml.Descendants()
    |> Seq.filter byForecastElements
    |> Seq.collect elementToAttributes
    |> Seq.filter byHighAndLowAttributes
    |> Seq.map attributeValueToDouble
    |> Seq.average
  averageForecastTemp

let avgRomeovllTmp = 2484280 |> getYahooWeather
printfn "Avg Forecast Temp for Romeoville, IL is %g" avgRomeovllTmp
```

*Code snippet XmlDemo.fs*

Although this last step does not add much functionality to the query, it does make it simpler to understand what the query is doing. It also provides a means to perhaps compose other queries out of the parts that were used to build this one.

## Processing

Of course, simply taking a forecast from a source and republishing it is not terribly useful. Many applications that deal with XML want to process the XML in some way that adds value to the original document.

In this use case, the goal is to take the weather information from Romeoville, IL, and add some useful information about such a "vacation destination." Let's start again by writing a function that creates the weather `XDocument` based on the Yahoo "Where on Earth ID" of a locality:

```
let getYahooWeather id =
    sprintf "http://weather.yahooapis.com/forecastrss?w=%d" id |>
    XDocument.Load
```

To add the information, we need to create an `XElement` that represents information about a community:

```
let makeCommunityInfoElement (s:string) =
    new XElement(XName.Get("communityinfo"),s)
```

One notable thing about this statement is that if `s` is not constrained to `string`, the `XElement` constructor will not determine which constructor overload to call. This is because there are two constructors that have an `XName` as a first parameter combined with a second parameter.

When we have these tools, all that is needed is a function that will insert an `XElement` in some location in the document that makes sense. If what is wanted is an element to be inserted after all the individual forecast elements, write the following:

**Available for download on Wrox.com**

```
let insertCommunityInfo (doc:XDocument) (commInfo:XElement) =
  let last sequence =
    sequence
    |> Seq.skip( (sequence |> Seq.length) - 1 )
    |> Seq.head
  let lastForecast =
    doc.Descendants()
    |> Seq.filter (fun(e) -> e.Name.LocalName = "forecast")
    |> last
  do commInfo |> lastForecast.AddAfterSelf
```

*Code snippet XmlDemo.fs*

One thing that is quickly found is that there is no `last` method on seq<a'>, so one will need to be written. Doing so is a matter of skipping to the next to last item using `Seq.skip`, passing it a length based on `Seq.length - 1`, and then taking the `Seq.head` of the resulting one item sequence.

When a workable implementation of `last` is written, we can much more easily get the last forecast by taking all elements via `document.Descendants()`, filtering by forecast, and taking the last item using `last`.

With `lastForecast`, the next step is to take the `communityInfo` `XElement` and pass it to the `AddAfterSelf` method. In this case, the `do` syntax is used to more clearly specify that what follows will cause a side effect. Although we could achieve the same result by passing the result of `AddAfterSelf` to `ignore`, using the `do` syntax more explicitly signals the reader of the code that we are doing something that causes a side effect, namely, mutating the XML structure by adding an element.

Next, put this all together using the following:

```
let townDoc = 2484280 |> getYahooWeather
let townInfo =
    "Fine Bedroom Community with Two Sushi Bars" |>
    makeCommunityInfoElement

do insertCommunityInfo townDoc townInfo
```

Here the code is simply getting an XDocument to manipulate, getting an XElement to add to the tree, and then affixing the new XElement to the XDocument using insertCommunityInfo. Again, the do statement is used to indicate that we expect the line to cause a side effect.

This is just one example of many things you can do to process XML. The following methods can also be called to provide various means of processing the XML tree.

| METHOD | PURPOSE |
| --- | --- |
| Add | Adds the specified content as a child |
| AddAfterSelf | Adds the specified content immediately after this node |
| AddAnnotation | Adds an object to the annotation list |
| AddBeforeSelf | Adds the specified content immediately before this node |
| AddFirst | Adds the specified content as the first child |
| Remove | Removes this node from its parent |
| RemoveAll | Removes all nodes and attributes |
| RemoveAnnotations | Removes all annotations |
| RemoveAttributes | Removes all attributes |
| RemoveNodes | Removes all nodes |
| ReplaceAll | Replaces the child nodes and the attributes of this element with the specified content |
| ReplaceAttributes | Replaces the attributes of this element with the specified content |
| ReplaceNodes | Replaces the children nodes with the specified content |
| ReplaceWith | Replaces this node with the specified content |
| SetAttributeValue | Sets the value of an attribute, adds an attribute, or removes an attribute |
| SetElementValue | Sets the value of a child element, adds a child element, or removes a child element |
| SetValue | Sets the value of this element |

http://msdn.microsoft.com/

Of course, the standard warning about programming with side effects is true for any code where you are mutating the XML document using these methods. Using these methods with async workflows or any other technology like PLinq that may do the operations in a different order can result in bugs that are hard to re-create.

## Writing

In the .NET framework, writing XML uses similar techniques, nearly all of which involve having a method that does XML serialization using the XmlWriter class. The simplest way to write out an XML file would be to simply do the following, given an XDocument named townDoc:

```
let writeToXml (doc:XDocument) (file:string) =
  use xmlWriter = file |> XmlWriter.Create
  do doc.WriteTo xmlWriter

do writeToXml townDoc "yourOutput.xml"
```

Running this code will serialize the contents of townDoc to a copy of yourOutput.xml in the current directory, overwriting the file if it already exists. One particularly important step here is to use the use binding with the xmlWriter so that the xmlWriter object will be closed when writeToXml completes, thereby flushing the underlying stream buffer.

 *Note that none of these examples worry about handling exceptions. Because these examples have nothing they can do in response to any thrown exception (such as a file being locked that we want to write to), it is assumed that the exceptions will be handled by something further up the call stack.*

## Writing XML to Memory or Other Stream-Based Resources

Frequently, the need arises to serialize to something other than a file. The following code will serialize a document to a MemoryStream:

**Available for download on Wrox.com**

```
let writeToMemory (doc:XDocument) =
  use stream = new MemoryStream()
  use xmlWriter = stream |> XmlWriter.Create
  do doc.WriteTo xmlWriter
  //do something with the memory stream

do writeToMemory townDoc
```

*Code snippet XmlDemo.fs*

In the preceding case where we are writing to memory, we can create a stream (note the use of use binding again), create an XmlWriter using the stream, and use the same WriteTo method with the resulting XmlWriter. The only difference here when compared to writing XML to a file is that we explicitly create the kind of stream we want to write to. Most other types of XML output will work in a similar fashion.

## F# AND XML DOM

F# just as easily supports XML DOM, and for that matter, any other .NET-based API for working with XML content. Although LINQ-to-XML is certainly convenient, many developers (or their managers!) prefer to stick with DOM because of the status of XML DOM as a W3C standard.

> Note that, technically, Microsoft's implementation of DOM isn't 100% compliant with the W3C DOM specification, because it takes a few of the DOM APIs and transforms them into something more C#/.NET-appropriate. Having said that, conceptually, they are identical.

## Reading

Reading XML using XML DOM in F# is somewhat similar to the way you would do it using LINQ-to-XML:

Available for
download on
Wrox.com

```
let getYahooWeatherDOM id =
  use xmlReader =
    sprintf "http://weather.yahooapis.com/forecastrss?w=%d" id |>
    XmlReader.Create
  let xmlDoc = new XmlDocument()
  do xmlReader |> xmlDoc.Load
  xmlDoc
```

*Code snippet XmlDemo.fs*

A key difference between the APIs is that the XmlDocument object itself is explicitly created, rather than using a factory method like we did with Linq to XML. The XmlReader object is also created separately. The load method of the XmlDocument then takes an XmlReader as a parameter, populating the XmlDocument.

Of course, there are other means of loading an XmlDocument object, such as the following:

| METHOD | PURPOSE |
|---|---|
| XmlDocument.Load | Create an XDocument based on a file, TextReader, XmlReader, or stream. |
| XmlDocument.LoadXml | Create an XDocument based on a string of XML content. Note that LoadXml is not part of the DOM standard. |

To start simply reading from the document, run the following:

```
let weatherDom = 2484280 |> getYahooWeatherDOM
do weatherDom.SelectNodes("*") |>
Seq.cast<XmlNode> |>
Seq.iter ( fun(e) -> do printfn "%s" e.Value )
```

There are a couple complexities that emerge when reading via XML DOM. The first complexity is that rather than the simple act of reading, XML means we are going to work with XPath, a standard query language for working with XML. The SelectNodes method of an XmlDocument object takes an XPath query as a parameter. The query for seeking all elements that are at the top level of a document is a simple wildcard ("*"), which is used above with SelectNodes.

Another complexity when dealing with DOM is that the results of XPath queries do not support the `IEnumerable<T>` interface, which is required to use most `Seq` methods to interact with the document. Should we want to use `Seq` methods, the result of any `SelectNodes` query has to be passed to `Seq.cast<XmlNode>`, which takes an `IEnumerable` and produces an `IEnumerable<T>`. Note that this will fail if any objects in the source collection do not derive from `XmlNode`; thankfully, everything that returns from `SelectNodes` does in fact derive from `XmlNode`, making this not an issue in this case.

## Querying

Going further with querying using XML DOM involves getting more familiar with XPath syntax. In the prior querying example with Linq to XML, solving the problem required retrieval of all the attributes with values equal to `high` and `low` in the document. Below are some queries that demonstrate different means of querying for the attributes of interest, including the `all high` or `low` query that is useful for solving the problem:

```
let weatherDom = 2484280 |> getYahooWeatherDOM
let allAttributesInTheDocument = weatherDom.SelectNodes("//@")
let allLowAttributes = weatherDom.SelectNodes("//@low")
//the query we really want...
let allLowOrHighAttributes =
    weatherDom.SelectNodes("//@low | //@high")
```

*Code snippet XmlDemo.fs*

Here are three different queries — all of which demonstrate, with increasing precision, ways to reach the attributes we are looking for. The `"//"` string tells XPath to recurse through the entire document hierarchy. The `"@"` symbol then tells XPath to look for attributes. In the second query, we further specify the name of the attributes we are looking for (`low`, in this case). The `"//@low | //@high"` query specifies both `high` and `low` attributes.

Recall that the problem criteria require retrieval of the average temperature. To get the average temperature again, do the following:

```
let weatherDom = 2484280 |> getYahooWeatherDOM
let allLowOrHighAttributes =
    weatherDom.SelectNodes("//@low | //@high")
let nodeValueToDouble (n:XmlNode) =
    n.Value |> Double.Parse
let averageTemp =
    allLowOrHighAttributes
    |> Seq.cast<XmlNode>
    |> Seq.map nodeValueToDouble
    |> Seq.average
```

*Code snippet XmlDemo.fs*

Like before when the solution was to simply read elements, this solution requires casting the result of the XPath query using `Seq.cast<XmlNode>`, so you can do further `Seq` operations on it. When casted to `XmlNode`, the next step is to cast the attribute strings that represent the temperatures into `double` (using our previous `nodeValueToDouble` function). When converted into a sequence of `doubles`, the average can be computed using `Seq.average`.

## Processing

XML DOM provides plenty of means to manipulate XML documents. In the previous example for LINQ-to-XML, information was added to the weather forecast. The process is similar in DOM, which starts by creating the `XmlNode` that should be added to the DOM:

```
let communityInfo = weatherDom.CreateElement("communityinfo")
do communityInfo.InnerText <- "Fine Community with Two Sushi Bars"
```

A key difference in DOM is that creation of elements in DOM happens via the parent document you want to create the element in, which is what is done in the previous `weatherDom.CreateElement("communityinfo")`. Setting the content is a separate line of code where the `InnerText` property is mutated to contain the content that we want.

```
let insertCommunityInfoDom (doc:XmlDocument) (commInfo:XmlNode) =
  let last sequence =
    sequence
    |> Seq.skip( (sequence |> Seq.length) - 1 )
    |> Seq.head
  let lastForecast =
    doc.SelectNodes("//*[local-name()='forecast']")
    |> Seq.cast<XmlNode>
    |> last
  do lastForecast.ParentNode.InsertAfter(commInfo,lastForecast) |>
  ignore
do insertCommunityInfoDom weatherDom commInfo
```

*Code snippet XmlDemo.fs*

The insertion routine works a bit differently as well. The implementation of `last` from the LINQ-to-XML example is borrowed (see the prior section on LINQ-to-XML). That is where the similarity ends though. Getting the last forecast element is a bit more involved, as there is a need to start by passing an XPath query into the `XmlDocument` that specifies forecast elements.

Note that the forecast elements are actually in the `yweather` namespace. In the LINQ-to-XML example, queries are easily based on `element.Name.LocalName`, because the name is scoped to the `yweather` namespace. When using XPath, we have to use the XPath `local-name()` function to achieve a similar result. We could also do work to attach a namespace to the `SelectNodes` query — however, it would be quite a bit more work to do so, and is probably unnecessary here.

When the weather nodes have been retrieved, the next step is a familiar cast to a sequence of `XmlNode` using `Seq.cast` and then grabbing the `last` element. When the `last` element is found, call `InsertAfter` on the `ParentNode`, whatever that might be, and pass it the new `XmlNode`, as well as the `lastForecast` node that is the node that will be appended. Although this call returns the `XmlNode` back, because nothing further is needed from the `XmlNode`, it can be safely passed to `ignore`.

## Writing

Writing XML out to a file, or a stream, using XML DOM is as simple, if not simpler, than LINQ-to-XML. To save to a file, it is as simple as calling the `Save` method, passing it a filename or a fully qualified path:

```
weatherDom.Save("yourOutput.xml")
```

Should you want to save to a stream, be it a `MemoryStream` or any other object that inherits from `Stream`, pass the Stream object as well:

```
weatherDom.Save(someStream)
```

It is notable that writing XML out largely builds on the .NET IO capabilities, nicely making sure that XML processing concerns are separated from concerns related to how such XML is persisted. This general feature helps make sure that any code you write to deal with XML is very much focused on XML processing and not IO concerns.

## F#, XML, AND ACTIVE PATTERNS

If we remove the fascination with angle-brackets and structure and look carefully at an XML document, a curious thing emerges: XML looks very much like name-value pairs, name-value-attribute triplets (where the attributes are a list of name-value pairs themselves), name-value-children triplets (where children are another list), or name-value-attribute-children quads. In other words, from a certain point of view, XML documents are basically lists of tuples, nestled in a hierarchical relationship.

Given this perspective, and the fact that active patterns (described in detail in Chapter 6) are used in F# to do "data decomposition," it seems reasonable to expect that active patterns can help break XML trees down into more palatable data structures that F# can process more easily. And as it turns out, it is but requires a slightly different approach to querying and processing than what the imperative programmer is used to.

Let's work with a slightly different XML model, one that's a bit simpler than the XML returned by the weather service (and, arguably, more like the XML that flies around inside a corporate intranet), that describes various famous (and/or infamous) characters:

```xml
<data>
    <item>
        <person gender="male">
            <name>Ted Neward</name>
            <age>38</age>
            <languages>
                <language>English</language>
                <language>French</language>
                <language>C#</language>
                <language>Java</language>
                <language>F#</language>
                <language>Scala</language>
            </languages>
        </person>
```

```
        </item>
        <item>
            <person gender="male">
                <name>Han Solo</name>
                <age>35</age>
                <languages>
                    <language>Imperial Standard</language>
                    <language>Wookiee</language>
                </languages>
            </person>
        </item>
        <item>
            <person gender="male">
                <name>Gaius Baltar</name>
                <age>35</age>
                <languages>
                    <language>Colonial English</language>
                    <language>Cylon</language>
                </languages>
            </person>
        </item>
    </data>
```

*Code snippet XMLActiveExample1.xml*

The goal here is to use active patterns to break this document down into the repetitive person structure that appears repeatedly and transform it into a form more easily used within an F# program.

Recall from the discussion on active patterns that three basic forms of active patterns are available:
the single-case active pattern, which converts data from one form to another; the partial-case active
pattern, which helps to match when data conversion failures are possible or likely; and the multi-case
active pattern, which can take the input data and break it down into one of several different data
groupings. Although only one structure appears in the preceding example (the person structure), it
remains a reasonable assumption to imagine that other data structures can, will, or do appear in the
document later. This implies that either the partial-case or the multi-case active pattern will be best
suited for extracting the data out of the document; the decision between the two will rest on whether
the F# programmer believes they know the full set of data types that the document contains.

This is not a casually discarded decision — XML documents are often used where a certain amount
of ambiguity in the data is expected or desired. Yet, much of the XML sent back and forth between
organizations is intended to be a closed-set of data types nestled in between angle-brackets, with
unrecoverable errors thrown when an unknown XML document is received. If ambiguity is
expected or desired, then the partial-case should be considered, and if not, then the multi-case active
pattern becomes the weapon of choice.

Just for pedagogical purposes, both approaches are considered.

## Multi-case Active Patterns

The multi-case active pattern requires a single function, written in "banana clips" style, which
contains all the possible atoms that the XML document can be decomposed into. For an easy

start, consider an active pattern that breaks the document down into `Node` and `Leaf` elements, showing the basic tree structure of a document:

```fsharp
let (|Node|Leaf|) (node : #System.Xml.XmlNode) =
    if node.HasChildNodes then
        Node (node.Name, seq { for x in node.ChildNodes -> x })
    else
        Leaf (node.InnerText)
```

Because the parameter to this active pattern can be either an `XmlNode` or any of its subtypes, the type descriptor is prefixed with a `"#"` to indicate subtype availability (as described in Chapter 9).

Using this pattern-match rule in a pattern-match statement becomes relatively trivial, allowing us to print the contents of any XML document in nicely indented form:

**Available for download on Wrox.com**

```fsharp
let printXml node =
    let rec printXml indent node =
        match node with
        | Leaf (text) ->
            printfn "%s%s" indent text
        | Node (name, nodes) ->
            printfn "%s%s:" indent name
            nodes |> Seq.iter (printXml (indent+"  "))
    printXml "" node
```

*Code snippet XMLActivePatternDemo.fs*

As might well be predicted, because the tree structure responds so well to a recursive-descent traversal through the nodes of the tree, the outer `printXml` function is made up of an inner recursively aware function to do the actual work, threading an "indent" string (made up of nothing but whitespace) through the descent to give nicely formatted text printed to the console.

Of course, a breakdown of `leaf`s and `node`s isn't itself useful; more useful would be to extract the `<person>` elements and their children into an easy-to-use structure in F#. Given the relatively simple structure of the `<person>` element, it's easiest to imagine the data extracted as a tuple, specifically a `string * string * int * seq<string>` tuple type, representing the person's gender, name, age, and the list of languages they speak. Extracting this via an active pattern would thus look like:

**Available for download on Wrox.com**

```fsharp
let (|Node|Leaf|Person|) (node : #System.Xml.XmlNode) =
    if node.Name = "person" then
        let pGender = node.Attributes.ItemOf("gender").Value
        let pName = node.Item("name").InnerText
        let pAge = Int32.Parse(node.Item("age").InnerText)
        let pLangNode = node.Item("languages")
        let pLangs =
            seq{ for l in pLangNode.ChildNodes -> l.InnerText }
        Person (pName, pGender, pAge, pLangs)
    else if node.HasChildNodes then
        Node (node.Name, seq { for x in node.ChildNodes -> x })
    else
        Leaf (node.InnerText)
```

*Code snippet XMLActivePatternDemo.fs*

This can then be used to get the various "parts" out of the XML via traditional pattern-match construct:

```
let printXml node =
    let rec printXml indent node =
        match node with
        | Person (n, g, a, ls) ->
            printfn "%sPerson: %s, %s, %d, speaks %d langs"
                indent n g a (Seq.length ls)
        | Leaf (text) ->
            printfn "%s%s" indent text
        | Node (name, nodes) ->
            printfn "%s%s:" indent name
            nodes |> Seq.iter (printXml (indent+"  "))
    printXml "" node
printXml xmlDoc
```

*Code snippet XMLActivePatternDemo.fs*

The `Leaf` clause from the pattern-match and active pattern rule can be removed if needed, but the `Node` clause is going to have to stay, unless specific rules to match on the `DocumentElement` that forms the root `XmlNode` of an `XmlDocument` are written. In general, it seems prudent to keep the `Node` clause around, with a match that forces the recursive descent further into the tree:

```
let (|Node|Person|) (node : #System.Xml.XmlNode) =
    if node.Name = "person" then
        let pGender = node.Attributes.ItemOf("gender").Value
        let pName = node.Item("name").InnerText
        let pAge = Int32.Parse(node.Item("age").InnerText)
        let pLangNode = node.Item("languages")
        let pLangs =
            seq{ for l in pLangNode.ChildNodes -> l.InnerText }
        Person (pName, pGender, pAge, pLangs)
    else if (node.HasChildNodes) then
        Node (seq { for x in node.ChildNodes -> x})
    else
        failwith ("Unexpected data: " + node.ToString())
let printXml node =
    let rec printXml node =
        match node with
        | Node (nodes) ->
            nodes |> Seq.iter printXml
        | Person (n, g, a, ls) ->
            printfn "Person: %s is %s, %d, " +
                "and speaks %d languages"
                n g a (Seq.length ls)
    printXml node
printXml xmlDoc
```

*Code snippet XMLActivePatternDemo.fs*

Typically, printing to the console is only done during development and debugging — most of the time, it is more useful to pull the data out of the XML document as a sequence of tuples or other strongly typed objects. This means rewriting the pattern-match itself to return a sequence of tuples:

```
let extract node =
    let rec extract node =
        match node with
        | Person (n, g, a, ls) ->
            Seq.singleton (n, g, a, ls)
        | Node (nodes) ->
            Seq.collect (fun (n) -> extract n) nodes
    extract node
let results = extract xmlDoc
for r in results do
    Console.WriteLine("Result: {0}", r)
```

*Code snippet XMLActivePatternDemo.fs*

Of course, after a certain point, tuples may want to become fully fledged domain objects:

```
type Person(name : string, gender : string,
            age : int, langs : seq<string>) =
    member p.Name with get() = name
    member p.Gender with get() = gender
    member p.Age with get() = age
    member p.Languages with get() = langs
    override p.ToString() =
        String.Format("[Person: {0} is {1}, {2}," +
            ", and speaks {3}]",
            name, gender, age.ToString(),
                (Seq.reduce (fun (l) (s) ->
                    l + ", and " + s) langs))
```

*Code snippet XMLActivePatternDemo.fs*

When that happens, the active-pattern rule takes that into account, returning a `Person` object instead of a tuple:

```
let (|Node|Person|) (node : #System.Xml.XmlNode) =
    if node.Name = "person" then
        let pGender = node.Attributes.ItemOf("gender").Value
        let pName = node.Item("name").InnerText
        let pAge = Int32.Parse(node.Item("age").InnerText)
        let pLangNode = node.Item("languages")
        let pLangs =
            seq{ for l in pLangNode.ChildNodes -> l.InnerText }
        Person (new Person(pName, pGender, pAge, pLangs))
    else if (node.HasChildNodes) then
        Node (seq { for x in node.ChildNodes -> x})
    else
        failwith ("Unexpected data: " + node.ToString())
```

*Code snippet XMLActivePatternDemo.fs*

which in turn makes the transformation from XML to a sequence of domain objects just a bit different:

```
let extract node =
    let rec extract node =
        match node with
        | Person (p) ->
            Seq.singleton p
        | Node (nodes) ->
            Seq.collect (fun (n) -> extract n) nodes
    extract node
let results = extract xmlDoc
for r in results do
    Console.WriteLine("Result: {0}", r)
```

*Code snippet XMLActivePatternDemo.fs*

The results of the extract function will be a seq<Person>, which is about as straightforward an extraction result as the F# programmer could want. Things get a tad more interesting (thanks to F#'s type-inference) when more than one domain object can appear in the XML; the F# type-inferencer right now assumes that extract produces a sequence of Person objects out of the XML document. If a new domain type is introduced into the system, such as:

```
type Ship(name : string, jumpCapable : bool) =
    member s.Name with get() = name
    member s.Jump with get() = jumpCapable
    override s.ToString() =
        String.Format("[Ship: {0}, jump={1}]",
            name, jumpCapable.ToString())
```

*Code snippet XMLActivePatternDemo.fs*

then extracting it from the XML is ridiculously simple, as we'd hope:

```
let (|Node|Person|Ship|) (node : #System.Xml.XmlNode) =
    if node.Name = "person" then
        let pGender = node.Attributes.ItemOf("gender").Value
        let pName = node.Item("name").InnerText
        let pAge = Int32.Parse(node.Item("age").InnerText)
        let pLangNode = node.Item("languages")
        let pLangs =
            seq{ for l in pLangNode.ChildNodes -> l.InnerText }
        Person (new Person(pName, pGender, pAge, pLangs))
    else if (node.Name = "ship") then
        let sName = node.Item("name").InnerText
        let sJump = node.Attributes.ItemOf("jump").Value
        Ship (new Ship(sName,
            if sJump="true" then true else false))
    else if (node.HasChildNodes) then
        Node (seq { for x in node.ChildNodes -> x})
    else
        failwith ("Unexpected data: " + node.ToString())
```

*Code snippet XMLActivePatternDemo.fs*

But the pattern-match rule has to change slightly; if the Ship clause is simply inserted into the pattern-match, the compiler complains:

```
let extract node =
    let rec extract node =
        match node with
        | Person (p) ->
            Seq.singleton p
        | Ship (s) ->
            Seq.singleton s
        | Node (nodes) ->
            Seq.collect (fun (n) -> extract n) nodes
    extract node
let results = extract xmlDoc
for r in results do
    Console.WriteLine("Result: {0}", r)
```

*Code snippet XMLActivePatternDemo.fs*

specifically, that the Ship clause doesn't return a Person object. This is because the type-inferencer in F# has assumed that the extract function wants to take in an XmlNode and return a sequence of Person objects, which obviously the Ship object isn't. If Ship inherits from Person, then obviously the compiler will be OK with this, but as written right now, Ship doesn't.

Fortunately, Ship and Person do both inherit from a common base class, System.Object, so it's simply a matter of telling the F# compiler this, doing the upcast from the domain object to System.Object during the pattern-match, and asking the compiler to see the result as a sequence of Object rather than a sequence of Person:

```
let extract node : seq<obj> =
    let rec extract node : seq<obj> =
        match node with
        | Ship (s) ->
            Seq.singleton (s :> obj)
        | Person (p) ->
            Seq.singleton (p :> obj)
        | Node (nodes) ->
            Seq.collect (fun (n) -> extract n) nodes
    extract node
let results = extract xmlDoc
for r in results do
    Console.WriteLine("Result: {0}", r)
```

*Code snippet XMLActivePatternDemo.fs*

And now, any number of domain types can be added to the active pattern rule and returned from the extract function.

Unfortunately, the drawback to the multi-case solution comes when the upstream source of the XML document throws something "new" into the XML stream. Not that clients would actually ever do that, of course, but still, a more robust solution would allow for a certain amount of forgiveness.

## Partial-Case Active Patterns

Operating on a slightly different XML example from before, we can introduce some "unknown" structure into the XML document that is to be parsed and extracted into domain objects:

```xml
<data>
    <item>
        <person gender="male">
            <name>Ted Neward</name>
            <age>38</age>
            <languages>
                <language>English</language>
                <language>French</language>
                <language>C#</language>
                <language>Java</language>
                <language>F#</language>
                <language>Scala</language>
            </languages>
        </person>
    </item>
    <item>
        <person gender="male">
            <name>Han Solo</name>
            <age>35</age>
            <languages>
                <language>Imperial Standard</language>
                <language>Wookiee</language>
            </languages>
        </person>
    </item>
    <ship jump="true">
        <name>Millenium Falcon</name>
    </ship>
    <fairyTalePrincess>
        <name>Sleeping Beauty</name>
        <ending>Happy</ending>
    </fairyTalePrincess>
    <fairyTalePrincess>
        <name>Cinderella</name>
        <ending>Happy</ending>
    </fairyTalePrincess>
    <item>
        <person gender="male">
            <name>Gaius Baltar</name>
            <age>35</age>
            <languages>
                <language>English</language>
                <language>Cylon</language>
            </languages>
        </person>
    </item>
```

```
    <ship jump="true">
        <name>Galactica</name>
    </ship>
</data>
```

*Code snippet XMLActiveExample2.xml*

Where'd those `fairyTalePrincess` elements come from? Clearly, as the children's television show implied, they are the "one of these things that doesn't belong," but what can we do? Clients sometimes don't send the data that is expected.

The partial-case active pattern requires a function for each "thing" that the XML might be extracted into, with a wildcard at the end of the name to indicate that this might not always succeed, and this is where the partial-match will be of better benefit. Because the partial-match pattern doesn't assume that it has all the possible cases the source (the XML node) can extract into, it will neatly and efficiently bypass any source that it doesn't understand.

To start, create the partial-match active pattern rules for the two types we do know about, `Person` and `Ship`:

```
let (|Person|_|) (node : #System.Xml.XmlNode) =
    if node.Name = "person" then
        let pGender = node.Attributes.ItemOf("gender").Value
        let pName = node.Item("name").InnerText
        let pAge = Int32.Parse(node.Item("age").InnerText)
        let pLangNode = node.Item("languages")
        let pLangs =
            seq{ for l in pLangNode.ChildNodes -> l.InnerText }
        Some(new Person(pName, pGender, pAge, pLangs))
    else
        None

let (|Ship|_|) (node : #System.Xml.XmlNode) =
    if (node.Name = "ship") then
        let sName = node.Item("name").InnerText
        let sJump = node.Attributes.ItemOf("jump").Value
        Some (new Ship(sName,
                       if sJump="true" then true else false))
    else
        None
```

*Code snippet XMLActivePatternDemo.fs*

Bear in mind, again, that the partial-match must yield an Option type, either `Some<T>` or `None`, from each rule. Other than that, the partial-match rules for extracting the domain objects out of the XML document are remarkably similar to the ones used for the multi-case match. This is actually comforting — it means that refactoring from one style to the other will be relatively trivial.

Still present is the problem of the nodes that the code will hit before the person or ship elements and the unrecognized elements like `fairyTalePrincess`. These are covered in the pattern-match itself:

```
let extract node : seq<obj> =
    let rec extract node : seq<obj> =
        match node with
        | Ship (s) ->
            Seq.singleton (s :> obj)
        | Person (p) ->
            Seq.singleton (p :> obj)
        | node when node.HasChildNodes ->
            let children = seq{ for n in node.ChildNodes -> n }
            Seq.collect (fun (n) -> extract n) children
        | _ ->
            Seq.empty
    extract node
```

*Code snippet XMLActivePatternDemo.fs*

Again, we just have to help the F# compiler along just a little bit by defining the returned sequence to be a sequence of Objects. And rather than creating an explicit partial-match rule for `Node` objects, which really isn't a data type we're trying to work with, it's easier in this case to use a pattern guard to determine if the node has any child objects, and if so, just walk through each of those and recursively call extract on them. And, the stunning *coup de grace*, if the node doesn't match any of these three conditions, an empty sequence can be returned.

Later, if there is an element that is known to be ignorable — that is, one for which it can be stated with certainty that it has nothing of interest to us, the parser can recognize that element and use it as a signal to prune the XML hierarchy that is being parsed:

```
let extract node : seq<obj> =
    let rec extract node : seq<obj> =
        match node with
        | Ship (s) ->
            Seq.singleton (s :> obj)
        | Person (p) ->
            Seq.singleton (p :> obj)
        | node when node.HasChildNodes ->
            let children = seq{ for n in node.ChildNodes -> n }
            Seq.collect (fun (n) -> extract n) children
        | node when node.Name = "fairyTalePrincess" ->
            Seq.empty
        | _ ->
            Seq.empty
    extract node
```

*Code snippet XMLActivePatternDemo.fs*

This will prevent the traversal of the nodes underneath the `fairyTalePrincess` element and save a few matches and recursive calls. For a small element like `fairyTalePrincess`, it won't make a huge difference; in a multi-megabyte XML document consisting of elements of hundreds of child elements long, it will.

Regardless of whether the partial-case or multi-case approach is used, the net result is a relatively easy, scalable way to parse XML documents and extract the data into strongly type domain objects for further processing:

```
let results = extract xmlDoc
for r in results do
    Console.WriteLine("Result: {0}", r)
```

And because the results of the extracting are a sequence of strongly typed objects, we could use pattern-matching again to walk through the sequence and do something more meaningful with the objects contained therein:

```
let results = extract xmlDoc
for r in results do
    Console.WriteLine("Result: {0}", r)
    match r with
    | :? Ship as s ->
        Console.WriteLine("The ship {0} {1}",
            s.Name,
            if s.Jump = true
                then "is jump-capable"
                else "is slower-than-light")
    | :? Person as p ->
        Console.WriteLine("Found {0}", p.Name)
    | _ ->
        ()
```

*Code snippet XMLActivePatternDemo.fs*

Regardless of what work needs to be done, the active patterns feature of F# allows for some easily read and easily maintained code.

## SUMMARY

In this chapter, we have covered how you deal with XML using F# employing two of the most common methods that F# programmers will use, LINQ-to-XML and XML DOM. LINQ-to-XML approaches that eschew XPath can certainly work; however, XPath, especially if others you are working with understand XPath, tends to produce more concise queries. Which you use is a matter of choice that is made most commonly by the group you are working with, any organizational standards you might have, or lacking any of those constrains, personal preference.

# 21

# ASP.NET MVC

**WHAT'S IN THIS CHAPTER?**

➤  Building websites

➤  Integrating C# views with F# controllers and models

➤  Keeping concerns properly separated

➤  Understanding the MVC pattern applied to F#

While F# is a strong contender in many areas of the development stack, it has not been traditionally thought of as a great candidate for development of code on the UI layer. This is especially true for platforms like WinForms, which promote a sense of statefulness that flows through not just the UI, but through the object model that a UI might be bound to. Most UI technologies of the WinForm era (including ASP.NET WebForms) are tied to the idea of mutating control objects as a core mechanism by which you promote interaction between a presentation object (MVP pattern) or ViewModel (MVVM pattern), and mutable UI objects (like controls with a .Text property). For such a stateful model, F# is merely an average OO language on the .NET framework, with no real compelling application besides being yet another language option.

For other models, however, that depend less on state maintenance — such as MVC frameworks — F# is far more compelling. In this chapter, you learn how to use F# with the ASP.NET MVC framework. We demonstrate an example of writing an ASP.NET MVC application that demonstrates how to use F# to simplify web development.

## OVERVIEW

It is not that controversial to say that ASP.NET WebForms was designed in a manner to make web development "safe" for programmers from the world of Windows development, with events tied to controls where processing happens on the server. Unfortunately, this attempt at

abstraction is a great example of what Joel Spolsky calls a "leaky abstraction" (http://www
.joelonsoftware.com/articles/LeakyAbstractions.html). That is, despite how hard we try
to hide that development is being done over the Web, the latency between, say, a user's click on
the client side, and the response handled on the server side, means that most developers end up
worrying about concerns related to the detail that the framework tries to abstract away.

Put another way, we don't have to do much coding in ASP.NET WebForms before Requests,
Responses, and plumbing that makes web programming actually work rear their heads. There is
little you can do in ASP.NET WebForms without having to realize that the application is on the
Web. The abstraction of a window with click events breaks down very quickly!

ASP.NET MVC grew from a premise that developers are better off admitting that web apps are
best thought of as the HTTP-based services they actually are, rather than as an abstraction of
a programming model designed for a very different set of assumptions. It does not hurt that the
framework is designed with testability in mind. However, this moving from a stateful model to a
service-based model has other important ramifications to the F# programmer.

As is covered in Chapter 23, F# is a great language for service development. ASP.NET MVC is
merely a more complex type of service that, rather than serving up JSON or XML, serves up HTML
based on a HTTP request. In this chapter, we demonstrate writing a completely stateless application
using F# and the ASP.NET MVC Framework.

## FORECAST'R — THE WORLD'S SIMPLEST WEATHER FORECAST SITE

To demonstrate this, this chapter builds on the weather example started with Chapter 20 to build
out a website that implements the following user story:

> *As a human, to quickly determine whether I should wear a light jacket, a parka,
> a raincoat, a bikini, or in the case of a forecasted Zombie takeover, body armor. I
> want to know what weather to expect.*

To build this out, the following steps apply:

➤ Build out a domain that models a weather forecast.

➤ Create a repository that can populate the domain.

➤ Build a controller that provides a means for an outside service to access the domain.

➤ Add an ASP.NET MVC website that leverages the controller and makes the system usable by
humans.

To get started, I encourage you to become familiar with the project setup steps described by Tomas
Petricek on his blog: http://tomasp.net/blog/fsharp-mvc-web.aspx. This setup explains how
to set up an F#/C# hybrid project that uses C# for views but F# for everything else.

# Modeling the Domain

If we are going to have a weather forecasting site, it will probably need to have a model that covers different types of possible weather. Such a model might start as follows:

```
namespace FSharpBook.Models
type SkyType =
    | Sunny
    | Overcast
    | PartlyCloudy
    | Snow
    | Rain
    | Hurricane
    | Zombies
```

*Code snippet ForecastModel.fs*

`SkyType` is a discriminated union that represents different types of weather that are possible. Others may be added, but this is a good initial list that allows a developer to know whether a parka is needed. Others could be added (that is, `PartlySunny`, `Showers`, and so on), but the current set should be enough for a really simple site.

Of course, it is not enough just to give an indication of temperature, knowing just because it is sunny, it does not mean that a coat isn't needed. Without a temperature, it could be sunny, but a bone chilling -30 degrees outside! It would also be useful to know the location of our forecast, in case the user entered Paris, but got Paris, Texas instead of Paris, France. The following is added to the same file, `ForecastModel.fs`:

```
type Forecast = { Location:string; AverageTemperature:double; Skies:SkyType }
```

To implement a simple forecast model as asked for in the user story, a simple record type with a `Location`, `AverageTemperature`, and `Skies` — will determine whether it will be wet and how cold or hot it will be.

Of course, something is needed that will provide a means to get a forecast. For that, a repository should be created from which forecast information can be obtained.

It isn't just what the model does, but it is also what the model *does not* do. It is not doing any work to retrieve actual forecast data from outside sources — that is a concern for the repository. Nor does it care about how anything is rendered — that is a concern for the view — not the model. The only things that belong in the model are considerations about how it is going to internally represent weather, and any behavior that might be added. For example, behavior can be added to `Forecast` that allows it to return something that specifies what kind of attire should be worn. Assume the following choices of attire the user might be interested in wearing:

```
type Attire =
    | Bikini
    | Normal
    | LightJacket
```

```
      | Coat
      | Raincoat
      | Parka
      | BodyArmor
```

The definition for `Attire` is a discriminated union, much like the definition for `SkyType`. Given the above attire, it would be useful to add behavior to specify what kind of attire should be worn in different weather conditions. Such a specification may look like this:

```
type Forecast with
  member forecast.ToAttire() =
    match forecast.AverageTemperature,forecast.Skies with
      | temp,sky when temp > 75.0 && sky = Sunny || sky = PartlyCloudy -> Bikini
      | temp,sky when temp > 65.0 && sky = Sunny || sky = PartlyCloudy -> Normal
      | temp,sky when
          temp > 45.0 && sky = Sunny || sky = PartlyCloudy -> LightJacket
      | _,Rain -> Raincoat
      | temp when temp < 20.0 -> Parka
      | _,Hurricane -> Coat
      | _,Snow -> Parka
      | _,Zombies -> BodyArmor
      | _ -> Coat //when in doubt, wear a coat...
```

A conversion from a `Forecast` to `Attire` is based on mapping the appropriate `AverageTemperature` and `Skies` combinations to the appropriate `Attire`. So in a case where there are temperatures over 75 and at least `PartlyCloudy` skies, the recommendation will be `Bikini`. There are various other recommendations, including `BodyArmor` in the event of `Zombies`.

Note the reopening the `Forecast` type later on in the model definition, in this case, to add new behavior. This is not that uncommon in F#, as frequently, a method needs to be added that uses a type that was not known earlier because of sequential evaluation. (Remember, types can't be used prior to being defined.)

For a simple website that models a weather forecast and attire recommendations, this is certainly a good model to start with. With this in place, the next phase is to move on to implementation of a repository from where a forecast can be retrieved.

## Creating a Repository

A repository is generally considered a source for information that can be used to populate a domain. In many applications, a repository can take the form of a relational database, such as Postgres, MS SQL Server, or Oracle. CouchDB, MongoDB, db4o, among others, are also great candidates for repositories.

Whatever technology is chosen, the domain objects should never have a need to be aware of it. That is, they should be **persistence ignoranant**. This is especially important given the increasing rate of innovation in the world of storage and the increasing likelihood you may want to swap out, say, a SQL Server repository at some point for one based on a technology more oriented toward the cloud in the future.

In this case, however, there is no need for traditional data storage. The simple "Forecast'R" site merely uses various Yahoo APIs to gather weather and location information. The signature for the repository method is as follows:

**Available for download on Wrox.com**

```
namespace FSharpBook.Repositories
open System
open System.Xml.Linq
open FSharpBook.Models

type YahooForecastRepository() =
  static member GetForecastByLocation locationName =
```

*Code snippet ForecastRepository.fs*

## Retrieval of "Where On Earth ID"s

The goal, of course, is to retrieve a single forecast based on a name of a location. Chapter 20 provided a means to gather information from a weather forecast based on a Yahoo "Where On Earth ID" (WOEID), but only a specific number for that ID as provided to keep things simple. However, this application is going to need to get such an ID, based on a textual location query, to be of much use. Thus, this first line in the repository routine:

```
let yahooWhereOnEarthIds
  = YahooForecastRepository.GetWhereOnEarthIdsByLocation locationName
```

For more about Yahoo "Where On Earth ID"s, please visit `developer.yahoo.com/geo/geoplanet/`.

This routine will be expected to return one or more "Where On Earth ID"s. In this case, it is implemented as a static member of the repository, because the repository has no state of its own. The implementation is as follows:

**Available for download on Wrox.com**

```
static member GetWhereOnEarthIdsByLocation locationName =
//visit http://developer.yahoo.com/geo/geoplanet/ to get your
// own appId
  let appId = ""
  let yahooUrlLocationLookup
    = sprintf "http://where.yahooapis.com/v1/places.q('%s')?appid=%s"
        locationName appId
  let locationsDoc = yahooUrlLocationLookup |> XDocument.Load
  let yahooWhereOnEarthIds =
    locationsDoc.Descendants()
    |> Seq.filter (fun e -> e.Name.LocalName = "woeid" )
    |> Seq.map (fun e -> e.Value |> Int32.Parse )
  yahooWhereOnEarthIds
```

*Code snippet ForecastRepository.fs*

The Yahoo Geoplanet API, as of time of writing, works by passing a simple HTTP GET to a specific URL. For example, if one wanted to find a WOEID for New Jersey, issue an HTTP GET request to the following:

```
http://where.yahooapis.com/v1/places.q('New Jersey')?appid=YourAppID
```

In this example, replace `YourAppID` with your ID provisioned by the Yahoo Geoplanet service.

What is returned is XML content that has a lot of information about New Jersey. The requirement, however, is to ignore most of this information and simply return a set of integers related to the "Where On Earth ID"s in the response. The file itself contains a set of elements with the local name `woeid`, each of which (there may be more than one) contains the integer of interest. After filtering by the `LocalName`, and then parsing into an `Int32`, a sequence of "Where On Earth ID"s related to the location is returned.

### From "Where On Earth ID"s to Weather Content

The next four lines of the main repository routine allow retrieval of the specific document that relates to the first "Where On Earth ID" returned from `GetWhereOnEarthIdsByLocation`:

```
static member GetForecastByLocation locationName =
  let yahooWhereOnEarthIds
    = YahooForecastRepository.GetWhereOnEarthIdsByLocation locationName
  let getForecastDoc id =
    let yahooWeatherRSSUrl =
      sprintf "http://weather.yahooapis.com/forecastrss?w=%d" id
    yahooWeatherRSSUrl |> XDocument.Load
  let weatherDoc = yahooWhereOnEarthIds |> Seq.head |> getForecastDoc
```

*Code snippet ForecastRepository.fs*

The first step is to implement a function scoped to `GetForecastByLocation` called `getForecast-Doc`. It takes an `id`, expected to be an integer that refers to a "Where On Earth ID". The next step is to compose a URL by combining the public Yahoo Weather forecast RSS URL template with the "Where On Earth ID". Next, pass the composed URL to `XDocument.Load`, which provides the Yahoo Weather content related to the given "Where On Earth ID".

The last line is where the function is called that was defined on the previous three lines. Starting with a sequence of "Where On Earth ID"s, the top one is taken (making an executive decision that the first result is the one the user most likely wanted), and it is passed to the `getForecastDoc` function, with the result being an `XDocument` with the weather information that can be used to populate a forecast domain.

### Digging Out the Content

The next set of lines of the routine use skills developed in Chapter 20 to dig into the content and find information about the weather:

```
let firstLocationElement (elems:seq<XElement>) =
   elems |> Seq.filter ( fun(e) -> e.Name.LocalName = "location" ) |> Seq.head
let locationNameFromElement (elem:XElement) =
   XmlHelpers.getAttr elem "city"
      + ", " + XmlHelpers.getAttr elem "region"
      + ", " + XmlHelpers.getAttr elem "country"
let currentConditions (elems:seq<XElement>) =
   let findFirstConditionElement (elems:seq<XElement>) =
      elems |>
      Seq.filter (fun(e) -> e.Name.LocalName = "condition") |> Seq.head
   let forecastText
      = XmlHelpers.getAttr ( elems |> findFirstConditionElement) "text"
   forecastText |> YahooForecastRepository.ForecastTextToSkyType
let averageTemperatures (elems:seq<XElement>) =
   elems
      |> Seq.map (fun(e) -> e.Attributes())
      |> Seq.concat
      |> Seq.filter (
        fun(a) -> a.Name.LocalName = "low" || a.Name.LocalName = "high")
      |> Seq.map (fun(a) -> a.Value |> Double.Parse)
      |> Seq.average
```

*Code snippet ForecastRepository.fs*

To populate the domain, the location name is needed that the search resolved to, the current conditions specified, and the average temperature. The preceding lines use Linq to XML to gather the required information.

The only real interesting thing being done here, from a domain standpoint, is that the raw text provided by the API is converted into the domain language for weather. This conversion goes through `YahooForecastRepository.ForecastTextToSkyType`:

```
static member private ForecastTextToSkyType (text:string) =
   match text with
   | t when t.Contains "Partly Cloudy" -> SkyType.PartlyCloudy
   | t when t.Contains "Rain" -> SkyType.Rain
   | t when t.Contains "Snow" -> SkyType.Snow
   | t when t.Contains "Hurricane"
        || t.Contains "Tropical Storm" -> SkyType.Hurricane
   | t when t.Contains "Overcast" -> SkyType.Overcast
   | _ -> SkyType.Zombies
```

*Code snippet ForecastRepository.fs*

This allows for conversion of an arbitrary string into a given `SkyType` that ultimately becomes the basis for the `Attire` recommendation. This example starts with a small number of mappings that provide a good starting point. Inclusion of this in the repository is a choice made here because this particular mapping is likely specific to this repository. Other repositories (say, some foreign language weather service), may have different terms that represent different `SkyType` values.

## Returning the Weather Result

Of course, a great deal of setup and parsing routines have already been done, setting up the conditions needed for the following:

```
static member GetForecastByLocation locationName =
    let yahooWhereOnEarthIds =
 YahooForecastRepository.GetWhereOnEarthIdsByLocation locationName
    let getForecastDoc id =
      let yahooWeatherRSSUrl = sprintf
        "http://weather.yahooapis.com/forecastrss?w=%d" id
      yahooWeatherRSSUrl |> XDocument.Load
    let weatherDoc = yahooWhereOnEarthIds |> Seq.head |> getForecastDoc
    let firstLocationElement (elems:seq<XElement>) =
      elems |> Seq.filter ( fun(e) -> e.Name.LocalName = "location" ) |> Seq.head
    let locationNameFromElement (elem:XElement) =
      XmlHelpers.getAttr elem "city"
        + ", " + XmlHelpers.getAttr elem "region"
        + ", " + XmlHelpers.getAttr elem "country"
    let currentConditions (elems:seq<XElement>) =
      let findFirstConditionElement (elems:seq<XElement>) =
        elems |>
        Seq.filter (fun(e) -> e.Name.LocalName = "condition") |> Seq.head
      let forecastText =
        XmlHelpers.getAttr ( elems |> findFirstConditionElement) "text"
      forecastText |> YahooForecastRepository.ForecastTextToSkyType
    let averageTemperatures (elems:seq<XElement>) =
      elems
         |> Seq.collect (fun(e) -> e.Attributes())
         |> Seq.filter
         (fun(a) -> a.Name.LocalName = "low" || a.Name.LocalName = "high")
         |> Seq.map (fun(a) -> a.Value |> Double.Parse)
         |> Seq.average
    let convertDocToForecastModel (doc:XDocument) =
      {
        Location = doc.Descendants()
           |> firstLocationElement
           |> locationNameFromElement;
        AverageTemperature = doc.Descendants() |> averageTemperatures;
        Skies = doc.Descendants() |> currentConditions
      }
    weatherDoc |> convertDocToForecastModel
```

*Code snippet ForecastRepository.fs*

These last lines provide a function for conversion of an XDocument from the Yahoo Weather API into a domain model for Weather. The function convertDocToForecastModel is a composition of other functions that have been defined. The last line simply passes the actual document to the function, so the actual result can be returned.

It is important to note that this repository is fairly complex compared to many repository implementations we may write. More typical repositories might be based on more traditional database code, as is demonstrated in Chapter 19.

# Creating the Controller

When a domain is set up and a repository has been written that is capable of populating a domain, the next step is to implement a means to connect the domain to something more interesting. In the ASP.NET MVC framework that takes the form of a controller. The controller is, to put it simply, a means for a domain to be exposed to the outside world, typically a `View` somewhere.

A good way to think about a controller is to think about how a user somewhere may interact, logically, with the application. A simple site for viewing a forecast will definitely need an `Index` page, which likely has instructions on it, and perhaps a box where someone can enter a query. Certainly something will be needed to handle the query. It would probably also be a wise idea to have a page that shows a result somewhere — one that is preferably a result from the aforementioned query.

## Setting Up the Controller

Start a controller by adding a file, perhaps `controllers.fs`, and adding the following code:

**Available for download on Wrox.com**

```
namespace FSharpBook.Controllers
open System.Web.Mvc
open FSharpBook.Models
open FSharpBook.Repositories
open System.Web.Routing

[<HandleError>]
type ForecastController() =
    inherit Controller()
```

*Code snippet Controllers.fs*

By convention, all controller classes in ASP.NET MVC end in the word `Controller`. The part of the name before `Controller`, `Forecast` in this case, will become the name of the controller that is used by the `View` logic when mapping routes to controllers. The controller should be aware of the domain (in `FSharpBook.Models`), as well as the repositories (in `FSharpBook.Repositories`). The initial implementation will use concrete versions of those classes, though it is certainly possible (and ultimately desirable!) to use dependency injection to map controllers to a domain and a repository.

Of course, it is worth noting that the class derives from `Controller`, which provides it with a good deal of default controller functionality out of the box that will be used as this sample site is built.

## The Index Action

The index page, frankly, will not do much. It is expected to probably have some text on it, and perhaps a form that might take in some information. However, neither the controller nor the actions defined in a controller care much about that form. What the form actually contains is a responsibility of the `view`. It is known that the index page displays the same thing, no matter who or what is using it. The index is defined as follows within the `forecastController`:

```
member forecastController.Index() =
    forecastController.View()
```

The preceding code dictates that when the `Index` is asked for, provide a default view for that index. Note that the member must always have the () attached to indicate to the framework that will call the routine that there are zero parameters — as while it is common to leave off the parens in pure F# programs, the framework expects that the signature be a proper zero parameter member and will not map properly without the parens.

## The DoQuery Action

Of course, it would be useful to actually have some code that does something. The `Submit` action, the second written in this example, will perform that role.

When the form is submitted, be it by the `Index` page, or in theory, any other page that has a form that posts to the `Submit` action of the `Forecast` controller, something useful needs to be done with it. There are a couple of options. One naive approach many use is to simply do the work right on the submit action, returning a `View` that renders the forecast. Although this approach is simple, it causes the great annoyance of the type of message shown in Figure 21-1.

**FIGURE 21-1**

To get around this, the form processor is going to implement what is often called the PRG Pattern. PRG stands for Post, Redirect, and Get. This has a couple of advantages — one of which is that it gets away from having the browser complain that it is going to need to re-post the form. Another though, and probably more compelling than that, is that it allows separation of form processing from the view rendering that is the result of that processing. The code to implement a PRG pattern is actually quite simple:

```
member forecastController.Submit(locationQuery:string) =
    let rvd = new RouteValueDictionary()
    rvd.Add("locationQuery",locationQuery)
    forecastController.RedirectToAction("for","forecast",rvd)
```

A forecast controller always takes a `locationQuery` as a parameter. This may be a form field from some form that posted to this page, but how it looked on such a form does not really matter to the controller — the controller just needs to know that by the time this routine is called, something mapped it in properly. What is needed is to create a redirect to the controller and action that is actually going to render the result.

One technique to do that is to create a `RouteValueDictionary` object that has the parameter. The first two lines of the method that create the dictionary and add the item accomplish that goal. The third line is a call to `RedirectToAction`, a method on the `Controller` base class that knows how to redirect a new GET request based on an action, a controller name, and optionally, a `RouteValueDictionary` that holds the parameters.

## The For Action

The last action is named `For`, as it helps when visualizing a URL that might read `/Forecast/For?someQuery`. The job of `For` is to actually render the forecast the user is interested in. As it turns out, the method to do so is actually pretty tame:

```
member forecastController.For(locationQuery:string) =
    locationQuery
        |> YahooForecastRepository.GetForecastByLocation
        |> forecastController.View
```

Again, it is expected that `locationQuery` will be passed as a parameter from the view. The repository knows how to retrieve a single forecast based on the query, so the simplest thing to do is to pipe the query into the repository, providing the forecast. That result is then piped into a `View`, which presumably is structured in such a way as to render the domain object.

Of course, there are a couple schools of thought about rendering domain objects directly on views. It works fine for a simple case like this one, where the object is not terribly complex. However, sometimes, one may want a less complex object than the entire domain object to be sent to a view. `Presentation` objects, `ViewModels`, or other abstractions come to the rescue in such situations. However, even in the presence of one of those, it belongs squarely in the domain model part of the MVC framework, not in the `Controller`, lest you end up inadvertently ending up with a "fat controller" that is typically a code smell that happens when one mixes domain and controller concerns.

## Creating Some View Helpers

It should be noted that the view is not quite ready for implementation. There are a couple of things that need to be done to have the domain objects render nicely in the views. The `Attire` and `SkyType` objects, although definitely in a nice form useful for the domain logic, do not have a reliable means to convert to strings. Of course, we could interrogate their type and push out a string based on that, but then there would still need to be a means to convert from something like `"PartlyCloudy"` to, say, `"Partly Cloudy"`, or perhaps if the website needed to render in Spanish, `"Parcialmente Nublado"`.

It would be bad practice to put such view-specific concerns in the same place as the main controller or model, so to keep the concerns separate, put these in a separate area of the project called `ViewHelpers`. The first new file will help us render various `SkyType` values:

```
module SkyTypeRenderer
open FSharpBook.Models

let ToWeatherString sky =
  match sky with
  | Sunny -> "Sunny"
  | Overcast -> "Overcast"
  | PartlyCloudy -> "Partly Cloudy"
  | Snow -> "Snow"
  | Rain -> "Rain"
```

```
    | Hurricane -> "Hurricane"
    | Zombies -> "Oh NO! ZOMBIES!!!"
let ToImageFileName sky =
 match sky with
    | PartlyCloudy -> "PartlyCloudy"
    | Zombies -> "Zombies"
    | _ -> ToWeatherString sky
```

*Code snippet SkyTypeRenderer.fs*

This first file allows us to do two view-specific things. It creates a string for each state of sky (to be rendered in a specific view), and it maps sky types to filenames, which again, are known when dealing with a specific view.

The second file will help map various Attire definitions to strings:

```
module AttireRenderer
open FSharpBook.Models

let ToAttireString attire =
    match attire with
        | Bikini -> "Bikini"
        | Normal -> "Normal"
        | LightJacket -> "Light Jacket"
        | Coat -> "Coat"
        | Raincoat -> "Raincoat"
        | Parka -> "Parka"
        | BodyArmor -> "Body Armor"
```

*Code snippet AttireRenderer.fs*

Of course, what is being done here with these renderers, in a production system, would be best done with locale-specific resource files, so that when a system is internationalized, such internationalization is more easily done by swapping out the appropriate resource.

## Creating the View

If everything has been done right, there should be almost no reason to have code, other than perhaps a few very trivial binding helpers, in the view. The Holy Grail in this kind of system is a view that lacks any code at all. That is, the view should consist of markup that is the province of the user interface designer, and anything that such a designer would have a hard time understanding should go in some other kind of component.

The example site has two views. It has the Index view that is rendered when the user goes to the default page, and the results view (For.aspx, in this case) that shows the result. The Index view (Index.aspx) is very simple:

```
<%@ Page Title="" Language="C#" MasterPageFile="~/Views/Shared/Site.Master"
    Inherits="System.Web.Mvc.ViewPage" %>

<asp:Content ID="titleContent" ContentPlaceHolderID="TitleContent" runat="server">
    Forecastr - The simplest weather forecast system in the Universe!
</asp:Content>
```

```
<asp:Content ID="mainContent" ContentPlaceHolderID="MainContent" runat="server">
<div id="queryText">
<% using (Html.BeginForm("DoQuery","forecast", FormMethod.Post)) {%>
    I want to know the weather forecast for:
    <%= Html.TextBox("LocationQuery") %>
    <input type="submit" value="Get Forecast" />
<% } %>
</div>

</asp:Content>
```

*Code snippet Views/Forecast/Index.aspx*

It is notable that what little code is here is written in C#, not F#. Although it may be possible to get markup to work in F#, doing so requires a lot of work with `web.config` files and certainly does not work easily out-of-the-box as of the time of writing. Given the intent is to minimize code in the view anyway, in this case, a decision is made to keep view-only code in C# — but do as little as possible.

The code that *is* here, frankly, does very little. Simple helpers are being used from the framework to generate some html code. `Html.BeginForm` is a framework helper function for spitting out form elements; `Html.TextBox` does the same for `Input` elements that represent text boxes. The only thing that really needs to be done here is to specify a controller that should be posted to, as well as an intended action. We could just as easily write:

```
<form action="/forecast/DoQuery" method="post">
```

Of course, the benefit received in using the helper is that it can provide some help in making sure the output is correct, because the preceding code might not be correct if we were in a situation that involved writing a site that ran from a virtual directory. That said, there may be cases where a designer will want more control over the output and will opt for writing the raw html. Given that the only responsibility of the html helper is to spit out appropriately formatted html, having an html designer hand-code it would not break the site.

The code for the `Forecast` view is a slightly bit more complex, but not horribly so:

**Available for download on Wrox.com**

```
<%@ Page Title="" Language="C#" MasterPageFile="~/Views/Shared/Site.Master"
Inherits="System.Web.Mvc.ViewPage" %>
<%@ Import Namespace="FSharpBook" %>
<%@ Import Namespace="FSharpBook.Models" %>

<asp:Content ID="titleContent" ContentPlaceHolderID="TitleContent" runat="server">
    <%
        var forecastModel = (Forecast) ViewData.Model;
    %>
    Forecast for <%= forecastModel.Location %>
</asp:Content>

<asp:Content ID="mainContent" ContentPlaceHolderID="MainContent" runat="server">

    <%
        var forecastModel = (Forecast) ViewData.Model;
    %>
    <table><tr>
    <td>
```

```
    <div id="weatherIcon">
        <img src="../../Content/<%=
SkyTypeRenderer.ToImageFileName(forecastModel.Skies) %>.gif" alt="<%=
SkyTypeRenderer.ToWeatherString(forecastModel.Skies) %> Graphic" />
    </div>
    <div id="weatherText">
        <%= SkyTypeRenderer.ToWeatherString(forecastModel.Skies)%>
    </div>
    </td>
    <td>
    <div id="weatherIntroText">We are forecasting that the weather in <%=
forecastModel.Location %> will be:</div>
    <div id="averageTemperatureDisplay">
        <%= forecastModel.AverageTemperature %> degrees with <%=
SkyTypeRenderer.ToWeatherString(forecastModel.Skies)%>
    </div>
    Consider wearing <%= AttireRenderer.ToAttireString(forecastModel.ToAttire()) %>
    </td>
    </tr></table>
    <%= Html.ActionLink("Back to Index","Index","Forecast") %>
</asp:Content>
```

*Code snippet Views/Forecast/For.aspx*

Again, this is being done in C#, but doing so using the minimum of executable code. Starting with the title part of the page, it starts off with a user friendly title so that when the end user has multiple browser windows open, they will know which one is the Forecast page. ViewData.Model carries an object that represents the thing that the page should bind to. In this case, to make this work a strongly typed reference to the model is useful:

```
<%
    var forecastModel = (Forecast) ViewData.Model;
%>
```

This allows the following snippet that sets the title text to be written:

```
Forecast for <%= forecastModel.Location %>
```

The body of the page is a little more work. Note that each page content area, delimited by <asp:Content> tags, has independent scope, so it is necessary to put in a strongly typed declaration for forecastModel again:

```
<%
    var forecastModel = (Forecast) ViewData.Model;
%>
```

The first bit of code that is encountered is for the icon used to display the weather. The view helper has a routine to provide the name of a file. The page is going to leverage that to provide the html that will be used to show the image:

```
    <div id="weatherIcon">
        <img src="../../Content/<%=
SkyTypeRenderer.ToImageFileName(forecastModel.Skies) %>.gif" alt="<%=
SkyTypeRenderer.ToWeatherString(forecastModel.Skies) %> Graphic" />
    </div>
```

In this case, the code is appending the string for the image file to the Content path and then adding .gif at the end. Like all good web citizens, the site provides alt text as well that leverages the `ToWeatherString` method that was written in the view helper so that the site has a text representation of the image as well.

The same code will be used to generate alt text for the weather headline:

```
<div id="weatherText">
    <%= SkyTypeRenderer.ToWeatherString(forecastModel.Skies)%>
</div>
```

Again, the page is using the `SkyTypeRenderer` to translate from a logical type of weather represented by `forecastModel.Skies` to the actual string the page should use for rendering.

The next couple sections follow the same pattern:

```
<div id="weatherIntroText">We are forecasting that the weather in <%=
forecastModel.Location %> will be:</div>
    <div id="averageTemperatureDisplay">
        <%= forecastModel.AverageTemperature %> degrees with <%=
SkyTypeRenderer.ToWeatherString(forecastModel.Skies)%>
    </div>
```

*Code snippet Views/Forecast/For.aspx*

The last section is where a clothing recommendation is made. Again, the logic is not terribly complex; just render the model:

```
Consider wearing <%= AttireRenderer.ToAttireString(forecastModel.ToAttire()) %>
```

If the view is much more complex than this, say, rendering a simple domain model, it might be advisable to write a ViewModel — and some classes to convert from the more complex domain to a ViewModel so that the chance of that complex logic getting added to the view is minimized. Code that goes in views tends to not be reused and tends to allow concerns that are not specific to a particular view to leak into views, leading to duplication and difficult maintenance.

## SUMMARY

In this chapter, we learned how to leverage F# in our ASP.NET MVC applications — and in so doing, use F# and the fact that F# discourages mutation to our advantage in building a simple yet robust website. One of the striking things you will notice in our implementation of a simple ASP.NET MVC site is that there are zero cases where we change the value of a variable once assigned. A reality of web development is that state across multiple requests, although sometimes useful, is not an inherent part of the medium, like it is on an ordinary WinForm or WPF application. If you have little or no state, each request action type becomes like a separate program with a much more limited scope. Although this does not make bugs go away, it does provide a layer of isolation between the details of various requests, making the code for any given action easier to understand, manage, and test.

# 22

# Silverlight

**WHAT'S IN THIS CHAPTER?**

➤  Working with Visual Studio Project Templates

➤  Using the Silverlight Toolkit

➤  Working with data binding

Silverlight is one of the most popular new facets of .NET and is used to broadcast the Olympic Games, Netflix HD streaming, and financial analyst dashboards and is quickly gaining popularity as a principal enterprise application development platform. Silverlight is a web browser plug-in runtime environment for executing .NET code. Originally dubbed WPF/E for Windows Presentation Framework Everywhere, Silverlight offers a powerful vector-based presentation engine for creating dynamic content. Most development in Silverlight is done in C# or VB.NET. But because the underlying runtime environment is a special CLR that is compatible with F# code, a few tweaks can unleash the full power of F# in Silverlight applications.

## OVERVIEW

Silverlight is a Rich Internet Application (RIA) platform for developing both enterprise and public Web-based applications. Silverlight 3 and later versions include support for out-of-browser applications and network status awareness for enabling offline mode. Silverlight 4 supports printing, local fonts, webcam, microphone, group policy object support, and many other features that make it an excellent platform for both Web and enterprise development.

The recommended architecture for Silverlight development separates the application into two tiers not including the database tier. The client tier includes presentation logic, for example client-side validation and animation, plus potentially some client-side business logic needed for lightweight calculations to reduce round trips to the server. See Figure 22-1. The application server tier includes server side validation, business logic, and database interaction. The client tier is implemented in Silverlight and deployed as a XAP file that is executed in the Silverlight CLR runtime in the browser. The application server tier can be implemented using RIA Services or any number of service platforms including Azure, XML Web Services, and OData. Sensitive intellectual property is one consideration when determining where to place the business logic. Also, data that requires secure access should be filtered on the server. For example, it would not be wise to cache project names on the client if the user is not allowed to have access to them. The business logic to filter the project names would run on the application server.

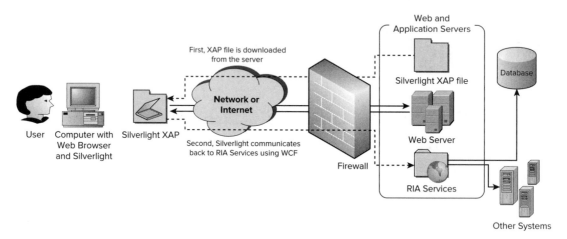

**FIGURE 22-1**

By leveraging the processing power of the user's computer to handle any quick response of presentation data, Silverlight has an advantage over other web development platforms such as ASP.NET. Because the CLR is multithreaded and GPU-accelerated, it also is a richer development platform than Flash. Because of F#'s built-in constructs such as asynchronous workflows, F# can easily take full advantage of Silverlight's multithreading capability on the client, exploiting the increasing number of cores per system produced by the many-core era of computing.

Using Isolated Storage, a Silverlight application can cache data and user preferences on the client machine for offline use or quicker responsiveness while the application connects to the backend systems. Be aware though, it is wise to keep sensitive data, sensitive logic, and intellectual property behind the firewall. A XAP file is just a ZIP file with a different name, and the contents can be reverse engineered. Enterprise applications built on Silverlight may present less concern regarding reverse engineering if only employees can access and download the Silverlight application as opposed to a publicly accessible application hosted on the Web open to anyone with an Internet connection. During the system design phase, it is important to plan how and where the code executes in a Silverlight application. Proper planning and architecture accounts for security, scalability, and performance.

## Software Runtime and Developer Requirements

As mentioned earlier, Silverlight is a web browser plug-in runtime environment for executing .NET code. It uses a special CLR that is portable on both Windows and Macintosh computers. Also, through the Mono project called Moonlight, Silverlight is also available unofficially on Linux. Officially, Silverlight 3 and 4 are supported on Windows XP through Windows 7 in IE 7, IE 8, and Google Chrome. For the Mac, Silverlight 3 is supported in Safari on Intel hardware. The following table shows official support for Silverlight versions:

|  | IE 6 SP2 | IE 7 & 8 | Firefox 3 | Safari | Google Chrome |
|---|---|---|---|---|---|
| **Windows Vista/7** |  | Silverlight 1, 2, 3, and 4 |  | Silverlight 1 and 2 | Silverlight 2, 3, and 4 |
| **Windows XP/2003** | Silverlight 1, 2, 3, and 4 | Silverlight 1, 2, 3, and 4 |  | Silverlight 1 and 2 | Silverlight 2, 3, and 4 |
| **Mac OS 10.4/10.5 Intel** |  |  | Silverlight 1, 2, and 3 | Silverlight 1, 2, and 3 |  |

Silverlight 1.0 released to Web in 2007 only supported JavaScript. Since Silverlight 2, released in 2008, Silverlight has included a .NET runtime environment. Because Silverlight requires a special lightweight CLR, a compiler target is required to generate Silverlight-compatible MSIL. Visual Studio provides templates for making the build process easier.

Visual Studio 2010 includes a project template called the "F# Silverlight Library" for creating code that can execute in the browser in a Silverlight application. Unfortunately, Visual Studio 2010 does not include a template for building the entire Silverlight application in F#, but it is possible to use C# or VB.NET templates to build the Silverlight application project and reference an F# class library for all the logic. An F# Silverlight application template written by Dmitry Lomov, a developer on the F# team, has been available on MSDN Code Gallery with limitations and documented issues. Perhaps as it continues to mature it will be included in one of the Silverlight or F# releases.

One of the best free extensions for developing Silverlight is the Silverlight Toolkit. The Silverlight Toolkit from CodePlex provides rich graphing tools and controls for building Silverlight applications. Additional Silverlight controls are also available from various third-party component venders.

F# Silverlight development with Visual Studio 2008 requires the F# CTP and the Microsoft Silverlight 3 Tools for Visual Studio 2008 SP1 found on Microsoft Download Center plus Luke Hoban's "F# for Silverlight" project templates for Silverlight 3.0 found on MSDN Code Gallery at

```
http://code.msdn.microsoft.com/fsharpsilverlight
```

Depending on which version of Visual Studio will be used for development (2008 or 2010) and which version of Silverlight (3 or 4) is targeted, various downloads are required. Note that Silverlight 4 development is not supported on Visual Studio 2008. Figure 22-2 shows the necessary components.

| Visual Studio 2008 SP1 | Visual Studio 2010 | |
|---|---|---|
| **Silverlight 3 Development** | **Silverlight 4 Development** | |
| F# 2.0 CTP **(download from Microsoft Download Center)** | (Visual Studio 2010 includes F#) | |
| Silverlight 3 Tools for Visual Studio 2008 SP1 **(download from Microsoft Download Center)** <br> • Includes SDK <br><br> F# Silverlight templates for Silverlight 3.0 **(download from code.msdn.microsoft.com)** | (Visual Studio 2010 includes Silverlight 3 and the F# Runtime for Silverlight 3 as well as F# Silverlight Library project template) | Silverlight 4 Tools for Visual Studio 2010 **(download from Microsoft Download Center)** <br> • Includes SDK <br> • Includes F# Runtime for Silverlight 4 |
| Silverlight 3 Toolkit November 2009 **(download from CodePlex)** | | Silverlight 4 Toolkit **(download from CodePlex)** |

**FIGURE 22-2**

# VISUAL STUDIO PROJECT TEMPLATES

The key project template in Visual Studio that hosts the XAML files and builds the XAP file is called the Silverlight Application project template. The template for a Silverlight application creates two projects, one for building the Silverlight XAP file and another for building a web site that will host the Silverlight binaries and any services needed for communicating back to the server from the client application.

The C# or VB Silverlight application includes XAML files for laying out the user interface. Silverlight and WPF (Windows Presentation Framework) both use XAML for user interface development. There are only minor differences between Silverlight and WPF and, in fact, it is possible to write applications that can be compiled into both Silverlight and WPF. The similarities between the two are no accident; the original name for Silverlight was WPF/E or Windows Presentation Framework Everywhere. So skills gained from using one framework easily translate to the other.

The web site project by default includes an ASP.NET page for testing the Silverlight application, even though Silverlight does not require ASP.NET for hosting, only HTML. This project template is handy for rapid application development, because it facilitates building and running a Silverlight application and automatically connecting the debugger to both the web server process in the Visual Studio "Cassini" service and the Silverlight process on the browser. It also deploys the XAP file to a ClientBin folder that the HTML references.

When the build environment is set up, creating some sample data in F# and binding it to a chart provides a basic understanding of the chart tools. To demonstrate the ease and power of combining F# and Silverlight, this chapter demonstrates how to manipulate the chart by running the data through a moving average algorithm implemented in an F# function in just three lines of code. Moving average is often used in financial applications to visualize trends when the data series is volatile and erratic. F# provides not only a great way to express and manipulate data, but also to analyze data. Combined with Silverlight, F# can be a powerful tool for manipulating and visualizing data.

# The Silverlight Application

A Silverlight application template is a special Visual Studio project template that compiles and builds into a package designed to run in the browser in the Silverlight runtime. The project includes XAML (XML for describing the UI), .NET assemblies, and other resources such as images that are packaged into a XAP file to be deployed to a web server. The XAP file is downloaded by a browser using HTML tags referencing the XAP file on the Web server. When the XAP file has been downloaded by the browser, it executes the XAP in a special .NET CLR designed to be portable across operating systems including Macintosh and Linux. This model is similar to other browser plug-ins such as the JVM (Java Virtual Machine) and Adobe Flash.

 *One major advantage for F# programmers that Silverlight has over Flash is that it allows an F# developer to use a single language for both browser client logic and server side logic. This reduces the need for JavaScript, AJAX, and other client-side scripting languages and frameworks. It also allows for better usage of client-side resources such as Memory and CPU.*

## Creating the Silverlight Application

For both C# and VB there are three Visual Studio project templates in the Silverlight category:

➤ Silverlight Application

➤ Silverlight Class Library

➤ Silverlight Navigation Application

The first template is the simplest template to get a full Silverlight application started. It includes two XAML files (one for the application in general and one for the page.) The second template, the C#/VB Silverlight Class Library, is equivalent to the F# Silverlight Library template. The third template is useful for applications that require multiple screens by providing a navigation framework using the Visual State Manager from the `System.Windows` namespace in Silverlight 3 and .NET 4. The navigation application template is useful when building multiple page navigation without the overhead of browser post backs and full-page reloads.

The Silverlight Application Template Wizard prompts for the version of Silverlight. Visual Studio 2010 includes only Silverlight 3. Silverlight 4 Tools for Visual Studio 2010 is required for Silverlight 4 development. With Visual Studio 2008, the Visual Studio Tools can be installed to support Silverlight 3 (not 4.) The examples in this book use Silverlight 3 but will work with Silverlight 4 without any changes. The result of the Template Wizard is a single solution with two projects. Both projects by default have the same name except the web project has a .Web suffix to distinguish between the Silverlight application (which creates the XAP file) and the website hosting the application (hosting the XAP, HTML and/or ASPX, and other server-side services such as RIA Services or web services.) In fact, this second project is optional because the first project can be compiled and run in Visual Studio without a website project. The web project is unnecessary because, when the Silverlight application is set as the startup project instead of the .Web project, and is started with F5, a test HTML page is placed in the bin directory and Visual Studio launches a browser/debugger instance for debugging the XAP file.

In the Solution Explorer, the Silverlight project includes two XAML files: App.xaml and MainPage .xaml. These two files include code behind written in C# (or VB.) A later example in this chapter includes only a single line of C# required to delegate all the work to an F# library.

## XAP

When the Silverlight project is compiled, the build process packages it into a XAP file. As mentioned previously, the XAP file is actually a zip file with a .xap extension. Changing the extension to .zip facilitates the ability to examine the contents. In fact, this technique is often handy when debugging deployment issues.

### Testing Silverlight in the Browser

The web project includes two TestPage files in the Solution Explorer, one ASPX TestPage (ASP.NET) and the other HTML. It doesn't matter which one is used, but initially the ASPX page is set as the default startup page. The Set As Start Page in the context-sensitive menu can be used to switch between the two. After the project is built, the web project includes a folder called ClientBin where the build process copies the XAP file created by building the Silverlight project.

With Visual Studio 2010, the designer window for the MainPage.xaml starts out with a blank rectangular surface, 300 pixels by 400 pixels, ready for UI components. One way to confirm that the build process is working and the Silverlight prerequisites are installed and configured properly is to drag a Button control from the toolbox onto the surface, place it in the top-left corner, and hit F5 to run the application. If everything is working properly and the build is successful, a browser window pops up with a single button on the page.

Visual Studio 2008 may require manipulation of the XML directly or a designer tool such as Microsoft Expression to lay out the components visually. To add the button directly in the XML, place a Button element inside the Grid element (between the `<Grid x:Name="LayoutRoot">` tag and the `</Grid>` tag):

```
<Button Content="Button" Height="23" HorizontalAlignment="Left"
Margin="14,14,0,0" Name="button1" VerticalAlignment="Top" Width="75" />
```

## XAML

XAML is an XML implementation that stands for eXtensible Application Markup Language and is used in Silverlight applications to describe the UI elements, layout, and behavior such as animation.

The XAML file includes a code-behind file in a similar fashion to Web Forms. The XML is used to declare the graphical components such as buttons and charts and important attributes including name and type.

Examining the XAML for MainPage.xaml created in the previous section reveals:

```
<UserControl x:Class="SilverlightAppTest.MainPage"
 xmlns="http://schemas.microsoft.com/winfx/2006/xaml/presentation"
 xmlns:x="http://schemas.microsoft.com/winfx/2006/xaml"
 xmlns:d=http://schemas.microsoft.com/expression/blend/2008
 xmlns:mc="http://schemas.openxmlformats.org/markup-compatibility/2006"
 mc:Ignorable="d"
 d:DesignWidth="640"
 d:DesignHeight="480">
  <Grid x:Name="LayoutRoot">
    <Button Content="Button"
            Height="23"
            HorizontalAlignment="Left"
            Margin="14,14,0,0"
            Name="button1"
            VerticalAlignment="Top"
            Width="75" />
  </Grid>
</UserControl>
```

The XAML for this user control includes several namespaces that need to be added to in order to support additional controls and libraries. The UserControl element is the root XML document element and contains all the other elements. The Grid element has a name attribute assigned the value LayoutRoot that is used in examples later in this chapter to pass to F# a handle on the UI. Inside the grid is the button added in the previous section. The button contains attributes to describe its size and position, but most important has a name attribute that is used inside F# for acquiring a handle to this component to register events such as the Click event.

After the basic Silverlight build environment is prepped, it is easy to start building an F# Silverlight Library and get instant feedback verifying that the Silverlight Library is functioning properly in the Silverlight CLR.

## The F# Silverlight Library

The F# Silverlight Library is similar to an F# Library except that the build script targets the Silverlight CLR, which has more limitations than full .NET CLR. Because it is targeted at the Silverlight CLR, this project cannot be referenced from other non-Silverlight projects.

The library project can include Silverlight event handling code, application logic, service calls to the host server, and all the Silverlight application code. It is possible to build the entire Silverlight UI in F# as well, although because Silverlight utilizes XAML for presentation separation to enable designer tools such as Microsoft Expression that enable parallel graphic design and development by separate teams, it is wise to refrain from UI code as much as possible by implanting it declaratively in XML.

To verify that the F# Silverlight Library is wired up properly and executing in the browser, create a simple `HelloWorld` function in the Module1.fs provided by the project template and call the function from the Silverlight application.

```
module Module1

let HelloFromFsharp =
    "hello from F# at " + System.DateTime.Now.ToString()
```

Reference the Silverlight library from the Silverlight application project and add an event handler to the button. This can be done by double-clicking a button added to the designer surface in Visual Studio 2010 and adding the following line of code to the event hander generated by the designer:

```
button1.Content = Module1.HelloFromFsharp;
```

For Visual Studio 2008, wire up the event handler using XML in the XAML by adding the following attribute and value to the Button element.

```
Click="button1_Click"
```

Then in the code-behind for the `MainPage`, add a method in C# to handle the event:

```
private void button1_Click(object sender, RoutedEventArgs e)
{
    button1.Content = Module1.HelloFromFsharp;
}
```

To move the event handler over to F#, pass a root object in the XAML tree such as the `UserControl` and find the controls to register events as demonstrated later in the `WireUpEvents` function. With a reference to a control, event handlers can be added using F# as follows:

```
control.EventName.Add( fun(_) ->
    // event handler code here
    )
```

The `UserControl` along with all controls inheriting from `System.Windows.FrameworkElement` in Silverlight include a useful method to find a control by name called `FindName`. A downcast to the control type needed is required:

```
let button1 : Button = downcast container.FindName("button1")
```

Wire up the controls by finding them and then adding event handlers.

```
static member WireUpEvents (container:UserControl) =
    let button1 : Button = downcast container.FindName("button1")
    button1.Click.Add(fun(_) ->
        button1.Content <- Module1.HelloFromFsharp
        )
```

Now the C# code in the Silverlight application can be a one line of code addition in the `MainPage` partial class constructor, after `InitializeComponent`:

```
public MainPage()
{
    InitializeComponent();
    SilverlightEvents.WireUpEvents(this.LayoutRoot);
}
```

The full source for the SilverlightEvents.fs file contains a namespace and an open statement to qualify the Silverlight controls:

```
namespace FSharpPro

open System.Windows.Controls

type SilverlightEvents() =
    static member WireUpEvents (container:UserControl) =
        let button1 : Button =
            downcast container.FindName("button1")

        button1.Click.Add(fun(_) ->
            button1.Content <- Module1.HelloFromFsharp
            )
```

## Unit Testing F# Silverlight Library

The previous section described how to build a Silverlight application using a C# template that can be used to test a Silverlight Library. Good unit tests exclude dependencies and focus only on a single unit of functionality. Unfortunately, because the Silverlight Library is compiled to DLL (.NET Assembly) that can only be referenced by Silverlight applications, simply referencing this project from a test project will not build. One technique to test the F# Silverlight Library without using the Silverlight application is to create a regular F# Library and place a file link in the project to each F# source file in the Silverlight Library. This new project includes all of the source code but has settings to compile it against the regular CLR. The new library can be referenced to build and run other test projects using any .NET testing library including NUnit or Visual Studio Team Test.

The Silverlight Toolkit includes unit testing templates for C# and VB for Silverlight projects. These could also be used to test an F# Silverlight Library.

# THE SILVERLIGHT TOOLKIT

To use the chart controls described next, download and install the Silverlight toolkit from CodePlex located at http://www.codeplex.com/Silverlight.

There are two versions of the Toolkit: one for Silverlight 3 and one for Silverlight 4. Download the appropriate one or both if needed and install them.

The Silverlight Toolkit offers a full set of rich controls including mature components such as the DatePicker, TabControl, and TreeView. It also includes data visualization controls for creating scatter, pie, bubble bar, and line charts.

As mentioned earlier, the toolkit also includes a Silverlight Unit Test Application project template for C# and VB.

## Line Charts and Area Charts

Line charts are fairly straightforward to work with. Simply place a chart on the XAML surface, and add a LineSeries to it. To create an area chart, simply use an AreaSeries instead of a

LineSeries. The `LineSeries` can be declared with XAML, loaded from a static resource at design time, or created at runtime programmatically. See Figure 22-3 for an example of a line chart.

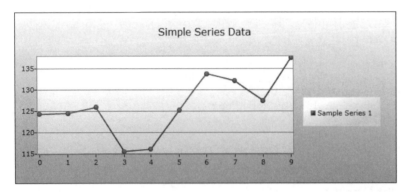

**FIGURE 22-3**

To add the chart to the user control, an XML namespace is added to the `UserControl` element.

```
xmlns:chartingToolkit="clr-
namespace:System.Windows.Controls.DataVisualization.
Charting;assembly=System.Windows.Controls.DataVisualization.Toolkit"
```

Then add the `Chart` element to the contents of the `Grid` element.

```
<chartingToolkit:Chart
    Title="Chart Title"
    Name="chart1"
    Margin="12,41,12,0"
    Height="274">
</chartingToolkit:Chart>
```

XAML is used to declaratively add a line series using a point collection by placing it inside the `Chart` element. Visual Studio 2010 automatically displays the chart in the designer (see Figure 22-4).

```
<chartingToolkit:LineSeries
    DependentValuePath="Y"
    IndependentValuePath="X">
    <chartingToolkit:LineSeries.ItemsSource>
        <PointCollection>
            <Point>0,15</Point>
            <Point>35,5</Point>
            <Point>60,3</Point>
            <Point>75,35</Point>
            <Point>100,50</Point>
        </PointCollection>
    </chartingToolkit:LineSeries.ItemsSource>
</chartingToolkit:LineSeries>
```

## Designer Tools

Visual Studio 2010 includes a built-in designer to enable WYSIWYG (what you see is what you get) design of the Silverlight XAML. (See Figure 22-5.) This allows for adjusting the background gradients and other design elements for getting rapid feedback without rebuilding and running the application in the browser.

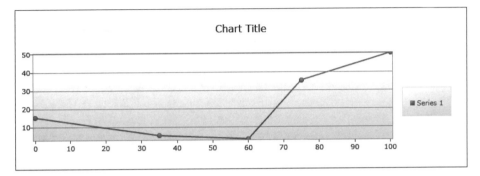

**FIGURE 22-4**

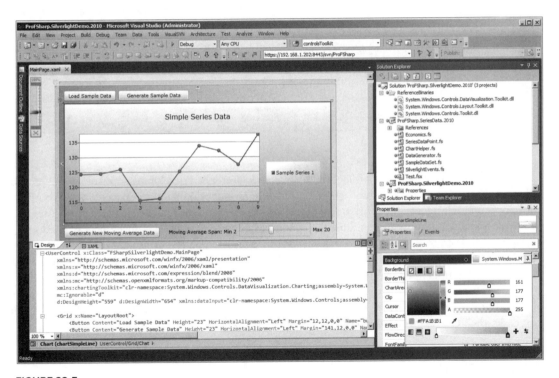

**FIGURE 22-5**

With Visual Studio 2008 there is no XAML designer for Silverlight built in. Expression Blend allows designers to open Visual Studio solution files and modify the XAML and even launch the application without Visual Studio (see Figure 22-6). It is possible to use Expression Blend as a designer tool to get the same WYSIWYG functionality found in Visual Studio 2010 and in some ways more.

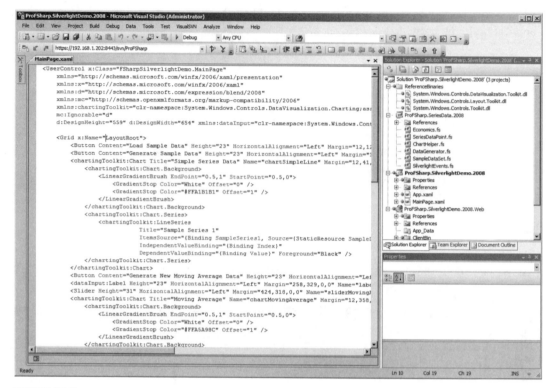

**FIGURE 22-6**

Expression Blend 3 is targeted at Visual Studio 2008 and Silverlight 3 development and design. Expression Blend 4 is targeted at Visual Studio 2010 and Silverlight 4 development and design. When both developers and designers can work on the same files at the same time, there is more opportunity to work together and provide rapid feedback and development cycles. If a developer is also doing design work, both tools can be used together at the same time on the same solution. When switching between Visual Studio and Expression Blend, each tool prompts when the other updates. This prompt can be suppressed in Visual Studio under Tools ➪ Options so that Visual Studio automatically detects and updates the display without nagging dialogs. There is no such setting in Expression Blend. But if Expression Blend is used for XAML modification and Visual Studio is used for writing F# code, then the two work together quite nicely when used in concert.

## DATA BINDING

Data binding in Silverlight (as with WPF) can be done declaratively using XAML or programmatically using the Binding class.

## Design Time Data Binding

One nice aspect of Silverlight is the ability to bind data at design time. This can be helpful for designers to understand what the application looks like with sample data. To bind chart data at design time, one approach is to provide a series of points that can be loaded by Visual Studio 2010's designer. A series data point can be defined using a type with object-oriented members. Note that it is possible to make these data points immutable. The following sample F# code defines a data type to store each data point:

```
type SeriesDataPoint(index, value) =
    member this.Index with get() = index
    member this.Value with get() = value
```

A sample data set modeled after the C# samples provided in the following Silverlight Toolkit example exposes a static member that can be loaded by the XAML designer. This uses an `ObjectCollection` instance (from the `System.Windows.Controls` namespace) with 10 data points using the `SeriesDataPoint` type defined earlier. A reference to the `System.Windows.Controls .Toolkit` assembly is required to access the `ObjectCollection` type.

Available for download on Wrox.com

```
open System.Windows.Controls

type SampleDataSet() =
    static member SampleSeries =
        let data = new ObjectCollection()
        data.Add(new SeriesDataPoint(0, 124.1))
        data.Add(new SeriesDataPoint(1, 124.3))
        data.Add(new SeriesDataPoint(2, 125.7))
        data.Add(new SeriesDataPoint(3, 115.4))
        data.Add(new SeriesDataPoint(4, 115.9))
        data.Add(new SeriesDataPoint(5, 125.0))
        data.Add(new SeriesDataPoint(6, 133.6))
        data.Add(new SeriesDataPoint(7, 131.9))
        data.Add(new SeriesDataPoint(8, 127.3))
        data.Add(new SeriesDataPoint(9, 137.3))
        data
```

*Code Snippet SilverlightDataSet.fs*

For the XAML designer to load this `ObjectCollection`, declare the `SampleDataSet` class as a resource in the App.xaml file.

## Adding a Resource to the Application XAML Element

To provide design time binding, the `Application.Resource` element must be added to the Silverlight application using XAML. Modifying the App.xaml file, which is provided by the Silverlight Application template, results in the following XAML:

Available for download on Wrox.com

```
<Application
xmlns="http://schemas.microsoft.com/winfx/2006/xaml/presentation"
            xmlns:x="http://schemas.microsoft.com/winfx/2006/xaml"
            x:Class="FSharpSilverlightDemo.App"
            >
    <Application.Resources>
        <!-- put resources here -->
    </Application.Resources>
</Application>
```

*Code Snippet App.xaml*

An additional XML Namespace to reference the `SampleDataSet` type applied to the `Application` element is required to load the data. Note that this XML namespace includes the CLR namespace and the assembly name.

```
xmlns:sampleData="clr-
namespace:ProFSharp.SeriesData;assembly=ProFSharp.SeriesData"
```

When the XML namespace has been properly added to the App.xaml file, then it is possible to insert the resource. This allows referencing the `SampleDataSet` class in the MainPage.xaml for design time binding.

```
<Application.Resources>
    <sampleData:SampleDataSet x:Key="SampleDataSet"/>
</Application.Resources>
```

Finally to see what the chart looks like at design time, include a `LineSeries` element with binding to the `SampleDataSet.SampleSeries` member using the curly brace syntax `{Binding SampleSeries, Source={StaticResource SampleDataSet}}`

```
<chartingToolkit:Chart
   Title="Simple Series Data"
   Name="chart1"
   Margin="12,41,12,0"
   Height="274">
   <chartingToolkit:Chart.Series>
     <chartingToolkit:LineSeries
       Title="Sample Series 1"
       ItemsSource="{Binding SampleSeries,
           Source={StaticResource SampleDataSet}}"
       IndependentValueBinding="{Binding Index}"
       DependentValueBinding="{Binding Value}" />
   </chartingToolkit:Chart.Series>
</chartingToolkit:Chart>
```

*Code Snippet MainPage.xaml*

In the preceding example, the `IndependentValueBinding` attribute binds the line series to the `Index` property of the `SeriesDataPoint` class. The `DependentValueBinding` attribute binds the `Value` property. With these two properties, the chart can display the points on a Cartesian coordinate system with an x- and y-axis. The `Index` is plotted on the x-axis and the `Value` on the y-axis.

```
type SeriesDataPoint(index, value) =
    member this.Index with get() = index //IndependentValueBinding
    member this.Value with get() = value //DependentValueBinding
```

When compiled, the XAML designer in Visual Studio 2010 can load the static resource and bind the series to the chart. Note that Visual Studio 2008 does not have designer support, so this chart will not be visible without running the application. If a development team is limited to Visual Studio 2008 for Silverlight 3 development, design time support can be found in Expression Blend 3. Expression Blend 4 is designed to work with Visual Studio 2010 solutions.

## Programmatic Data Binding

To add a series programmatically at runtime to the chart, assign the data (the `ObjectCollection`) to the `LineSeries.ItemSource` property. The following code defines a helper function to bind the `DependentValueBinding` to the `"Value"` property and the `IndepenentValueBinding` to the `"Index"` property. Note that this helper function takes the data as a parameter:

```
namespace ProFSharp.ChartHelper

open System.Windows.Controls.DataVisualization.Charting
open System.Windows.Data //for data binding

type DataConverter =
    static member CreateLineSeries title data =
        let series = new LineSeries()
        series.ItemsSource <- data
        series.DependentValueBinding <- new Binding("Value")
        series.IndependentValueBinding <- new Binding("Index")
        series.Title <- title
        series
```

Following is an example of adding another event handler and wiring up a button to add a second line series from a second static sample series using the helper function previously defined:

```
buttonLoadSampleData.Click.Add(fun(_) ->
    let data = SampleDataSet.SampleSeries2
    let series = DataConverter.CreateLineSeries "Series 2" data
    chart.Series.Add(series)
    )
```

Adding a series to a chart automatically updates the Silverlight display. The problem with using this approach to update an existing chart is that it requires that the series be cleared and a new series created and added to the chart. This approach causes the new series to appear in a different color, because the chart assumes that it is a whole new series. To modify a series in place, and have Silverlight Toolkit chart animate the change, the `SeriesDataPoint` must implement the `INotifyPropertyChanged` interface:

```
namespace ProFSharp.ChartHelper

open System.ComponentModel

type SeriesDataPoint(index:int, value:float) =
    let mutable v = value
    let propertyChanged = Event<_, _>()

    member this.Index
        with get() = index
    member this.Value
        with get() = v
        and set(value) =
            v <- value
```

```
        propertyChanged.Trigger(this,
            PropertyChangedEventArgs("Value"))
    interface INotifyPropertyChanged with
        [<CLIEvent>]
        member this.PropertyChanged = propertyChanged.Publish
```

*Code Snippet SeriesDataPoint.fs*

The `INotifyPropertyChanged` interface contains only one member, the `PropertyChanged` event. One way to implement this event is using the `CLIEventAttribute` to decorate the event and use the event `Publish` property to publish the event. A setter has been added to the `Value` property to make the `SeriesDataPoint` mutable. In the preceding example, if a change is made to the `"Value"` property, the setter triggers the event using the `Trigger` method and passes the property name as part of the `EventArgs`.

If the Silverlight Toolkit sample application is executed, several charts update by themselves every two seconds. This effect was accomplished by implementing the `INotifyPropertyChanged` interface. With a framework for updating the graph, now it is possible to visualize some interesting data manipulation using the Silverlight Toolkit.

## CALCULATING MOVING AVERAGE

Data by itself can be interesting to visualize, but often the trends or patterns in data can be more useful. In the financial sector and in economics, the moving average is a common model often applied to time series data to assist analysts in understanding trends and help predict future directions of a series. But looking for patterns in data can be useful for a range of solutions including security attack detection or business intelligence applications. An algorithm for calculating moving average in F# takes the data and chunks it into windows and calculates the average of each window:

**Available for download on Wrox.com**

```
let MovingAverage period data =
    Seq.windowed period data
    |> Seq.map Array.average

let testdata = [1.0 .. 10.0]
let result = MovingAverage 4 testdata
```

*Code Snippet Economics.fs*

The output of these three `let` statements to the F# Interpreter are:

```
val MovingAverage : int -> seq<float> -> seq<float>
val testdata : float list =
  [1.0; 2.0; 3.0; 4.0; 5.0; 6.0; 7.0; 8.0; 9.0; 10.0]
val result : seq<float>
```

Viewing the result in FSI displays the first few items in the sequence.

```
> result;;
val it : seq<float> = seq [2.5; 3.5; 4.5; 5.5; ...]
>
```

The result is a moving average based on the period applied. The average of the first four points are $(1 + 2 + 3 + 4) / 4 = 2.5$, which is the first value of the series result. The second set is $(2 + 3 + 4 + 5) / 4 = 3.5$ and so on through the sequence. The Seq.windowed function returns a sequence that produces sliding windows of the input elements as arrays of the size specified.

If the testdata value contains ten elements (the floating point numbers 1 through 10) then Seq.windowed 4 testdata returns ten arrays each containing four elements:

```
> Seq.windowed 4 testdata;;
val it : seq<float []> =
  seq
    [[|1.0; 2.0; 3.0; 4.0|]; [|2.0; 3.0; 4.0; 5.0|];
     [|3.0; 4.0; 5.0; 6.0|]; [|4.0; 5.0; 6.0; 7.0|]; ...]
>
```

Take that sequence of windows and using the pipe forward operator, pipe it into the Seq.map function to apply the average of each array.

```
Seq.windowed period data
|> Seq.map Array.average
```

Overlaying the moving average on the chart provides an augmented view of the original data. Using a slider control or other input control, the user interface can provide input for the moving average period function and provide a parameter to animate the chart.

## PUTTING IT ALL TOGETHER

Using a C# or VB Silverlight Application project to host the XAML and build the XAP file, an F# Silverlight Library project to put all the application logic, and the Silverlight Toolkit to provide visualization, the application framework is ready to generate some interesting charting. Leveraging the INotifyPropertyChanged to provide animation to the data points and a slider control to give the user the ability to change the range of the moving average period window, the following example puts together a MovingAverageModel to store the SeriesDataPoint collection as a generic List. When the UpdateSeries method is called as a result of a mouse event, a new moving average is calculated and the data point Value property is updated.

```
type internal MovingAverageModel(chart:Chart, slider:Slider) =
    // used for animated data bining
    let mutable m_dynamicItemsSource =
        new System.Collections.Generic.List<SeriesDataPoint>()
    // stores the original data
    let mutable m_data = []
    // stores the moving average range (window size)
    let mutable m_range = 1

    member private this.GetMovingAverageSeries movingAverage =
        let title = String.Format("{0} Moving Average", m_range)
        DataConverter.ConvertSequenceToAreaSeries title movingAverage

    member private this.InitSeries =
        chart.Series.Clear()
        // generate moving average using range and data
```

```
    let movingAverage = MovingAverage m_range m_data
    // build both AreaSeries sets
    let series1 =
        DataConverter.ConvertSequenceToAreaSeries "Original Data" m_data
    let series2 = this.GetMovingAverageSeries movingAverage
    chart.Series.Add(series1)
    // generate dynamic item source used for animated data binding
    let array = List.toArray(m_data)
    let max = array.Length - 1
    for i in 0..max do
        m_dynamicItemsSource.Add(new SeriesDataPoint(i, array.[i]))
    series2.ItemsSource <- m_dynamicItemsSource
    chart.Series.Add(series2)
    this.UpdateSeries()
    ()

member this.Init() =
    //initialize members
    m_dynamicItemsSource <-
        new System.Collections.Generic.List<SeriesDataPoint>()
    m_range <- (int slider.Value)
    m_data <- List.ofSeq <| GenerateData 200.0 50.0 50
    this.InitSeries

//naive forcast algorithm based on historical flow
member internal this.Forcast last index =
    let distance = index - last + 2
    let pastPoint = m_dynamicItemsSource.Item(last - distance)
    let lastPoint = m_dynamicItemsSource.Item(last - 1)
    let trend = lastPoint.Value - pastPoint.Value
    lastPoint.Value + trend

member internal this.UpdateSeries() =
    m_range <- (int slider.Value)
    let movingAverage = MovingAverage m_range m_data |> Seq.toList
    for point in m_dynamicItemsSource do
        if point.Index < movingAverage.Length then
            point.Value <- movingAverage.Item(point.Index)
        else
            point.Value <- this.Forcast movingAverage.Length point.Index
        ()
    let legend = chart.Series.[1].LegendItems.Item(0) :?> LegendItem
    legend.Content <- m_range.ToString() + " Moving Average"
    ()

member
this.UpdateMovingAverage(args:RoutedPropertyChangedEventArgs<float>) =
    let oldVal = int args.OldValue
    let newVal = int args.NewValue
    if oldVal = newVal then
        ()
    elif (Math.Abs(oldVal - newVal) > 4) then
        m_range <- newVal
        this.UpdateSeries()
```

```
            ()
    else
        m_range <- newVal
            ()
```

*Code Snippet SilverlightEvents.fs*

To complete the application, wire up the model to the chart. Add a slider and buttons and add event handlers to trigger the model to generate new data. The sample code downloadable from the book's site at www.wrox.com will product the graph seen in Figure 22-7.

```
static member WireUpMovingAverageChart (container:UserControl) =
    let chart : Chart = downcast container.FindName("chartMovingAverage")
    let slider : Slider = downcast container.FindName("sliderMovingAverage")

    let model = new MovingAverageModel(chart, slider)
    model.Init()
    let buttonNewData : Button = downcast container.FindName("buttonNewData")
    buttonNewData.Click.Add(fun(_) -> model.Init())

    slider.MouseLeftButtonUp.Add(fun(_) -> model.UpdateSeries())
    slider.ValueChanged.Add(fun(callback) -> model.UpdateMovingAverage(callback))
    ()
```

*Code Snippet SilverlightEvents.fs*

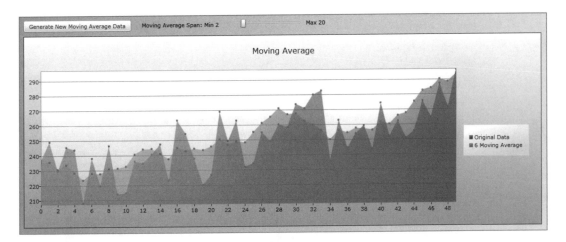

**FIGURE 22-7**

This example generates the data randomly. For a true application, the next step would be to add a server-side component using RIA Services or another Silverlight-accessible service. Silverlight has the capability to consume restful services, WCF, Web services, and more. By placing the data source on the server, the data can be controlled and protected. Perhaps the service may require a monthly subscription, may be throttled by priority, or may provide limited access based on security roles. All these scenarios are possible by building services. And those services can also be built in F#.

## SUMMARY

This chapter leverages the powerful capabilities of F# to build rich, dynamic, and responsive Silverlight applications. Currently the tools are limited for F# Silverlight Application templates, but a C# or VB Silverlight Application template can be used to delegate all the important code to an F# Silverlight Library. Because Microsoft has implemented the FSharp.Core.dll (the F# runtime) for Silverlight, F# code can run in a multitude of browsers on multiple operating systems including Macintosh OS, Firefox, and Google Chrome browsers. Silverlight is a flexible application framework for both public Web applications and for Enterprise applications. Because Silverlight is a client-side technology, it can be easily deployed on any web server, including Linux and UNIX-based systems. As long as the users have installed the Silverlight plug-in in their browser, they can take advantage of all the power it offers. That is why Silverlight has been used for everything from the broadcast of the Olympics to real-time dashboards for financial advisors. Together F# and Silverlight make a powerful pair.

# 23

# Services

**WHAT'S IN THIS CHAPTER?**

➤ Defining service contracts

➤ Hosting F# services

➤ Implementing contracts

➤ Consuming services

It is amazing to see that, even at the time of publication in 2010, most applications currently in production tend to interface with other systems through mechanisms that create extraneous coupling. It is still common to see mechanisms such as file polling (system A polls an FTP server until system B drops a file in the right place) and shared databases. The former is wasteful, and the latter presents all sorts of pain as systems grow and evolve. Shared databases are particularly bad because they present what is often an "unprotected door" through which data can enter without any sort of validation or business rules applied. They also effectively become a giant API, with every table, every column, and every row adding to the surface area of what must be tested when changes are made.

## OVERVIEW

To avoid this fate and to provide a better alternative for interoperation, Service Oriented Architecture (SOA) was invented. Services are developed that provide interfaces between platforms so that we can open the functionality of a system to other systems, while preserving the integrity of those systems. Services can take the form of web services, but they do not always need be served up via the web, an idea that has deep support in the Microsoft Windows Communication Foundation. The form of the service is less important than what it does, and making sure it is written in the right way to be relevant (meet a business need), reusable, scalable, and secure.

An important aspect of many services is that, all things being equal, stateless services are preferred over stateful ones. As has been emphasized many times in this book, F# is a great fit for applications that do not require state. In the world of services, there is almost never a need for state. Even in the case of stateful services, state is usually persisted in either an application database, or some sort of state server so that if the next requests comes in from a different server, it can pick up the context and continue work. This makes F# programs particularly well oriented toward service-oriented applications, as was pointed out in Chapter 21, where a comparison is made between services that serve HTML over HTTP, and services that serve other stuff (be it XML, JSON, or something else) on some other protocol over application service boundaries.

This chapter focuses on implementation of services in F#. Particular attention is paid toward using F# to define service contracts in WCF, implementing contracts, and fulfilling those contracts through an F #-based domain model. It then goes into how to configure and host services. Finally, it presents an example of F#-based service consumption.

## AN F#-BASED WEATHER SERVICE

Although having a basic site that provides a forecast may be of some utility, it would not be inconceivable that there would be other uses of weather data in other systems. Say, for example, there is a need for a service that alerts farmers in Florida about the need to protect their citrus crop. Such a system may want to call out to a weather service that averages the expected temperature over a short-term period, so that the crops can be protected with reasonable lead time.

## The Service Contract

Just like it is considered good practice to use tests to make sure development "begins with the end in mind" (apologies to Stephen Covey), it also makes sense to do so when writing services. In other words, it is helpful to ask the question, before writing implementation code, *what is it that this service should do?*

To that end, start with an assumption that the service should provide the user with information about a weather forecast, including such items as an average expected temperature, recommended attire, and weather to expect. If the general shape of what is required is known, the next step is to start by writing a data contract to define the shape of the result:

```
namespace ProFSharp.Services
open System
open System.ServiceModel
open System.Runtime.Serialization

[<DataContract>]
type Forecast() =
    let mutable _city : string = String.Empty
    let mutable _averageExpectedTemperature : double = 0.0
    let mutable _recommendedAtture : string = String.Empty
    let mutable _weather : string = String.Empty
    [<DataMember>]
    member public f.City
      with get() = _city and set(v) = _city <- v
```

```
[<DataMember>]
member public f.AverageExpectedTemperature
  with
    get() = _averageExpectedTemperature and
    set(v) = _averageExpectedTemperature <- v
[<DataMember>]
member public f.RecommendedAttire
  with get() = _recommendedAtture and set(v) = _recommendedAtture <- v
[<DataMember>]
member public f.Weather
  with get() = _weather and set(v) = _weather <- v
```

*Code snippet ServiceContract.fs*

Note the presence of a couple things here that are not normally present in idiomatic F# code. First, in the world of Microsoft WCF Services, things that are not primitive types (that is, strings, ints, doubles, and the like) need to be described in a `DataContract`. The type gets marked as a `[<DataContract>]`, and each member that is to be passed over the wire is marked with the `[<DataMember>]` attribute.

It is also worth noting that these data contracts take the form of mutable types. The chief reason this is needed is for purposes of serialization, because it is expected that the client using the service will need to use serialization to repopulate the object when it is received. WCF, as of this writing, does not hydrate objects through means F# would consider typical (that is, the way you might populate a record), and therefore, to allow for the client to set the properties, the data contract has to define mutable properties.

A data contract can also be defined as an interface, which would allow us to build a nonmutable version on the F# side for the concrete implementation of the data contract. Although it would be slightly more idiomatic for F#, the added code in such a case for an object that acts as a simple DTO is typically not worth the trouble.

Of course, a `DataContract` alone isn't terribly useful. Also needed is a means to retrieve an object or objects that will match the `DataContract`. These are defined using `ServiceContract` and `OperationContract`:

```
[<ServiceContract>]
type IWeatherService =
  [<OperationContract>]
  abstract member GetForecastFor: place:string -> Forecast
```

Generally, a weather service will implement something that turns a `string` into a `Forecast` that matches the `DataContract` definition. On the surface, `OperationContract` is pretty straightforward. However, it is important to note that, as a consequence of the way WCF works, any parameters in an `OperationContract` *must be named*, or else exceptions will be raised when the service is hosted.

When a `ServiceContract` is in place, the next step is to think about how to fulfill the conditions of the `ServiceContract`. A good place to start is to use any domain models that might have been developed previously.

# LEVERAGING THE DOMAIN MODEL

One of the nice things about domain models is that they can easily be reused in different contexts. The forecast domain model was previously used in the context of an ASP.NET MVC website in Chapter 21. The domain model was expressed as follows:

```fsharp
namespace FSharpBook.Models
type SkyType =
    | Sunny
    | Overcast
    | PartlyCloudy
    | Snow
    | Rain
    | Hurricane
    | Zombies

type Forecast = { Location:string; AverageTemperature:double; Skies:SkyType }

type Attire =
    | Bikini
    | Normal
    | LightJacket
    | Coat
    | Raincoat
    | Parka
    | BodyArmor

type Forecast with
  member forecast.ToAttire() =
    match forecast.AverageTemperature,forecast.Skies with
        | temp,sky when temp > 75.0 && sky = Sunny || sky = PartlyCloudy -> Bikini
        | temp,sky when temp > 65.0 && sky = Sunny || sky = PartlyCloudy -> Normal
        | temp,sky
          when temp > 45.0 && sky = Sunny || sky = PartlyCloudy -> LightJacket
        | _,Rain -> Raincoat
        | temp when temp < 20.0 -> Parka
        | _,Hurricane -> Coat
        | _,Snow -> Parka
        | _,Zombies -> BodyArmor
        | _ -> Coat //when in doubt, wear a coat...
```

*Code snippet ForecastModel.fs*

The preceding model constitutes the recommendation engine that the service will provide an interface to. In a sense, all that is being done is replacing the user interface developed in the context of an ASP.NET MVC website with a system interface that will provide the same information.

It is worth noting that the ability to reuse a model from the previous example in the MVC context is a big reason why staying true to the principle of separation of concerns is so important. Had things like `HttpRequest` objects slipped into the model, or worse, tied the model to specific types of presentation logic, it would have required significant rework to reuse the model. Moreover, if someone wanted to update the model, the updates would have to be done in two places. Very bad indeed!

## WRITING THE SERVICE CONTROLLER

Just as one developer is a controller for MVC applications so that requests in http can be converted to the appropriate calls into the domain model, when developing services, controllers are used that can take external requests and route them appropriately. Although it is tempting to reuse the same MVC controller, chances are, it likely brings in more complexity than we need, because the needs in MVC to map a complex set of parameters from an http request into routes is not present. As such, a much less complex controller model for a service controller shall be used.

### Rendering Weather

There are some needs on the service controller that are going to be similar to things that were needed on the ASP.NET MVC controller. Specifically, a means to convert from algebraic data types on the domain into the appropriate string in the service contract will be needed. The following methods are carried over from the view helper project in Chapter 21 to help with that task:

```
module WeatherRendering
open FSharpBook.Models

let ToWeatherString sky =
  match sky with
  | Sunny -> "Sunny"
  | Overcast -> "Overcast"
  | PartlyCloudy -> "Partly Cloudy"
  | Snow -> "Snow"
  | Rain -> "Rain"
  | Hurricane -> "Hurricane"
  | Zombies -> "Oh NO! ZOMBIES!!!"

let ToAttireString attire =
  match attire with
  | Bikini -> "Bikini"
  | Normal -> "Normal"
  | LightJacket -> "Light Jacket"
  | Coat -> "Coat"
  | Raincoat -> "Raincoat"
  | Parka -> "Parka"
  | BodyArmor -> "Body Armor"
```

*Code snippet ForecastModelRendering.fs*

The preceding code converts the weather types into strings for ease of consumption on the client. Of course, it is conceivable that future versions of the service could specify a preferred culture for results to be rendered in. Were that to happen, it would simply mean that these methods would take a parameter, and likely, look up the appropriate string in a resource file.

### Helping the Service Controller

ASP.NET MVC comes stocked with objects like ModelBinder that help the programmer take a model and, so long as various conventions are followed, renders that model in a view. In the world of service controllers, there is no such concept. As a result, service controllers tend to use libraries, or otherwise contain routines, that convert model concepts into terms that the service contract can understand. In this case, a `Forecast` from the model is needed to convert into the type `Forecast` that was defined in the data contract:

```
namespace ProFSharp.Services
open FSharpBook.Models
open WeatherRendering

type ForecastServiceRenderer() =
    static member Render (forecast:Forecast) =
      let renderedForecast = new ProFSharp.Services.Forecast()
      renderedForecast.AverageExpectedTemperature <- forecast.AverageTemperature
      renderedForecast.City <- forecast.Location
      renderedForecast.RecommendedAttire <- forecast.ToAttire()
        |> WeatherRendering.ToAttireString
      renderedForecast.Weather <- forecast.Skies |> WeatherRendering.ToWeatherString
      renderedForecast
```

*Code snippet ServiceRenderer.fs*

The goal here is to convert an `FSharpBook.Models.Forecast` into a `ProFSharp.Services` `.Forecast`. Thankfully, doing so is not that hard, merely a matter of providing a function that creates a `ProFSharp.Services.Forecast` and maps the properties from the `FSharpBook.Models` `.Forecast`. This is a fairly common type of thing to do when converting from the F# world of records to the world of objects in the broader CLR and beyond.

## Service Controller Implementation

Thankfully, in the context of a WCF service that does not have to worry about rendering to such complex creatures as humans, the implementation of a service controller is far simpler:

```
namespace ProFSharp.Services
open FSharpBook.Repositories

type ForecastServiceController() =
    member forecastController.For(locationQuery:string) =
      locationQuery
        |> YahooForecastRepository.GetForecastByLocation
        |> ForecastServiceRenderer.Render
```

*Code snippet ServiceController.fs*

There are two routines that are particularly interesting. We are reusing our `YahooForecastRepository` `.GetForecastByLocation` (see Chapter 21) to provide a means to retrieve the model. The next step is to pass said model to `ForecastServiceRenderer.Render` so that they can pass back something in the form of an `Object` that conforms to the `DataContract` back at the service host.

## Service Implementation

The last piece, a controller is in place, is to write something that will implement the
IWeatherService:

```
namespace ProFSharp.Services
open System.ServiceModel
[<ServiceBehavior(ConfigurationName="Weather")>]
type YahooWeatherService() =
   interface IWeatherService with
      member s.GetForecastFor place =
         (new ForecastServiceController()).For(place)
```

*Code snippet ServiceImplementation.fs*

The service implementation usually defers to a controller that will provide most of the details. The
purpose here is to map what the controller does with specific operations from the service contract. It
is hard not to notice the lack of code here — the service implementation itself is not unlike a view in
the world of ASP.NET MVC — it is something ideally composed of as little code as possible. Most
of the action for dealing with a domain should (and is) deferred to the controller. With the implementation in place, it is time to get into the implementation of the service host itself.

## Implementing the Service Host

Services have come a long way since 2001, when most people in the world of .NET thought the
word Service was synonymous with Web Service, and that SOA was a matter of sprinkling a
WebMethod attribute in various places around a codebase. WCF is an important technology for
moving away from having to bring the baggage of IIS and all its administrative overhead to host a
service. In fact, the code that is written to host a service is amazingly simple:

```
module ServiceHost
open System.ServiceModel
open ProFSharp.Services

let startServicing() =
   let host = new ServiceHost( typeof<YahooWeatherService>, [||] )
   host.Open()
   printf "Press the 'any' key to stop hosting the service"
   System.Console.ReadKey() |> ignore

startServicing()
```

*Code snippet ServiceHost.fs*

This example has been provided because it works in the context of a console application. We could
just as easily run this in the context of a Windows Service (aka a Daemon running in the background, not to be confused with a WCF Service), and not interact with an end user. The really

important lines of code are not the ones that print to the console and ask you to press the 'any' key, but the following lines:

```
let host = new ServiceHost( typeof<YahooWeatherService>, Array.empty )
host.Open()
```

The `ServiceHost` class knows how to read a configuration file and use that to start servicing requests according to said configuration. It is only at this point that all those attributes that were included in prior code written in this chapter start to get interpreted. Of course, the `.Open()` method will fail if there is not a configuration file present that tells the `ServiceHost` what to do:

```xml
<?xml version="1.0" encoding="utf-8" ?>
  <configuration>
    <system.serviceModel>
      <behaviors>
        <serviceBehaviors>
          <behavior name="serviceBehavior">
            <serviceMetadata httpGetEnabled="false" />
          </behavior>
        </serviceBehaviors>
      </behaviors>
      <services>
        <service behaviorConfiguration="serviceBehavior" name="Weather">
        <clear />
        <endpoint
          address="WeatherService"
          binding="basicHttpBinding"
          name="basicHttp"
          contract="ProFSharp.Services.IWeatherService" />
        <endpoint binding="mexHttpBinding" name="mex"
contract="IMetadataExchange" />
          <host>
            <baseAddresses>
              <add baseAddress="http://localhost:8000/WeatherService" />
            </baseAddresses>
          </host>
        </service>
      </services>
    </system.serviceModel>
  </configuration>
```

*Code snippet App.config*

The preceding code, typically in something like `app.config`, specifies how a service host will do its work. Much of this is boilerplate, but of particular importance are the attributes in `<endpoint>` and `<host>`. The `<endpoint>` maps a URL to a contract (in this case, `WeatherService` to `ProFSharp .Services.IWeatherService`). The `<host>` provides information to the `ServiceHost` about what port and URL will be used to access the service.

Of course, there are many ways to configure a service, and the goal here isn't to go through each one. The book *Wrox Professional WCF 4: Windows Communication Foundation with .NET 4* is a great resource for further understanding of the details of WCF Service Host configuration.

Now, there are some provisions we need to account for before this stuff will actually work. Namely, most systems are not configured to simply let any identity start serving requests at any random port. One thing that needs to be done is to set up permissions that allow the app — or the Windows Service, if that route is chosen — to host requests, which in this case, are http requests. The following command is typical for allowing a given identity to service http requests:

```
netsh http add urlacl url=http://+:8000/WeatherService user=YourUserId
```

When permissions allow for the `ServiceHost` to serve up http requests, the service host can be started. To make sure the service is responsive, open a browser and point it to `http://localhost:8000/WeatherService` to make sure a valid response is returned from the http request.

## CONSUMING SERVICES

Consuming services, in the world of WCF, is typically a matter running `svcutil.exe` against a URL, which will generate a C# file that can be compiled into something usable for consuming a service.

## Generating a Service Stub

If the URL `http://localhost:8000/WeatherService` returns a valid response, it can pass that as a parameter to svcutil.exe (from your .NET Framework SDK), which will generate a file with the following code:

```csharp
//------------------------------------------------------------------------------
// <auto-generated>
//     This code was generated by a tool.
//     Runtime Version:2.0.50727.4927
//
//     Changes to this file may cause incorrect behavior and will be lost if
//     the code is regenerated.
// </auto-generated>
//------------------------------------------------------------------------------

namespace ProFSharp.Services
{
    using System.Runtime.Serialization;

    [System.Diagnostics.DebuggerStepThroughAttribute()]
    [System.CodeDom.Compiler.GeneratedCodeAttribute("System.Runtime.Serialization",
 "3.0.0.0")]
    [System.Runtime.Serialization.DataContractAttribute(Name="Forecast",
Namespace="http://schemas.datacontract.org/2004/07/ProFSharp.Services")]
    public partial class Forecast : object,
System.Runtime.Serialization.IExtensibleDataObject
    {

        private System.Runtime.Serialization.ExtensionDataObject
extensionDataField;
        private double AverageExpectedTemperatureField;
        private string CityField;
```

```csharp
private string RecommendedAttireField;
private string WeatherField;

public System.Runtime.Serialization.ExtensionDataObject ExtensionData
{
    get
    {
        return this.extensionDataField;
    }
    set
    {
        this.extensionDataField = value;
    }
}

[System.Runtime.Serialization.DataMemberAttribute()]
public double AverageExpectedTemperature
{
    get
    {
        return this.AverageExpectedTemperatureField;
    }
    set
    {
        this.AverageExpectedTemperatureField = value;
    }
}

[System.Runtime.Serialization.DataMemberAttribute()]
public string City
{
    get
    {
        return this.CityField;
    }
    set
    {
        this.CityField = value;
    }
}

[System.Runtime.Serialization.DataMemberAttribute()]
public string RecommendedAttire
{
    get
    {
        return this.RecommendedAttireField;
    }
    set
    {
        this.RecommendedAttireField = value;
    }
}
```

```
            [System.Runtime.Serialization.DataMemberAttribute()]
            public string Weather
            {
                get
                {
                    return this.WeatherField;
                }
                set
                {
                    this.WeatherField = value;
                }
            }
        }
    }


[System.CodeDom.Compiler.GeneratedCodeAttribute("System.ServiceModel", "3.0.0.0")]
[System.ServiceModel.ServiceContractAttribute(ConfigurationName="IWeatherService")]
public interface IWeatherService
{

    [System.ServiceModel.OperationContractAttribute(Action="http://tempuri.org/
IWeatherService/GetForecastFor", ReplyAction="http://tempuri.org/IWeatherService/
GetForecastForResponse")]
    ProFSharp.Services.Forecast GetForecastFor(string place);
}

[System.CodeDom.Compiler.GeneratedCodeAttribute("System.ServiceModel", "3.0.0.0")]
public interface IWeatherServiceChannel : IWeatherService,
System.ServiceModel.IClientChannel
{
}

[System.Diagnostics.DebuggerStepThroughAttribute()]
[System.CodeDom.Compiler.GeneratedCodeAttribute("System.ServiceModel", "3.0.0.0")]
public partial class WeatherServiceClient :
System.ServiceModel.ClientBase<IWeatherService>, IWeatherService
{

    public WeatherServiceClient()
    {
    }

    public WeatherServiceClient(string endpointConfigurationName) :
            base(endpointConfigurationName)
    {
    }

    public WeatherServiceClient(string endpointConfigurationName, string
remoteAddress) :
            base(endpointConfigurationName, remoteAddress)
    {
    }
```

```
      public WeatherServiceClient(string endpointConfigurationName,
System.ServiceModel.EndpointAddress remoteAddress) :
            base(endpointConfigurationName, remoteAddress)
      {
      }

      public WeatherServiceClient(System.ServiceModel.Channels.Binding binding,
System.ServiceModel.EndpointAddress remoteAddress) :
            base(binding, remoteAddress)
      {
      }

      public ProFSharp.Services.Forecast GetForecastFor(string place)
      {
          return base.Channel.GetForecastFor(place);
      }
  }
```

*Code snippet YahooWeatherService.cs*

Yes, it is a lot of generated code; when a closer look is taken, it is simply a lot of boilerplate that hides the ugly implementation details of putting together the appropriate request to the service that was just implemented. It can be ignored for the most part, other than to use it, it needs to be put into a .NET C# Windows DLL project so that it can be easily used from F# code that needs to consume this functionality.

The generated code defines a `WeatherServiceClient` that is capable of reading a configuration — telling it what address to make requests to — and handling the response so that the result matches the form specified in the `DataContract`.

## Writing the Service Consumer

Assuming the previous example has been put in a project we can reference from an F# project, calling the service is not too difficult. However, to use this, there is the matter of configuring the client with a mapping so it can know where to make the call to:

```xml
<?xml version="1.0" encoding="utf-8"?>
<configuration>
  <system.serviceModel>
    <bindings>
      <basicHttpBinding>
        <binding name="basicHttp" closeTimeout="00:01:00" openTimeout="00:01:00"
            receiveTimeout="00:10:00" sendTimeout="00:01:00" allowCookies="false"
            bypassProxyOnLocal="false" hostNameComparisonMode="StrongWildcard"
            maxBufferSize="65536" maxBufferPoolSize="524288"
maxReceivedMessageSize="65536"
            messageEncoding="Text" textEncoding="utf-8" transferMode="Buffered"
            useDefaultWebProxy="true">
          <readerQuotas maxDepth="32" maxStringContentLength="8192"
```

```
         maxArrayLength="16384"
                      maxBytesPerRead="4096" maxNameTableCharCount="16384" />
                 <security mode="None">
                   <transport clientCredentialType="None" proxyCredentialType="None"
                       realm="">
                   <extendedProtectionPolicy policyEnforcement="Never" />
                   </transport>
                   <message clientCredentialType="UserName" algorithmSuite="Default" />
                 </security>
               </binding>
             </basicHttpBinding>
           </bindings>
           <client>
             <endpoint address="http://localhost:8000/WeatherService/WeatherService"
                 binding="basicHttpBinding" bindingConfiguration="basicHttp"
                 contract="IWeatherService" name="basicHttp" />
           </client>
         </system.serviceModel>
       </configuration>
```

*Code snippet App.config*

The preceding example provides a means for the code that will create a `WeatherServiceClient` to know what address to make calls to, as well as various parameters around things like timeouts and the like. The `<endpoint>` configuration is of particular note and should match the `<endpoint>` that was specified on the host configuration. Most good WCF books will provide adequate detail on how to use all the provided settings. Thankfully, the default settings are good enough for us to see how F# code will work when using a `WeatherServiceClient`:

```
open ProFSharp.Services

let getWeatherFor place =
    use myWeatherService = new WeatherServiceClient()
    let theWeather = place |> myWeatherService.GetForecastFor

    printf "The weather in %s should average %g degrees with %s, wear %s!"
      theWeather.City
      theWeather.AverageExpectedTemperature
      theWeather.Weather
      theWeather.RecommendedAttire
    printf "\n\nPress any key to continue"
    System.Console.ReadKey() |> ignore

getWeatherFor "Romeoville, IL"
```

*Code snippet Program.fs*

The client itself is an `IDisposable` resource, so it is important to make sure to use the `use` binding when retrieving it. Outside of that, the mechanics of using the service are mere idiomatic F# code.

## SUMMARY

Services, among other things, are a way that programmers can provide outside systems a window into a domain model. They are a key to making interoperability happen in a more predictable manner. Without reliable services, experience demonstrates interoperability will happen — through the database, which for anyone who has maintained a legacy "integration database" knows, is far more error prone than it is through services. If you doubt that, ask yourself what happens when you start to have programs that read data that is frequently modified in hard-to-predict ways by other programs, and what the testing load on programs like that is like.

# INDEX

<< (backward composition), 274–275
<| (backward pipe), 271–272
>> (forward composition), 273–274
|> (forward pipe), 270–271
_ (underscore) as wildcard, 86

## A

abbreviations, types, 105–106
abstract inheritance, 210
abstract keyword, 168, 170
abstract members, overriding and, 168–169
AbstractClass attribute, 168, 201
abstraction, 95
    collection abstractions, 257–258
    leaky abstraction, 342
access
    arrays, 62
    list elements, 68–70
    maps, 80–81
    properties, 135
access modifiers
    members, 155
    types, 156
accumulators, 263–264
    fold function, 265–266
    reduce function, 264–265
    scan function, 266–267
active patterns, 95–96
    multi-case, 99–101
    partial-case, 97–99
    single case, 96–97
    XML and, 329–330
        multicase, 330–335
        partial case, 336–339
ADO.NET
    data retrieval, 298–302
    database connections, creating, 298
    delete operations, 301–302
    filtering data, 300–301
    insert operations, 301–302
    reading data, 299–300
    update operations, 301–302
allHighAndLowAttributes function, 321
ambiguously typed data, 247–248
AND patterns, 90
APIs (Application Programming Interfaces), writing, 294–295
AppDomain, 150
application operations
    arrays, 64–65
    lists, 71–72
    sequences, 78–79
area charts (Silverlight Toolkit), 365–366
arguments, functions, 211–215
    automatic generalization, 211–212
    generic type, 214
    partial application, 215–218
    statically resolved type parameters, 215
    type constraints, 214
arithmetic conversions, 41–42
arity of methods, 142
array patterns, 93
Array.create function, 60
arrays
    access, 62
    brackets, 60
    construction, 60–61
    functions, 62–65
        application operations, 64–65
        meta functions, 63–64
    immutability and, 242
    literal byte arrays, 42
    range expressions, 60
    syntax, 61
    using, 72–73
arrow-based notation, 168
as clause, 128
as keyword, 92
as patterns, 92
ASP.NET MVC
    Forecast'r, 342
        controller, 349–351

model, 343–344
repository, 344–348
view, creating, 352–355
view helpers, 351–352
weather result, 348
Where On Earth ID, 345–346
overview, 341–342
assembly attributes, 201–202
asynchronous workflows, immutability and, 228
attributes
AbstractClass, 168
custom, 197–198
AbstractClass, 201
assembly attributes, 201–202
AutoOpen, 202
Class, 201
Conditional, 200
consumption, 205–206
creating, 203–205
DefaultMember, 202
EntryPoint, 198–199
GetCustomAttributes( ) method, 205
Interface, 201
NonSerializable, 202
Obsolete, 199–200
ParamArray, 200–201
Serializable, 202
Struct, 201
Obsolete, 198–199
RequiresQualifiedAccess, 107
Serializable, 198
automatic generalization, 211–212
AutoOpen attribute, 202

**B**

backward composition (<<), 274–275
banana clips around functions, 96
Base Class Library, 42
BeginInvoke method, 151
bigint type, 38
binary operators, 148
BinaryTree type, 112
bindings
let, 130, 140
member, 140
bitwise operators, 40
BlameAttribute class, 203
bool type, 37
Boolean types, 37
boxing/unboxing, 174–177
brackets, arrays, 60

browser, Silverlight testing, 362
bubble and assign, 235–236
business objects, 3
byref keyword, 238

**C**

C#
calling F#, 290
discriminated unions, 292–293
events, 288–289
F# tuples, 290–291
functions, passing to F# functions, 292
libraries, calling from F#, 284–289
methods, delegates, 287–288
objects, constructing, 285–286
option types, 293–294
overview, 283–284
records, 291–292
C# 2.0
Database<T>, 13
Filter, 13, 15
Func, 15
Func<T>, 13
functions, 211
IEnumerable<T>, 14
Map, 13
Predicate<T>, 13
Reduce, 13, 15
C# 3.0
lambda expression, 17
List<T>, 16
methods, new, 16
calling
functions, 209–210
methods, 140–141, 145
interface, 179–180
scenarios, 284–285
carried type, 56
casting, 171
boxing/unboxing, 174–177
downcasting, 172–173
flexible types, 173
upcasting, 172
chaining constructors, 127
character types, 42
choose function, 262–263
Church, Lorenzo, 17
Class attribute, 201
class libraries, 4
class marker, 125–126
class methods, currying, 217

ClassCastException, 173
classes
    access modifiers, 155–157
    BlameAttribute, 203
    class marker, 125–126
    constructor methods, creating, 126–131
    constructors, multiple, 127
    creating, 131
    DelegateEvent types, 152–154
    delegates, 149–152
        MulticastDelegate, 151
        subscribing, 150
        types, 151
    end marker, 125–126
    events, 149
        subscribing, 150
    Exception, 205
    fields, 126
        mutable, 126
        static, 147
        val keyword, 126
    functions, 211
    members
        member keyword, 132
        methods, 140–146
        properties, 132–140
        static members, 146–149
    methods, definition, 140
    System.String, 42
    type extensions, 157–158
    type keyword, 125
clauses
    as, 128
    elif, 48
    inherit, 164
CLI Producer, 203
Clojure, 283
cloning records, 121–122
closures, 222
CMYK (cyan/yellow/magenta/black) color, 109
collection abstractions, 257–258
    foreach statement, 258
collections, subsets, 258
    filter function, 259
    partition, 259–260
color values, 109
COM+/Enterprise Services, 4
comments, 31–32
    documentation, 32
        XML and, 32
    multi-line, 32
    single-line, 32
comparison, 174–177

comparison constraint, 188
comparison operators, 39–40
compile-time-only type constraints, 215
complex composite types
    abbreviations, 105–106
    discriminated union types, 109–114
    enum types, 106–109
    record types, 119–123
        implicit members, 123
    structs, 114–117
        pattern-matching and, 118–119
        value type implicit members, 117–118
component containers, 4
composite types
    arrays
        access, 61
        construction, 60–61
        functions, 61–65
        using, 72–73
    lists, 65
        access, 68–70
        construction, 66–68
        methods, 70–72
        using, 72–73
    maps
        access, 80–81
        construction, 79–80
        functions, 81–82
    option types, 55–58
        functions, 57–58
    sequences, 74–79
    sets, 82–83
    tuples, 58–60
composition, 272–273
    advanced, 278–279
    applying, 275–279
    backward composition (<<), 274–275
    forward composition (>>), 273–274
Conditional attribute, 200
Console.WriteLine method, 129
constant patterns, 88–89
constants, decimal, 38
constraints. See type constraints
constructor constraint, 188
constructors
    chaining, 127
    creating, 126–131
    definition, 127
    derived types, 164
    inheritance, 163–166
    multiple, 127
    primary, 128
        copying data, 129

logic, 129
self-identifiers, 128
value types, 116
consuming services
service stub generation, 385–388
writing service consumer, 388–389
consumption of custom attributes, 205–206
containers, 4
control flow, expressions, 47
create function, 60
CreateTableFor function, 308
Curry, Haskell, 20
currying, 20, 216
custom attributes, 197–198
AbstractClass, 201
assembly attributes, 201–202
AutoOpen, 202
Class, 201
Conditional, 200
consumption, 205–206
creating, 203–205
DefaultMember, 202
EntryPoint, 198–199
GetCustomAttributes( ) method, 205
Interface, 201
NonSerializable, 202
Obsolete, 199–200
ParamArray, 200–201
Serializable, 202
Struct, 201
CustomComparison, 175
CustomEquality, 175

### D

data binding
design time, 368–370
programmatic, 371–372
data mutation, 232–233
avoiding, 233–235
bubble and assign, 235–236
message passing, 238–239
passing by reference, 238
reference calls, 236–238
data structures, custom, 8–9
data types, 247
recursively redefined, 253–254
databases
adding data, FAR, 304–305
connections, creating, 298
delete operations, 301–302
deleting data, FAR, 305–306

filtering, 300–301
insert operations, 301–302
overview, 297–298
predicates, 304
queries, FAR, 304
reading data, 299–300
FAR, 303–304
table creation, FAR, 308
update operations, 301–302
updating data, FAR, 305
debugging, 229–230
decimal constants, 38
decisions, 47–49
declarations, static members, 146
DeepClone( ) method, 232
DefaultMember, 202
defining
interfaces, 180–181
operators, 147–148
delegate constraints, 189
delegate strategy, 12–17
DelegateEvent types, 152–154
delegates, 149
methods and, 287–288
MulticastDelegate, 151
subscribing, 150
types, 151
delete operations in databases, 301–302
deleting database data, FAR, 305–306
dependencies, FAR, 306
derived classes
constructors, 164
methods, customizing, 169
properties, 164
Descendents( ) method, 320–321
design patterns, 4
designer tools (Silverlight Toolkit), 366–368
destructive update operator, 134
directives, preprocessor, 33–34
discriminated union patterns, 93
discriminated union types, 109–114,
292–293
pattern-matching, 110
tree-based structures, 111
do expression, 130
documentation comments, 32
XML and, 32
domain types, 3
DoQuery action, 350
downcasting, 172–173
DRY (Don't Repeat Yourself), 8
duck typing, 99
DumpInternals method, 200

## E

element transformations, 260
    `choose` function, 262–263
    `map` function, 260–262
elif clauses, 48
#else directive, 33
encapsulating state in types, 249–251
end marker, 125–126
#endif directive, 33
`EndInvoke` method, 151
Enterprise Java Beans, 4
`EntryPoint`, 198–199
enum types, 106–109
enumeration type constraints, 189
equality, 117, 174–177
equality constraint, 187
`Equals( )` method, 117
`Equals` method, 174
`Event.add` function, 154
`Event.filter` function, 154
Eventing, 210
events, 149, 210, 288–289
    `ProcessExit`, 150
    subscribing, 150, 289
`Exception` class, 205
exceptions, 50–51, 251–252
    raising, 52–53
    throwing, 52–53
    try...finally, 52
    try...with, 51
    types, defining, 53
explicit member constraint, 189–190
expressions
    control flow, 47
    `do`, 130
    lambda, 222–223
    `let`, 130
    object expressions, 181
    pattern matching, 86–87
    range, arrays, 60
    sequence, 61
    *versus* statements, 27–28
extensions
    members, 157
    methods, 157

## F

F#
    called by C#, 290
    lexical structure, 31

F# Silverlight Library, 359, 363–365
failing fast, 248
FAR (F# Active Record)
    adding data, 304–305
    deleting data, 305–306
    dependencies, 306
    library, 308
    queries, processing, 309–314
    querying data, 304
    reading data, 303–304
    table creation, 308
    updating data, 305
    use case, 315
    utility routines, 307–308
`faultyMethod` method, 205
fields
    classes, 126
        inheritance, 163–166
        mutable, 126
        `static`, 147
        `val` keyword, 126
    initializing, 121
FIFO (first-in-first-out), 184
`Filter`, 15
`filter` function, 259
filtering, databases, 300–301
first class functions, 218–223
flexible types, 173
floating-point types, 40–41
`fold` function, 265–266
for loops, 50
FOR operations, implementation, 314–315
`ForEach` function, 220
`foreach` statement, 258
Forecast'r, 342
    controller, 349
        DoQuery action, 350
        For action, 351
        index action, 349–350
        setup, 349
    model, 343–344
    repository, creating, 344–348
    view, creating, 352–355
    view helpers, 351–352
    weather result, 348
    Where On Earth ID, 345–346
forward composition (>>), 273–274
forward pipe (|>), 270–271
frameworks, 4
`FSharpLibrary`, 291
`Func<T>`, 13
function calls, 209–210
    abstract inheritance, 210

Eventing, 210
function pointers, 210
function pointers, 210
functions
    allHighAndLowAttributes, 321
    arguments, 211–215
        automatic generalization, 211–212
        generic type, 214
        partial application, 215–218
        statically resolved type parameters, 215
        type constraints, 214
    Array.create, 60
    arrays, 62–65
        application operations, 64–65
        meta functions, 63–64
    banana clips, 96
    C#, 211
    choose, 262–263
    classes, 211
    create, 60
    CreateTableFor, 308
    currying, 216
    Event.add, 154
    Event.filter, 154
    filter, 259
    first class, 218–223
    fold, 265–266
    ForEach, 220
    getWorldStateChanges, 236
    higher-order, 17, 219–221
    inline keyword, 212–213
    lambda calculus, 19–20
    leastFactor, 235
    map, 260–262
    Map.ofList, 79
    maps, 81–82
    mathematical, 210
    methods and, 140
    module functions, 258
    nextParam( ), 311
    option types, 57–58
    paramList( ), 311
    ParseCriteria, 310
    partition, 259–260
    passing, 17
    passing to F# functions, 292
    pipelining, 21–22
    pow, 218
    recursive, 218–219
    reduce, 264–265
    removeDuplicates, 250
    restrictions, 217–218
    return values, 211–215

    runtime creation, 221
        closures, 222
        lambda expressions, 222–223
        partial application and, 223
    scan, 266–267
    storing, 221
    tail recursion optimization, 211
    type annotations, 213–214
    type inference, 211
    usdToEuro, 44
functors, 19

**G**

generic types, 214
generics, 9
    overview, 183–184
    statically resolved type parameters, explicit member
        constraint, 189–190
    type constraints, 186–187
        comparison constraint, 188
        constructor constraint, 188
        delegate constraints, 189
        enumeration type constraints, 189
        equality constraint, 187
        null constraint, 188
        reference type constraints, 188–189
        type constraint, 187
        unmanaged constraints, 189
        value type constraint, 188–189
    type parameters, 185–186
get( ) method, 133
GetCustomAttributes( ) method, 205
GetEnumerator( ) method, 74
GetHashCode( ) method, 118
GetHashCode method, 174
getWorldStateChanges function, 236
guarded blocks, 50

**H**

hash tags, 33–34
hashing, 174–177
higher-order functions, 17, 219–221

**I**

IClonable interface, 179
IComparable interface, 179
IComparable.CompareTo( ) interface method, 149
IDbConnection interface, 298

identifiers, 32–33
    illegal, 33
    self-identifiers, 128
IEnumerable<T>, 14
IEnumerator, 74
if construct, 47–49
#if directive, 33
illegal identifiers, 33
immutability, 26–27
    asynchronous workflows and, 228
    data mutation, 232–239
    performance considerations, 239–245
        arrays, 242
        lists, 239–242
        records, 243
        sequences, 242–243
        structs, 243–245
        tuples, 243
immutable classes, outputs, 228
implicit conversions, 172
indexer properties, 136–140
inequality, 117
inferred relativity, 117
inherit clause, 164
inheritance
    abstract, 210
    casting, 171
        boxing/unboxing, 174–177
        downcasting, 172–173
        flexible types, 173
        upcasting, 172
    constructors, 163–166
    fields, 163–166
    interfaces
        definition, 180–181
        implementation, 177–180
        method calling, 179–180
    object expressions, 181
    overriding and, 166–167
        abstract members, 168–169
        default, 169–171
    overview, 161–162
    structs, 117
    System.Object class, 162
initialization
    fields, 121
    named properties, 135–136
    properties, 285–286
inline keyword, 211–213
inlined functions, 213
input type, converting to output type, 271
input validation, partial-case active patterns, 97
insert operations in databases, 301–302

instances, InterestType, 186
int property, 133
InterestType instance, 186
Interface attribute, 201
interface keyword, 178
interface methods, IComparable.CompareTo( ), 149
interfaces
    defining, 180–181
    IClonable, 179
    IComparable, 179
    IDbConnection, 298
    implementation, 177–180
    methods
        calling, 179–180
        defining, 180
    properties, defining, 180
    query interface, implementing, 313–314
intrinsic extensions, 157
IS-A relationship, 162
Isolated Storage, 358
iter method, 112
iteration, foreach statement, 258

## J-K

JVM (Java Virtual Machine), 361
keywords, 32
    as, 92
    with, 134
    abstract, 168, 170
    byref, 238
    inline, 211–213
    interface, 178
    member, 132
    module, 193–195
    mutable, 116, 126, 131
    new, 131
    open, 191–192
    override, 166
    protected, 155
    rec, 218
    seq, 74
    then, 47, 127
    type, 106, 114–115, 125
    val, 126

## L

lambda calculus, 17–22
    functions, 19–20
lambda expression, 17, 222–223
language-wide type inference, 25

Leaf element, 331
leaky abstraction, 342
leastFactor functions, 235
let binding, 130
    methods, 140
let expression, 130
lexical closures, 222
lexical structure, 31
libraries
    C#, calling from F#, 284–289
    calling from C#, 289–294
    class libraries, 4
LIFO (last-in-first-out), 185
line charts (Silverlight Toolkit), 365–366
#line directive, 33
linear data, 257
LINQ (Language-Integrated Query), 16
LINQ-to-XML
    processing XML, 322–324
    querying XML, 320–322
    reading XML, 318–320
Linux, Silverlight, 359
list patterns, 92
lists, 65, 239–242
    access, 68–70
    construction, 66–68
    methods
        application operations, 71–72
        meta functions, 70–71
    using, 72–73
List<T>, 17
literal byte arrays, 42
literal patterns, 90–91
literal values, 44–45
local data state safety, 229–232
looping
    for, 50
    sequences and, 74
    while/do, 49–50

**M**

map function, 260–262
Map.ofList function, 79
mapping, object relational mapping, 302–303
maps
    access, 80–81
    construction, 79–80
    functions, 81–82
mathematical functions, 210
member binding, 140
member-declared elements, 156
member keyword, 132

member type parameters, 186
members
    extension members, 157
    member keyword, 132
    methods
        arity, 142
        calling, 140–141
        definition, 140
        functions and, 140
        let binding, 140
        member binding, 140
        named parameters, 143–144
        optional parameters, 144–146
        overloaded, 142–143
        return type, 141
    properties, 132–140
        indexer properties, 136–140
    static members
        declaring, 146
        operator overloading, 147–149
    type extensions, 158
MemoryStream, 325
message passing, data mutation and, 238–239
meta functions
    arrays, 63–64
    lists, 70–71
    sequences, 76–77
method signatures, syntax, 168
methods
    arity, 142
    BeginInvoke, 151
    calling, 140–141, 145
        scenarios, 284–285
    Console.WriteLine, 129
    DeepClone( ), 232
    definition, 140
    delegates, 287–288
    Descendents( ), 320–321
    DumpInternals, 200
    EndInvoke, 151
    Equals, 174
    Equals( ), 117
    extension methods, 157
    faultyMethod, 205
    functions and, 140
    get( ), 133
    GetCustomAttributes( ), 205
    GetEnumerator( ), 74
    GetHashCode, 174
    GetHashCode( ), 118
    interface
        calling, 179–180
        IComparable.CompareTo( ), 149

iter, 112
let binding, 140
lists
    application operations, 71–72
    meta functions, 70–71
member binding, 140
named parameters, 143–144
optional parameters, 144–146
overloaded, 142–143
overriding, 117
parameters, order, 143–144
remove, 289
restrictions, 217–218
return type, 141
TestMethod( ), 199
ToString( ), 111, 166
Microsoft.FSharp.Core.LanguagePrimitives, 118
Microsoft.FSharp.Core.Operators module, operators, 39
*ML Programming Language,* The, 168
module functions, 258
module keyword, 193–195
modules
    defining, 193–195
    referencing, 193
Moonlight, 359
moving average calculation, 372–373
multi-case active patterns, 96, 99–101
    XML and, 330–335
multi-core, 4
multi-line comments, 32
MulticastDelegate, 151
multiline string literals, 42
mutable keyword, 116, 126
    let binding, 131
mutation. *See* data mutation

named parameters, 143–144
named patterns, 89–90
named properties, initialization, 135–136
namespaces
    defining, 192–193
    nesting, 193
    referencing, 191–192
nativeint type, 39
nesting, namespaces, 193
.NET programs, immutability, 26
new keyword, 131
Neward, Ted, 302
nextParam( ) function, 311

NHibernate, 302
NoComparison, 175
Node element, 331
NoEquality, 175
NonSerializable attribute, 202
notation, arrow-based, 168
null
    constant value, 89
    constraint, 188
    parameter, 286–287
numeric types, 38–40

object-oriented languages
    edges, 4
    goals, 3–4
object relational mapping, 302–303
objects
    C#, constructing, 285–286
    expressions, 181
    Reflection, 205
Obsolete attribute, 198–200
OCaml, 31
open keyword, 191–192
operators
    algebraic, 38
    binary, 148
    bitwise, 40
    comparison, 39–40
    defining, 147–148
    destructive update operator, 134
    Microsoft.FSharp.Core.Operators module, 39
    overloading, 147–149
    right-associative, 67
    unary, 148
    upcase, 68
option types, 55–57, 249
    from C#, 293–294
    functions, 57–58
optional parameters, 144–146
Option<T>, 249
OR patterns, 90
ORMs (object relational mapping), 302–303
overloaded methods, 142–143
overloading operators, 147–149
override keyword, 166
overriding
    inheritance and, 166–167
        abstract members, 168–169
        default, 169–171
    methods, 117

**P**

packaging
  modules
    defining, 193–195
    referencing, 193
  namespaces
    defining, 192–193
    referencing, 191–192
ParamArray attribute, 200–201
paramEnumerator, 311
parameterized types, 184
parameters
  member type, 186
  named, 143–144
  null, 286–287
  optional, 144–146
  type parameters, 185–186
paramList( ) function, 311
parse tree, 309–314
ParseCriteria, 312–313
ParseCriteria function, 310
parsing, syntax, 25–26
partial application of arguments to functions, 215–218
  runtime creation and, 223
partial-case active patterns, 96, 97–99
  XML and, 336–339
partition function, 259–260
passing by reference, 238
passing functions, 17
  to F# functions, 292
passing messages, data mutation and, 238–239
pattern guards, 94–95
pattern matching
  discriminated union types, 110
  expressions, 86–87
  overview, 85–88
  structs and, 118–119
  syntax, 85–86
patterns, 4
  AND, 90
  as, 92
  active, 95–96
  array, 93
  constant patterns, 88–89
  discriminated union, 93
  list, 92
  literal, 90–91
  named, 89–90
  OR, 90
  record, 93–94

  tuples, 91
  variable-binding, 89–90
  when clause, 94
performance considerations, immutability and, 239
  arrays, 242
  lists, 239–242
  records, 243
  sequences, 242–243
  structs, 243–245
  tuples, 243
performance-sensitive code, 67
Petricek, Tomas, 342
pipelining
  applying, 275–279
  backward pipe (<|), 271–272
  converting to, 276–277
  forward pipe (|>), 270–271
  functions, 21–22
Point value type, 115–116
pointers, function pointers, 210
pow function, 218
predicateParser routine, 310
predicates, 304
Predicate<T>, 13
preprocessor directives, 33–34
PRG Pattern, 350
primary constructor, 128
  copying data, 129
  declaring, 115
  logic, 129
primitive types, 37
ProcessExit event, 150
processing XML
  LINQ-to-XML, 322–324
  XML DOM, 328
program-wide state safety, 226–229
programmatic data binding, 371–372
properties
  accessing, 135
  declaration, 23
  defining, 132–133
  derived classes, 164
  get( ) method, 133
  indexer properties, 136–140
  initializing, 285–286
  int, 133
  named, initialization, 135–136
  read/write, member definition, 133
  static, 146
  string, 133
  TargetSite, 205
protected keyword, 155

## Q

queries
    FAR, 304
    interface, implementing, 313–314
    LINQ-to-XML, 320–322
    processing, FAR, 309–314
    XML DOM, 327–328
queryString, 311

## R

rachel, 90
raising exceptions, 52–53
range expressions, arrays, 60
RBG (red/green/blue) color, 109
read/write properties, member definition, 133
reading data, 299–300
    FAR, 303–304
reading XML
    LINQ-to-XML, 318–320
    XML DOM, 326–327
rec keyword, 218
record patterns, 93–94
record types, 119–123
    cloning records, 121–122
    implicit members, 123
records
    from C#, 291–292
    cloning, 121–122
    immutability and, 243
recursive functions, 218–219
recursively redefined data types, 253–254
reduce function, 264–265
reference calls, 236–238
reference type constraints, 188–189
ReferenceEquality, 175
references, passing by, 238
referencing
    modules, 193
    namespaces, 191–192
Reflection objects, 205
remove method, 289
removeDuplicates function, 250
repository, Forecast'r, creating, 344–348
RequiresQualifiedAccess attribute, 107
restrictions
    functions, 217–218
    methods, 217–218
return type, methods, 141
return values, 211–215

RIA (Rich Internet Application), 357
right-associative operators, 67
runtime
    function creation, 221
        closures, 222
        lambda expressions, 222–223
        partial application and, 223
    preconditions, 248

## S

scan function, 266–267
Scheme, 283
scoping, 115
searches, 13
self-identifiers, 128
seq keyword, 74
sequence expressions, 61
SequenceFrom, overload, 314
sequences, 74–79
    application operations, 78–79
    immutability and, 242–243
    loops, 74
    meta functions, 76–77
Serializable attribute, 198, 202
service controller
    helping, 381–382
    rendering weather, 381
Service Oriented Architecture. *See* SOA (Service-Oriented Architecture)
service stub generation, 385–388
services, 4
    consuming
        service stub generation, 385–388
        writing service consumer, 388–389
    domain models, 380
    weather service
        contract, 378–379
        implementation, 383
        service controller, 381–382
        service host implementation, 383–385
sets, 82–83
significant whitespace, 34–35
Silverlight
    application, 361–363
    data binding
        design time, 368–370
        programmatic, 371–372
    developer requirements, 359–360
    F# Silverlight Library, 359, 363–365
    Isolated Storage, 358

Linux, 359
moving average calculation, 372–373
overview, 357–358
Silverlight Toolkit, 359
    area charts, 365–366
    designer tools, 366–368
    line charts, 365–366
software runtime, 359–360
testing in browser, 362
XAML, 362–363
XAP, 362
Silverlight Application Template Wizard, 361–362
single-case active patterns, 96–97
single-line comments, 32
SOA (Service-Oriented Architecture), 4, 377
SpecificCall, 310
specificity, 248–254
Spolsky, Joel, 342
Spring, 4
SQL (Structured Query Language), 297–298
    command objects, executing, 313
StackoverFlowException, 219
state, 225–226
    encapsulating in types, 249–251
state flow, 252–253
state safety
    local data, 229–232
    program-wide, 226–229
statements
    foreach, 258
    *versus* expressions, 27–28
static fields, 147
static members
    declaring, 146
    operator overloading, 147–149
static property, 146
statically resolved type parameters, 215
    explicit member constraint, 189–190
storing functions, 221
Strategy, 10–12
    delegate, 12–17
string property, 133
string types, 42
strings, concatenating, 42
Struct attribute, 201
structs
    immutability and, 243–245
    inheritance, 117
    pattern-matching and, 118–119
    value type implicit members, 117–118
    value types, 114
structural equivalence, 58
StructuralComparison, 175

StructureEquality, 175
subscribing to delegates/events, 150, 289
subsets, 258
    filter function, 259
    partition function, 259–260
syntax, 24, 33
    arrays, 61
    method signatures, 168
    parsing, 25–26
    pattern matching, 85–86
System.Collections.IStructuralEquatable interface, 175
System.IEquatable, 175
System.Object class, inheritance, 162
System.String class, 42

**T**

tables, creating, 308
tail recursion optimization, 211
TargetSite property, 205
TestMethod( ) method, 199
then keyword, 47, 127
throwing exceptions, 52–53
ToString( ) method, 111, 166
transformations, 260
    choose function, 262–263
    map function, 260–262
tree-based structures, discriminated unions and, 111
try...finally block, 52
try...with block, 51
tuple patterns, 91
    structs and pattern matching, 119
tuples, 58–60
    immutability and, 243
    in C# programs, 290–291
type abbreviations, 105–106
type annotations, functions, 213–214
type constraints, 186–187, 214
    comparison constraint, 188
    compile-time-only, 215
    constructor constraint, 188
    delegate constraints, 189
    enumeration type constraints, 189
    equality constraint, 187
    null constraint, 188
    reference type constraints, 188–189
    type constraint, 187
    unmanaged constraints, 189
    value type constraint, 188–189
type declaration syntax, 23
type extensions, 157–158
    extension members, 157

intrinsic extensions, 157
member access, 158
type inference, 22–26, 184, 211
language-wide, 25
type keyword, 106
classes, 125
value types, 114–115
type parameters, 185–186
member type parameters, 186
type patterns, 51
type-safe collections, 184
types
access modifiers, 156
ambiguously typed data, 247–248
bigint type, 38
bool type, 37
Boolean types, 37
carried, 56
complex composite
abbreviations, 105–106
discriminated union types, 109–114
enum types, 106–109
record types, 119–123
structs, 114–119
composite, 55
option, 55–58
tuples, 58–60
DelegateEvent, 152–154
delegates, 151
domain types, 3
encapsulating state, 249–251
enum types, 106–109
exceptions, defining, 53
flexible, 173
floating-point, 40–41
language-wide type inference, 26
nativeint type, 39
numeric types, 38–40
option types, 249
parameterized, 184
UDTs (user-defined types), 3–4
unativeint type, 39
unit, 43
units-of-measure, 43–44

unit type, 43
units-of-measure types, 43–44
unmanaged constraints, 189
upcast operators, 68
upcasting, 172
update operations in databases, 301–302
update operator, destructive update operator, 134
updating database data, FAR, 305
usdToEuro function, 44
utilities, paramEnumerator, 311
utility routines, FAR, 307–308

## V

val keyword, 126
validation, abstracting, 18
value type constraint, 188–189
value types
constructors, 116
creating, 114–115
implicit members, 117–118
Point, 115–116
structs, 114
variable-binding patterns, 89–90
Vietnam of Computer Science, The, 302
Visual Studio
project templates, 360–361
Silverlight
application, 361–363
F# Silverlight Library, 363–365
testing in browser, 362
XAML, 362–363
XAP, 362

## W

WCF (Windows Communication Foundation), 202
weather forecast site, 342
controller, 349
For action, 351
DoQuery action, 350
index action, 349–350
setup, 349
model, 343–344
repository, creating, 344–348
view, creating, 352–355
view helpers, 351–352
weather result, 348
Where On Earth ID, 345–346
weather service
contract, 378–379

## U

UDTs (user-defined types), 3–4
unary operators, 148
unativeint type, 39
unbox call, 174
underscore (_) as wildcard, 86

service controller
  helping, 381–382
  implementation, 382
  rendering weather, 381
service host implementation, 383–385
service implementation, 383
when clause, patterns, 94
Where On Earth ID, 345–346
while/do loops, 49–50
whitespace, 34–35
wildcard character, partial-case active patterns, 98
wildcard clause, 90
wildcard pattern, 52
wildcards, _ (underscore), 86
with keyword, 134
WPF (Windows Presentation Framework), 360
writing XML, 325
  to memory, 325
  XML DOM, 329

## X-Z

XAML, 362–363
  files, 360
  resources, 369–370
  Silverlight, 361–363

XAP files, 358, 362
XAttribute objects, 321
XDocuments, 319–322
XElement, 323
XML DOM, 325–326
  processing XML, 328
  querying XML, 327–328
  reading XML, 326–327
  writing XML, 329
XML (eXtensible Markup Language)
  active patterns, 329–330
    multicase, 330–335
    partial-case, 336–339
  documentation comments and, 32
  LINQ-to-XML, reading XML, 318–320
  overview, 317–318
  processing
    LINQ-to-XML, 322–324
    XML DOM, 328
  reading, LINQ-to-XML and, 318–320
  writing, 325
    to memory, 325
    XML DOM, 329
XmlDocument object, 326
XmlReader object, 326
XmlWriter, 325
zero-bit-pattern initialization, 116